The object of this volume is to make available articles concerned with European economic history which were not previously translated into English or are difficult of access. As there is a considerable amount of appropriate material, certain criteria have been applied to aid the editors' task of selection. Coverage is limited to the period from the French Revolution to the First World War, which coincides with the beginnings and the development of European Industrialization. In order to illustrate the different approaches by 'national schools' of economic history, essays from a variety of countries in Western and Central Europe (and one Russian article) have been chosen. However although a balance has been maintained between different topics, languages, countries and sub-periods, quality is the chief criterion for selection: articles which had broken fresh ground when they appeared or revised traditionally accepted ideas, which are not purely factual but deal with problems of general interest while maintaining a high standard of scholarship, have been chosen. There are inevitable gaps in coverage because space is limited, but this volume is intended as an eclectic selection of viewpoints on nineteenth-century economic developments in continental Europe, rather than a textbook of economic history.

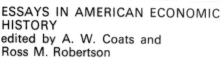

## ESSAYS IN AMERICAN ECONOMIC HISTORY
edited by A. W. Coats and Ross M. Robertson

The nineteen essays reprinted in this volume are by the foremost scholars in Britain and America, and are seminal to the study of American economic history. Some of the essays are recent; others are classics written long ago, but still repeatedly cited in current writing and discussion. While the collection provides a composite picture of many important aspects of the history of the American economy, at the same time it both reflects tendencies and preoccupations in the literature and provides illustrations of the evolution of American economic theory.

# ESSAYS IN
# EUROPEAN ECONOMIC HISTORY
## 1789-1914

# ESSAYS IN EUROPEAN ECONOMIC HISTORY
## 1789-1914

edited by

F. CROUZET

W. H. CHALONER

and

W. M. STERN

EDWARD ARNOLD

© The Economic History Society 1969

First published 1969 by
Edward Arnold (Publishers) Ltd.,
41 Maddox Street, London W.I.

SBN: 7131 5461 6

Printed in Great Britain by
Robert Cunningham and Sons Ltd., Alva

# Contents

# Preface

The three volumes of *Essays in Economic History* published for the Economic History Society in 1954 and 1962 under the editorship of Professor E. M. Carus-Wilson were so favourably received and so widely used by scholars and students that in 1964 the Society's Council decided, in association with Messrs Edward Arnold, to put in hand a further collection of reprints in English, to be devoted to Continental economic history. The study of this field, though developing in British universities, was hampered by students' reluctance to read work in foreign languages and by the location of important articles in periodicals which many university libraries do not possess. The editorship was entrusted to W. H. Chaloner and F. Crouzet, who were later joined by W. M. Stern; the editors worked in close touch with the Society's Publications Committee, chaired first by Professor E. M. Carus-Wilson, later by Professor W. Ashworth.

In order to combine usefulness with manageable size and to avoid too wide a chronological spread, the editors and the Committee decided to limit the coverage of the present volume to the period from the French Revolution to the First World War, which coincides with the beginnings and the development of European industrialization. From the main journals which publish articles on modern economic history and from suggestions and opinions contributed by many experts in a number of countries, the editors were able, not without some misgivings, to compile a 'long list' of over 100 articles to be considered for inclusion. These articles differed widely in length and quality. Economic history developed much later on the Continent than in Britain; in several countries it remains a field incompletely explored; in others, research of real importance and scholarship is not usually published in the form of articles, as is the practice in Britain.

The most difficult and laborious task was the process of final selection which, out of a shorter list of 40 articles, eventually resulted in the twelve included in this volume. As in all such anthologies, selection involved a number of rather arbitrary decisions; we explain therefore some of the criteria used.

First, it was decided not to include articles originally published, or already reprinted, in English (an exception was subsequently made for the essay of a Swedish scholar published in a journal difficult of access) or appearing in works easily available, such as the proceedings of the recent International Conferences on Economic History. The editors have also tried to limit the number of articles originating from any one country and to present work by historians indigenous to the countries concerned, in order to illustrate the different approaches by 'national schools' of economic history.

On the other hand, it was impossible comprehensively to cover within the restricted scope of a single volume all the problems which interest economic historians and to include articles dealing individually with every European country

or even with all the main geographical areas. A broad international or comparative approach would have enjoyed preference, but such essays were rarely encountered, most research work having been done within a narrow national framework. Eventually it was decided to concentrate on Western and Central Europe,
but to include one article on Russian economic history. Though some balance had
to be maintained between different topics, languages, countries and sub-periods,
quality was the criterion for selection. The editors and the Committee tried to
select articles which had broken fresh ground when they appeared, which revised
traditionally accepted ideas, which were not purely factual, but dealt with problems of general interest, while maintaining a high standard of scholarship. However, some practical considerations had also to be taken into account: several first-
rate articles had to be excluded because they were far too long and could not be
abridged; others suffered the same fate because, though brilliant, they were too
narrow in scope and confined to problems of local or regional history.

An informed reader may well wonder why some articles have been included
rather than others which he would have preferred. Gaps in coverage may also
give rise to criticism; this volume is intended, however, not as a textbook of Continental economic history, but as an eclectic selection of viewpoints on nineteenth-
century economic developments in Continental Europe. The articles have therefore
been arranged in an approximate chronological order.

The editors have benefited from the help of the Publications Committee and
from suggestions and advice of many fellow economic historians to whom they are
heavily indebted. They wish further to express their gratitude to the authors of the
articles reprinted—two of them, Marcel Blanchard and Gino Luzzatto, alas!, no
longer alive, to the editors and publishers of the journals in which the essays
originally appeared, for permission to reprint, to the translators who have per-
formed a difficult and thankless task, and to Mr Anthony Hamilton and Miss Mary
Arnold who saw the volume through the press.

As in the three previous volumes of *Essays*, the articles have generally been reproduced unaltered and reflect their authors' views at the time they were written.
However, authors were invited to add a brief note or to make minor corrections,
if they so wished, to call attention to any aspects in the light of subsequent research; they had an opportunity of seeing the translations and of approving such
abridgements as were necessary in one or two cases to bring the essays within the
framework of the volume. The editors are most grateful for all this co-operation
from various quarters, which has enabled a collection of essays from different
sources and countries to be published, and hope that, despite imperfections of
which the editors are only too well aware, this volume will be useful both to
students and to teachers.

F. M.-J. CROUZET
*Professor of Economic History, in the University of Paris–Nanterre*
W. H. CHALONER
*Reader in Economic History in the University of Manchester*
W. M. STERN
*Senior Lecturer in Economic History, London School of Economics*

# 1848–1830–1789:
# How Revolutions are Born

E. LABROUSSE

Translated by Max A. Lehmann

# I

Revolutions are made in spite of revolutionaries. When the event has occurred, governments do not believe in it. But the 'average' revolutionary does not want it. Consider the events of 1848, 1830 and 1789. What person of rank was more assured of the future than Louis-Philippe? Who was more confident than Charles X on the eve of the Three Glorious Days? To say nothing of the court between May and July 1789. On the other hand, our 'average' revolutionary hesitated to take the decisive step. Or rather, as was the case in 1848, he refused to take it. Remember Louis Blanc, or the parliamentary majority in 1848; or, eighteen years earlier, the majority of the 221, or the future 'average minister' Laffitte; or the 'average' deputy of the Paris Third Estate in 1789. This hesitation occurred to such an extent that to contemporaries all these revolutionaries appear to have been taken by surprise.

Furthermore, I know of nothing more significant than the record of the press on 25 February 1848. Let me open with you the newspapers you would have unfolded in Paris, amidst the tumult and shouting, at the Palais-Royal, or on the Boulevard des Italiens, at a table at the Café Foy or the Café Tortoni. Here is *Le Constitutionnel* of 25 February 1848. You will see here that because of a few minutes, the régime has just fallen. 'The recent government has fallen in the same way as its predecessors, for having realized its interests and duties a day, an hour, a minute too late.' Here now is the right-wing opposition press. *L'Union Monarchique* writes: 'A revolution was accomplished in a matter of hours. Four carriages taking Louis-Philippe, his family and the debris of his fallen house towards Cour-la-Reine have just disappeared over the horizon. It was no longer a royal procession...Justice has been done!'

And now, briefly towards the Left of the political spectrum, here is *La Démocratie pacifique* of the Fourierists and Victor Considérant, not really 'burning' for universal suffrage: 'The hours which have passed since our last number are in effect years. Time has never marched forward so quickly! Paris has just shown Europe which was astonished by its silence that its awakening had to be an explosion!' And further on: 'The consequences are incalculable. Sympathetic shocks will reach the farthest extremes of the Continent.' And again: 'The federal, liberal unity of Europe becomes simple, irresistible.'

As for *La Réforme*, it tells us simply: 'Events follow each other too quickly for there to be time to comment on them.' And *Le National*—this is my last example— writes in its number of the 25th: 'Never has a revolution been so sudden, so unexpected. Let the People be proud of their victory! Let fortunate France learn that the Parisians have just administered justice to a government caught red-handed in a flagrant outrage against liberty! Let Italy, Switzerland and the other peoples who are our brothers applaud our triumph, which we hope will be fruitful in its results.'

So much for the press of 25 February . . .

We are told that social problems were of little importance in the opinions of the men of 1848. We must be careful not to judge men by what they thought of themselves. We must be careful to look for evidence to which contemporaries have no reply. Remember the cinema! The audience in the front row does not always have the best view. In any case, all our observers in the front row on 25 February were bad witnesses. Was this classic revolution, with its classic symptoms, this repetition of 1830 and 1789, a surprise?

Without doubt many types of revolution can be distinguished. There are the principally popular revolutions and those inspired by manifestos, mass revolution. and palace revolutions. 1848, like 1830 and 1789, was a revolution of the massess But there are varieties of this type of revolution: it can be 'spontaneous' or 'organized'—spontaneous and improvised by the vital impulse of the populace, or stage-managed by, for example, the determining influence of a popular party. But 1848, 1830 and 1789 were nothing like this. There was no organized army of revolution. What took place was a mass uprising of a voluntary, improvised nature. So the second characteristic of these three revolutions was that they were spontaneous mass revolutions.

But there are variants of this sort of revolution, too: for example, the 'endogenous' and the 'exogenous' type. An 'endogenous' revolution is one produced by an internal situation and by that alone, which develops freely to the end. This was the case in the three French revolutions: the events of 1789, 1830 and 1848 were not influenced by invasion or occupation or by some external shock, as were the movements of the Fourth of September (1870) and the Liberation (1944). The former were more social in character, the latter more national, or more a mixture of national and social pressures. This, then, is the third characteristic which I distinguish in the three revolutions we are studying: they were 'endogenous', predominantly social revolutions.

Finally, powerful force was required to achieve a revolution of the kind that took place in 1789, 1830 or 1848, to get the masses into motion in the absence of a watch-word from a great popular party, in the absence of the traumatic shock of defeat or occupation of which I spoke just now. Here economic force is the most obvious.

Is it necessary to restate the subject of this paper, to redefine my intentions? The title on its own is clear enough. I am not going to investigate the long-term origins of our three revolutions, but merely, so to speak, the process, the technique of the days of revolution, in the strictest sense; I shall limit this exposition to the facts of the explosion itself.

The first element in explaining the revolutionary outburst is the existence of a state of economic tension. The factors of the economic tensions of 1789, 1830 and 1848 were, it is true, very different. Nonetheless, they are closely related. The history of our economic difficulties at those three dates is astonishingly repetitive.

The tension of 1789 began with a well-known natural accident, two successive bad grain harvests. At the root of the economic difficulties, therefore, I shall attempt to discover a natural, spontaneous factor beyond the control of man, and not the 'infernal conspiracy of greed' of which Louis Blanc spoke when he pointed out the rising price of grain and the violent rise in the cost of living for the common people in 1788-9; it is an index of the crucial importance of this rise in price that the average worker or manual labourer spent on bread about 50 per cent of his total income, whether the year was good or bad.

The poor harvests of 1788 and 1789 therefore resulted in a considerable rise in food prices. It varied regionally; for the country as a whole it was a rise of 50 per cent compared with the average annual figure, but if we follow the curve from month to month—or, better still, to get a more accurate view, from event to event, from week to week—we discover, in times when difficulties were extreme, increases of 100 per cent for the kingdom as a whole and 200 per cent in certain areas.

Here, then, in the first instance, was a natural disaster. Here was a people which depended on basic food, the price of which rose above the purchasing power of the great mass of consumers as a result of the disaster. Bad harvests and rising prices cause the purchasing power of a large social group to collapse. The first to suffer were the peasantry: the purchasing power of the peasant producers disappeared because they had precisely nothing to sell in years when the harvest was bad. The rise in prices was far from compensating for the reduction to virtually nothing of the volume of output they had for sale. On the other hand, the purchasing power of day labourers, who constituted the mass of agricultural consumers, collapsed because wages did not rise as fast as the cost of grain.

And now this spontaneous economic tension, beyond the control of government, manifested itself with all its consequences, its repercussions on all aspects of industrial life. France in 1789 was essentially rural. Imagine the effect of stopping up the outlets of the rural market on industrial markets entirely dependent on them.

We must draw attention, in this context, to the excellent work of our predecessors, in particular to an article by Charles Schmidt which appeared forty years ago in the *Revue historique* describing the different phases of the government's agony from the beginning of 1788 onwards, what with unemployment and the crises in textiles and other industries. The situation became considerably worse during the course of the year, so much so that by its end catastrophes were piling up on each other: agricultural catastrophe, industrial catastrophe, unemployment, the fall in wages. Let us consult the fiscal statistics of the *plombs de marque*, lead seals used as a sort of fiscal visa affixed to a piece of merchandise to show that it had undergone the formalities of control. In 1789, in the provinces, there were only half the number of seals there had been in 1787. The fall in industrial production can therefore be presumed to have been 50 per cent. Other facts confirm this figure. Consequently, industrial and urban unemployment can be assumed to have been around 50 per cent. Add the fall in wages—15–20 per cent. All this at a time when the cost of living was rising by between 100 and 200 per cent. This was the atmosphere of economic crisis in which the revolution of 1789 was born.

The situation was much the same in 1830. True, the crises which occurred were not exactly the same. The crises of 1830 began long before that year, in the prosperous and easy period of the Restoration. The turning point in the economic life of the Restoration took place around 1825. It began with the crisis in England in 1825 which spread to France by the end of the year. So far it was only a crisis by contagion, a sort of imported ill-health, but attenuated and moderated and without real roots in France. But in 1827–8 the crisis became tragic and we can see all the important symptoms of 1789 reappearing. First, bad harvests, above all a whole series of bad potato crops, at a time when potato consumption was about three-fifths that of wheat by weight and the potato had become an important element in the people's diet.

After the potato crisis—or rather, in addition to it—came a grain crisis, of relatively moderate proportions—prices rose very little more than 50 per cent— but for a much longer duration than that of 1789. Compare the curves: in 1789 the dramatic price rises reaching a high point in June and July; in 1830 a curve like a dome following a bleak plateau of high prices, difficulties and suffering which had begun in 1828. The industrial consequences of these agricultural difficulties were the same as before: closure of the rural market involved a reduction in the sale of manufactured goods and a considerable fall in industrial output. Bankruptcies followed: this was the time when the *Banque de France* refused to accept bills of exchange bearing Alsatian signatures, because these signatures were suspected to be those of cotton merchants and because the second stage of the crisis was, as in 1789, in the textile industries. As a result, the profits of the bourgeois classes fell, as did the purchasing power of the working classes. For this period we have information of a sort not available for 1789. In the building trade in Paris, for example, wages fell by 30 per cent between 1825 and 1830; in a sample of the provincial textile industries, they fell by 40 per cent; in the metallurgical industries, they fell by more than a third. And naturally unemployment became acute, notably in the winter of 1828, the time when the price rise of 50 per cent occurred.

It is true that there was this difference: unlike in 1789, the 1830 revolution did not break out when pressure of social and economic crises was at its most acute; but nonetheless, the prices of 1830 were at an abnormal crisis level. Here again we find the same complex of misery and difficulty: unemployment, falling wages, rising cost of living, in a word, the annihilation of the purchasing power of the public.

What quotations from newspapers could be cited on this point! Here is the shortest, of 2 January 1830:

'The harsh, early winter, the high cost of bread, the shortage of work and the distress of the lower classes of society have excited the generous sympathy and pity of the upper classes.' Subscriptions were opened, balls were organized. 'Whether we want to or not, we must dance for charity!'

Nevertheless, social crisis persisted in this atmosphere of economic crises. And in, or close to, this social crisis burst the revolutionary crisis of July. The social crisis covered notably the years 1828 and 1829. The worst aspect of it was the food question. A map shows that it was at its most extreme in the west, north-west and centre of the kingdom. At some stages riots took place almost daily. For the month of May 1829 alone, there were 25 reports informing the government of fresh outbreaks, in other words, almost one a day. It is true that by the end of 1829 agitation was dying down and the political revolution did not coincide exactly with the months of social upheaval. Even so, it was close enough. If the culminating point of social crisis was past, the cause persisted: economic tension continued, aggravated by the Revolution, up to 1832.

Next, the crisis of 1847. This was characterized by the persistence of tensions of the old kind plus the appearance of a new form; several instabilities coincided: the natural instability in grain and textiles with an artificial imbalance in the new metallurgical economy.

The crisis was first of all of the old variety, that is to say, in agriculture and textiles: 1847 was a repetition of 1830! It began, once again, with a potato blight— and potatoes now comprised a much larger part of the diet of the majority of the people than they had in 1830. The blight began in 1845–6, and the corn harvest of 1846 was a bad one. You will understand the importance of this 'duo': high potato prices were matched by the price of bread, the only alternative food available to the people. The rise in price of an important article of popular consumption like the potato will, even in the absence of a bad cereal harvest, lead to a considerable rise in the price of grain; the more so when, as was the case in 1846, that harvest is bad. France saw in 1847 an almost exact repetition of the economic events of 1830 and 1789. The economic map of 1847–8 is ominous in the extreme. In the north and north-east is a great dark stain, signifying a rise of between 100 and 150 per cent in the price of grain; towards the east, the stain is less serious; as we move down towards the south-west and the slopes of the Massif Central, the atmosphere clears and the disaster decreases; it decreases still more towards the south and the sheltered shores of the Mediterranean. In 1847, as in 1789—and here is the best proof of our economic model—there was a vast difference between the corn market in Lorraine and that in Provence, between the extreme tensions of the inland areas and the moderation in the economic life of the coastal regions. The Mediterranean, that balanced sea, was a sort of world market in miniature to which corn from the north was brought down the corridor of the Saône and which received corn also from Italy and, even farther afield, from Africa and the Levant, in such quantities that the supply was never seriously deficient. Marseilles has always been a sort of miniature universe, a miniature commercial world enjoying the compensation of its 'meteorological luck'.

1848! 1789! Identical facts! Almost exactly similar economic structures and circumstances! And in the textile market there appeared the repercussions with which we are familiar. As the cost of living rose, so profits from textiles fell; and we saw just now the effect of this on wages! Thus was reborn the old sort of crisis. But the Revolution of 1848 broke out because of a combination of the old sort of crisis with a new kind. The crisis in the metal industries must be added to the grain and textile crises.

The French economy was undergoing its first serious crisis originating in heavy industry. 1847 is very close to 1841, the date of the great law of expropriation, the statute of compulsory purchase which was indispensable to the construction of our railway network; and it is also very close to 1842, which saw the passing of the statute which was the charter of this network. A plan of construction had been drawn up, but it had been drawn up in the illusion of prosperity, almost at the moment when that prosperity came to an end, in 1846. But who believed that a crisis was on the way? The plan would make the rapid construction of railways possible by a combination of private, local and national credit. The economic age of iron and steel was beginning.

Modern metallurgy, using coke, was already making rapid progress. But the crisis broke out, and there were no more funds available; lack of credit forced suspension of the plan. The expenditure of one thousand million francs on public works was postponed, that is to say, about 500 million working days were given up, at a rate of two francs a day. Consequently the iron industry collapsed. The same thing happened in the mines. Between 1847 and the beginning of 1848 the value of iron production fell by a third; it was soon to fall by a half. The figure for the mines fell by 20 per cent. And the amount of business fell even further, because sales did not equal total output. Finally, profits fell even further, because overhead costs of production remained effectively the same: for example, rents, taxes and interest on the enormous sums of capital invested.

What could the bourgeoisie think at the beginning of 1848? We shall find out in a moment.

The changes which we have already analysed exerted severe pressure on the wage-earner. In the main industries, for example the textile industry, the drop was about 30 per cent. Add to this unemployment and falling production, destruction of purchasing power and rises of 100 to 150 per cent in the price of grain. It is true that the social crisis was at its height in 1847, and that the price of grain fell considerably in the second half of 1847 and at the beginning of 1848, when it returned almost to the level of 1844—which even so was not a low price. Nonetheless, violent pressure on the price of grain was at an end. But the wave of high prices had swept over the country like a flood, and falling back like a flood, it left behind it a population whose savings had been destroyed in the disaster. Often, as the *monts de piété* show, even personal property had been affected. The revolution broke out in a world suffering from economic shipwreck.

As in 1830, it broke out not at the time of the social convulsions, those convulsions which in 1847 swept the whole country, but immediately afterwards. The social pressures of January 1848 were not those of April or May 1847. But economic pressure remained, bourgeoisie and proletariat were without funds and without work.

How did bourgeoisie and proletariat react to the crisis? In other words: what is the effect of crises on revolutions?

The crises were attributed to the government. How can a bad harvest be attributed to a government?—you will ask. But it was said: if prices had risen, it was because the government had allowed too much grain to be exported in previous years—or because it had not imported enough in the year of the deficiency. If smelting stopped or there was a textiles crisis, it was because import taxes on raw materials were too high and because exports had not been sufficiently encouraged. The crisis was similar to that of 1788–9 when, instead of blaming nature, one blamed the Anglo-French trade treaty which, though not entirely innocent, cannot be considered wholly responsible. In a word, I detect at the origins of our three revolutions this view of the crisis as personified by a minister or ministry. I could give many examples of 1789 and 1830, but in the interest of brevity I shall turn straight to 1848.

For example, what did *La Réforme* say?

The working class and the bourgeoisie have been hit by economic disasters which the government has not been able to foresee or resist. So who can congratulate themselves on France's well being? Those who have not suffered because they control the budget.

The crisis was not blamed on the government alone, but on the régime itself. Let me cite a characteristic quotation, from Ledru-Rollin's speech on the occasion of the speech from the throne in 1847. What did he say about the economic situation, and whom did he hold responsible?

If our industries, trade and financial credit are in an alarming state, I could even say, in immediate danger of ruin, who is to blame? The system which has been weighing on us for the last sixteen years! . . . In vain they invoke, as the cause of this distress, a calamitous but temporary accident: the shortage of cereals. On the eve of 1789, the same excuses were made to mask other plans and cover other disorders in the same way. This is merely the last drop which makes an already full cup overflow. There are more general fundamental permanent causes for the distress of the working classes, the sickness of trade and the shortage of currency. Look at the customs statistics [of the last five years] . . . France exported 551 millions' worth of goods less than she imported, with the result that in a mere five years 551 millions of currency have left France to enrich foreign countries. This sum is bad enough, but it may be necessary to add another 200 millions to arrive at the true figure, since we know that a good deal of flexibility is allowed in export and import declarations.

And the newspapers noted a change here.

Do the young members of the conservative party who are undertaking to introduce reform believe that the decay of our trade has nothing to do with the government's foreign policy? This is the servile and convenient policy which they support with their votes!

Equally, it is the government which has precipitated these conditions of ruin in our manufacturers, these disasters to our commercial middlemen, by allowing the greater part of our industry to be monopolised by the great capitalists, thereby creating with its own hands a moneyed aristocracy, a financial feudalism.

This same government has sunk a thousand million francs in railways as fodder to the tax farmers and speculators of all sorts, of which 600 millions went to French firms and 400 millions to the capitalists of England and Germany . . .

Instead of waiting for reforms from a régime like this, what is necessary above all is to stop defending, and start reforming, the régime itself.

. . . The difficulties which our trade and industry are in are explained by the government's weaknesses abroad and faults at home!

This was the accusation. In the difficult circumstances of a serious crisis, here was a government being made the object of a solemn and effective charge.

But, you may say, this applied only to the parliamentary world! The accusation obviously went much further. It reveals a propaganda affecting the whole of the middle and lower bourgeoisie and the masses. The crisis awoke, intensified, brought together and synchronized all existing forms of discontent. People spoke, with reference to recent troubles, of a mysterious 'conductor'. This conductor was none other than the anonymous rhythm of capitalist production in 1848, as in the two preceding revolutions: the periodic, cyclical, ten-year rhythm of production, long ago identified by economic science from Marx to Aftalion and Simiand.

We must be careful what we say. Does this mean that the revolutionary, the leader at the barricade, climbed it to conquer bread? Is a revolution only a *jacquerie* of starving people? By no means. But all the political grievances against the government are awoken by the occasion; all the economic and social grievances are aroused by a crisis which aggravates all forms of social inequality.

The psychology of the insurgent is, without doubt, a large subject. Here I can do no more than outline its dimensions and sketch in replies to its questions. The best method is to study and explain the present influence of the fluctuations and rhythms of capitalist production on general and political opinion, and then to call Marc Bloch's regressive history to our help. In present-day society, as in the past, two main categories appear in the insurgent masses: the believers and the followers. The believers certainly do not need an economic crisis to attempt a revolution, but it makes all their grievances and hostilities more acute. However, by themselves they can achieve nothing. They need an uprising of the people as a whole. It is the believers who make revolutions, but they cannot win them without the drifters. By the weight of their numbers the drifters turn the riot into a victorious move-ment. An innumerable mass, a sort of popular 'unanimism' is necessary.

Victor Hugo, in I think *Les Misérables*, put the problem very well. What a con-trast between the opposed forces of government and riot! On the one side divisions, on the other unorganized bands of men; arsenals and cannon against a few barrels of powder and a motley collection of guns. To tip the balance against the army and onto the side of the unarmed crowd needs an enthusiastic mass of people and the support, whether active or passive, of opinion in general.

In a word, what is necessary is the asset of the weight of the masses. The econo-mic phenomenon, which is pre-eminently a mass phenomenon, can provoke this sort of burst of indignation by its sharpness and the general scope of its applica-tion.

Crisis will thus synchronize all forces hostile to the government. At the same time, it disperses the government forces. Sometimes materially and militarily, as in 1789 when food riots had to be faced everywhere at once; and as also in 1830 (though to a lesser degree), for example in the incendiarism in Normandy. And in an indirect and passive way, it was the case in 1848 when the National Guard re-fused to fight; this was a National Guard composed of shopkeepers hit by the crisis and forced to sell goods at a loss, and it handed its guns over to the rioters. Remem-ber the Days of February, the participation of the Twelfth Legion, the Twelfth Legion of the *rue Mouffetard* which left its post near the *place du Panthéon*, dragging after and pushing before it a number of its representatives who had been among the least glorious figures in the conciliation of the opposition the day before.

# II

Thus crisis was concentrating the forces against the government at the same time as it dispersed the governmental forces. But it only contributed to the creation of the political crisis. It only explains one aspect of it . . . Perhaps this aspect is the greatest, so vital does it appear to be in the process of triggering off revolution.

How limited, in effect, is the explanation of revolutions by crises? These crises, as I have indicated, recur, by and large, every ten years or so. There are decennial economic crises. There are not revolutions every ten years. Therefore, for this explosive mixture to occur, other elements are necessary. Notably, the economic crisis must coincide with a political crisis. This political crisis shows itself in the decomposition of governmental and military forces, as we have just seen; and also in the disintegration of political, parliamentary and ministerial forces, as we shall see.

First of all, financial difficulties act as a powerful catalyst and compromise the government in the eyes of parliament and the public. These difficulties are, of course, connected with economic problems. Whoever says economic crisis at the same time says budgetary crisis, whether latent or overt. In an economic crisis, tax revenues fall off, receipts are reduced, public credit is weakened. By contrast, expenses rise with the cost of public assistance. So much so that in times of financial crisis governments experience a sort of instability, a particular vulnerability. Ministers follow each other in quick succession. For example, count the number of controllers-general between 1787 and 1789, and try to remember something about Lambert or Laurent de Villedeuil! Even inside governmental circles, a minister of finance who cannot balance the budget is not held to be a very welcome associate!

These three crises of 1789, 1830 and 1848 were so distinctively—even if unequally—marked by the effects of severe financial crises on the government that government stability was compromised. From 1787 to 1789 this was the case. Equally, we must not forget that there was a deficit between 1827 and 1830, that the budget of 1828 was only balanced by levying fifty million francs of extraordinary imposts, and that in the first third of 1830, a strong surplus appeared; but against this must be set the costs of the expeditions to Morea and Algeria. It was at this point that new grievances appeared and the opposition enjoyed its heyday. Remember the famous incident of the Peyronnet dining-room which was the more scandalous for occurring during a year of 'lean kine'. And there was some justification for denouncing the 'liberalities' of the régime, for example, the payment of 15,000 francs to a Swiss colonel (there was money for Swiss colonels, for the privileged troops of the royal household!)—compared to the 6,000 francs paid to some French colonels! The financial aggravated the political crisis, or contributed to its aggravation. And it is natural that, in view of the record deficit of 258 millions (20 per cent of ordinary receipts) in 1847, we should find the same thing in 1848.

Political crisis is also characterized by extreme fragmentation among supporters of the régime, while the opposition makes considerable headway. The political crisis before 1789 is well known. The forces of the régime disintegrated, first in the 'aristocratic revolution' which M. Georges Lefebvre has exposed as such in his *1789*, then in the revolution of the bourgeoisie. Furthermore, at the same time as this bourgeois revolution, the bourgeoisie attracted to itself a section of the nobility and the clergy, while the working classes formed a bloc with the bourgeoisie. Thus the forces on the side of the government disintegrated, and some of them went over to the opposition.

And before 1830 there was the *Défection*. In 1830, in the Polignac ministry, there was dissension and last-minute ministerial shuffles took place; while in contrast the liberal coalition increased its strength when the '221', in accord with Cavaignac and the republicans, joined forces and became the 274. While in 1848 the opposition made great progress as the political crisis in the property-franchise Chamber of 1846 grew. I have here a long list of votes, from which I will cite a few examples.

Guizot's majority was enormous at first, about three-quarters against a quarter. But there are some other votes, for example, on the question of electoral reform. The young conservatives hesitated, and although the government's majority was comfortable enough, it was already much reduced: 252 votes to 154. Here now is a vote on Rémusat's proposals with regard to electoral reform. The government vote fell to 219, while the opposition rose to 170. In February 1848, in the debate on the Address, the government's majority fell to 43 votes: 228 against 185, a record figure. This majority was even further reduced in the vote on the Sallandrouze amendment: as a result of the attitude of a few conservatives, it fell from 43 to 33.

So, during the course of our three great Revolutions, the political crisis comes to reinforce the economic crisis and constitutes a second and formidable element in the mixture.

I am not, however, proposing a dualist explanation. I am not saying that at the origins of the revolutions we can see simultaneous social, economic and political crises, without going into the question of how far the political crisis was itself an expression of a social crisis.

This is not to say that I reject the dualist explanation; for my own part, I would go even further: a revolution, like any other historical event, has innumerable antecedents. There are personal, moral, and sentimental causes in every revolution, not to mention the influence of accident and chance, and the inevitable uncertainty of the men of the centre parties. There is moral agitation as the result of resounding scandals, like those at the end of the July Monarchy, when a whole collection of thefts and assassinations among the nobility were brought before the highest court of law in the kingdom: the effect on public morale was devastating. Finally, there is the nation itself, the predominant emotional factor. Take, for example, the passionate excitement in 1830, at the sight of the tricolour, or the hatred Guizot and his régime incurred for their complicity by action or abstention in the treaties of 1815. But the tricolour agitation was a form of social agitation; the flag of the revolution had a social significance in that it was the flag of the progressive middle classes. What is more significant than the European debate, the comments of the chancelleries immediately after the events of 1830 or 1848? Never had Europe been more clearly divided into two blocs. Never had it been so apparent that the old Europe must co-exist with the new. The impact was not merely between two classes, but between two civilizations, between landed property and industry, between immovable and movable wealth; the conflict was between permanence, heredity and tradition on one side, the active circulation of élites on the other, the old world of conservative aristocracy against the new world of bourgeois daring. I know of no more accurate analogy than Metternich's comparison of the events of 1830 to the breaking of a dam. He declared that society was in danger; in fact the course of the French Revolution was being taken up again to the extent that national self-determination, the tricolour flag and the extension of the French Revolution to the international stage were basically social questions.

Furthermore, these political crises which we have been studying have underlying social origins. These political divisions and conflicts were largely the expression of permanent social conflicts which, though in existence almost since the beginning of time, now came to a head.

I will not go into the details of how the shocks of 1789 set the aristocracy and bourgeoisie by the ears. The bourgeoisie was becoming increasingly rich, not merely by the accumulation of capital and profits, but also through the range of its activities: its control of economic activity, of the labour market, of employment and of production. I know of no greater contrast than that between the industrial activity of the bourgeoisie and the absenteeism of aristocratic landlords. Here, too, there was an accumulation of wealth, but passive in character. The bourgeoisie, in addition to growing in wealth and economic power, was becoming more cultured and increasing in numbers. We must not forget that the bourgeoisie proliferated physically, and also, and much more, economically, as a class in the growing towns, while the nobility, on the other hand, was a limited caste. Finally, the bourgeoisie became increasingly self-conscious, and this new class-consciousness made itself felt noticeably most at the end of the eighteenth century. It was a healthy consciousness, for the bourgeoisie was bringing prosperity to the country as a whole. It was in a sense a class with a mission, an élite charged with guiding humanity towards all forms of progress. It knew this, and it said so. Literature did nothing but repeat it. The bourgeoisie exerted the attraction of a growing and victorious class on society in general drawing towards itself elements of the disintegrating forces of the *ancien régime*. And its ambitions and prestige as the rising and progressive class provide the basic explanation of the political struggles of May to July 1789.

In 1830, the situation of 1789 repeated itself in relatively simple form, in spite of the additional overtones. The conflict between the bourgeoisie and the aristocracy continued in the struggle between the 221 and the old monarchy, even though the latter had been renovated by the Charter: the difference was that the bourgeoisie was afraid of the terrible egalitarianism of the Year II.

The situation was more confused in 1848. The conflict was no longer between bourgeoisie and aristocracy, but it was not yet between bourgeoisie and proletariat. It was a sort of triangular class struggle between two bourgeoisies (the upper and the lower) and the people. But the rising class was no longer the bourgeoisie. It was now the proletariat. The urban proletariat of the rapidly growing towns, the 'congealing' proletariat of the factories and the artisans of the suburbs were no longer the old dispersed proletariat of eighteenth-century industry—an abstract term embracing workers scattered about the countryside, a system which was the forerunner of the factories. In 1848 the proletariat of the factories was born; this was a concentrated working class in which class-consciousness was to develop to a higher degree than ever before—though this is not saying much.

Thus the proletariat was emerging as the rising class and political opinion was defined in relation to it. With the exception of the staffs of *Le National* and *La Réforme*, and among the Christian Socialists, there was no real programme of social reform independent of socialist sects. The questions of the limitation of the working day, a minimum wage, the beginnings of labour legislation and pension funds, these were the issues which distinguished and classified parties. Universal suffrage was itself part of the proletarian question: it meant votes for the poor. It did not matter that the proletariat was still in its infancy and continued to be politically subordinate; it was nonetheless the up-and-coming class, while the bourgeoisie was more divided and disorganized than ever.

Much could be said about this disorganization, but I will attempt only a brief description. It was expressed by resistance on the part of the small bourgeois, who might be called the 'competitive' bourgeois, to the great bourgeois monopolists. It is characteristic of socialist authors that, after the economic difficulties of 1837–40, they stressed the dangers of large-scale enterprise and industrial concentration for small enterprises, for the artisan and for the small-scale textile producer. It is true that Sismondi had already pointed to this sombre outlook. But now there was a whole school, a whole current of thought proclaiming the danger from the upper bourgeoisie to the lower. In contrast to this, the government visibly and openly sided with the upper bourgeoisie when it came to railway companies, banking, mines and blast furnaces. It refused to apply the law against combinations—and from the legal point of view, its position appeared unassailable —to great combinations of capital. It prosecuted working-class associations and drove miners into strike action against tribunals, but refused to look upon a great mining company formed by the absorption of small enterprises as an association of employers. The same thing happened when great banks began to absorb local banks. The privileged monopolistic railway companies were allowed to ruin small transport enterprises. And in the smelting industry for the first time the vast coke-fired blast furnaces began to cause a reduction in the numbers of charcoal furnaces. For this reason certain elements in the bourgeoisie felt their existence menaced, and became angry and worried at the favours accorded by the July monarchy to monopolistic capitalists who were already formidable enough in their own right.

Foreign policy was another question on which the bourgeoisie was divided. At the beginning of 1848 a numerically very important section accepted the dangers involved in continuing the work of the French Revolution on a European scale, and with it, the risk of provoking the revolutionary spirit everywhere—even, on the rebound, in France itself. Finally, there was disunity among the bourgeois classes on issues of internal policy: the unenfranchised *petite bourgeoisie* and artisans wanted the right to vote. Ultimately, the disintegration of the bourgeoisie showed itself when the Chamber of 1848 split into two almost equal blocs. But this is not to say that the opposition group of 'competitive' bourgeois, in spite of its national and liberal ideals, could have united to form a government. Molé and Garnier-Pagès could never have ruled together, and it is impossible to imagine a partnership between Barrot and Ledru-Rollin! One of the essential aspects of 1848 was that with the proletariat still under age politically and the bourgeoisie divided, there was a vacuum at the centre of power.

Lastly, what were the effects of this grave political crisis of 1848, of which we have outlined the social causes, on the Revolution? As economic crisis gave the political crisis an immense social force, so this in its turn gave social crisis a social objective. We can now see the real nature of our explosive mixture. In all three cases, it involved the combination of an economic upheaval with serious political difficulties; of a great economic with a great political crisis, the latter being to a great extent the result of pre-existing social antagonisms which produced deep divisions within the ruling class or classes.

But even all this is not enough to cause revolution. If the two forces of economic and political tension are to result in a total upheaval, they must meet with some sort of resistance. In 1789 this was provided by the preparations for a royal *coup de force*; in 1830 by the Ordinances; and in 1848 by the refusal to make any concessions to demands for reform and by the prohibition of reformist demonstrations.

It is remarkable how British governments have known how to avoid this 'resistance' at the critical moments! I am referring to the British Conservative Party's extraordinary technique of cutting the ground from under revolutionary movements. In Britain politics are supple: they give way in time to avoid catastrophe. In France there is resistance, and things get out of hand as a result. This is not, of course, meant as an explanation of the differences between the British process of evolution and our revolutions in France. It is only one aspect of the question, and a secondary, almost improvised one at that. But even so I wonder whether it does not at least partly explain the tendency towards upheaval in our internal history, and its remarkable absence during the last few centuries in Britain.

But that is a form of historical speculation which I do not propose to undertake. My purpose is to study the three examples of the French case . . . and the 'explosions' themselves, for I have limited my study to the revolutionary outbreaks themselves. This is a simplified exposition; its purpose is to make some suggestions which I hope will be worth looking at again, following up and completing.

I have found myself faced with a category of revolutions most easily explained in economic terms. Even so, we have seen that other factors besides the economic ones are involved: personal, moral, and those which are both ideological and social —for example, those which derive from national consciousness. *A fortiori*, the part played by non-economic forces would be larger if we were concerned with other types of revolution.

I do not propound some sort of unitary, total explanation of history. In my view the economic factor is the most important, but by no means the only one involved. I myself do not recognize the materialist attitude to history any more than I recognize the idealist explanation of it. I recognize only the positive approach which applies itself to the whole range of problems, goes into them as deeply as possible, and neglects neither what is on the surface nor what lies underneath: a historical approach which ranges from infrastructure to superstructure, from economics to ideology.

In other words, my interpretation of history is at once sociological and traditional. It is traditional because it does not neglect the individual nor the influence of chance; it involves innovation in that it tends to require sociological techniques, to study the overall picture, to look for dominant factors. But in borrowing from sociology and other allied disciplines, it revives and revolutionizes them; notably it substitutes a positive approach to economics, based on statistical observation and a social psychology reconstructed by enquiry into its permanent and variable factors, for the old method based on abstract introspective concepts. The result is a science of economics which bases every statement on substantial evidence. To put it briefly, I believe in complete history, in historical method which must be complete to be true. I believe that working hypotheses must be verified.

# The Cotton Industry
# at Ghent during the French Régime

## J. DHONDT

### Translated by Michael B. Palmer

At the beginning of the French régime, Ghent was a town of some 55,000 inhabitants.[1] It was the capital of Flanders, a district of small farms whose yield was insufficient to provide for the farmer and his family.[2] Consequently, flax spinning and weaving were carried on in their homes by this rural population. These factors explain the structure of the Ghent economy: it included the numerous small industries characteristic of the country town.[3] Some of these industries exceeded strictly local needs. This was true of the sugar and salt refineries and of the tanneries.[4] But, with the exception of printed cotton goods, Ghent was not, on the

---

[1] On the demographic history of Ghent in the nineteenth and twentieth centuries, M. E. Dumont, *Een stedenaardrijksundige studie*, Bruges, 1951. For an introductory outline of the general trends of social development from the Middle Ages to the nineteenth century, H. Van Werveke, *Gand, Esquisse d'histoire sociale*, Brussels, 1946.

[2] Faipoult, *Mémoire statistique du Département de l'Escaut adressé au ministre de l'Intérieur*, Paris, Imprimerie Impériale, An XIII, p. 80: '... the farms are all very small and the majority do not exceed 2 or 3 ha ...'. (The French Revolutionary calendar began theoretically on 22 September 1792, and the year had the same number of days as the Gregorian year; for example, Year II ran from 22 September 1793 to 21 September 1794 inclusive. There was a reversion to the Christian style as from 1 January 1806, i.e. during the fourth month of Year XIV. Eds.)

[3] There is a survey of these for Year V, Paris, *Arch. nat.* F⁷ 7445. Another survey can be found in *L'Annuaire statistique ou Almanach des autorités constituées du département de l'Escaut pour l'an XI*.

[4] When discussing the career of Bauwens we shall evaluate the importance of the tanneries. The first of the sugar refineries dates back to 1750; on them, cf. H. Coppejans-Desmedt, *Bijdrage tot de Studie van de gegoede burgerij te Gent in de 18ᵉ eeuw*, Verhand. Kon. VI Academie, Kl. Lett XIV–17, particularly pp. 59–63. The survey of Year V, referred to in note 3, mentions 13 industrial firms. The beginning of the wars between France on the one hand, Austria and Britain on the other, endangered the growth of this industry for which raw materials from the 'French Islands and India' were imported via French and British ports. The raw materials could only be obtained by 'very costly blockade-running measures'. However, annexation to France opened the enormous French market to the Ghent sugar industry. At the time of the treaty of Amiens, exports from Ghent sugar refineries were sent 'throughout the republic, and as far as Switzerland'. This information is taken from a report drawn up by the Chamber of Commerce of Ghent, undated but relating to the period of the treaty of Amiens (*Arch. nat.* F¹² 1164). On the salt industry, the same report notes that the *Liègeois* exported salt as they did oils, to the Rhineland.

whole, the centre of large-scale industries. Above all, it was a major market for linen cloth and this trade was the chief cause of the town's prosperity.[5] At the close of the Empire, Ghent had become a large manufacturing centre, dominated by manufacturers.

In this article we shall study this transformation.[6] During the French occupation, the lines of future development of the town which was ultimately to become a major centre of cotton (later also of flax) spinning, were not yet determined. The woollen, flax and cotton industries developed simultaneously and not only was cotton spun, but woven and printed there.[7] In any case the importance of other industries was small compared to that of the cotton industry which alone concerns us in the present study.

Memories of the prosperity of Ghent in the Middle Ages never faded; the city's rulers tried on several occasions to resurrect the town's textile industry through tax exemptions and privileges awarded to entrepreneurs. As early as the beginning of the seventeenth century, a variety of textile industries developed: first, woollens followed by bombazines, and in the eighteenth century fustians, pioneered by a certain Coene. Towards the middle of the century, the printing of cottons began to develop due to the activity of the 'haberdasher' J. Clemmen. Manufacture had replaced trading by 1778 to the extent that he was at the head of a concern of 500 workers. Clemmen had his imitators and each year in the 1780s witnessed the establishment of one or more new cotton printing works.[8]

The yearly almanac—*Wegwijzer der stadt Gent*—mentions eight 'cotton manufacturing establishments' in 1781, nine for 1789, ten for 1790, 13 for 1793. It notes 12 in 1795, 15 in 1797, 19 in 1799. We may add that the municipal archives record the establishment in 1790 of three cotton printing works, of four in 1791, of three in 1793. A report of fructidor Year V notes the existence at Ghent of '12 factories of printed cloth which compete with those of Switzerland and England'.[9] In the *Mémoire Statistique*, the prefect Faipoult, discussing Year IX, records:[10]

Nothing is more surprising than the spread, within the last few years, of cotton printing works in this *Département*. 30 years ago, there was only that of M. Clemmen. 20 years ago, a few had been established, but they were small, installed in shabby buildings, and the fear of risks limited capital investment. At that time, cotton cloth was little known to the general public. Just before 1789, investors became more daring but soon all speculation ceased with the beginnings of requisitions and the hardships of the period. Capital investment

[5] Thus there was a large merchant class at Ghent; in 1751 there were 218 'wholesale dealers'; however, a survey of 1771 noted that at Ghent there were 140 traders with international ties compared with 217 at Brussels and 149 at Antwerp; H. Coppejans-Desmedt, *op. cit.*, pp. 23–4.
[6] Until now, studies of this change have been few and superficial; only the career of L. Bauwens, the founder of cotton spinning, has been frequently studied; cf. in this connection A. Desplechin, *Liévin Bauwens et sa famille*, Bruges, 1954, which lists earlier works. J. Voortman, in *L'industrie cotonnière gantoise sous le régime français et le régime hollandais*, Ghent, 1940, chiefly uses the archives of his own firm. L. Varlez, *Les salaires dans l'industrie gantoise. I. Industrie cotonnière*, Brussels, 1901, touches briefly on the subject as does J. B. Nève in *Gand sous la domination française*, Ghent, 1927.
[7] In this study, we shall occasionally allude to the development of the Ghent woollen and linen industries. The reader will be able to verify our remarks in a study of these industries which we hope to publish shortly.
[8] On all this, cf. L. Varlez, *op. cit.*, pp. 7–9, 17ff. and H. Coppejans-Desmedt, *op. cit.*, pp. 65–8.          [9] *Arch. nat.* F⁷ 7445.          [10] pp. 132–3.

began again in Year V. It is since that date that the established cotton printing works have expanded their workshops and new ones have been founded. The owners of these firms had the happy idea of devoting their first energies to providing for the needs of the people. They undertook the manufacture of all the standard makes that are in use . . . large fortunes were the just rewards of the efforts of the pioneer founders of the first concerns . . . the majority of cotton printing works use only thin wooden blocks . . .; in some cases, machinery is used. But when mechanical power is applied, thin engraved copper sheets are generally employed. A more rapid, but little-known method replaces the thin copper sheet by a cylinder likewise engraved which rotates on its axis. The cloth unwinds from a roller and passes under a certain force onto the copper cylinder. Then the latter prints the cotton by a continuous movement; the whole piece can be printed without interruption. The secret of the process thus summarized is still known only to the manufacturers who use it.

The following extract from a report drawn up in 1803 by the Chamber of Commerce of Ghent[11] says of this 'secret' process: moreover each manufacturer is very secretive as to the source and use of his colours 'and the same attitude prevails towards cotton thread'; 'it is not known whence they are exported' (same report). A survey of nivôse Year III[12] speaks of ten firms[13] 'before the war', the largest—belonging to Clemmen and Son—employing 230 workers, the second largest—belonging to Smeulders and Lousbergs—205, the third—belonging to Voortman—144 workers, and the fourth—belonging to Villiot—110.

In nivôse Year III, the industry suffered a severe depression, the number of factories in operation falling from ten to seven and that of workers from 881 to 178. The crisis lasted until at least fructidor Year V, since a report bearing this date[14] notes 'the stagnation throughout the industry' following the wars. On the other hand a report dated 2 fructidor Year VIII[15] pointed out that 'the Ghent cotton printing works have resumed large-scale production'.

This new expansion was a definite trend as is clear from the *Mémoire Statistique* by the prefect Faipoult, already quoted, surveying Year IX. In the *Département* as a whole, in Year IX, there were 44 cotton and linen printing works,[16] 16 of them located in Ghent. These 44 concerns employed some 2,500 workers, an average of 56 adults per factory. Comparing these figures with those of the pre-war period (when the largest factory employed 85 adult workers, the second largest 72, the third largest 65 and the fourth 56, with an average of 42 to a factory), it can be seen that the Ghent cotton printing industry advanced considerably in this period, in spite of severely adverse circumstances.

These cotton printing works, whose activity was to increase,[17] were responsible for the change in Ghent's position from being the leading trading to being the leading industrial centre.

[11] *Arch. nat.* F[12] 1614.
[12] *Arch. Mod. Gand,* K 1–2, file A–B.
[13] There is not always complete agreement between the number of figures given in this document and in others cited below. This is obviously due to a deficiency in the statistics hurriedly compiled for the report. But the numbers do not vary greatly.
[14] The same document as the one cited in n. 9.
[15] *Arch. nat.* F[20] 139.    [16] p. 133.
[17] Let us say straight away that the industry developed rapidly in the early years of the nineteenth century: a document of 10 February 1806 (*Arch. dép. Escaut,* No. 1654³) notes six cotton printing works, set up between 1800 and 1806: the factories of De Smet (1803), Van der Broecke (1801), De Rudder (1800), Job (1800), Janssens-Leenaert (1800) and Poelman (1800).

What turned these traders into manufacturers? It is difficult to be precise, but the following considerations may be noted: for one thing, it seems that cloth exports to Spain may have begun to decline even before 1789. This would have led to a search for profitable economic alternatives. This was the time when the use of cotton goods was *beginning* to spread in this very region, as noted by the prefect Faipoult. Thus, prospects for the sales of printed cottons must have been considered good. Clemmen had been a trader in printed cottons before becoming a manufacturer. A market was thus opening, and the reader will recall Faipoult's remarks that Ghent cotton printers were producing mass consumption articles. The annexation to France did not count for much in the immediate development of the cotton printing industry. In fact, the report of the Chamber of Commerce of Ghent already referred to, drawn up soon after the conclusion of the Treaty of Amiens, notes in the section on markets for printed cottons that 'exports are sent to the *Départements réunis*, to the left bank of the Rhine. Exports to the Republic are beginning.'

A clear picture emerges from all this; when the traditional trade of cloth exports had reached its peak, a new textile, the printed cotton fabric, began to enter the market. A few enterprising business men in Ghent, beginning with Clemmen, realized the potentialities of this new product and, wishing to exploit them to the full, became printers of cotton fabrics, while at the same time continuing as traders. The success of their factories impressed other merchants. At first attempts were made to satisfy local demand[18] by producing a cheap article for mass consumption. This probably explains why the disturbances of the period between 1789 and the short period of the Consulate interrupted the expansion only temporarily. Markets expanded progressively as appears from the Chamber of Commerce. Under the Empire, there was uninterrupted growth in the prosperity of cotton printing, but this expansion was eclipsed by the lightning progress of spinning and weaving mills. However, the growth of the latter two can be fully explained only by that of cotton printing which psychologically, financially and industrially blazed the trail for the new industries.

The eighteenth century witnessed the establishment in Ghent of several weaving factories in which cotton thread played at least a useful part: fustian, bombazine, velveteen, striped calico. These works were modest in the extreme. At first, women were employed to produce the cotton yarn. Ten at least were needed to feed a loom weaving these composite fabrics. The spinners were soon replaced by power-driven frames.[19] The survey of nivôse Year III notes the existence of four 'cotton mills' that are in fact spinning mills.[20] This section of the industry suffered from the general depression: in nivôse Year III, the number of workers had fallen from 144 to 81. A survey of fructidor Year V notes five spinning mills, two for striped calicoes, one for knitting cotton.[21] A census of the manufacturing population[22] notes that there were at Ghent 221 men, eight women and 172 boys employed in weaving

[18] One must not stress the local market too exclusively. Clemmen exported part of his production (H. Coppejans-Desmedt, *op. cit.*, p. 81).
[19] Varlez, *op. cit.*, p. 20.
[20] *Arch. Mod. Gand*, K 1–2, file A–B. Varlez, who also used these, seems to have known of some documents that were a little more detailed than those I have been able to find.
[21] The same survey as quoted in n. 20.
[22] The survey already quoted.

cotton and composite fabrics. 288 women spinners (of cotton and flax) are also noted. Such are the modest beginnings of what was to become an industry of world importance. This rapid development is intimately connected with what we may call the epic story of Liévin Bauwens.

We need not dwell too long on the general career of Liévin Bauwens. Indeed it has been re-assessed quite recently.[23]

Liévin Bauwens belonged to a family that for several generations had been involved in the tanning industry in Ghent. Although probably operating in the framework of the guild system, they were not small craftsmen. Theirs was a large concern, and the marriage in 1768 of the father of the future industrialist to a woman who belonged to the family of a rich wine merchant increased the financial power of the family still further. 12 children, of whom Liévin was the eldest, were born of this marriage. In accordance with sound eighteenth-century tradition, wife and children participated actively in the family business. Liévin in particular was sent to England to learn the trade of tanner and was said to have returned with several secrets that considerably helped his father's business. On the father's death in 1789 his widow took over the management of the business, helped by Liévin and his elder brother François, born of an earlier marriage of his father. Either then or even earlier, the firm of Widow G. J. Bauwens and Son became importers from the colonies in addition to tanning and the wine trade.

A few years later, the soldiers of the Republic conquered the Austrian Netherlands. How did the Bauwens react to the new situation? True to form, they rallied to the new order. This can be seen from several well authenticated facts: the Bauwens brothers became contractors for cloth and leather goods to Pichegru's army. In 1796 they obtained the concession of the leases and income of the national lands of the nine Belgian *Départements réunis*; lastly, they purchased many national lands in Belgium (the convent of the Norbertins, Tronchiennes near Ghent, and the convent of the Chartreux in Ghent) as well as in Paris (including the Hôtel de Richelieu and above all, the convent of the Bonshommes at Passy, where their first spinning mill was to be built). Such operations leave no doubts at all: the Bauwens were openly rallying to the new order. Obviously it was in their interest to do so, but it is clear that they would not have acted thus had they not had confidence in the soundness of the Republic which their conservative compatriots refused to share. Moreover we may add that, at the beginning of the Consulate, Liévin Bauwens was not only the friend of many of the influential men in Paris, but also mayor of Ghent at a period when few were anxious to accept such compromising honours. Were the Bauwens the only ones to act thus? Certainly not among their own class, for at this very period, members of the family so openly partisan married other representatives of the Ghent industrialist class. Thus, in 1792 one of Liévin Bauwens' sisters married François de Vos, then owner of one of the chief Ghent cotton printing works, who was to become one of the leaders in cotton spinning. In 1798, another of Liévin's sisters married the Frenchman Jean Guinard, another future leading cotton spinner. In 1797, yet another sister married Ferdinand Heynderickx, also to become foremost among cotton spinners. Anne Bauwens, a fourth sister, married in 1801 Charles de Smet, who belonged—a notable excep-

---

[23] Most of the information about Bauwens that is stated here comes from the work of A. Desplechin, cf. n. 6.

tion—to an old legal family. In 1800, Sophie, another of our hero's sisters, married her cousin Bernard de Pauw, her brother's trusted adviser, who was also soon to become master of a sizeable spinning mill. It is pointless to continue this list of marriages; those that we have mentioned show that the Bauwens in no way suffered the social ostracism that their expressed opinions would have brought, had these opinions appeared scandalous in the milieu to which our industrialist's family belonged.

Liévin Bauwens was not destined to remain a manufacturer; his main interest did not lie in textiles, he was a tanner, and a tanner on a large scale. Around 1800 the prefect Faipoult announced: 'Such is the skill with which leather hides are prepared and cured there that they compete in foreign markets with the best that England has produced';[24] meanwhile the jury of the industrial exhibition of Year IX wrote in its report:

the Bauwens brothers have exhibited their leather goods . . . that are the despair and envy of England. Their superiority in no way worries other tanneries because most of their orders come from abroad, and their prices in general are higher . . . moreover, their warehouses are always empty.[25]

Besides, this tannery was of some importance, for Ghent was one of the chief tanning centres of the Republic; a report of 1812 recorded that 'the production of the tanneries of the *Département* of the Scheldt is second only to that of the Eure'.[26]

Henceforth, Liévin Bauwens was not content to control important tanneries; he had glimpsed the possibility of more grandiose schemes. As an international trader on the grand scale he possessed close ties with England. Trade with Great Britain was conducted through the Hamburg branch of his firm, controlled by one of Liévin's brothers. The origin of the scheme is not known, but, with the full approval of the French authorities, Liévin decided to import from England all the equipment necessary for a spinning mill, including a steam engine, and not, as is generally thought, only a mule-jenny.

The scheme was only partly successful—only a small part of the machinery that had been bought reached its destination. It was necessary to assemble the components of the machinery. Parts lost *en route* had to be replaced. The machinery had been smuggled out of England at the end of 1798; the first mule-jennies were ready for operation only by the beginning of 1800. Bauwens opened his first factory not at Ghent, but at Passy. This was doubtless because, on his return from England, he found Belgium suffering from the Peasants' War, a rising of the countryside against France; accordingly, it seemed expedient to set up at Passy, where his family owned the convent of the 'Bonshommes' as we have already said.

In 1801, Liévin Bauwens established in Ghent a second cotton spinning works in the former convent of the Chartreux. As we know, there were at this time in Ghent a few modest 'cotton mills', but of course, none of them used mule-jennies. At first, the mill in the convent of the Chartreux was small in scope, numbering a hundred odd workers. But as new mule-jennies were built, so the spinning mill expanded and in thermidor Year XI, it employed 227 workers.[27]

---

[24] *Mémoire statistique*, p. 146.
[25] *Procès-verbal des opérations du jury pour examiner les produits de l'industrie départementale, réunis au salon de la mairie de Gand à l'occasion du passage du premier consul* (Gand, An XI).
[26] *Arch. nat.* F¹² 1602.        [27] Varlez, *op. cit.*, p. 26.

Like most of the Ghent industrialists of this period, Bauwens never seems to have considered confining himself to one manufacturing process, in this case spinning. Not only was he obliged to build his machines but he also organized the weaving of the cotton yarn manufactured in his factory and the bleaching of the resultant cloths. He did not have weaving sheds but used as weavers the inmates of the prison of which he was warden.[28] He was the first to introduce the fly shuttle into Flemish cloth mills; although long in use elsewhere, it was still unknown in Flanders. He completely modernized the other processes of cloth production: he introduced mule-jennies,[29] steam as a new source of power,[30] the Chaptal-Berthollet process (steam and immersion) for bleaching.[31] Moreover, as early as this, Bauwens had begun his attempts to adapt mule-jennies to flax spinning.[32]

In Faipoult's *Mémoire statistique*, mention is made of Bauwens' spinning mill:[33]

the Bauwens, who have established at Passy near Paris such a fine spinning mill, possess another one almost as large in the town of Ghent. Until now they have hardly manufactured any textiles but plan to do so ultimately. At present their supply of weavers is provided by the inmates of the prison, where very beautiful quilts and bombazines are manufactured and then bleached by new processes.

These quotations refer to the beginnings of the Bauwens' concerns. It will be noted that the Passy firm is still referred to as the largest. Bauwens was only feeling his way, experimenting both with linen thread and cotton weaving. The report of the Chamber of Commerce of 1802 or 1803 revealed the same state of affairs, saying of the cotton industry:

Giant strides are being made in this sector. Passy and Ghent provide the most striking examples. To weave cloth in such a multiplicity of ways, to print it in all the colours of the rainbow . . .[34]

Clearly cotton printing was still the leading industry.

However the Bauwens were expanding; speaking of spinning mills and cotton fabrics, bombazines and quilts, the jury of the Industrial Exhibition of Year XI[35] stated:

The citizens François and Liévin, the two eldest of the Bauwens family (from Ghent), in Year IX obtained the gold medal of Paris, despite the fact that they were competing against the whole of France. The jury considers that their workshops of the Chartreux, of the prison and of Tronchiennes should become model workshops . . . It awards them the grand gold medal.[36]

This extract, along with other proofs, shows that the Bauwens' factories had by now undergone far-reaching changes: the tanneries were now run by the younger brothers as the same jury said in the section on the tanneries. On the other hand,

[28] Faipoult, *Mémoire statistique*.
[29] Bauwens was not the first to introduce mule-jennies into France. It is known that such machines had been brought to France before 1789, in particular to Amiens and Melun, but it seems clear that Bauwens' factories were responsible for their widespread adoption by the industry.
[30] Liévin Bauwens had bought a steam engine in England at the same time as the mule-jennies.
[31] Faipoult, *Mémoire statistique*, p. 130.
[32] *Ibid.*, p. 134.        [33] pp. 133–4.
[34] Cf. the report quoted in n. 11.
[35] n. 25 above.        [36] *Arch. nat.* F[20] 184.

the cotton spinning mills had become the exclusive property of the two elder Bauwens, Liévin and François. In addition to the Passy and Chartreux workshops, they had founded a third firm at Tronchiennes near Ghent, in the former convent of the Norbertins.

A second *Mémoire statistique* by Faipoult, surveying the end of Year XII,[37] also mentioned the Tronchiennes factory:

The splendid installation that Liévin Bauwens has just opened at Tronchiennes in an abbey . . . is a cotton spinning mill similar to the one he has created at Ghent. He has houses built for his workers, and his factory at Tronchiennes is becoming the centre of a new village. At present he is engaged on the establishment of an even larger spinning mill. He devotes part of his stock of yarn to the weaving of bombazines, quilts and velveteen.

It seems likely that for several years the equipping of the factories at Ghent and Tronchiennes absorbed the output of the Bauwens' construction works. Many have remarked on the unselfishness of Bauwens, who, it is claimed, allowed anyone to copy the machinery that he had introduced on the Continent of Europe at such danger and expense.

The truth is very different: Bauwens exploited to the full his *de facto* monopoly of construction of mule-jennies so as to obtain shares in the newly created spinning mills founded mostly, indeed, by his relatives. The first such mill belonged to François de Vos Bauwens, Liévin's brother-in-law. This large factory was equipped with machinery supplied by Liévin.[38] But Liévin made his brother-in-law sign a contract of partnership guaranteeing Liévin one-third of the profits.[39]

It is possible that this very large factory—it was one of the three spinning mills in Ghent using a steam engine—may be the one referred to above. And this is not all; the next spinning mill to be built belonged to Heynderickx (1805). Heynderickx was another brother-in-law of Bauwens. The Rosseel spinning mill was set up in the same year—the third to use steam power. Rosseel was a partner of L. Bauwens.[40] And the latter was in partnership with the Lousbergs brothers[41] who, originally tanners, became cotton spinners around this time, doubtless in 1803. We may conclude this survey of firms linked to Bauwens by family or partnership by adding that De Pauw (brother-in-law of Liévin Bauwens and a former manager of the tannery)[42] also founded a spinning mill; that one of Liévin's brothers, Charles, erected a spinning mill at Vonèche, near Dinant, and that another mill belonging to Jean Guinard, brother-in-law of Liévin, was also equipped with machinery furnished by Bauwens.

Until the middle of 1806, Bauwens was to be the sole maker at Ghent of mule-jennies.[43] Thus we can see that he took the utmost advantage of this *de facto*

[37] A. Desplechin, *op. cit.*, p. 58.
[38] It was set up in the castle of the Counts at Ghent.
[39] Varlez, *op. cit.*, p. 27.        [40] *Ibid.*        [41] *Ibid.*
[42] De Pauw himself is an interesting example of a manufacturer: a cousin of L. Bauwens, in 1798 he was manager of L. Bauwens' works at Ghent, clearly the tannery (N. De Pauw, *Liévin Bauwens*, p. 28). Later he was to found a spinning mill and also a large tannery, a gum factory, and above all a factory producing cards for wool and cotton, which Nemnich greatly praised: 'The same hard-working Pauw for the last three years has been manufacturing all sorts of cards for wool and cotton which are already considered the best in France. He has indeed the requisite number of machines to sharpen the ends of the combs some of which are very advanced and costly.'
[43] One concludes this from the letter of Faipoult cited below, n. 48.

monopoly to equip himself, his partners and relatives, thus creating a group of family or associate businesses that constituted a real industrial empire. Doubtless the reader will have been struck by the amazing rapidity of the expansion of these concerns. At the end of 1798, the separate parts of the mule-jenny were brought to Passy. We can assess the situation seven years later thanks to a survey[44] of cotton spinning, weaving and printing works in the *Département* of the Scheldt on 1 January 1806:

SPINNING MILLS

| Owner | Date of establishment | Number of workers 1804 | Number of workers 1 January 1806 | Annual production (in kg) |
|---|---|---|---|---|
| *Ghent:* | | | | |
| Bauwens | 1800 | 200 | 15 | 55,000 |
| De Vos Bauwens | 1804 | 400 | 115 | 166,000 |
| Rosseel | 1805 | 0 | 0 | 106,000 |
| Heynderickx-Bauwens | | | | |
| Geirnaert | 1805 | 0 | 0 | 28,000 |
| *Tronchiennes:* | | | | |
| Bauwens | 1804 | 350 | 0 | 90,000 |
| *Audenaerde:* | | | | |
| X | 1805 | 0 | 25 | 28,000 |
| *Ghent:* | | | | |
| 250 Miscellaneous | | | 600 | 95,000 |
| *Termonde:* | | | | |
| 350 Miscellaneous | | | 800 | 14,000 |
| *Waesmunster:* | | | | |
| 150 Miscellaneous | | | 360 | 55,000 |
| *Renaix:* | | | | |
| 200 Miscellaneous | | | 450 | 70,000 |

There is no record in the survey of any weaving factories at Ghent. Apart from the many artisan workshops, there was only the mill of the Lousbergs brothers, set up at Renaix in 1803. There follows a table relating to this firm:

| *1 Vendémiaire Year XII* | | *1 January 1806* | |
|---|---|---|---|
| *Looms* | *Workers* | *Looms* | *Workers* |
| 180 | 280 | 45 | 70 |

Two facts emerge from these tables: firstly, from the dates of the establishment of the spinning mills, that the use of machinery in cotton spinning, introduced on a large scale by Liévin Bauwens in 1800, was not widely adopted before 1804; 1805 appears to have been especially propitious for its spread. Secondly, this industry immediately suffered a depression: Bauwens' two mills at Ghent and Tronchiennes were almost at a standstill at the beginning of 1806. The factories of Rosseel and Heynderickx, established in 1805,[45] were already idle by the end of the year. The extent to which Bauwens suffered from this temporary crisis is significant. This is the first indication of what will soon become increasingly evident, the weak financial position of these mills.

[44] Published in Voortman, *op. cit.*, pp. 65–9. The dates given for the foundation of the concerns do not seem to me totally reliable. Works showing an annual production in spite of a labour force of 0 on 1 January 1806 were closed down on that date, owing to lack of orders. [Ed.]

[45] The spinning mills of Rosseel, Heynderickx and Geirnaert cost respectively over 400,000 fr., 80,000 fr. and 90,000 fr.

This was only a short-lived depression; very quickly a real boom began, sparked off by the intensification of economic warfare with England. One must remember that Ghent was still a centre for cotton printing. The works used grey India cotton fabrics.[46] The description of the weaving factories in 1806 which provided us with information about the Lousbergs brothers' mill, concludes as follows:

In this *Département* two manufacturers only make the cloths known as calicoes, suitable for printing. Were there an embargo placed on textile imports from India, the *Département* would soon be able to produce sufficient to satisfy the needs of the numerous printing works of this and other *Départements* because of the abundance of weavers in the area and because the spinning mills could produce all that is needed.

By the decree of 22 February 1806, the emperor did indeed ban imports of English yarn and textiles into the Empire. Vast possibilities opened for the Ghent industry, because of the difficulties encountered by Indian cotton textiles entering the French market. The industry was quick to grasp these possibilities. Whereas, on 23 March 1806, the Lousbergs brothers still spoke of 'stagnation in trade'[47] and how 'bad business is', on 5 November 1807, the prefect Faipoult sent the following letter to the Minister of the Interior[48] at that time, Crétet:

When you came to Ghent, there was only one spinning mill of any note, that of Messieurs Bauwens; today, within the *Département* there are seven or eight establishments as large if not larger. Judging from the growth rate of the last 18 months, there will be 30 within three years. Engineering works are increasing daily. 15 months ago, only M. Bauwens built textile machinery. Today three other engineering works are active. The annual productive capacity of all the workshops is 250 mule-jennies or *continues*, that is 40,000 new spindles or the means of spinning annually 4,000,000 pounds of thread (in Paris weight units) more than at present. Three new workshops have been set up in the last 15 months, there is no reason why within the next 15 months three or six more should not be established, for an existing workshop always employs two or three workers qualified to become managers of other workshops. Present annual production is 800,000 pounds of cotton thread. Textile machinery is being built, and spinning takes place on a large scale at Brussels, Mons, Tourcoing, Dinant, Saint-Quentin and other centres in neighbouring *Départements*. No industrial progress has ever taken place more rapidly.

Turning to weaving:

It did not exist or, if so, hardly at all eighteen months ago. Today, every one builds looms, trains children in the use of the fly shuttle, and weaves. Home consumption absorbs all the home-produced yarn without difficulty. These, then, are the results of the decree of 22 February 1806.

The above passage is unashamedly expansionist. Future prosperity is never in doubt. Unlimited growth of production is adduced as proof. Yet Faipoult was not easily given to such enthusiasm. Confidence within Ghent manufacturing circles must indeed have been running high for him to write such an optimistic letter.

[46] This is explicitly stated in the *Rapport du conseil de commerce* of Ghent drawn up at the time of the Treaty of Amiens from which we have already frequently quoted: 'Purchases are made at the various sales by East India companies held from time to time in London, Gothenburg, Copenhagen and Lorient.' The position was unchanged at the beginning of 1806 (*Arch. dép. Escaut*, no. 16543, 10 Feb. 1806: *Etat des manufactures de toiles peintes de Gand*): 'Grey cottons used by these print works come, without exception, from India via Antwerp and Holland.'
[47] Voortman, *loc. cit.*
[48] *Arch. nat.* F$^{12}$ 164.

This document also throws light on another aspect, the development of cotton weaving. Cotton weaving was not unknown to these parts. Faipoult alludes to it in his *Mémoire statistique* of Year IX,[49] but the industry discussed here is of another nature altogether. Weavers of the earlier period sought to manufacture quilts and bombazines or mixtures of flax and cotton, cotton and wool or wool and flax, such as 'siamoises', kerchieves, fustians and a cloth known as 'vlaeminck'. The output of this industry was 'used either by country or town folk'. These goods were both manufactured and absorbed locally.

This was not the industry that now developed; production concentrated on calicoes for printing.[50] This seems logical: Ghent, already a centre for spinning and printing cotton, appeared particularly suitable to become also a weaving centre. But this did not make sense in manufacturing terms; there was no connection at first between cotton printing and weaving, in that the fabrics to be printed were not local cloths but grey cottons bought at the sales of the large East India companies in London, Gothenburg, Copenhagen or Lorient.[51] As late as the Year XI Faipoult believed that European textile manufacturers were unable to manufacture calicoes that could compete with those from India[52] and indeed, these latter were so much lower in price that they worked out far cheaper than local textiles, even when cotton printing works had to rely on smuggling for their raw materials.[53]

It is true that there was one exception to this: as early as 1803 it appears that the pioneering Lousbergs brothers set up a plant in which the different processes were collected under one roof, spinning, weaving and printing of cotton,[54] but this was an isolated example.

[49] p. 134.

[50] The traditional fabrics did not disappear, but calico production became the most important. This can be seen, for example, in *L'état de situation des fabriques de manufactures de coton de la ville de Gand* (*Tableau général récapitulant la production depuis 1810 jusqu'en 1813*. Arch. Mod. Gand, K 1–2, file V), from which I take at random production figures for the first six months of 1810:

| | |
|---|---|
| Cotton textiles | 12,619 pieces |
| Calicoes | 33,000 |
| Mignonettes | 4,000 |
| Percales (cotton cambrics) | 2,700 |
| Quilts and bombazines | 680 |
| Total | 53,059 |

(of which 35,786 were printed):
During the periods of depression there was a considerable fall in the proportion of calicoes to the whole (2nd quarter 1813):

| | |
|---|---|
| Cotton textiles | 9,460 pieces |
| Calicoes | 6,470 |
| Quiltings | 30 |
| Total | 20,600 |

[51] Cf. above, n. 44.

[52] *Mémoire statistique*, p. 133.

[53] Letter from Faipoult (as quoted in n. 48). 'A person who weaves at Ghent offered a Ghent cotton printer 60,000 calicoes at the rate of 12 Brabant sols the ell, whereas the net price at Ghent is 12.50 sols and the weaver has to sell at 14 sols to cover his overheads. The person who made the offer was himself unable to manufacture such quantities, for he would need 700–800 looms, and does not even have 150.' The prefect quotes this example to illustrate the importance of smuggling in English cotton goods.

[54] Voortman, *loc. cit.*: 'They do not sell any of the fabrics they make, for all are used in their own printing works', and elsewhere, a letter from Lousbergs brothers on 8 April 1808

B

The most momentous consequence of economic warfare was gradually to make the above-mentioned exception into the rule. This meant first the establishment of many weaving mills; second, spinning mills made yarn for these weaving mills which, third, produced the calicoes necessary for the printing works. This led to a double process of consolidation: several 'vertical' concerns were created (comprising spinning, weaving and printing in one establishment), at the same time that the Ghent textile industry became vertically fully integrated, the weaving mills of Ghent using yarn produced in Ghent and the Ghent cotton printing works using cloths woven on the spot.

Integration of the different processes was an important reform in the structure of the Ghent textile industry, thus marking a decisive phase in its development. One must not exaggerate the speed at which it occurred. The letter from Faipoult quoted above might suggest that cloth weaving was already a major activity by the end of 1807. That this is untrue appears clearly from the survey of the state of the Ghentish textile industry on 1 May 1808, given below.[55] This shows that there were only 282 looms in operation at the time in Ghent. Later it will be shown in the surveys for 1812 that the number of looms was then approximately 3,000.[56] Thus it is clear that the expansion of weaving at Ghent—and accordingly the change in the structure of the industry—occurred several years after 1806, at a time when the first blows were struck in economic warfare.

Anything else is indeed inconceivable: until 1808, cotton fabrics from India were still plentiful and only disappeared during that year.[57] As 1808 ended in a depression which lasted during at least most of 1809, it is clear that the expansion of the weaving industry occurred chiefly in 1810, and again, after the depression of 1810–11, in 1812. There is conclusive evidence on this point: in a report of 14 October 1812,[58] the mayor of Ghent notes that the number of looms which he reckons at 500 in 1808 rose to 2,900 in 1810 and to 3,600 in 1812. He tells us also in this report about the progressive change of structure of the textile industry and of the progressive integration of its three sectors:

Manufacturers engaged in bombazines and quilts concentrated solely on calico production during 1811. Almost all these cloths were woven outside the mills, within the town, on its outskirts, in the neighbouring countryside and large villages.[59] Only yarn spun by their own mills is supplied by manufacturers to their weavers. Machine spinners employ one and every weaver. Each gives work to a number proportionate to the amount of yarn produced by his mill and there are even some who, unable to find weavers sufficient to work the yarn by their mill, have their weaving done in adjoining *Départements*, as far as

records (*Arch. nat.* F¹² 1614): 'As owners of one of the largest cotton printing businesses on the Continent, we have established weaving and spinning mills to supply our printing works.'
[55] p. 29.
[56] It must be pointed out that these figures are not wholly reliable, because the designation 'Ghent looms' includes both those located within the town and those which, while owned by Ghent manufacturers, were as likely to be situated in the countryside as in the town. In any case, this change is not open to doubt since on 1 May 1806 there were 1,100 looms in the whole of the *Département*, and in 1812 the town alone harboured 3,000.
[57] Cf. p. 30.     [58] *Arch. Mod. Gand*, K 1–2, file I.
[59] Nearly all reports agree on this: *Statistique industrielle et manufacturière de 1811* (*Arch. Mod. Gand*, K 1–2, file V), *Tableau général*: 'Cotton fabrics; the labour force is scattered throughout the countryside.' The entry for this year in another survey even noted: 'Workers are scattered throughout rural districts, they work as they choose, on a piece-work system . . .'

Saint-Quentin . . . Almost three-quarters of these cloths are printed at Ghent as cottons, chintz and kerchieves. The actual printing is contracted out to establishments whose owners do nothing else. Moreover, quite recently a few cotton printers have established their own weaving mills. Already the two concerns which at present are the most important—those of the Desmet brothers and of M. De Vos-Bauwens—have concentrated within their respective premises spinning, weaving and printing.[60]

Thus two features stand out clearly: the progressive development of weaving and the steady integration of the different processes of cotton manufacture. First machine spinners—followed soon after by owners of cotton printing works—put the yarn out to weavers; thus in the large textile firms weaving was fully integrated from beginning to end. It must be pointed out that there did exist certain independent weaving mills. There were already ten of them in May 1808 (Bauwens, Coppens, Greban and Co., Van Gheluwe, De Coninck, Buyck, Autheunis, Godefroy, Metdepenningen and Verspeyen);[61] by the end of the French régime they numbered 28. As well as these new weaving mills built between 1806 and 1808, there were the three engineering workshops noted by Faipoult and De Pauw's factory producing carding machines, evidence of economic expansion in Ghent at this time.

However, the increase in the numbers of spinning mills is even more striking. If one adds to Ghent, as do the authorities, the two neighbouring towns of Tronchiennes and Ledebourg, there were on 1 May 1808 eight large spinning mills: De Vos and Co., Rosseel and Co., L. Bauwens (Ghent and Tronchiennes), Heynderickx-Bauwens, Delebeque and Co., Poelman and Co., Guinard. A comparison of this list with that of 1 January 1806 reveals that if the Geirnaert firm, founded in 1805, had disappeared during this time, three new mills had been built. Thus there was a distinct advance. This growth was sharply arrested; a severe depression began some time between 1 May and 1 November 1808. It lasted until the end of 1809 or the beginning of 1810. Thus, within approximately two and a half years, the Ghent cotton industry passed through a complete cycle: stagnation in the industry, beginning at the end of 1805 and still in evidence in March 1806,[62]

Another survey of the same date: 'The majority of spinning mill owners use their yarn to make cotton fabrics, MM. Bauwens, Rosseel, De Vos-Bauwens, Desmet Brothers and Coppens are the leading manufacturers. They operate the domestic system. Workers are scattered about the town and in the surrounding rural districts.' The same survey says of 1812: 'It is noticeable that several spinning mill owners have their yarn woven in towns or villages outside the *Département* of the Scheldt. Many looms in Saint-Quentin among other towns work for manufacturers at Ghent. As a rule, weavers do not work in workshops, but in their homes on the domestic system.' In 1816 (*Arch. Mod. Gand*, K 1–2, C.C.), the mayor of Ghent, describing the organization of the cotton industry, noted that weavers did their work in their homes and that weaving accounted for 15,570 workers, of whom 5,000 lived in Ghent. However, it is said in the section of a survey of 1811 covering one of the town districts and, particularly as far as weaving is concerned, the Nuytens firm, that 'a quarter of the workers weave in the factory, the other three-quarters are scattered amongst the rural districts'.

[60] Cf. also *Tableau général de 1812* (*Statistique industrielle et manufacturière*, 1812, *Arch. Mod. Gand*, K 1–2, file Z): 'The leading cotton manufacturers are MM. De Vos-Bauwens, Bernard de Paepe, Desmet Brothers, Van de Woestijne-De Cuyper; they are also machine spinners.' 'The chief cotton printers are MM. De Vos-Bauwens, Lousbergs, Desmet Brothers and Story, most of whom own both spinning and weaving mills.'
[61] Cf. the table on p. 29.
[62] Voortman, *op. cit.*, p. 69.

gave way to a period of rapid expansion, only to relapse into severe depression at the end of 1808.

It is desirable, but difficult, to define the different phases of this economic movement more accurately. Detailed information—half-yearly or quarterly surveys—is available only for subsequent periods. Thus we can trace the industry's development only approximately.

It is certain that the decrees of 22 February 1806 did not stimulate immediate expansion. An explicit statement by the Lousbergs brothers, dated 24 March 1806, affords proof of this:

Until now the ban has had no effect on the prices of foreign textiles, for two reasons: large stocks were already in the country and owing to business stagnation the need to sell was imperative. Raw cotton prices have moved little; they did not rise in proportion to the new duties because trade is bad and a fall in prices abroad is expected.[63]

It is very obvious that, despite the intention announced in the decrees of 22 February to increase prices, shortage of money prevented industrialists from raising prices immediately, all the more because there were already large stocks of imported goods on the market. When did this sluggishness in the industry give way to an upward turn? It is difficult to be precise. The letter from prefect Faipoult dated 5 November 1807, unrestrainedly optimistic about the state of the economy, implies that existing prosperity was not a recent phenomenon. It places the establishment of new engineering works turning out mule-jennies in the preceding 15 months (that is, from August 1806 onwards). Thus one may date the beginning of the upward turn to the last months of 1806. Doubtless the rise was at first no more than steady, being limited, at least in so far as spinning mills were concerned, by the amount of machinery the engineering workshops could produce, and by the existence of large stocks of imported fabrics. Although the evidence is thin, letters from the manufacturer Voortman, dated 27 November 1806 and 11 February 1807, give the impression that manufacturers were canvassing for orders at this time.[64] Anyhow, the unbounded enthusiasm expressed in the letter of prefect Faipoult of 5 November 1807 indicates that manufacturing activity increased rapidly at this time. This letter also provides us with an indication of prices:[65] it notes, incidentally, that spun cotton, 'Georgia' no. 20, sells at 5.50 francs per pound. According to evidence supplied by L. Bauwens,[66] the same yarn cost 5.25 francs per pound on 1 May 1808. Thus there has been no rise in the price.[67]

Whereas the price of yarn (and thus of raw cotton) remained unchanged, by the beginning of 1808 prices of printed fabrics were rising noticeably. A series of letters from the Voortman firm from 24 February to 9 July 1808 show prices steadily increasing, both for grey and printed cloths.[68]

---

[63] *Ibid.*      [64] *Ibid.*, p. 198.
[65] Letter quoted in note 48, in a passage not reproduced here.
[66] *Arch. Mod. Gand*, K 1–2, file G.
[67] In his letter of 27 March 1809, Liévin Bauwens seems to suggest that the price of cotton had not risen in 1806: 'Doubtless it would be in their interest that the price of cotton remain at the same price as two years ago . . .'
[68] Voortman, *op. cit.*, pp. 227–8: '. . . our goods will rise steeply in price' (24 November 1808). 'Our goods have become dearer; the copper plates for which you paid 25 are now 26 and 26½ and will go still higher' (15 March). 'We are completely out of stock so that when sales begin again in September, prices will be very high' (8 July). 'Prices will go up considerably round about 1 September.' These references are all to printed cottons. For grey

Ultimately, in the months following 1 May 1808, cotton yarns themselves began to rise markedly in price, climbing from 5.25 francs the pound (for yarn 'Georgia' no. 20) to 11 and 12 francs.[69]

Not surprisingly, such a situation encouraged manufacturers to press for maximum output. All of them noted that production was at its peak in May 1808.[70] In addition new factories were set up in this period, such as Greban and Co. and

## COTTON SPINNING

| Firm | 1 May 1808 | | | | 1 November 1808 | | | |
| | Spindles | | | | Spindles | | | |
| | Mule-jennies | Looms | Labour force | Kilos of yarn per day | Mule-jennies | Looms | Labour force | Kilos of yarn per day |
| --- | --- | --- | --- | --- | --- | --- | --- | --- |
| *Ghent:* | | | | | | | | |
| De Vos & Co. | 14,880 | — | 436 | 235 | 7,584 | — | 243 | 80 |
| Rosseel & Co. | 13,728 | — | 348 | 208 | 9,768 | | 220 | 74 |
| Bauwens | 11,928 | — | 340 | 200 | — | — | — | — |
| Heynderickx | 4,416 | 216 | 185 | 120 | 3,648 | | 103 | 26 |
| Delebecque & Co. | 5,928 | | 144 | 80 | 2,964 | | 78 | 38 |
| Poelman & Co. | 1,920 | | 70 | 50 | 3,360 | | 108 | 80 |
| *Tronchiennes:* | | | | | | | | |
| Bauwens | 17,466 | | 416 | 215 | 13,080 | | 230 | 83 |
| *Ledeberg:* | | | | | | | | |
| Guinard | 7,540 | | 315 | 150 | 5,030 | | 210 | 100 |

The following are the totals for the *Département*, including those of Ghent firms:

| | 88,702 | 4,266 | 2,783 | 1,543 | 52,736 | 2,250 | 1,547 | 631 |
| --- | --- | --- | --- | --- | --- | --- | --- | --- |

## COTTON WEAVING

| Firm | 1 May 1808 | | | 1 November 1808 | | |
| | Looms | Labour force | Pieces of cloth per day | Looms | Labour force | Pieces of cloth per day |
| --- | --- | --- | --- | --- | --- | --- |
| *Ghent:* | | | | | | |
| Bauwens | 102 | 153 | 26 | — | — | — |
| Coppens | 72 | 215 | 30 | 72 | 215 | 30 |
| Greban & Co. | 80 | 110 | 7 | 50 | 80 | 5 |
| Van Gheluwe | 12 | 24 | 4 | 12 | 14 | 4 |
| De Coninck | 4 | 12 | 2 | 4 | 12 | 2 |
| Buyck | 4 | 10 | 2 | 4 | 10 | 2 |
| Antheunis | 3 | 7 | 1 | 8 | 22 | 2 |
| Godefroy | 15 | 36 | 5 | 33 | 80 | 10 |
| The *Département* as a whole: | 1,109 | 2,273 | 222 | 779 | 1,657 | 160·5 |

cloth: 'Because I had had no reply from you, I reckoned that you were unable to sell me your fifty grey pieces at the 33 I had offered you. I shall pay you an extra sou, that is 34 sous the ell' (28 May 1808). 'Cloths are forever rising in price' (8 July).

[69] Cf. letter from L. Bauwens quoted above: 'It is easy to understand the situations experienced by mills producing cotton fabrics when one knows, for example, that Georgia no. 26 yarn, which had risen since 1 May from 5.25 francs to 11 and 12 francs, has fallen to 6.50 to 7 francs per 5 hectogrammes.'

[70] *Arch. Mod. Gand*, K 1–2, file G (manufacturer De Vos): 'In May 1808, employees worked 5/4 (100%) a day to meet the demand.' This is echoed in the remarks of manufacturers Rosseel and Heynderickx.

Delebecque and Co. At this time, still quoting from Bauwens, 'sales of manufactured goods were profitable and easy'.[71]

However, the sharp rise in prices was followed by a fall almost as steep: from 11 to 12 francs the pound, yarn Georgia no. 20 fell to 7 and 6.50 francs.[72] By 1 November 1808, there was a severe depression in the Ghent textile industry. This is clearly seen in the above tables, which show the state of the industry on 1 May and 1 November 1808.[73]

At first it seems difficult to explain the rapid climb and sudden fall of prices. On closer examination certain reasons seem to appear. In short, in 1808 manufacturers and speculators misinterpreted the first apparent effects of the economic war. The French decrees against English goods put into operation from 22 February 1806 seeking to bar English and Indian supplies of raw cotton, cotton thread and cotton goods from entering the Empire had little immediate effect. This was because of abundant stocks within the Empire[74] and because smuggling continued to provide France with sizeable quantities of all these goods.[75] Voortman's commercial correspondence shows that it was possible to obtain grey cotton cloth from India until at least March 1808.[76] As for cotton, it was much later that supplies became scarce, at the end of 1812. The same commercial correspondence records purchases of American cotton (from Louisiana and above all from Georgia) as late as 1810,[77] and as we shall see,[78] each depression in the textile industry witnessed a fall in cotton prices. In so far as cotton yarn was concerned, English goods entered the market via neutral countries.[79] All these factors explain why the economic measures of the war were not as drastic as one might have expected. Nevertheless, they ultimately had some effect, chiefly in 1808; in that year there were increases first in the price of printed cotton goods,[80] then of the yarn[81] which implied that of raw cotton.[82]

[71] Same letter as above.

[72] Same letter, passage quoted above, note 67.

[73] Collection of surveys of firms, on the situation on 1 May and 1 November 1808 (*Arch. Mod. Gand*, K 1–2, file G). For spinning and weaving mills: *Arch. nat.* F[12] 1561.

[74] Cf. above, p. 28, the observations of the Lousbergs brothers on this subject.

[75] The letter from prefect Faipoult dated 5 November 1807, from which we have often quoted, was written mainly to secure from the government measures against smuggling, the chief obstacle, according to Faipoult, to full expansion of the Ghent industry. Faipoult cites an actual case which reveals the size of the smuggling trade: cf. n. 53.

[76] *Op. cit.*, pp. 198–9 and 207.          [77] *Ibid.*, pp. 216–21.

[78] Cf. p. 32 and p. 34. Although some complaints about shortage of cotton are recorded for 1808, no more occur until 1812 when all manufacturers were complaining. The following letter from Voortman (*op. cit.*, p. 212) dated 6 December 1809, is typical: 'I am not interested in textiles that are made of Levant cotton.'

[79] In the oft-quoted letter of Liévin Bauwens: 'We should not ignore the well-known fact: only English spinning mills are more advanced than ours, and thus foreign cotton yarns of finer counts that are imported into France must be English in make.' The manufacturer Delebecque states in his explanation of the causes of the depression of 1808 (*Arch. Mod. Gand*, K 1–2, file G): 'The present stagnation is caused by the fact that large supplies of English cotton yarn entered the port of Trieste; Switzerland and Germany are flooded with them at present, and they are offered there at more competitive prices than we can quote.'          [80] Cf. above, p. 28, n. 68.

[81] In the same letter, Bauwens notes: 'Cotton rose in price from 1 May onwards. Around 1 November 1808, the fall in the value of cotton prices more than offset the previous exaggerated rises.'

[82] *Arch. nat.* F[12] 1614: 'As owners of one of the largest cotton printing works on the Con-

A full understanding requires appreciation of the picture as a whole, first, the drop in imports both of raw cotton and grey cottons from India. A letter from the Lousbergs brothers, dated 8 April 1808, adduces proof of the first phenomenon.[83] A letter from Voortman of August 1808 testifies to the second;[84] in it, the cotton printer seeks to convince his customers that goods printed on home-produced cloths successfully compete with those that use textiles from India. Another letter from Voortman, dated 19 August 1809, states explicity that 'there are no more Indian cloths'.[85]

This shortage of the necessary raw materials in both the cotton spinning and printing industries produced understandable panic among manufacturers. To stay in business, they employed two expedients, one long, the other short term; the first entailed a search for alternative raw materials. Thus American cotton was replaced by Levantine cotton in spinning mills.[86] In cotton printing, home-produced cloths were used instead of Indian textiles.[87] But the immediate problem was not solved by these measures: modifications in the machinery were necessary as a result of the use of Levant cotton,[88] and home production of cotton textiles was insufficient at first. Accordingly, to meet immediate needs, manufacturers amassed sizeable reserves of cotton and grey cotton cloth. We possess proof of the existence of cotton stocks.[89] We infer the existence of cloth in stock from the fact that from the beginning of 1808—long before the cotton price began to rise—grey cloths and printed cottons rose steeply in price, as is shown by the price level of yarn. Given that at this time neither raw cotton nor yarn had begun to rise markedly in price, the sole explanation of the rise in the price of cloth is that large purchases of it were being made.

There is no need to emphasize the fact that the laying-in of reserves of cotton and cotton fabrics simply stimulated the price rise. This price rise of 1808 was certainly caused by shortage of raw materials and manufacturers' precautionary

tinent, we have built weaving and spinning mills. In them, we employ 2,000 workers. Fears as to supplies of raw cotton led us to lay in a year's supply.'

[83] *Op. cit.*, p. 202.        [84] Cf. above, n. 68.

[85] *Ibid.*, p. 199.

[86] This will be clear from the following passages. In his letter of 27 March 1809, Bauwens writes: 'It is claimed that French spinning mills are not able as yet to spin as fine a thread as foreign mills. The improvement of methods in French spinning mills seems to prove quite the reverse. Once the manufacturer decides that it is in his interest, he will soon be able to produce thread as fine as that of other countries. Present developments in French spinning are a good example of what necessity and hard work can do: when spinning mills were first set up in France, this country could not use cotton from Georgia in the production of standard types of cloths. Only Louisiana cotton was used by the mills. Soon after the mills were successful in spinning Georgia cotton. A year ago, it was thought impossible by many people to use Levant cotton for spinning. By now, experience has shown that Georgia cotton is well up to standard to make ordinary cloth and French spinning mills are now using enormous supplies of it.' The Lousbergs brothers, in a letter from which we have already quoted, note: 'Fears for our supplies of raw cotton led us to build up a year's reserves. Then we thought of substituting a mixture of half cotton and half flax for pure cotton. After this, we examined the possibility of supplies of cotton from the Levant, which seemed abundant; we were able to invent a process to use it by having them spun 40–46 pounds per hank which made them suitable for the production of semi-fine goods.'

[87] Letter by Voortman, quoted above (*op. cit.*, p. 202).

[88] Cf. letters from the Lousbergs brothers and L. Bauwens, quoted above.

[89] Cf. the letter from the Lousbergs brothers; the passage quoted in n. 86.

stocking-up. How, then, does one account for the abrupt fall in prices and the depression in the industry?

This can perhaps be explained by many different factors operating in conjunction. For one, it is clear that the increase in production must have been very large; we know that existing mills expanded[90] and new ones were set up. This is understandable because manufacturers anticipated steady growth in a market from which war-time protectionist tariffs increasingly eliminated English competition. The letter from Faipoult already quoted[91] shows that this was the common expectation. The sharp rise in prices in 1808 must have considerably strengthened this expansionist trend. Thus we may repeat that production tended to exceed if not demand, at least prospects for immediate outlets.

Secondly, the price rise probably led at some time to a slowing down in consumption.

Thirdly, English goods which entered the market either through smuggling or via neutral countries, must have become increasingly competitive as prices rose within the Empire; the factors which caused that rise had no effect at all on the English prices.[92] Accordingly, English goods must have flooded the French market, thus robbing manufacturers within the Empire of much of their market. Probably, the latter firms—in particular those of Ghent—had only small profits. These firms founded very recently in difficult technical conditions,[93] requiring enormous financial outlay from their owners,[94] had not had time to accumulate reserves. Money was rare and dear;[95] because the stockpiling of raw materials must have led to the immobilization of resources, these firms must have operated with the smallest possible liquid assets, especially as manufacturers reckoned that their products would be sold immediately upon manufacture. In such a situation the slightest stoppage in sales was bound to lead to disaster. This stoppage may have been due to the narrowness of outlets, to second thoughts on the part of consumers provoked by the price rise or to competition from English goods; the important fact was that the stoppage occurred and prices plummeted.[96]

[90] Five spinning mills, Heynderickx, Rosseel, De Vos, Bauwens and Delebecque increased the total number of workers between 1806 and 1808 as follows:

|      |              |
| ---- | ------------ |
| 1806 | 883 workers  |
| 1807 | 1,221        |
| 1808 | 1,405        |

[91] Cf. p. 24 above.

[92] This is explicitly stated by the prefect Faipoult about cotton fabrics and by Delebecque for spun yarn (above, note 79).

[93] Often the new machinery functioned badly.

[94] The spinning mill of Rosseel cost over 400,000 fr.; those of Heynderickx and of Geirnaert 80,000 and 90,000 frs. (Voortman, op. cit., p. 66).

[95] We have seen in the preceding note the size of capital investment necessary to establish a spinning mill; between 1804 and 1808, six or seven large spinning mills were established at Ghent.

[96] Cf. above, the comparative table for 1 May and 1 November 1808, cf. also certain observations of the manufacturers themselves, added to a survey that they drew up at the request of the authorities. J. Coppens (weaving works, 378 looms, 827 workers): 'I estimate that output will fall by a half because of the cost of raw materials, which prevents us supplying the factories.' De Vos and Company (spinning mill, 14,880 spindles and 436 workers in May, 7,584 spindles and 243 workers in November): 'Workers only work three-quarters of the day because of the shortage of outlets.' Total wage expenditure of the firm, which

When exactly did the crisis occur? How long did it last? How did it finish? L. Bauwens states explicitly that on 1 May 1808, the prospects for the industry could not have been better and that the price of spun cotton, static until then, from that date began to rise sharply.[97] Moreover, the tables published above show that by 1 November, the crisis was widespread. The correspondence of the Voortman firm appears to suggest that prices were still rising in July,[98] whereas the position had changed by the beginning of September.[99] Thus, the turning point would seem to have occurred some time in August.

How long did the depression last? A letter from Bauwens, dated 27 March 1809, and one from Voortman, dated 29 August 1809, reveal that it was still rife at both those dates.[100] However, this manufacturer wrote on 10 March 1810: 'Prices are picking up.' Thus the turning point came somewhere between August 1809 and March 1810. During 1810, Ghent textiles climbed to new peaks.

This is not surprising. The seeds of recovery were inherent in the depression itself. It was caused more by the mistakes of manufacturers than by a saturated market.[101] Too many mills had been set up too quickly and production indiscriminately increased without paying attention to the prospects for immediate sales, at a time when the financial situation of firms was very weak.[102] Everything depended on immediate sales of the finished article at any price. Prices in fact were artificially inflated by the speculative rise in the price of cotton, not based on a real shortage. As the conversion of raw cotton into consumer goods took about six months,[103] it was inevitable that as soon as the market contracted,[104] if only be-

was 4,000 fr. a week in May fell to 1,800 francs in November. Heynderickx (spinning mill, 4,362 spindles and 185 workers in May, 3,648 and 103 in November): 'In November the workers worked a day of only six to seven hours. Because of the stagnation current at that time it was impossible to find an outlet for their goods, for my mill as well as others.' Rosseel & Co. (spinning mill, 13,728 spindles and 348 workers in May, 9,768 and 220 in November): 'We work at only three-quarters capacity per day in November.' Delebecque & Co. (spinning, 5,928 spindles and 144 workers in May, 2,964 and 78 in November): 'Production was cut by half because the deep stagnation in the industry meant it was impossible to dispose of our goods. In November, a day of only six to seven hours was worked.'

[97] Cf. above, n. 69.          [98] *Op. cit.*, pp. 207, 227.
[99] *Ibid.*, pp. 212, 218.
[100] *Op. cit.*, p. 233: 'It is very true that the situation does not inspire optimism, but a depression never lasts long.' However, in his letter of 27 March 1809, L. Bauwens gives a more complicated view of affairs: 'The fear of an increase in the price of cotton fabrics did not stop the government from allowing exports of cotton yarn. Thereafter, some activity returned to the mills that had been cutting down production and had been preparing to shut down.' 'Some activity' does not suggest that the depression was over (which is refuted by the later letter from Voortman), but we may perhaps infer that the worst of the depression had been overcome by March 1809 at the latest. It is possible that at this time the recovery was confined to spinning as the permission to export yarn was accorded only to spinners and not to printers and weavers. This is also suggested by a letter from the mayor quoted above, dated 14 October 1812 (*Arch. Mod. Gand*, K 1–2, file I): 'Since 1809, when the government began to allow exports of cotton yarn, there has been a large increase in the numbers of mills of the town.' This does not signify, however, that there was a sudden recovery in 1809; for this observation applies to the whole period up to 1812.
[101] This is substantiated by the fact that production in 1810 and 1812 far exceeded that of May 1808 even though, in May 1812 at least, the Ghent textile industry produced almost exclusively for the home market.
[102] The financial state of the Bauwens concerns gives an idea of the general picture.
[103] Cf. the letter of the Lousbergs quoted above, n. 63.
[104] Cf. the letter of Bauwens from which we have already quoted: 'because they were
B 2

cause of increased competition from English goods, these marginal firms were in trouble. Money was desperately needed; to get it, it was imperative to lower selling prices. This meant that articles made of very expensive cotton had to be sold cheaply. Some firms could not survive this blow; but their disappearance helped those that remained. Moreover, the lowering of prices stimulated consumption. Furthermore, reserves of Indian cotton fabrics were by now completely exhausted, which soon led to an increased demand for home-produced cloth. Finally, the price of raw cotton had fallen substantially[105]—doubtless speculators feared they would burn their fingers as demand slackened. Indeed, the same speculators also feared that imports of English cottons might be resumed.[106] Finally, the government took certain measures to stimulate recovery, such as allowing exports of cotton yarn.[107] All this led to a sharp recovery by the Ghent textile industry, which became clearly visible in the first half of 1810.

It is generally held that the industry entered a further depression in 1810 which continued until the end of the French occupation. The 'surveys' of spinning and weaving at Ghent over the period from the beginning of 1810 to the end of 1813, tabulated on the following page, show that this is an oversimplified view.[108] These figures are disturbing at first sight because they do not bear out the theory, dear to historians, of a Ghent textile industry assailed from 1810 onwards by severe depression. To test their figures we reproduce a survey of the leading spinning mills, based on information provided by manufacturers themselves for the authorities.

An examination of these surveys reveals the following general phenomena: the Ghent industry successfully overcame the depression of 1808 and began a new expansion. Indeed, it was more substantial in 1812 than in May 1808. In May 1808

horrified by such a sudden change (the fall in cotton prices) and feared a further price fall and because they could not sell their goods, the manufacturers . . .'

[105] Cf. above, n. 69, a passage from L. Bauwens' letter on the precipitate fall in the price of cotton. Cf. also a letter from Voortman (Voortman, *op. cit.*, p. 228) dated 25 May 1809: 'because of the sizeable fall in the price of cotton'. Cf. proofs of the fall of the raw material in the firm of Voortman, *op. cit.*, pp. 212 (7 October 1808) and 216 (1 November 1808).

[106] Cf. several letters by Voortman, quite typical of the fears on this subject (*ibid.*, pp. 217, 220). Speculators feared that one way or another, cotton might again infiltrate into the market.

[107] Cf. above n. 105, a passage from Bauwens' letter.

[108] These surveys are found in the file K 1–2, G *bis* of the Modern Archives of Ghent both for individual firms and the entire industry. Doubts exist as to the accuracy of these statistics; some documents are suspect because of manufacturers' unwillingness to provide the required information: they were afraid that their evidence would be used for tax purposes. On 12 October 1812, the prefect wrote to the mayor: 'We must convince manufacturers that these enquiries are not motivated by tax purposes, but seek solely to provide His Excellency with regular surveys of the state of French industry' (*Arch. Mod. Gand*, K 1–2, file I). The mayor noted that manufacturers would not cooperate in providing necessary statistical information about the industry in 1813; they nearly always understated their production figures and the capacity of their mills (6 June 1813, same file). Therefore, can no credence be given to this evidence? This would be too extreme a view. We are not concerned with exact figures of total output, but with the pattern of production. We may assume that these statistics, doubtless inaccurate in absolute terms, do reflect trends and volume of production: this assumption would be false only if we adopted the absurd view that all manufacturers had agreed to falsify the statistics in the same proportion. Besides, nearly all the statistics corroborate one another; this applies both to developments in particular firms and to the pattern of industry as a whole at any given period.

WEAVING

| Period | Rosseel | Total output in Pieces De Vos-Bauwens | Guinard | Desmet | De Paepe | Bauwens |
|---|---|---|---|---|---|---|
| 1st half yr. 1810 | 125 | 10,000 | — | 5,400 | — | 1,973 |
| 2nd half yr. 1810 | 910 | 10,000 | — | 8,800 | — | 1,000 |
| 1st half yr. 1811 | 153 | 10,000 | — | 3,500 | — | 2,829 |
| 2nd half yr. 1811 | 570 | 10,000 | — | 3,500 | 3,900 | — |
| 1st half yr. 1812 | 850 | 10,000 | 5,000 | 6,200 | 6,500 | — |
| 3rd qrtr yr. 1812 | | | | | | |
| 4th qrtr yr. 1812 | 410 | 10,000 | 1,300 | 4,800 | 1,800 | — |
| 1st qrtr yr. 1813 | 260 | 4,000 | 1,300 | 2,000 | 2,100 | — |
| 2nd qrtr yr. 1813 | 260 | 3,500 | 700 | 3,600 | 3,000 | — |
| 3rd qrtr yr. 1813 | 120 | — | 1,200 | 2,860 | — | — |

SPINNING

| Period | Spindles | Kilos of yarn | Frames | Pieces manufactured | Pieces printed |
|---|---|---|---|---|---|
| 1st half yr. 1810 | 110,756 | 288,970 | 2,908 | 53,059 | 35,786 |
| 2nd half yr. 1810 | 115,810 | 276,866 | 2,703 | 48,378 | 39,842 |
| 1st half yr. 1811 | 75,266 | 169,193 | 2,800 | 49,572 | 29,665 |
| 2nd half yr. 1811 | 74,682 | 187,075 | 2,956 | 58,241 | 31,135 |
| 1st half yr. 1812 | 103,020 | 264,260 | 3,617 | 69,894 | 35,943 |
| 2nd half yr. 1812 | 103,644 | 273,160 | 2,996 | 68,894 | 34,024 |
| 1st half yr. 1813 | 60,798 | 193,610 | 1,979 | 40,473 | 39,738 |
| 3rd qrtr yr. 1813 | 64,056 | 84,944 | 1,367 | 15,990 | 28,852 |

QUANTITY OF YARN PRODUCED (IN KILOS)

| Period | Van De Woestijne | Rosseel | De Vos-Bauwens | Guinard | Desmet | De Paepe | Bauwens (Ghent & Tronchiennes) |
|---|---|---|---|---|---|---|---|
| 1st half yr. 1810 | nil | 32,080 | 30,000 | 20,000 | 12,000 | nil | 67,267 |
| 2nd half yr. 1810 | 5,352 | 26,740 | 30,000 | 20,000 | 21,000 | 13,890 | 55,048 |
| 1st half yr. 1811 | 4,800 | 15,454 | 30,000 | 10,000 | 8,000 | 5,079 | 21,299 |
| 2nd half yr. 1811 | 4,896 | 19,315 | 30,000 | 10,000 | 8,000 | 11,344 | ? |
| 1st half yr. 1812 | 4,896 | 28,388 | 30,000 | 20,000 | 13,000 | 17,480 | 13,500 |
| 4th qrtr yr. 1812 | 6,115 (sic) | 11,163 | 30,000 | 5,200 | 8,400 | 7,200 | 13,500 |
| 1st qrtr yr. 1813 | 2,415 | 7,125 | 15,000 | 1,733 | 4,800 | 8,300 | 2,420 |
| 2nd qrtr yr. 1813 | 3,000 | 7,125 | 14,000 | nil | 7,460 | 9,000 | not |
| 3rd qrtr yr. 1813 | 2,850 | 6,125 | 7,000 | 3,900 | 5,000 | 7,200 | available |

FIGURES FOR THE WHOLE OF
GHENTISH FIRMS

| Period | Mule-jennies | Looms | Total machines | Spun yarn | Cotton spinners |
|---|---|---|---|---|---|
| 4th qrtr yr. 1812 | 102,650 | 994 | 103,644 | 141,061 kg | 1,185 |
| 1st qrtr yr. 1813 | 68,000 | 2,042 | 70,042 | 118,413 | 624 |
| 2nd qrtr yr. 1813 | 58,852 | 1,946 | 60,798 | 75,197 | 506 |
| 3rd qrtr yr. 1813 | 60,764 | 3,292 | 64,056 | 86,944 | 316 |

the number of spindles engaged in the spinning of cotton 'for the whole *Départe-ment*' was 88,702. 'For Ghent alone' (including the neighbouring communes of Ledeberg and Tronchiennes) in 1810 they numbered 113,000, and in 1812, 102,650. Furthermore, in 1808 there were eight spinning mills in Ghent; in 1812 there were 25. Weaving factories rose from ten to 15 in this period.

Thus it is clear that the Ghent textile industry recovered from the depression of 1808 to enter a new and dynamic expansion. But secondly, the industry did not expand without interruption between 1810 and 1813. The statistics clearly show that a depression began in the second part of 1810 and intensified during the first half of 1811. A new period of prosperity began at the end of 1811 and lasted until the end of 1812. Then in the first half of 1813, a new acute depression began.

Let us examine these developments in more detail. There is much corroborating evidence for the depression of end 1810, early 1811.[109] An unidentified manu-facturer who owned a spinning mill of 1,100 spindles and a weaving factory of 94 looms, notes as an addendum to his replies for the second half of 1810: 'Circum-stances have forced cuts in the labour force'; for the first half of 1811, he notes, 'because business has not improved, am forced to halt production.' Another manu-facturer, M. Van Huffel (engaged solely in spinning) successively noted: (*a*) first half of 1810: 'we were the first to build cotton spinning machines'; (*b*) second half of 1810: no comment; (*c*) first half of 1811: not all the machines have been active throughout the six months period, first because of stagnation, second because the machines were occasionally without the necessary spare parts, third 'the prevailing gloom and the small output discourage production'.

M. De Waele-Van den Broeck (cotton weaving and printing works) was even more precise:

During the first half of 1810 and at the beginning of the second half, we encouraged our weavers to work as long as they could and our printers worked every day from sunrise to sunset, save at midday. During the second half of 1810, we were forced to cut down production. In the first half of 1811, workers' hours were steadily reduced. During these six months we discharged all our weavers and reduced the number of printers from 13 to four. In both the first and second halves of 1810, demand at first substantially fell to a point where sales at present are almost at a standstill.

M. Heynderickx-Bauwens reported that from 1 April to 1 November 1811 his spinning mill ceased production. M. Van de Woestyne (spinning mill) wrote:

Our mill had not yet been set up in the first half of 1810. We began spinning operations in September 1810 with four mules; by October there were eight, by November 13 and by December 16. In January, February and March 1811, 16 were in operation, in April eight, in May five, and in June six.

Lousbergs, the weavers, stated:

By the end of 1810, the firm suspended production and did not resume it until the second half of 1811.

Moreover, on 28 September 1810, the prefect of the *Département* of the Scheldt wrote to the Minister of the Interior[110] that 'factories and mills threatened by

---

[109] Taken from the column of 'Special Remarks' in the survey of industrial firms which were the basis of the tables given above and referred to in the preceding note.

[110] *Arch. dép. Escaut* (in the Archives at Ghent), no. 1656.

bankruptcy and by the depression ask for immediate and effective measures to be taken'. On 13 March 1811 the same government official adds:[111] 'Things have far from improved since the last report on the state of the factories of the *Département*. Several concerns have ceased operation, and others are threatened by total disaster. The view of most manufacturers is that they will suspend production sooner or later.' On 22 March the mayor wrote to the prefect[112]:

I have to report that one of the most important cotton manufacturers of the town of Ghent, M. Rosseel, has just dismissed 97 of his workers. Nearly all the cotton spinners have dismissed some of their workers and announce plans to cease production as soon as present stocks of raw materials have run out.

On 20 March the manufacturer De Vos wrote:

In the last few months we have halved our labour force.

On 13 May, the mayor wrote to the prefect:[113]

M. Bauwens has just dismissed all the workers of his factory at the Chartreux monastery: his workshops have closed down and in his Tronchiennes factory he has kept on only 12 spinners who will also be dismissed in a few days. These discharged workers cannot find work in other spinning mills which are themselves due to be shut. M. De Vos' mill will probably close during next week.

It is possible to date these happenings even more exactly: on 6 February 1811, a sudden cut of roughly 20 per cent was made in spinners' wages[114] which provoked considerable unrest. The significance of such a move is thrown into relief by recalling the eagerness with which manufacturers had earlier sought labourers and the lengths to which they would go to keep their labour force intact lest it prove insufficient.

All this evidence makes it possible to follow the different stages in the developments of the textile industry; prosperity reigned in the first half and also at the beginning of the second half of 1810. New mills were opened and the labour-force worked at maximum capacity. A regression began during the second half of 1810 and became more severe during the first half of 1811. Expansion was resumed sometime between June and November 1811.

It emerges from this survey that the new period of prosperity of the Ghent industry was very short. The boldness of Ghent businessmen should be stressed here: we have established that on 1 May 1808 there were eight spinning and ten weaving mills. The survey of the whole industry for 1811 shows 23 spinning mills and 15 weaving works. Thus, at the first indication of a new spell of prosperity, Ghent capitalists made large, rapid and undoubtedly rash investments. It may well be that the statistics of 1808 do not take into account small firms, whereas the survey of 1811 does. In this case the contrast between the two figures would be less striking than appears at first; nonetheless, it is undeniable that several new and large concerns were created in 1810.[115] Particularly remarkable were the large manufacturing concerns created during the same period in the linen and woollen sectors of the textile industry.[116] They afford striking proof of an unusual preoccupation

---

[111] *Ibid.*    [112] *Ibid.*    [113] *Loc. cit.*, no. 1655.    [114] Varlez, *op. cit.*, proofs p. 19.
[115] In particular, that of Van Muffet and Van de Woestyne, as is shown by their own testimony, quoted above, p. 36.
[116] The firms of Maes (wool) and Gamard-Verhegghen (flax).

current at that time: everyone wanted to manufacture as much and as rapidly as possible. As soon as the depression of 1808–9 began to recede, factories sprang up like mushrooms after the rain! The splendid work by E. Labrousse and P. Lebrun[117] has made this more clearly apparent. The turning point came during the 1810-11 period: the price of corn rose rapidly in 1811, causing a fall in the output of industrial goods. Elsewhere, P. Lebrun has noted that, for the woollen industry of Verviers, the expansionist period (phase A) finished in 1810, more specifically in the middle of that year.[118] Because depression occurred in Ghent at the same time, but in a different sector, it is clear that this period witnessed a turning point in economic activity. And this happened at the very moment when Ghent cotton firms, established as rapidly as possible, were multiplying and working at full capacity. It was inevitable that sudden contraction of the market in an industry where production was quickly expanding would lead to a sharp fall in sales; the manufacturer Voortman summarized the situation thus on 7 November 1810: 'We can take our pick of goods that are abundant and not in demand.'[119]

It is not difficult to foresee the effects of this sudden crisis on so young an industry still lacking a solid financial basis: there was a plethora of bankruptcies. The pioneer, L. Bauwens, was the hardest hit. Thereafter he was in a desperate situation and doubtless he was typical of other manufacturers.[120] Bauwens was heavily in debt. He had borrowed from a Parisian capitalist, Armand de Vérac, 245,000 francs, with his mills as security. He had repaid part of the loan but in 1811, 110,000 francs were still outstanding. Moreover, an old debt of 45,000

---

[117] *Mouvement des prix et des revenus au XVIIIe siècle. Le prix du blé en France de 1781 à 1817.*

[118] *L'industrie de la laine à Verviers pendant le XVIIIe et le début du XIXe siècle,* Liège, 1948, p. 334. The Verviers industry also experienced a slight improvement in 1812 (*ibid.,* p. 339, n. 5). However, the recovery in the Ghent textile industry appears much greater than that of Verviers, because in 1812 production at Ghent undeniably exceeded former peaks. I have based this enquiry solely on production figures; I have made only occasional use of price variations. This is so because in this provisional survey I have refrained from compiling price figures; moreover, prices of cotton goods are too heavily influenced by a fortuitous element and the varying degrees of the application of the Continental Blockade.

[119] Voortman, *op. cit.,* p. 73.

[120] His financial position had always been precarious. Debts had plagued Bauwens since 1801; they were to increase. They were contracted thus (explained in detail in Nève, *Gand sous la domination française,* pp. 177–9): in 1801, Bauwens had entered a competition held in Paris—he had exhibited four mule-jennies. The prize money totalled 105,000 francs, in three parts: he was given 40,000 as a reward, 20,000 to pay for the machines exhibited (which are kept in the *Conservatoire des Arts et Métiers*) and 45,000 francs to pay for two further orders of machinery that Bauwens was to construct. It is likely that Bauwens received all the money in 1801; probably most of it was invested in his firms which were expanding fast in 1801. However, Bauwens never delivered the two sets of machinery for which he had been paid. In 1805, the Minister of the Interior demanded that he either deliver the machinery or repay the 45,000 francs. Bauwens did neither. The minister, growing impatient, began legal proceedings in 1807. As the industry was experiencing a boom at this time one would expect Bauwens to have met his obligations. This did not happen and Bauwens was saved from an immediate law-suit only by the active intervention of the prefect. All the evidence suggests Bauwens' inability to pay. Thus it is not difficult to see why Bauwens closed down his mills at the very beginning of the depression. This is proved by a survey of his mills accompanying the letter mentioned above (1 May, 1 November 1808). This makes it clear that he had to close the mills at Ghent and Saint-Quentin; the mill at Tronchiennes continued to operate but yarn production fell from 430 to 116 kg.

francs which he had contracted in 1801 had still to be paid. Thus the depression occurred when he was financially very vulnerable. His financial position was even worse than appeared, for on 11 February 1811 he obtained a loan of 300,000 francs from the government—again on the security of his mills. Thus he was in debt to the tune of at least 455,000 francs, more than Rosseel had had to spend in 1804 on setting up his large textile plant. Moreover, Bauwens' debts must have been even greater; for he was unable, even with the loan from the government in 1811, to repay De Vérac. In September 1811, on the latter's orders, Bauwens' property was seized; at the same time, the government opened proceedings to recover the 45,000 francs owing since 1801. Bauwens was driven to desperate measures. He tried to sell his mill at Tronchiennes to the government which wanted to establish an asylum for vagrants. The government was at first well disposed to this offer as a means of recovering the money, but rejected it on discovering that De Vérac's mortgage on Bauwens' mills ranked before its own. Thus the founder of Ghent's economic prosperity met with total bankruptcy.

Nève has shown that Bauwens was by no means alone in this. Let him tell the tale[121]: 'Bankruptcies proliferated. After that of M. Lousbergs[122] the banker De Paepe suspended payments and thus occasioned the bankruptcy of the merchants MM. de Bas-de Hert and Van de Waele and of the cotton spinner Schrijver. The prefect was visibly concerned and demanded an explanation from the president of the Tribunal of Commerce, M. Serdobbel, about the rash of sizeable bankruptcies. On 8 June 1811, the latter replied, blaming these bankruptcies on speculation and on businessmen's 'lack of capital and perhaps of knowledge for such undertakings . . . He reckoned that excluding those of under 50,000 francs, bankruptcies totalled fifteen millions . . .'

There is no point in further elaboration; the year 1810 which had opened so promisingly, ended in a financial catastrophe which shook the very foundations of the Ghent economy. However, the very severity of the depression implied the possibility of recovery through the sharp fall in production which it provoked: as demand for raw cotton slackened, its price fell (proof that supplies were still ample) and wages tumbled. One proof of this is furnished by the letter from manufacturer Vortman dated 18 July 1811: 'I find that prices [doubtless of cotton goods] have not fallen in proportion to those of cotton or as much as wages.'[123] Prices of finished goods certainly conformed to the trend; thus this combination of falling wages and prices explained the recovery of the industry, which in 1812 was to reach new peaks. Despite all these depressions, production inevitably rose, adequate proof that up to 1812, the market had not yet reached saturation point for textile goods. Successive stoppages in sales were due to a too rapid rate in the rise of prices rather than of production. Each fall in selling prices gave a new boost to production, and thus to demand.

[121] *Ibid.*, p. 186.

[122] On 28 December 1810, the prefect referred to 'the most famous and most important manufacturer of this town who integrated in his factory all three processes of cotton spinning, weaving and printing of the cloths produced from this material' (*Ibid.*, p. 185). According to a letter from Voortman dated 18 January 1810 (Voortman, *op. cit.*, p. 235): 'The financial statement shows that assets cover only 35 per cent of debts' (he is speaking of the bankruptcy of the Lousbergs).

[123] *Ibid.*, p. 215.

It is apparent from the table reproduced above that 1812 was another year of great prosperity for the industry. Then came a further depression. A manufacturer, M. Greban, wrote on 11 September, 1812:[124]

The price of the raw material has risen alarmingly; it has not been accompanied by a proportionate increase in the price of the finished product. The excessive price of raw cotton is not due to speculation but to a real shortage. If this state of affairs continues, it is to be feared that mills will dismiss many of their workers as winter approaches.

M. Rosseel wrote of the first quarter of 1812:

It hurts us to see that the cotton shortage will force us to dismiss half of our workers before the end of next month and to close our workshops before two months are out.[125]

Similarly, M. Voortman noted for the first half of 1812:[126]

Unless supplies of raw cotton arrive, it is so expensive a raw material that consumers cannot afford it and production will have to be cut down in the first half of 1813.

Finally, M. Heyman, also speaking of this period, noted that 'dearth and costliness of cotton will bring the spinning mills to a halt unless more cotton is brought in from abroad to supply them'.[127] Moreover, official statistics covering the whole of 1812,[128] therefore drawn up during 1813, echo the above:

The cost and difficulty of obtaining this raw material have led to a dangerous fall in the activity of the mills. Cotton costs from 12 to 14 francs the kilogramme. The shortage is acute . . . ,

and elsewhere:

The prosperity of cotton spinning mills has notably increased in the last ten years, but the lack of raw materials and of outlets will bring them almost to a standstill.[129]

These complaints and observations were borne out when the authorities, obviously prompted by the manufacturers, cast doubts on the value of the policy of the economic blockade—as emerges from the following note accompanying an official survey devoted to the third quarter of 1812:[130]

Both the spinning and weaving mills of cotton manufacturers have been quite busy until now, but their raw materials are exhausted and their present situation gives cause for alarm. Cotton manufacturers employ such a large number of workers that it seems political considerations affecting imports of colonial produce ought to be waived to ensure confidence and the survival of a large number of manufacturers. Representations have been made on this score to His Excellency the Minister of Manufactures and Commerce and we are awaiting the results.

The predictions of manufacturers from the end of 1812 onwards were borne out; the year 1813 witnessed a new depression in the Ghent textile industry. A report on the second quarter of 1813[131] contains the following passage:

Cotton spinning mills and printing works are in difficulties. Because of the shortage of raw material and because manufacturers can only obtain it at very high prices, goods are often manufactured at a loss which probably accounts for the smallness of production in these factories.

[124] *Arch. Mod. Gand*, K 1–2, file V. Surveys of firms, drawn up for the compilation of quarterly statistics.     [125] *Ibid.*
    [126] *Ibid.*          [127] *Ibid.*          [128] *Ibid., Tableau général pour 1812.*
    [129] *Ibid.*          [130] *Arch. dép. Escaut*, no. 1677.          [131] *Ibid.*

A report of 6 June 1813[132] states:

The information produced by the surveys is not as satisfactory as that for the previous quarter. The stagnation in cotton production is due to the dearth of material and to the difficulties of obtaining it.

On 10 November 1813, a letter from the mayor to the prefect[133] stated that 1,281 workers, of whom 723 were women, had been dismissed. In 1812, 10,600 workers had been employed in cotton manufacturing. In the following quarter this number had already fallen to 6,150. 'Most manufacturers have warehouses filled with products that they cannot get rid of.' In his chronicle[134] the contemporary J. F. Laval noted that

from 4 March 1813, manufacturers dismissed their spinners and weavers because they could not get raw material and because buyers had cancelled their orders.

Thus all agree on the shortage and high price of cotton. It is clear that the industry suffered severely from this shortage. However, the situation is more complex: manufacturers also complained of lack of sales; to some extent this contradicts the explanation of a halt in production due to lack of raw materials. Of course, both causes may have operated: high cotton prices drove up those of yarn and thread which limited sales and produced stagnation. However, if this is the correct explanation, the manufacturers' attitude had changed; when cotton prices soared in 1808, they had expanded their firms, but in 1813 they closed them. Clearly manufacturers had learnt the lessons of previous depressions and no longer persisted in maintaining production regardless of consequences. They had lost their former optimism. The mayor says precisely this in his letter of 14 October 1812, from which we have already quoted:[135] 'Manufacturers anticipate that this growth cannot be sustained.' This strikes a very different note from that of the prefect Faipoult in his letter of 1807 or of the manufacturer Voortman writing in 1809: 'Certainly the situation is not promising, but depression never lasts long and can hold up sales only for a few months.'[136] Thus at last manufacturers had learnt from painful experience. Nonetheless, the Ghent textile industry recovered yet again, as is shown by the following table:

| Period | Spinning mills | Weaving factories | Printing works | Spinners | Weavers | Printers | Total |
|---|---|---|---|---|---|---|---|
| | | | | *Number of cotton* | | | |
| 1 Jan 1806 | 6[137] | — | 16 | 155 | — | 1,135 | 1,290 |
| 1811[138] | 23 | 15 | 10 | 3,700 | 3,400 | 790 | 7,890 |
| 1812[139] | 25 | 13 | 13 | 3,880 | 4,810 | 1,910 | 10,600 |
| 1816[140] | 28 | ? | 20 | 4,671 | 5,000 | 2,257 | 11,928 |

[132] *Ibid.*      [133] *Arch. dép. Escaut*, no. 335.
[134] The manuscript is preserved in the library of the University of Ghent.
[135] *Arch. Mod. Gand*, K. 1–2, file I.
[136] Voortman, *op. cit.*, p. 233 (29 August 1809).
[137] Table in Voortman, pp. 65–8. Ghent textiles were experiencing a depression at this time. The total number of workers was greater in 1804 than in 1806: 600 were employed in spinning mills, 1,866 in cotton printing works (*ibid.*).
[138] *Arch. Mod. Gand*, K 1–2, file V.
[139] *Ibid.*      [140] *Ibid.*, file Z.

Thus, both in terms of numbers of factories and size of labour force, the position in 1816 was healthier than in 1811 or 1812.[141]

We have come to the end of this very summary outline of developments in Ghent cotton. What conclusions can we draw from this study?

We must warn the reader against the widely accepted opinion to which we have ourselves subscribed by entitling this essay 'The Cotton Industry at Ghent during the French Régime': the French Régime does not constitute a properly self-contained period in the history of Ghent as a manufacturing centre. While it cannot be denied that this was a period of vast expansion for the Ghent textile industry, this growth cannot be limited to the 20 years of French rule.

The establishment at Ghent of large textile factories, looked upon normally as the cause of its changed economy, was only in fact the most spectacular element in a total transformation: trading centre politically tied to the Habsburgs and economically to Spanish markets[142] became a manufacturing centre[143] tied to France both politically and economically.[144] A system of production based on the guild, monopoly, manual labour in the home, was replaced by large-scale capitalist, mechanized and centralized industry.[145] A cluster of villages whose livelihood de-

[141] One last comparison: in 1812, the number of spindles actively employed in the Ghent cotton industry was 103,500. In 1815, there were 250,000.

[142] The most important element in the economic life of Ghent at the end of the *Ancien Régime* was the cloth trade; the chief trading partner was Spain. Cf. H. Coppejans-Desmedt, *op.cit.*, pp. 19ff. and Faipoult, *Mémoire statistique*, p. 128.

[143] This phrase is perhaps too uncompromising: there still existed businessmen who took no part in manufacturing projects, but were noted for their business sense, as emerges from the following extract from prefect Faipoult's *Mémoire* on the business activity of Ghent, quoted immediately above: 'Ghent is the town most actively engaged in business in all Belgium. Her export of weapons restarted as soon as the sea was reopened to trade [after the Treaty of Amiens]. Today, apart from chartered vessels, 38 of her own carry the fruits of her industry to America, Cadiz and the Mediterranean. A businessman decided to send his textiles in demand in the colonies or the United States to Cadiz where he bought wines, soda and other Spanish produce. The goods were taken from Cadiz to the Islands or the United States to be exchanged for colonial produce or precious woods; these, when sold in Europe, earned for him the profits of a triangular trade. The other trading firms of Ghent engaged in somewhat different undertakings but all were profitable and their second and third convoys left a long time ago. Probably there is no other French port on the Atlantic or Mediterranean coasts more active than Ghent. For example, Antwerp seems to have at most five or six vessels.'

[144] There is no need to insist on the political ties. On the economic links, cf. above, p. 18, for the exports of printed cottons to France. From this time onwards, all documents agree that cotton goods manufactured at Ghent are exported almost exclusively to the Empire. For example, it is recorded in the commercial correspondence of Voortman's firm (Voortman, *op, cit., passim*) that according to the account books for 1805–8, the firm Frans de Vos, one of the largest in Ghent, established in 1804, had three agents at Rouen, one each in Paris, Saint-Quentin and Amiens (Voortman, *op. cit.*, p. 53); there are more general indications of this trend of which the following is quite precise (*Arch. Mod. Gand*, K 2, enquiry into haulage contractors and commission agents, letters July–August 1811): 'The major trade links are with all of France; trade with Germany is one way—no exports are sent there.' The statistics for the entire industry in 1812 (*Arch. Mod. Gand*, K 2) in the subsection of cotton manufacturers testify to the same phenomenon: 'There are no direct exports; the kingdoms of Italy and Naples alone offer some prospects for exports of printed cottons.'

[145] This was not yet true for the period of French rule. Although linen production by artisans had long since disappeared and woollen production by artisans was in sharp decline, cotton weaving had considerably increased in the town—the number of Ghent weavers in 1816 was put at 5,000 (cf. above, p. 41). This does not include workers employed in large workshops.

pended on the exports of the output of rural industry had been transformed into a town in which production was concentrated.

No decisive break with the former state of industry occurred during the French régime; certain elements of the past survived; Ghent remained—though to a lesser degree—the market for textiles produced by the rural industry and the focus for their distribution. Even its own industry, in particular cotton weaving, continued to depend on the work of rural artisans.[146] Even in the organization of cotton spinning there remained traces of the past: from one point of view each mule-jenny was a small autonomous concern in which the spinner himself paid the other workers out of his basic wage, while the upkeep of his machine came out of his own pocket. Moreover, he was paid by the piece, not by the hour. In short, the factory was an aggregation of small concerns.

Some of these traces of the past survived for a long time, others disappeared soon, as was the case with the domestic system, both for linen and cotton. Nonetheless, the transformation of the industry had not been completed by the end of the French régime. Nor indeed had it started only with the arrival of the French. Traces of an initial slow and faint movement go back to a variety of more or less still-born firms founded at the end of the seventeenth[147] and the beginning of the eighteenth centuries—a few enterprising businessmen, speculators perhaps, tempted by the prospect of manufacturing. No one stopped them; indeed they were encouraged, but all ended in failure. The last of this generation was the Coene family. Clemmen[148] was the first of a new generation of manufacturers who did not burn their fingers. His activities in the cotton textile trade led him to found cotton printing works: the first large Ghent manufacturing plant to survive the early difficulties. It was at this time, round about 1780,[149] that the transformation occurred: some of the Ghent businessmen became cotton manufacturers and printers. They were very few at first, but their ranks successively swelled. From 1780, one or two Ghent capitalists left trading for industry. This trend became more general round about 1789—political and social difficulties experienced by the country did but delay the process. New cotton printing works were founded between 1789 and 1800, even more between 1800 and 1805. Indeed, round about 1800, if not earlier, cotton printing was already the most important and prosperous sector of the Ghent economy. From 1800 onwards, the march towards industrialization quickened.[150] It was during the Consulate that the first cotton spinning mills were set up and the first attempts made to spin flax by mechanical means, while woollen mills of some size were established. Before then, up to the peace of Amiens, the French market had never exerted a very strong pull. While textiles were still exported to Spain and printed cottons to southern Holland and to the Rhineland,[151] most production went towards local consumption. Ghent was still no more than a centre of provincial industry. Around 1804–5, the pace suddenly quickened, and henceforth there was a continual ebb and flow; the first period of modest growth occurred in 1804–5 with the establishment of several spinning mills; they had already ceased production by the end of 1805.[152] The giants of the industry were founded in the dangerous and uncertain climate of economic blockade; the moment of

[146] Cf. above, pp. 26–7.    [147] Cf. above, p. 16.    [148] Cf. above, pp. 16–17.
[149] Cf. above, p. 16.    [150] Cf. above, p. 17.
[151] Cf. above, p. 18.    [152] Cf. above, p. 23.

decisive expansion occurred when a ban was placed on both yarns and cotton fabrics from England: spinning mills, soon followed by weaving factories, were founded and prospered. The years from 1806 to 1808 were the turning point; many new manufacturing plants came into existence; above all, economic attitudes changed. Manufacturing concerns now decisively replaced the trading activity by which the town had hitherto existed. The mass conversion to this new doctrine occurred between 1806 and 1810. Everybody wanted to manufacture, to produce, and enormous sums were invested in the industry. These were painful as well as exciting years: manufacturers lacked experience, undoubtedly capital was in short supply, and new machinery often failed to function.[153] Market opportunities were badly miscalculated as though there were no limits either to expansion or profits. Harsh reality intervened: prices, after two years of steady rise, spiralled upwards.[154] Then, between July and November 1808 they plummeted.[155] Inflated by speculation and misleading rumours, prices crumbled. Factories lacking substantial reserves were forced to close. Depression reigned. The industry recovered because some of the mills disappeared, as a result of measures taken by the government and of the generally favourable business position. However, manufacturers learnt nothing from this experience. In 1810 entrepreneurial business zeal reached a peak because of rising prices; in the flax, wool and above all, cotton sectors of the industry gigantic firms requiring massive capital investments expanded as never before.[156] This was the year of the downturn; the crisis was terrible—bankruptcy dragged down the boldest of the innovators, such as the Bauwens and the Lousbergs.

At the end of 1811, production picked up.[157] However, it seems that a change had occurred at Ghent. Manufacturers became more prudent after their painful experience. There was no recurrence of the rapid creation of new firms which had accompanied each preceding period of prosperity. Ghent manufacturers, apparently convinced that the market could not absorb all they produced, became more cautious, however high prices might rise. They took advantage of the lowering of the cotton price in 1812 and of the reduction in labour[158] costs to recommence expansion, so that in 1812 their production attained new peaks;[159] but when cotton prices again began to spiral rapidly upwards,[160] pulling up prices of manufactured goods with them, they made no attempt to follow the trend,[161] but simply closed down their factories. Later, when the French had gone, the industry resumed its expansion which lasted throughout the nineteenth century until our own times, periodically interrupted by cyclical depressions and corresponding market readjustments. Such is the outline of changes in the industry. As a whole, despite severe depressions, progress was sustained; after each depression, production attained a peak higher than the previous best.

[153] Cf. above, p. 36, the observations of the manufacturer Van Huffel.
[154] Extracts from the correspondence of the firm of Voortman, cf. above, p. 28. If one takes L. Bauwens literally (cf. p. 29), prices shot upwards between 1 May and November 1808.         [155] Cf. above, p. 30.
[156] The new price rise was reflected in the correspondence of Voortman's firm (op. cit., p. 229). 10 March 1810: 'The price of our goods is rising, and the mignonettes [fine lace goods] are rising'. 15 March 1810: 'I can only provide you with such goods at a price increased by two to three sols the ell.' On 19 March 1810: 'Prices of our cotton cloths have risen 1½ sols to the ell.'
[157] Cf. above, p. 36.          [158] Cf. above, p. 37.          [159] Cf. above, p. 35.
[160] Cf. above, pp. 40-1.          [161] Cf. above, p. 41.

This trend of continual expansion was made possible by the interaction of three factors: first, access to a wider market as a result of measures of economic warfare against England; second, increasing productivity of the labour force; and finally the structure of the firms and the personal characteristics of the entrepreneurs. This is not the place to consider the full implications of the first point. Government measures included prohibitive or increased duties on foreign, especially English, textile goods, certain import and export embargoes, and inducements to export to French-occupied Europe—measures which had widespread and conflicting repercussions. Obviously the opening of the French and, to a much smaller extent, of the continental market[162] and the virtually total suppression of English competition were two of the most important factors in the growth of the Ghent cotton industry. Clearly these two measures reflected the wishes of Ghent manufacturers,[163] but they had severe drawbacks. Heavy import duties on cotton, resulting in difficulty in importing this indispensable raw material, led to a rapid increase in its price; this price-rise, due at first more to speculation than to a real shortage of cotton,[164] was the root cause of the principal troubles besetting Ghent manufacturers—they were faced with the recurrent dilemma of either stocking up with expensive raw materials, thereby running the risk of selling at a loss if the market collapsed in the four or five months necessary to process the raw cotton, or else of closing their factories and waiting for cotton prices to fall. The ban on Anglo-Indian textile goods at first seemed entirely advantageous, but in fact gave them a false sense of security; for goods at a price that undercut anything they could produce entered the continental market through the smuggling provoked by the ban.[165] The combined effect of the ban and their difficulties in obtaining cotton compelled manufacturers to adapt their factories to the production of goods, in particular the finest counts of yarn, from cottons (from the Levant) to which they were not accustomed.[166] All this led to an increase in production costs and prevented them from competing in markets where the English were operating. In a more general

[162] Cf. the above remarks, from which it is clear that little was exported to countries outside the Empire. The cause is found in the general survey of 1812, quoted in the same note, in the section dealing with cotton spinning mills: 'Yarn exports are non-existent, because the duty on imports of the raw material have made the product uncompetitive.'

[163] Throughout the period under consideration, or at least from 1806, manufacturers constantly pressed the government to take a series of measures that made sense to a manufacturer but which could not feasibly be applied at the same time: a ban on cotton yarn and English cloths (cf., for 1806, p. 23 above, and the letter from Bauwens of 1809 above, p. 30); no import limitation or at least a reduction on import duties, on raw cotton, cf. the letter of 1807 from prefect Faipoult, quoted, above p. 24, in a passage not reproduced in the text, and also the prefect's remarks accompanying the quarterly survey for 1811, above, pp. 35-6); effective measures against English smuggling (same Faipoult letter); no controls on textile exports (letter by Bauwens above); assurances that once manufacturers had sufficiently large reserves, controls would be placed on cotton imports. This last point was developed in the letter of 1806 from the Lousbergs brothers (quoted above, p. 28) written precisely in order to persuade the government to promise a guarantee that in the event of American cottons arriving, import duties would be levied to maintain the price of cotton high. There is nothing surprising in all this; but it is strikingly clear that the manufacturers were not conditioned by the concept of a free economy. They considered governmental intervention necessary to ensure their own prosperity.

[164] Cf. above, p. 30.

[165] Cf. above, p. 30.

[166] Cf. above, p. 31.

sense, they were held back[167] by uncertainty about measures that the government might take, for instance in the sphere of foreign trade.

We can only touch here on the complex question of the labour force. We may confine ourselves to noting that, on the positive side, manufacturers had at their disposal a large rural population, experienced in textile production.[168] Accordingly, they were able to increase weaving operations without any difficulty. Weavers were in ample supply; the sole modifications necessary were the transfer of weavers from flax to cotton by equipping their looms with fly shuttles.[169] Nonetheless the growth of their factories compelled Ghent manufacturers to recruit weavers from as far away as Arras and Amiens.[170] Moreover, the large population of Ghent contained an indigent class that met the needs of the Ghent manufacturers for spinners: men, women and children of this class, owing as much to the bribe of high wages as to measures against vagrancy and begging, were induced to work in factories. The one serious difficulty lay in retaining these workers once they had been trained; so rapidly was the industry developing that a manufacturer had hardly trained a worker before he was snapped up by a rival.[171]

In conclusion let us try to depict the nature of the factories and the business men themselves. The originality of the new firms lay not only in their immense size,[172] but also in their unique organization. There was a definite trend towards the

[167] This is clear from the letter of the Lousberg brothers quoted in note 163, which sought —as we stated above—a guarantee that the government would maintain existing high cotton prices if large supplies arrived. This way of thinking is revealed even more clearly in the correspondence of the Voortman firm, as shown in the following extracts. 8 February 1808 (Voortman, *op. cit.*, p. 217): '[an order of Georgia cotton is under discussion] If this rumour about import licences is substantiated, manufacturers will be forced to sell at lower prices.' On 5 August 1810 (p. 220): 'Several rumours are circulating about cotton: it is claimed that the only restriction to be placed on imports will be a duty, some say of three, others twenty [francs per quintal. Ed.]; if this is so, the buyer will be under a severe handicap.'

[168] Cf. above, p. 15.

[169] Cf. above, p. 21.

[170] Varlez, *op. cit.*, p. 28: 'The whole of the surrounding area was engaged in production for Ghent manufacturers. They had their own yarn woven for them in country areas deep in the *Département* of the *Nord*, as far as Arras, Saint-Quentin and Avesnes.'

[171] On the problem of the labour force in the spinning mills, cf. J. Dhondt, 'Note sur les ouvriers gantois à l'époque française', *Revue du Nord*, 1954.

[172] In their letter from which we have quoted (cf. above, n. 82), the Lousbergs brothers claim that they employ two thousand workers. This figure is undoubtedly exaggerated, emphasizing the size of their firm in order to obtain favourable economic measures. Moreover, theirs was a vertical concern comprising cotton spinning, weaving and printing works. A random selection among surveys of firms shows that in the first half of 1812 the number of workers was as follows:

| | |
|---|---|
| De Vos | 2,550 |
| Greban et Compagnie | 1,050 |
| Poelman-Vervaecke | 690 |
| De Paepe | 699 |
| Delebecque | 466 |
| Rosseel | 447 |
| Guinard | 380 |
| H. Lousbergs | 210 |
| Voortman | 186 |
| Heynderickx | 150 |

These figures seem much larger than those given in n. 96 for the same firms. This is because weavers were not included in the totals in the latter note.

creation of vertical concerns including every stage in the transformation from the spinning of the fibre to the manufacturing of the finished article, ready for consumption.[173] We have seen that factories comprising spinning, weaving and printing works were frequent in the cotton sector of the industry. In the wool and flax spheres of production, the same manufacturers concentrated on both spinning and weaving. They also undertook the dressing and bleaching. Furthermore, Ghent manufacturers to the exclusion of qualified middlemen themselves attended to the sale of their goods.[174] While it is true that L. Bauwens did not engage in cotton printing, he possessed the very first link in the chain of operations because he built his own machinery.

The complex nature of these firms should be stressed. The industrialist headed a spinning mill, where frequent failures of machinery obliged him to maintain a team of mechanics. He directed a weaving factory which brought him into contact with hundreds of weavers as far away as Saint-Quentin. He supplied yarn to hundreds of small artisans; they, in turn, sent him the woven cloth. He headed the printing works and organized sales.[175]

Rapid changes in the business world made the structure of the firm even more complex. In the traditional business world, industry had generally been controlled by statutory monopolies; there were very few large firms devoted solely to manufacturing; production was by hand in artisans' workshops and the manufactured article, cotton textiles, which was going to revolutionize this industrial world was still little-known.[176] Goods were sold on commission to distant countries (such as Spain and the Spanish colonies).

Radical changes were experienced by the immediate descendants of these traders

---

[173] This is not to say that this was the general rule. *L'état de situation des manufactures de coton de la ville de Gand pendant le premier trimestre 1813* (*Arch. Mod. Gand*, K 2) covers a total of 33 cotton firms. They are:

 3 spinning/weaving/printing works;
11 spinning/weaving mills
 1 spinning mill and printing works
 7 printing works
 6 spinning mills
 1 weaving factory

It is interesting to note that the only two firms that, at first sight, appear to have lasted from the French régime to our own times (Voortman and Story) were exclusively printing works throughout the French régime.

[174] Obviously, this refers not to direct sales to the consumer, but to the immediately preceding retailer. This is confirmed in correspondence of July–August 1813 (*Arch. Mod. Gand*, K 2), about commission agencies in Ghent: 'Our manufacturers nearly always dispose of their goods on the open market, and rarely to a middleman'. Another indication of this set-up is found in the correspondence of the Voortman firm, published by J. Voortman in his book, already quoted, on the cotton industry in Ghent, *passim*. Although Ghent manufacturers probably did not figure among them, it should be stressed that Ghent businessmen of the period were ship owners: they were sole masters of 38 vessels, whereas Antwerp had less than six at the moment of the Treaty of Amiens (Faipoult, *Mémoire pour le commerce de la ville de Gand*, quoted by Nève, *op. cit.*, pp. 353–4).

[175] Even firms engaged in only one of the manufacturing processes, such as cotton printing, had a complex structure. From documents published by Voortman, it is clear that his ancestor, a cotton printer during the French régime, bought raw cotton and had it woven on the domestic system; thus, while nominally a cotton printer, in practice he must have been in charge of spinning and weaving operations.

[176] On this last point cf. the observations of Faipoult above, p. 16.

of 1760: suppression of the guilds; loss of the Spanish and opening of the French market; appearance of revolutionary new techniques; manufacture of a product for mass consumption; governmental politico-economic measures occasioned by the war with England and their unexpected and varied consequences for the entry of raw materials; and the establishment of large firms with resultant enormous fluctuations in production and therefore in the state of the market. In addition, totally new problems of financing and labour recruitment[177] were posed by these large firms.

Thus the sons of Ghent business men of the earlier epoch created large manufacturing 'empires' in a world where little remained of the past, where all was new and constantly in flux, where nothing was stable or permanent. These conditions are sufficient to explain the failures, the abrupt changes, the bankruptcies. It was inevitable that so great a revolution would exact so high a cost.

The enthusiasm of this new generation for technical progress is remarkable. They could have been expected to approach innovations with extreme caution and suspicion. On the contrary, they made advances in technique in every branch of the textile industry; in spinning, not only were the new mule-jennies[178] installed in all the mills, but on at least two occasions machinery was used to spin flax and wool: attempts to mechanize flax spinning involved Liévin Bauwens in some costly experiments,[179] and at the end of the French régime, Gamard-Verhegghen invested a large sum in a spinning machine and a weaving works. As to the mechanization of wool production, as early as Year XI, Sybille was spinning 'with machinery' and at the end of our period, Maes founded a large spinning concern. As for weaving, we have studied the attempts made to propagate the use of the fly shuttle[180] and in particular, the experiments of the Lousbergs brothers with power looms.[181] New sources of power were harnessed: three cotton factories installed steam engines.[182] The characteristic innovation in printing techniques was the introduction of printing by metal cylinders.[183] Turning, in conclusion, to the bleaching of cloths, Liévin Bauwens introduced the Chaptal-Berthollet[184] process,

[177] Seemingly unimportant, this was in fact a real nightmare for manufacturers. The rapid training of a labour force of several thousands was required by the establishment, within a very few years, of all these spinning mills. Because they could not be found straight away, wages rose to fantastically high levels for the period. A worker trained in modern spinning methods was worth his weight in gold, and law courts resounded with the grievances of manufacturers accusing their rivals of poaching workers trained at great cost. Nothing is more striking than the attempts by manufacturers, especially Bauwens, to bind their workers to them by law—workers were to have no say in the choice of their master.

[178] Although some frames existed, there were few in Ghent.

[179] Cf. above, p. 16, n. 7.

[180] Cf. above, p. 21.

[181] The Lousbergs brothers installed at Renaix a machine-driven cotton weaving factory with some 400 power looms. No one followed their example (Varlez, *op. cit.*, p. 29).

[182] J. Mareska and J. Heyman, *Enquête sur le travail et la condition physique et morale dans les manufactures de coton à Gand*, Ghent, 1845, p. 44: 'In 1803 . . . Liévin Bauwens, followed by De Vos and Rosseel, began to use steam engines, but all the other manufacturers, for almost 15 years, continued to rely on manual—or horse—power, until after the fall of the Empire links with England were renewed. Two years ago, it was still possible to see the steam engine of Liévin Bauwens, constructed mainly of wood, in the factory of the Chartreux. M. Rosseel possesses to this day his very first wooden steam engines.'

[183] Cf. above, p. 17, the passage from the *Mémoire* by Faipoult.

[184] Cf. above, p. 21.

and we must not omit the many obvious if less well-known improvements that allowed the finest counts to be spun.[185]

What was the background of the entrepreneurs? Where did they get their capital? What did they think of the productive capacity of their factories?

It is not easy to discover their social background nor the original source of their capital. We have already seen that traders began to enter cotton printing from about 1780 onwards. Many of these cotton printers later entered spinning[186] and obviously used their large profits from cotton printing to finance their new activity. Other traders went straight to spinning and weaving without passing through cotton printing—notably the Bauwens; however, they were tanners as well as traders. Research shows that traders were thinly represented among cotton manufacturers,[187] less so in fact than the small manufacturers of the Austrian period (sugar and salt refiners, brewers, distillers, etc.). The prefect Faipoult gives us the valuable information[188] that the former nobility believed their income, substantially reduced by abolition of seigneurial rights, would increase by investment in industry. Finally, the example of Bauwens and others shows that profits from war contracts for the armies and from speculation inherent in periods of social upheavals also provided capital investment for the industry.

It is obvious that members of very varied social milieux would only have invested their money in industry,[189] if the latter appeared to offer quick and certain profits. At first sight, this seems improbable. On the one hand, wage expenditure was abnormally high, and labour shortage meant that it could not be reduced. In addition, machinery was very costly, nor were the new mule-jennies yet working satisfactorily. It is true that factory space was cheap; works were often housed in former convents, fit for nothing else, which would otherwise have remained

---

[185] Cf. above, p. 31, n. 86.

[186] Of the ten names of cotton printers mentioned in the 'list of cotton printers' (*Arch. Mod. Gand*, K 2), at least two ranked among the leading spinning and weaving industrialists of the Empire. They were De Vos and the Lousbergs.

[187] In the list of the chief Ghent traders, compiled in 1771 (published in H. Coppejans-Desmedt, *op. cit.*, pp. 195–9), I have found the names of Clemmen, Poelman, J. F. Smet, Villiot; these men also feature among Ghent manufacturers under the French régime. Because of the lack of genealogical information, I cannot say whether the families of Poelman and J. F. Smet were the same in the list of 1771 and under the French régime; it seems very probable, since the latter was a merchant dealing in cotton textiles in 1771. One must add the Bauwens to this list—although tanners, they were also traders in colonial produce.

[188] Faipoult, *Mémoire statistique, An* IX, p. 151: 'The number of factories and of sound investments is increasing; it is easy to understand why: those living on fixed incomes, former nobles, have suffered considerably from the abolition of annuities and feudal dues; some of them have already had the intelligence to become manufacturers or tradesmen and look to a sound business firm to restore their fortunes. The rise in the cost of living forces others to do the same, because their well-being is threatened, although they enjoy the same income as in the past.'

[189] Relatives often clubbed together to launch a company. This was true of the Bauwens, Lousbergs, and Desmet families, to name only three of the most important. Often these family firms later divided. Thus three of the Bauwens brothers had spinning mills (Ghent and Tronchiennes, Passy, Vonèche) which may have been united at first, but which later on appear to have separated. It seems that the same was true of the Desmet brothers. The family firm appears to belong to the earlier period. As the firm grew, the original unit divided so that several members of the same family were owners each of their own factory. But in addition to these family concerns, there were many others organized in a variety of

unused. As for supplies of raw materials, Ghent industrialists had no private source of supply; they wholly depended on sales by large trading companies. Administrative and sales services were strictly limited because industrialists themselves did most of the work; this meant that other 'general expenses' were probably small. Nonetheless, production costs must have been high. Thus, large-scale production ways. A list of firms, with their official trade names, in February 1816 (spinning and printing works) shows:

|  | *labour force* |  | *labour force* |
| --- | --- | --- | --- |
| SPINNING MILLS |  | *Companies* |  |
| *Individually owned firms:* |  | Veuve Antheunis et Cie | 72 |
| P. J. Banneville | 144 | Delebecque et Cie | 216 |
| J. Coppens | 270 | Dierman et Cie | 72 |
| F. de Hemptinne | 72 | De Vos et Cie | 621 |
| B. De Rudder | 72 | Godefroy et Cie | 144 |
| Previously engaged in bleaching |  | Rosseel et Cie | 576 |
| of cloth |  | Van Kuffel et Cie | 72 |
| De Paepe-Speelman | 297 |  |  |
| Heyman-Bauwens | 144 | PRINTING WORKS |  |
| Frans de Ruyck | 72 | *Individually owned firms:* |  |
| De Pird | 45 | J. Braeckman | 200 |
| Hovaere | 45 | Fr. De Vos | 180 |
| J. J. Hebbelinck | 72 | Hubert Lousbergs | 180 |
| Probably a descendant of the |  | G. van der Waerden | 147 |
| tradesman of the same name of |  | Van den Broecke | 40 |
| 1771 |  | Van den Broecke-Grenier | 20 |
| Marnef | 36 | Van de Vijvere-Goethals | 20 |
| Valentin van Loo | 90 | A. Voortman | 280 |
| Bernard van Loo | 90 | J. Vereecke | 50 |
| F. L. van Caneghem | 90 | De Vaere | 20 |
| Van de Woestijne de Kuyper | 216 | Onderheed | 20 |
|  |  | David | 40 |
| *Family firms:* |  | Rappe | 50 |
| Bossaert frères | 360 | B. Story | 160 |
| Desmet frères | 261 | B. Story fils | 40 |
| Speelman frères | 108 | Frans Speelman fils | 200 |
| Wanten frères | 90 |  |  |
|  |  | *Family firms:* |  |
| *Partnerships:* |  | De Hert et fils | 150 |
| J. Chrétien et Mouton | 90 | De Smet frères | 150 |
| Poelman et Fervaecke | 270 |  |  |
| Is this Poelman descendant of |  | *Partnerships:* |  |
| the tradesman of the same name |  | Ch. Alexis et veuve Sauvage | 250 |
| in 1771? |  | Snel et van Hoorde | 60 |

This shows that companies are on the whole larger than partnerships and family concerns which themselves are larger than individually owned firms. It also illustrates that one-man businesses are more numerous in the printing industry, the reverse of the situation in the spinning mills.

Ghent firms grew largely by ploughing back their profits; this emerges from the report by the prefect Faipoult at the opening of the session of the general council in Year XIII: 'In the past the cloth, lace and leather trades accounted for all capital investment. Only new sources of capital, accrued from the profits of past investment and from rigid economy measures, can account for the establishment of the many new refineries and printing works and the setting up of spinning mills that do not encroach upon existing concerns' (published in Nève, *Gand sous la domination française*, pp. 168–9).

There is one source of capital for which it seems impossible to find any evidence: these manufacturers probably did not only invest everything they and their associates possessed, but also borrowed additional sums, as did Bauwens (cf. above, p. 38).

or the possibility of very high selling prices alone can have coloured industrialists' assessments of possible profits.

How correct is it to speak of estimated profits? Surely it was rather a case of hopes and illusions. These new businessmen had never experienced the realities of economic activity. Their *naïveté* about economic matters is shown by what may be called their 'excessive expansionism'; the proliferation and growth of individual firms clearly suggests that this generation believed the market to be unlimited, as perhaps also would be the price rise. Liévin Bauwens said as much: 'a manufacturer must be able to devote all his energies to the expansion and improvement of his factories';[190] he considered that it was wrong for the manufacturer to have to pay when prices fell, but right for the consumer to pay the costs of rising prices. Faipoult, in his letter of 1807,[191] was reflecting the views current at that time: he clearly reveals the mentality of the manufacturers when, in an unrealistic estimate, he takes the unlimited growth of the industry for granted. The recurrence of the establishment of new firms at the beginning of any period of prosperity, however short-lived, is proof enough that most manufacturers held this view. Only the belief that every investment in industry would yield immediate and substantial profits can explain this phenomenon. Up to a point, this belief was justified: throughout and even after the French régime, production was greater, after every depression, than the previous best. Thus consumer demand was never wholly satisfied; but manufacturers underestimated the importance of certain vital factors, as is proved by successive periodic depressions responsible for the staccato rhythm of the industry during French rule: the cost price, sufficient reserves of capital at the foundation of the firm, and the outlet by which finished goods would reach consumers.

Thus it seems that this generation of Ghent manufacturers lacked neither boldness to invest nor receptivity to new ideas, but only experience and knowledge commensurate with the size of their undertakings. (Incidentally, they lived well and lavishly.[192]) They were forever short of money and—outside the brief periods of prosperity—concerned about future prospects; they were often forced to take risky short-term measures.[193] On the whole one may subscribe to the severe judgment of the President of the Tribunal of Commerce; in 1810 he blamed the plethora of bankruptcies on speculation and on involvements which 'exceeded the means and knowledge'[194] of manufacturers.

---

[190] In his letter of 1809, from which we have often quoted, cf. n. 66.

[191] Cf. n. 48 above.

[192] Varlez, *op. cit.*, p. 28. A contemporary noted that 'the money that had been easily earned and which was "ever changing hands", was spent with a prodigality never before known in the small town of Ghent. The Bauwens alone had seven *hôtels* in Paris, including *l'hôtel de Richelieu*, lavishly maintained.' In 1810 the President of the Chamber of Commerce in Ghent wrote: 'In the past the trader lived off the profits of his business; economy prevailed and show was never carried to the degree of recent extravagance . . .' (Nève, *op. cit.*, p. 186).

[193] We saw how, to wipe out his debt to the government, Bauwens contracted two heavy mortgages on his factories and later tried to sell one to the State, thus eliminating the first creditor (cf. p. 39). The President of the Chamber of Commerce (cf. preceding note) wrote: 'Previously, confidence in the industry was general; trade was not then the haggling of second-hand dealers—sincerity, probity, the word of the trader was worth as much as the tightest of contracts.' He obviously is suggesting that the opposite was the case at the time of writing, i.e. in 1810.    [194] Same document as quoted in preceding note.

This does not signify that they should be condemned out of hand. This Ghent industry of 1780–1814 must be seen for what it was: an enormous effort to modernize the economy, undertaken by a new generation that succeeded despite many mistakes in creating a major modern industry in very difficult circumstances.

# The Effects

# of Nineteenth-Century

# Liberal Agrarian Reforms on

# Social Structure in Central Europe

WERNER CONZE

Translated by Walter M. Stern

Central Europe's social structure has essentially been transformed since the beginning of the nineteenth century[1] from a developed agrarian society, tied in various feudal ways and stratified into classes, to an industrial society freed from these ties, subordinated in part directly to the State, in part to supra-national economic conditions. The metamorphosis is due above all to two important events:

(1) the dissolution of social ties in countryside and towns through the well-known reforms which took place chiefly in the second half of the eighteenth and the first half of the nineteenth centuries;

(2) the growth of the industrial system which reached Central Europe mostly later and assumed large proportions only towards the middle of the nineteenth century.

Both processes were rendered possible, pushed forward and accelerated, but not caused, by population pressure which increased in the course of the eighteenth century. Population strove for non-existent living space and found it in the great mobilization and widening of opportunities consequent upon liberal reforms and industrialization. However, this did not moderate the surge of population nor stabilize it, for, favoured by the new conditions, it soared beyond tolerable limits, thus engendering new pressures.

These two developments interacted and complemented one another in pushing forward the structural change of society. Their effects on the social order can therefore hardly be separately analysed. This interaction must be borne in mind,

[1] This article is a new edition of the lost manuscript of an inaugural lecture [customary in Germany on first appointment to university teaching. Transl.] delivered in 1943. Owing to immediate post-war difficulties in the use of libraries, it was unfortunately then impossible to check all the essential sources used.

though we deal here with one of its aspects only, the great work of liberal reform in its main sector, agrarian reform, and its repercussions on social order in Central Europe.

In the concept of agrarian reform we include:

(1) Peasant liberation in the narrower sense, i.e. abolition of peasant obligations, of all ties and dues of a personal, jurisdictional, feudal or manorial nature.

(2) Enclosure which has close logical connections with it—a collective concept including all measures aiming at rational reallocation of cultivable land, i.e. consolidation of strips scattered in the open field, redistribution of common lands (fields and pastures) to form private holdings, redemption of manifold servitudes attaching to the property of others, and finally—not necessarily in conjunction with, but following logically upon, enclosure—removal or development of farms out of ancient village settlements to occupy an economically preferable position at the centre of a consolidated holding.

The aim of all these measures, as visualized by reformers, was a cultivator pursuing agriculture rationally and autonomously on a holding freed from all feudal and corporate obstacles. The economic optimism of the period expected the free play of market forces to produce a favourable development, with the inefficient falling behind and progress bringing to the fore the 'best cultivator'.[2]

Consequent upon peasant liberation and enclosure, and aimed at from the outset, modern intensive agriculture developed, changing from its traditional to an improved three-field system and methods of crop rotation, cyclically alternating animal husbandry and arable in individual cultivation, employing mechanization and rationalization in the modern and capitalist meaning of these words.

It is of the nature of these liberal reforms, unless arrested half-way, that they affected the entire rural way of life, politically, socially and economically. Their intellectual foundations are manifold and will not be discussed here. In general they sprang from the following principal roots:

(1) The endeavour of territorial rulers to remove intermediate feudal forces and establish a direct relationship with all dwellers in their territories as equal subjects or citizens. Their efforts were in future to benefit the State direct and no longer to be intercepted by the aristocracy. This represented a centuries-old tradition of territorial rulership; it was also the ultimate outcome of the absolutist State, reached at a moment of time when it was already being superseded by liberal constitutional provisions.

(2) The demand for the liberation of man, especially of the peasant living in oppressive dependency—a demand operative already during the Reformation and developed by the philosophy of enlightenment. It was addressed both to feudal lords and to the State.

(3) The new doctrines of the physiocrats and, even more significant, of economic liberalism as formulated in Britain, especially the effects of rational agriculture of which Britain provided a model in theory and practice.

The heterogeneity of these currents, with sometimes one, sometimes another predominating in the interplay of forces and interests, explains the considerable differences displayed by reform movements in different countries and the dis-

---

[2] For its classical formulation, cf. e.g. A. Thaer, *Grundsätze der rationellen Landwirtschaft* Principles of Rational Agriculture), 1809–12.

similar social consequences. Their beneficiary was often the State of the territorial ruler who succeeded by means of reforms in establishing a viable peasantry. In other instances developments worked against him, when he might be unable to keep control of the course of events. In large areas the aristocracy, in general the main opposition at which reforms tilted, recognized very clearly the advantages flowing from agrarian liberalism, hence took charge of reforms and became their chief beneficiary.

To the manifold tendencies uniting and contending within the framework of reform corresponds the multiplicity of historical and social foundations on which reforms in the various States had to be erected.

Lastly, intensity varied greatly in individual instances. Instalments of the work of reform were mostly carried through separately and at different periods, sometimes compressed in concentrated haste, sometimes interrupted by long intervals of quiescence or reaction. Important reforms, particularly enclosure, might be omitted altogether or neglected, some not having been carried out up to the present day.

In spite of numerous local studies following the classical discussions by Knapp and Grünberg, the connection between reforms and their effects has by no means been equally clarified everywhere. There remains important scope for further research based on contemporary sources in individual countries and cultural areas.

The following description of the great and complex movement includes geographically the nineteenth-century area of the German Federation, including Prussia's eastern provinces which remained outside the Federation, Switzerland, the area of the Hungarian crown of St. Stephen, of the Polish-Lithuanian State before the partitions, and the Baltic provinces of the Russian Empire. This suggests the following scheme of presentation:

I    The area of feudal landownership (*Grundherrschaft*) west of the boundary line of a highly-developed manorial system.

II   The area of manorial system (*Gutsherrschaft*) of the German Federation, including the whole of the Prussian east.

III  Regions surrounding this area, either undertaking agrarian reforms of their own in conjunction with West or Central European developments or affected by Prussian and Austrian reforms.

IV   The 'western regions' of the Russian Empire in which the Russian peasant liberation determined the change in the agrarian order.

# I

Only in contrast with the manorial system of the east can the west and south German area be considered as a unit. Internal variations abound, but in spite of many territorial and regional differences we can distinguish some principal areas by prevailing types of agrarian order.[3]

---

[3] Cf. articles on 'Bauernbefreiung' (Peasant Liberation) in *Handwörterbuch der Staatswissenschaft* and *Wörterbuch der Volkswirtschaft* by F. Gutmann and J. Fuchs, and by way of correction F. Lütge, *Die mitteldeutsche Grundherrschaft. Untersuchungen über die bäuerlichen*

In the south-west German areas of physical land division,[4] the agrarian order was determined largely by small and miniature territorial rulers who had arrogated to themselves a large part of the rights flowing from servile, jurisdictional and feudal domination. We can rightly speak of 'ossification' of the agrarian order inasmuch as no radical change had occurred after the late Middle Ages; some medieval conditions even survived intact the period of liberal reforms. However, this much-discussed 'ossification' did not signify a rigid standstill. Rather did the picture change considerably in the course of centuries through a gradual shift of fragmented feudal rights from which peasants not infrequently benefited by improving their rights of possession. It was above all the custom of physical division which modified the agrarian order from the late Middle Ages onwards and started the ball rolling. A result of this custom of inheritance was, by the eighteenth century, a high density of rural population, to a large extent even rural overpopulation; further, a closing of the social gap between a substantial peasantry of long standing and the occupants of smallholdings; a craft diversification of the countryside springing from the need for additional earnings, facilitated sometimes by the erosion of urban guild privileges, lastly, the obliteration of boundaries between countryside and town. 'Serfdom' had become no more than an obligation to render dues on special occasions (death, marriage, permission to emigrate) and had here and there been abolished from the sixteenth century onwards.[5] Labour services derived from feudal or jurisdictional lordship were inconsiderable in the absence of a manorial system. In comparison to other German areas peasants enjoyed favourable rights of possession. Many restrictions had lapsed. If pressure and burden was nevertheless resented in the eighteenth century, this resulted not only from the multiplicity of dues which added up grievously, but even more from the fragmentation of holdings due to physical division.

The area of Bavaria and the Alps with its custom of primogeniture shows evidence of a stronger preservation or development of the feudal system, with peasant rights of possession mostly inferior to those in the south-west. Fundamentally however the agrarian structure was sounder, owing to undivided inheritance of peasant holdings. This preserved a sturdy medium and substantial peasantry as a class clearly distinct from smallholders and landless people. In the south-east, too, liberal agrarian reform had here and there pushed out roots over several centuries in that community of interest between territorial ruler and peasants, which often led to relief or freedom for the latter, most typically in the Tyrol. Enclosure also had had its harbingers, above all the movement towards separate holdings which began in Kempten in the sixteenth century.

Lütge[6] rightly claims the central German area of Thuringia and Saxony to re-

Verhältnisse (Agrarverfassung) Mitteldeutschlands im 16–18. Jh. (Feudal Landownership in Central Germany. Enquiries into Peasant Conditions (Agrarian Order) in Central Germany from the Sixteenth to the Eighteenth Centuries), Jena, 1934.

[4] For its extension into Central Germany, cf. maps in M. Sering and C. v. Dietze, Die Vererbung des ländlichen Grundbesitzes in der Nachkriegszeit (Inheritance of Agricultural Land in the Post-War Period), Munich, 1930, I.

[5] On the course of peasant liberation in south-west and south-east Germany, even before the reform period proper, cf. O. Stolz, 'Die Bauernbefreiung in Süddeutschland im Zusammenhang der Geschichte' (Peasant Liberation in Southern Germany in its Historical Context), V[ierteljahrschrift für] S[ozial- und] W[irtschafts] G[eschichte], xxxiii, 1940, pp. 1ff.

[6] F. Lütge, loc. cit.

present a special type of agrarian order, though it seems related in many aspects, particularly in the Thuringian areas of physical division, to the south-west; from other points of view it could be included in the Bavarian-Alps area. The particular characteristic of central Germany is the evolution of an especially pure type of feudal system in the eighteenth century with a complete absence of traditional servitude. Attempts at a manorial system of the east German type for which certain favourable conditions existed in Saxony were prevented in good time by a deliberate policy of peasant protection on the part of the Wettin rulers.

In the area of the north-west German feudal system from the Lower Rhine to the Guelph territories, there prevailed a form of tenancy, mostly rather favourable to peasants, under the overlordship of the ground landlord; sometimes all personal servitude had been abandoned in favour of clear rights over land (reeve's right in Lower Saxony), sometimes traditional servitude had been preserved.[7] A tendency towards terminable tenancies which in an attenuated form appears to have had repercussions in Westphalia had invaded the regions along the Lower Rhine from the Netherlands already in the Middle Ages. The Lower Saxon and Westphalian agrarian constitutions, in spite of contrasts in detail, remain linked in this context by the common factor of preserving in both territories a substantial and medium peasantry practising primogeniture. A wide social gulf existed between them and the agrarian proletariat which from the sixteenth to the eighteenth century had in some parts come to outnumber vastly the nucleus of original peasantry. Above all among Westphalian peasants with their loose settlements in widespread *Esch* villages [villages with scattered holdings] and the consolidated separate farm settlements,[8] there was from early times a propensity, rooted in history, towards the later endeavours to separate holdings by enclosure.

Common to all four areas was the absence of a manorial lordship or manorial system of any consequence. Only to an insignificant extent did peasant dependency therefore take the form of personal services. Further, the whole area, in spite of fundamental regional differences in the agrarian order, submitted to co-operative and common cultivation of open fields, with strips held in individual possession and decisions made in common; in the 'common rights', the agrarian proletariat participated *de facto*, if not *de iure*. Such common land obligations tied also the peasant on his separate farm in the Alps and Westphalia.

The entire German area of the feudal system had achieved peasant liberation by the middle of the nineteenth century.[9] This had given them freedom of person and movement, established direct relationships of free citizens with the State administration, the police and the courts of law and dissolved the feudal payments nexus beweeen aristocratic lord and peasant. Methods of cultivation had to be modified only where small manors here and there had to switch from peasant labour dues to wage labour. Such minor changes, notably in Lower and Upper

---

[7] For legal aspects of the agrarian order in the eighteenth century, the basic work is W. Wittich, *Die Grundherrschaft in Nordwest-Deutschland* (The Feudal System in North West Germany), Leipzig, 1896.

[8] From the ample literature following the pioneering work by R. Martiny, *Hof und Dorf in Alt Westfalen* (Farm and Village in Old Westphalia), Stuttgart, 1926, cf. above all H. Riepenhausen, *Die bäuerliche Besiedlung des Ravensberger Landes bis 1770* (Peasant Settlement in the Ravensberg Territory before 1770), Münster, 1938.

[9] O. Stolz, *loc. cit.*, and the above quoted articles on 'Bauernbefreiung'.

C

Saxony, Bavaria and Lower Austria, in total hardly amounted to anything. In general peasant liberation did not entail change in social stratification. That came substantially only as the result of freedom of crafts and industrialization.

It is characteristic of the parts of Germany under the feudal system that enclosure was not usually carried through in conjunction with peasant liberation and that there was generally a sharp factual and chronological gap between the consolidation of strips in the open fields and the division of common lands. The north-west took the lead. Both changes were carried out there conjointly in Schleswig-Holstein, largely already in the eighteenth century. From there the movement spread to Hanover. Lüneburg's Division of Common Lands Edict in 1802 was the first of its kind in Germany and became a model for those that followed. Towards the end of the eighteenth century the division of common lands was carried through energetically in Westphalia. Throughout the whole of the north-west the enclosure movement made good progress generally in the first half of the nineteenth century, propelled by governments as well as the interests of the participants. Central, south-east and above all south-west Germany with Switzerland lagged by comparison. A throwing together of strips did not usually occur in the reform period proper, but gained impetus only towards the close of the nineteenth century and in more recent times or became arrested halfway in the form of 'consolidation' (rationalization of holdings within an open-field system). Division of common lands on the other hand was pursued more vigorously.[10] In general however a period of resolute struggle against the 'serpent with three heads: open fields, common cropping decisions, common pasture',[11] with a strong tendency towards partitioning common lands, was followed by a considerable reaction leading to widespread maintenance of common lands, especially in the 'ossified' south-west. Particular variations of common lands systems often had considerable importance in determining the social stratification of the rural population, especially of the agrarian proletariat.

While in general neither the peasant liberation nor the widely omitted or arrested enclosure movement achieved a change in the social structure of Old Germany sufficiently substantial to be reflected in the statistics, liberal agricultural reform nevertheless resulted in fundamentally new situations and decisions for the groups and classes affected.

When land was freed, the aristocracy lost its feudal revenues. Whether rural or court nobility, it had hitherto been able to lead a life untrammelled by material care. Compensation for liberation provided a reasonably adequate substitute during the transition period. In the long run, however, established sources of income had dried up, and the erstwhile privileged aristocracy suffered absorption into the general body of tax-paying citizens. In consequence many noble families grew im-

---

[10] For examples in Bavaria, cf. F. X. Wismüller, *Geschichte der Teilung der Gemeinländereien in Bayern* (History of Division of Common Lands in Bavaria), Stuttgart and Berlin, 1904; in Switzerland, A. v. Miaskowski, *Die schweizerische Allmende in ihrer geschichtlichen Entwicklung vom 13. Jh. bis zur Gegenwart* (Swiss Common Lands in their Historical Evolution from the Thirteenth Century to the Present), Leipzig, 1879.

[11] O. Howald, *Die Dreifelderwirtschaft im Kanton Aargau mit besonderer Berücksichtigung ihrer historischen Entwicklung und ihrer wirtschaftlichen und natürlichen Grundlagen* (The Three-Field-System in the Canton of Aargau with special reference to its historical evolution and its economic and natural foundations), Bern, 1927, p. 47.

poverished or decayed completely, especially in Bavaria and south-west Germany. The necessity of earning a living enforced adoption of a commonplace bourgeois occupation; public employment in civil or military service came closest to a continuation of the old tradition of court service—the adaptation to adverse circumstances was not always successful. The alternative, chosen especially in north-west and central Germany, was as an estate owner to make a living out of the economic intensification of demesne farming, hitherto mostly insignificant. It was often possible effectively to enlarge the demesne in the course of division of common lands and through additional purchases. Rarely was this done by 'peasant clearances' at the expense of the peasant proprietor class. The numerically few instances of this kind are fully offset by the dissolution of estates in connection with redemption. In Hanover all peasant clearances were prevented from the outset through peasant protection enacted by the State as part of the reforms. Only in the Rhineland were there instances of large estates being formed, consisting of scattered holdings let to tenants, but the beneficiaries were not so much noble landlords as bourgeois capitalists.

Nor were the terms of peasant occupancy changed by abolition of feudal and judicial lordship. It is particularly relevant that changes in the law of inheritance removing all restrictions and introducing general inheritance principles did not as a rule lead to a break with hereditary custom. In some places legal limitations on complete freedom of testamentary disposal of immovable property were from the outset instituted by the State, successfully so especially in Hanover whose legislation altogether made its mark by its conservative tenor of maintaining the peasantry in its own interest. The best-known exception to the rule that 'among peasants custom takes precedence over law'[12] can be seen in the advance of physical division in the Eifel: the fragmentation of the so-called 'stock estates' [estates descending undivided to heirs] under the influence of the *code civil*.[13] Elsewhere too we encounter now and then beginnings of an increasing tendency towards physical division, arrested subsequently by legislation in favour of primogeniture. But in a general way we can say that, where the custom of primogeniture had prevailed, it remained in existence by virtue of testamentary disposition on the part of the deceased. Conversely, physical division had already been in existence for a long time[14] where it is still the rule today; at most it developed more freely and quickly after removal of long-standing ties. The impoverishment of the south-west German population in the first half of the nineteenth century due to reduction in the size of holdings and continued overpopulation, however, cannot be attributed primarily to such legislative reform which had not even everywhere been completed. Rather was it a straight continuation of a development dating from the eighteenth century, in

[12] W. H. Riehl, *Die bürgerliche Gesellschaft* (Bourgeois Society), Stuttgart, 3rd ed., 1855, p. 58.
[13] W. Hedemann, *Die Fortschritte des Zivilrechts im 19. Jahrhundert; 2. Teil: Die Entwicklung des Bodenrechts von der französischen Revolution bis zur Gegenwart, 1. Hälfte: Das materielle Bodenrecht* (The Progress of Civil Law in the Nineteenth Century; Pt. II: Development of the Law of Real Estate from the French Revolution to the Present, i: The Law of Real Estate), Berlin, 1930, pp. 89ff.
[14] F. Steinbach, *Beiträge zur bergischen Agrargeschichte* (Contributions to the Agrarian History of Berg), Bonn and Leipzig, 1922, thoroughly investigates the question and comes to the following conclusion: there can be no question of the penetration of French law having promoted the custom of equal division, p. 53.

which the insignificant increase of food-producing areas through intensive utilization of the land, especially in conjunction with division of common lands, stood in
no adequate proportion to the further increase in population in an overcrowded
countryside. When liberal reforms rendered possible free disposal and mortgaging
of real estate, the small peasantry of the south-west, financially weak, was not in a
position to bear the burden of debt and increasingly suffered want. This resulted
in forced sales, the carving up of holdings and a great wave of emigration. The
situation from the middle of the nineteenth century onwards was relieved by industry which in its wide dispersal provided the necessary additional means of
livelihood for the agricultural population.[15]

Overriding all differences, it remains valid for the entire German area subject
to feudalism that the peasantry in the different regions developed within a spectrum of which the extremes were on the one hand a complete immobility of traditional economic and social attitudes and ways of life, on the other the reformers'
ideal of perfection, the 'agriculturist', divorced from all traditionalism, taking his
place in the division of labour peculiar to a bourgeois society by the pursuit of
progressive economic activities. The conditions created by its existing agrarian
order, a more favourable market situation and the more intensive and complete
carrying-through of reforms drove the German north-west—not without links
with Britain, Denmark and the Netherlands—farther towards this prototype.
Even here, however, a *bourgeoisie rurale* was nowhere attained; a special peasant
class and peasant custom remained. German peasantry, with the exception of
certain manifestations of a degraded south-west German small peasantry, in-
stinctively declined identification with the liberal bourgeoisie; hence the bourgeois revolution of 1848 failed, not least because of the German peasant who 'came
to a stop in front of the thrones'.[16]

In spite of reforms, the class characteristics of substantial peasants after elimination of the wider ties of village, community and overlordship remained preserved
through the overriding and determining stabilizer of the farm. The significance of
the farm in preserving peasants as a class vis-à-vis the levelling tendencies of a
bureaucratic State and a bourgeois society was rendered possible by the maintenance of the custom of primogeniture and a new, more intensive, tightened method
of work which no longer fitted into a feudal and communal nexus, but into the
economic rhythm of the autonomous farm. Growing prosperity enabled a considerable increase in the value of liquid cash compensation payable to landless
heirs. Especially in the primogeniture area of the German north-west, the increase
in money incomes promoted an endeavour to grant such disinherited children
compensation appropriate to their status so far as the farm could afford it.[17] In
many instances, however, such compensation to heirs constituted the main reason
for peasant holdings falling into heavy debt. Thus the substantial peasant made use
of capitalist opportunities offered by reform in order to preserve his peasant class
in a bourgeois century with its new economic demands. That in this fundamental

[15] Cf. R. Kellner, *Strukturänderungen in der württembergischen Landwirtschaft* (Structural
Changes in Württemberg Agriculture), Leipzig, 1941.
[16] W. H. Riehl, *loc. cit.*, p. 41.
[17] For impressive examples of the increase of compensation payments cf. A. Hömberg,
*Siedlungsgeschichte des oberen Sauerlandes* (History of the Settlement of Upper Sauerland),
Münster, 1938, p. 88.

metamorphosis of peasant existence the 'peasant of good breed' (Riehl) made his transition into, and maintained himself in, the new capitalist environment, whereas contemporaries discerned widespread peasant 'degeneration' owing to greater mobility and increasing dependence on markets and capital, goes without saying. W. H. Riehl described particularly the effect of tithe redemption which freed for the market corn hitherto earmarked for tithes, enabling peasants henceforth to indulge in the 'gamble of the produce market'.[18]

The reforms, particularly the division of common lands, generally offered an opportunity for more intensive agricultural utilization of land; adoption of an improved three-field system alone increased the crop-bearing area by 50 per cent. In conjunction with division of common lands more intensive cultivation of arable and meadows was often pushed forward into areas used hitherto either only extensively as wood or pasture or even left waste. This led not only to the enlargement of existing holdings, but also to the establishment of numerous new ones, mostly smallholdings or allotments,[19] and served above all in large parts of the north-west, after the land improvement activities consequent upon the division of common lands, as the beginning of a new settlement movement continuing down to the present.[20] Wherever a degree of overcrowding had not yet been reached prior to reforms, liberal agrarian reforms, unless measures of enclosure remained completely in abeyance, led to a final phase of purely agricultural utilization which often marked a direct transition to industrial use of the area, thus rendering possible a population density in excess of that which agriculture had been able to support.

In contrast to such rural population increase, other regions experienced a reduction in the number of settlements possible hitherto on a subsistence basis, but unprofitable in the new conditions, because with increasing need for capital, subsistence farming no longer sufficed or came to be regarded as too laborious in comparison with easier ways of making a living. In conjunction with other reasons, above all with the relocation of industry and crafts, this forms the prime cause of the widespread phenomenon of the 'flight from the heights' in German upland areas, but above all in the Alpine countries.[21]

As structure of work and rural occupancy in the feudal areas of Germany had hardly been modified by peasant liberation, no essential changes were called for on the part of the cottar and squatter class, especially as dissolution of feudal ties and land redemption did not affect it. Of much greater, often decisive import-

---

[18] W. H. Riehl, *loc. cit.*, p. 41.

[19] In eleven districts of Lower Saxony surveyed, a comparison of size of holdings around 1830 with the statistics of 1933 showed an unchanged number for the nucleus of the old substantial peasantry (between 5 and 32 ha.), but a strong increase of smallholdings and allotments below 5 ha. (from *ca.* 9,000 to *ca.* 32,000) as the consequence of liberal reforms and additional opportunities to exercise crafts. H. Morgen, *Zur Frage der Übervölkerung ländlicher Räume* (On the Overpopulation of Rural Space), Prague, 1942, pp. 27ff.

[20] Statistics of population increase as the result of such land utilization interpreted down to district level by H. Haufe, *Die Bevölkerung Europas* (The Population of Europe), Berlin, 1935.

[21] H. Bernhard, A. Koller, Ch. Caflisch, *Studien zur Gebirgsentvölkerung* (Studies in the Depopulation of Mountain Areas), Bern, 1928. For a monograph example, F. Knotzinger, *Der Rückgang des Gebirgsbauerntums in Niederösterreich. Eine siedlungsgeschichtliche Darstellung seiner Grundlagen an Hand der Entwicklung im oberen Schwarzatal* (The Decline of the Peasantry in the Mountains of Lower Austria. The Principles of the History of Settlement, as illustrated by Developments in the Valley of the Upper Schwarza), Berlin-Vienna, 1938.

ance for these groups was the division, above all of common land and pastures. The effect of these measures on the agrarian proletariat varied substantially, according to its share in the benefits. Extreme examples can be seen on the one hand in the chronologically early, radical division of common lands in Westphalia,[22] on the other in the various forms of conscious preservation and utilization of common lands in wide regions of the south-west German area of land division. The ultimate aim in the former instance was complete abolition of ancient land communities and transfer of the land into the private property of the parties in proportion to the rights of participation formerly enjoyed in the common land—rights graded in accordance with their place in the class stratification of peasantry. This left empty-handed the wage labourers who had become more numerous from the seventeenth century onwards. They had carried on an existence dependent in practice on utilization of, though unsupported by legal rights to, woods and pastures. This heavy loss jeopardizing their survival was offset in the course of time by tenancy and clearance of allotments carved out of former common lands as well as more profitable hirings by peasants whom reforms had strengthened economically and who needed more labour. But in the first instance the loss of the use of common lands, coinciding as it did chronologically with the decay of domestic industry hitherto pursued and of seasonal employment in Holland, led during the further increase in wage labour to great economic suffering which found its safety-valve in the period from the thirties to the fifties in a large emigration surge to America.[23] The main gain from division of common lands accrued therefore to those groups among the larger peasantry who owed transport or at least personal services. Beyond Westphalia large regions of the north-west are characterized, as a consequence of dissolution of the old community of land, by a sharpening of class divisions within the rural population in a new sense which bore the seeds of capitalist class conflict. This development did not come to a head because the outlook of the peasants continued to be non-capitalist and the wage labourers maintained their desire for landed property: energy and thrift enabled many of them during the upswing of the nineteenth century to raise themselves into the class of small or medium peasants.

The other extreme was conscious preservation of common lands as the most natural basis of existence and provision for the relief of the small and allotment holders. It is no accident that this occurred above all in the 'ossified' south-west whose rural structure lay least open to rational reform tendencies aiming at agrarian capitalism. It was of the essence that common lands could be neither mortgaged nor otherwise charged with debt. Especially in the crisis caused by transition to a more capital- and market-dominated economy, they therefore offered to small debt-burdened peasants and to the part-time cultivators of allotments the additional and guaranteed living space without which they could not have subsisted. Some such common lands were no longer used as wood or pasture

[22] Cf. R. Middendorf, 'Der Verfall und die Aufteilung der gemeinen Marken im Fürstentum Osnabrück bis zur napoleonischen Zeit' (The Decay and the Division of Common Lands in the Principality of Osnaburgh up to the time of Napoleon), *Mitteil. d. Vereins f. Gesch. u. Landeskde. v. Osnabrück*, il, 1927, pp. 1ff.

[23] For part of an area, cf. A. Wrasmann, 'Das Heuerlingswesen im Fürstentum Osnabrück' (The System of Wage Labour in the Principality of Osnaburgh), *ibid.*, xlii, 1920 and xliv, 1922.

in common, as of old, but either let in allotments by the village community or transferred to individual cultivation as their share of arable land due to *all* inhabitants of the local village, irrespective of their landholdings. Such a change in the use of former common lands, turning them into compact holdings in which common rights continued, constituted an endogenous agrarian reform, born out of the pressure of overpopulation and developed directly out of the tradition of the old agrarian order. In strong contrast to Westphalian division of common lands, this solution benefited cottars and landless people who obtained a share as large as that of the peasants. The social gap between them and the peasants remained variable and narrowed subsequently. In this manner were tens of thousands of people owning no or little land rooted in the soil and preserved from emigration. They offered the firmest basis for the country's industrialization when it gained impetus in the middle of the nineteenth century.

Between both extremes there were many halfway houses. By and large social problems did not arise from the division of common rights until the second half of the nineteenth century, enabling industry to cope with crises of the agrarian proletariat as they emerged.

To sum up: reforms in Germany's feudal areas did not entail fundamental changes in social stratification or population movements clearly distinct from previous population development. In general a healthy compromise was struck between the forward push of economic and social tendencies and the perseverance of the established order. The danger of land fragmentation was avoided by maintaining traditional customs of inheritance. The threat of excessive indebtedness of the land however grew and jeopardized the external and internal substance of the peasantry. In carving up holdings, it assumed the most dangerous shape of all, the beginning of capitalist disintegration of the rural structure. But the dangers of free disposal and capitalization were in general not only defeated, but converted to increasing peasant well-being; for the immediate future this preserved the peasantry as a class in a century of social unrest, in spite of all the beginnings of disruptive decay clearly visible at a later stage. The outcome of reforms was a peasantry familiar with modern economic methods, well-established, strengthened in self-confidence and preserving its possessions undiminished, in the midst of general social ferment, when from the middle of the nineteenth century onwards industrialization subjected German society to really revolutionary structural change.

# II

Very much more incisive and revolutionary were the reforms in the entire manorial area east of that hitherto discussed. The reason was the strict and all-embracing manorial rule giving rise to self-contained economies centred on manors whose lords had concentrated in their own hands the labour, judicial and feudal rights which in the west had been divided and attenuated. 'Hereditary servitude' gripped the peasant subject far more firmly than in the west and south; he could not escape the manorial lord's comprehensive administrative and economic power. A manorial system relies to a high degree on peasant labour. In the whole manorial area, peasant liberation therefore meant redemption not only of money, but above all of labour dues.

From the eighteenth century onwards, two main factions confronted each other in Prussia in the struggle for the contents of reform legislation:

(1) The Prussian kings' policy of peasant protection, carried on and modified by Freiherr vom Stein, aiming at the creation and maintenance of a free and healthy peasantry.

(2) The conversion of manorial lords to capitalism, above all in coastal areas situated favourably vis-à-vis markets, where commercial interests and intellectual ties between the Province of Prussia and England played a special part. This faction initiated a vigorous drive for repeal of an agrarian order with economically restrictive ties in favour of modern large-scale agricultural enterprise, hoping to resume, in the guise of liberal reforms, the development towards large estates at the expense of peasant lands which had been interrupted by Prussian peasant protection.

Both factions coalesced in the Prussian reform legislation. In the last resort aristocratic manorial lords widely succeeded in pursuing their aims in spite of the State's obstructive intentions, the main trump cards in their hands being limitations on the right to participate in redemption, acquisition of peasant land (which in western Germany was unknown or at least hardly practised) and abolition of peasant protection. After 1816 peasant liberation by the State degenerated into a movement dominated by the interests of the emerging large estate owners.

This is very closely connected with the combination of peasant liberation with enclosure which characterizes Prussia in contrast to most other parts of Germany. Both form part of the same movement in Prussia and were carried out chiefly between 1816 and the middle of the century, in many instances to the extent of dispersing villages of long standing by the sweeping away of farms.

Consideration of this combination makes it clear that the pre-eminence assigned to Prussian peasant liberation in the knowledge and evaluation of our general historical understanding cannot be completely explained by Prussia's position in nineteenth-century Germany and the widely accepted idea of Prussian-German history. Owing to its intensity, the totality of its achievement and its particularly blatant consequences, the Prussian reform occupies indeed a prominent place in the total complex of liberal agrarian reforms. This particular position of Prussian agrarian reform has found classical expression in its treatment by G. F. Knapp;[24] its contents and the questions raised therein have provoked several further monographs, works of a more popular nature and a series of parallel researches into the question of peasant liberations in other parts of Central Europe. While contemporaries of reform, unless their interests happened to be directly engaged on the side of the big estates, saw in the liberation of the peasants from their oppressive obligations and the creation of a free peasantry the foremost characteristic, Knapp's work reflects the situation of the eighties, when the social problem had shifted from the position of peasants to that of workers and when the agricultural labourer was 'discovered'. Knapp looks upon the reform in the social and political context of the 'origin of agricultural labourers'; in discussing the consequences of

[24] G. F. Knapp, *Die Bauernbefreiung und der Ursprung der Landarbeiter* (Peasant Liberation and the Origin of Agricultural Labourers), Leipzig, 1887.

reform, he devotes his chief attention to this aspect. From this angle peasant liberation was made to appear decisively less meritorious. With the great emigration from the eastern provinces causing a shortage of agricultural labour, depopulation of the countryside and the mass inflow of seasonal foreign labour, with the national struggle for the soil entering its decisive phase, public opinion already before the First World War, and increasingly in the years after it, thought even less highly of the Prussian reforms. In peasant liberation it recognized the root of peasant weakness vis-à-vis large estates and *Junkertum* and developed polemical views for and against, inspired by partisan attitudes. All these varying evaluations and views contain partial truths on a subject which calls for a new comprehensive survey, in spite of Knapp's classical work and numerous further monographs.

The following sketches the main lines of change in the Prussian east.

Long before the reforms the aristocracy had for centuries been resident manorial lords on knightly estates worked by peasants in hereditary servitude. After its first expansion in the fifteenth and sixteenth centuries the surface area of such manors had been extended increasingly in the eighteenth century by peasant clearances until royal protection of peasants arrested the continuation of this movement. The size of individual manors did not in general yet exceed the surface of a medium village area. Abolition of servitude, of monetary and labour dues, did not mean for the aristocracy, as in the west, the loss of the class basis of existence as hitherto known; on the contrary, it cleared the path from the old manorial to a capitalist system of large estates. This transition was achieved by parts of the Prussian aristocracy as early as the eighteenth century, using the reform as a means to defeat decisively resistance both from its own ranks and from the State. Transfer of land from peasant use to peasant property and rights of lordship of long standing were sold at a high price in order to draw profit from the change. The former paternal authority could be retained within the 'manorial district', thus carrying part of the old overlordship into the new order. Separation of the demesne from the open fields with their peasant strips and from the common pasture had been effected in part already in the eighteenth century and was accelerated in the interests of more rational methods of husbandry, mostly without simultaneous enclosure of the remaining land in the interest of the peasants who still hesitated. The aristocracy, particularly in liberal east Prussia, pushed this development forward with all its might, whereas liberated peasants often could not sustain the pace and fell victims to their new lack of protection. Thus the aristocracy made headway on ever-growing estates, using modern economic methods of cultivation with an eye to markets, but the formation of a pure entrepreneurial type was impeded by family tradition, political ties with the royal house and a genuinely paternal relationship to old peasants and new agricultural labourers. In spite of an increasing interest in economy and the often unscrupulous pursuit of opportunities for money-making, the old Prussian aristocratic tradition of civil and military service to the State largely caused the class to survive. An ever-increasing market in landed property, however, blurred this ancient Prussian line and created a new type, that of the bourgeois owner of knightly estates, which corresponded more closely to the economic rationalism of new agrarian development.

The peasantry emerged weakened and changed from the pressure of the decades after 1816. Only the majority of those owning draught animals i.e. medium and

C 2

large peasants—ownership of draught animals was defined very differently in particular areas—had ever been admitted to land reform. In view of the general scarcity of capital, a large number of them as well as of the estate owners preferred redemption by cessation of land to the payment of quit-rents. Thereby they lost as a rule one-third or one half of their land. Beyond that, numerous peasants, often whole villages, owing to their inability to pay and to their excessive debts, succumbed to the drive for expansion of the large estates. Small peasants not owning draught animals and cottars used for labour services, excluded from land reform in order to retain manpower for manorial lords in the customary manner and tide them over the transition to a new system of work, overwhelmingly turned into a new category of agricultural labourers, partly coerced, partly voluntarily in their search for security. Over wide areas small peasants and independent allotment owners disappeared, and most of the holdings of the remaining peasants were reduced in size from 2–3 to 1–2 Magdeburg *Hufe*.

To this curtailment corresponded on the other side a frequently important gain from enclosures and subsequent improvements which partly reduced the loss suffered as regards surface area, while improvement in cultivation rendered possible after enclosure constituted a positive gain. Concentrated on a smaller space, population on peasant land increased in density through greater use of labour in a more intensive form of husbandry. Peasants who had weathered the difficulties of the twenties and thirties gained strength in the course of time. The main gainers from enclosure, besides estate owners, were the peasants, as the agrarian proletariat in general emerged empty-handed from the division of common lands. This formed one of the chief causes for the widening of the social gap between the new peasantry and the dependent cottars and agricultural labourers. Intermediate small peasant farms moreover had been widely destroyed by the reform. The repeatedly quoted slogan (preserved by Rodbertus-Jagetzow) of the excluded small folk of the East Prussian village—'division of common lands turned peasants into nobles and us into beggars'—hits the nail on the head.[25]

In general, the peasants of the Prussian east, having weathered all dangers and increased their economic strength, from the middle of the nineteenth century onwards represented a power by and large unchanging and firm. To them applies what has been said about the peasants of old Germany: within, and with the aid of the new economic system they maintained a substantial peasant class, though in the east, in contrast with the west and south, it was overshadowed by large estates, imitating after a time-lag their agricultural methods and within the smaller compass of the peasant farm their economic, social and political outlook. The two severed parts of the old manorial system, the estate and the 'substantial-peasant rump of the village', continued to exist side by side in a single village, the 'manorial village of an authoritarian constitution',[26] and co-operated as agricultural entrepreneurs new style. The peasant turned into an 'owner' and as such, like the estate owner, the master of his force of agricultural labourers and farm servants.

[25] Quoted from F. Christoph, *Die ländlichen Gemeingüter (Allmenden) in Preussen* (Rural Common Lands in Prussia), Jena, 1906, p. 72.
[26] Weber, *Über den Zustand der Landwirtschaft in den preussischen Staaten und ihre Reformen* (On the Condition of Agriculture in the Prussian States and their Reforms), 1808, quoted from G. F. Knapp, *loc. cit.*, I, p. 294.

The agrarian proletariat, not admitted to land reform until after 1850, mostly lost its independence and fell into a state of dependency, labouring for the 'owner' of the former manor or a peasant farm. A contemporary critic already pertinently enquired whether this represented any difference from 'substantially servile labour dues'.[27] Difficulties in the change-over of agriculture and of a system of work now using his own stock and equipment made it appear advantageous to the estate owner from the very outset to secure the firm settlement of the new labourers on favourable terms which dispensed as far as possible with cash payments. This had a special attraction because the first years of transition heard many complaints about lack of certain availability of labour on the suddenly enlarged estate lands. Thus there developed a bondsman relationship limited to a number of years, to a small extent even antedating reforms, corresponding in Upper Silesia to the institution of *Dreschgärtner* [sharecropper]. For the previously independent peasant or cottar, the advantage of the bond lay in the security, particularly in the years of agrarian crisis during the twenties, accompanied by a very tolerable standard of living guaranteed to people grown insecure and timid. In 1829 von Haxthausen reflected in relation to the Province of Prussia 'that the family of an efficient bondsman really did better than a peasant'. The author, himself the product of a north-west German environment, comments that men in Prussia by no means lost status through selling their farms and entering into bond. Acceptance of bond was regarded as 'neither degrading nor disadvantageous', an attitude unthinkable in the area of Low German peasantry.[28] These comments appear to illustrate aptly the state of affairs and the force of circumstances after 1820 east of the Elbe. Bondsmen tied to the soil, with their own small livestock and arable cultivation, represented to estate owners and substantial peasants a solution of the labour problem appropriate to a state of transition and obviating the need for cash payments; for disinherited peasants and cottars exposed to the cold wind of a novel lack of protection, it provided the best shield. Consistent development of a modern agricultural enterprise gradually led to the bondsman providing a deputy, the absorption even of bondsmen's smallholdings in the main estate, the strengthening of the cash nexus for the labour contract and a more complete utilization of labour power purely for the benefit of the main estate.

Enclosure, improvements in cultivation and intensification of agriculture increased both the power of resistance of agriculture east of the Elbe and its need for labour on the land. Apparently growing opportunities of obtaining holdings as bondsmen and of founding families after the conclusion of reform legislation led to a sudden increase in population. Obstacles to marriage arising from the old agrarian ties of dependence having disappeared, the new, ostensibly secure proletarian manner of life, freed from any burden of responsibility regarding inheritance or property, led to a leap in the birth-rate. From 1816 to the establishment of the Reich, the rural population of Prussia's eastern provinces more than doubled. This purely rural increase renders Germany east of the Elbe unique throughout Central Europe, if we except the movement in the Hungarian Alföld based on the opening up of the *steppe*. The population increase east of the Elbe must be attri-

[27] *Ibid.*
[28] A. Frh. von Haxthausen, *Die ländliche Verfassung in den Provinzen Ost- und Westpreussen* (The Rural Order in the Provinces of East and West Prussia), 1829.

buted solely and directly to liberal agrarian reform.[29] This repercussion of Prussian reform soon became a serious problem, as already in the thirties population had outrun the density which the new conditions could support. The overpopulation problem could be solved only by emigration as Prussia's eastern provinces, with the exception of Silesia, did not undergo substantial industrialization even at a later stage. The population increase represented a growth in the numbers of the agrarian proletariat alone; the peasantry, having emerged from the losses due to peasant liberation, remained stationary, hence proportionately lost ground. The class which had shown substantial growth was only inadequately rooted in the soil, and the agricultural labourer developed from a smallholder into a landless wage labourer; it therefore became possible after the middle of the century, and even more after the establishment of the Reich, not only for the surplus population to drain away, but for the suction of west German industry to accomplish the stabilization and diminution of rural population numbers in the Prussian east.

Development in the remaining manorial areas of north-east Germany, in Schleswig-Holstein, Mecklenburg and Swedish Pre-Pomerania differed from that in Prussia. In Schleswig-Holstein, where enclosures had been carried through to a great extent already in the eighteenth century,[30] peasant protection had from the outset been tied to peasant liberation, and manorial lords preferred sales and heritable tenancies of manorial lands in the shape of peasant holdings to the formation of large estates, so that the peasantry emerged strengthened from the reforms. Favoured by early enclosure and the country's market situation, the peasantry achieved a progressive, economically favourable development, similar to conditions described for north-west Germany, partly in conjunction with the development of Danish agriculture with its unusual degree of intensification and specialization. Frequent division of estates created many new holders, in size somewhere between medium peasants and cottars, who could make a living owing to favourable agricultural conditions, in spite of the fact that in some parts fragmentation went too far. Cottars did not emerge empty-handed from enclosures, hence mostly gained from reform. Altogether the course of events in Schleswig-Holstein can serve as an example of a healthy and responsible conduct of reforms. The manorial type of holding such as survived particularly in Holstein after the reform no longer determined the agrarian order of the province.[31]

In Mecklenburg and Swedish Pre-Pomerania the development of large estates and the far-reaching annihilation of the peasantry, which in Prussia had been arrested through protection of peasants before their liberation, had made so much progress already in the eighteenth century that nineteenth-century reforms constituted no more than the last step. The transition to the new working régime of large estates had already begun here before peasant liberation. This fact and the early absorption of the larger part of the ancient peasantry explain why the large-

[29] Statistical references in Haufe, *loc. cit.*

[30] F. Mager, *Entwicklungsgeschichte der Kulturlandschaft des Herzogtums Schleswig in historischer Zeit* (History of the Development of the Cultural Landscape of the Duchy of Schleswig in Historical Times), Breslau, 1937, II, pp. 58ff.

[31] G. Hanssen, *Die Aufhebung der Leibeigenschaft und die Umgestaltung der gutsherrlich-bäuerlichen Verhältnisse in den Herzogtümern Schleswig und Holstein* (Abolition of Serfdom and Re-casting of Relationships between Lord and Peasant in the Duchies of Schleswig and Holstein), St. Petersburg, 1861.

estate regions of Mecklenburg and Swedish Pre-Pomerania participated only weakly in the violent population increase of Prussia.[32]

The manorially orientated region of Bohemia, Moravia and Austrian Silesia occupied in many respects an intermediate position between the feudalism which pervaded west and south Germany and the manorial system of the north-east. Here also from the end of the Midddle Ages onwards a manorial economy had been carried on for centuries by means of servile peasant labour. But in lieu of knightly estates occupied by resident aristocracy, in Bohemia and Moravia the agrarian order revolved round the latifundia of an 'absentee' court nobility. This aristocracy adopted an attitude to landed property recalling west German rather than Prussian conditions, looking upon it as a source of rents to satisfy its demands for a high standard of living and taking little interest in cultivation which was left to specialists employed for the purpose or to stewards. The Bohemian aristocrat, with blood not only Czech and German, but to a great extent Latin, coursing in his veins, wanted to play a part in high politics, not to engage in agriculture. Thus the chief incentive for the formation of large estates on the lines seen east of the Elbe was absent, and the danger of peasant clearances hardly existed any longer in the eighteenth and nineteenth centuries.[33] Peasant liberation in Bohemia, with its harbingers in the eighteenth century and its final completion after 1848, did not therefore change the system of occupation. The extent of aristocratic and peasane property remained unchanged. Abolition of servitude merely meant the formation of an agricultural labouring class which however did not alter the structure as much as east of the Elbe, because different sizes of peasant holdings remained in existence. The subsisting agrarian constitution owes its preservation largely to two factors:

(1) Enclosure almost entirely failed to occur; it did not gain impetus legally until 1883 and in practice only after the turn of the twentieth century.

(2) Decrees limiting division of holdings from 1812 onwards in the Czech nucleus of Bohemia had made primogeniture customary. It was not abandoned even when after peasant liberation and the legislation of 1867–9 the law permitted free division of land.[34] Thus Bohemia assimilated its agrarian order to prevailing German conditions, as did the province of Poznan in the nineteenth century. This preserved the substance of the peasantry; disinherited children found ample opportunities for work and earnings in the rising industry of Bohemia and in Vienna. Industry here interacted with the process of freeing the peasant popula-

[32] C. J. Fuchs, *Der Untergang des Bauernstandes und das Aufkommen der Gutsherrschaften nach archivalischen Quellen aus Neu-Vorpommern und Rügen* (The Decay of the Peasantry and the Rise of Estate Ownership from Archival Sources in New Pre-Pomerania and Rügen), Strassburg, 1888. H. Haufe, *loc. cit.*

[33] W. Stark, *Ursprung und Aufstieg des landwirtschaftlichen Grossbetriebs in den böhmischen Ländern* (Origin and Rise of the Agricultural Large Estate in the Bohemian Lands), Brno-Prague, Leipzig-Vienna, 1934, p. 47. Stark's book supplements and criticizes the authoritative work by K. Grünberg, *Die Bauernbefreiung und die Auflösung des gutsherrlich-bäuerlichen Verhältnisses in Böhmen, Mähren und Schlesien* (The Peasant Liberation and the Dissolution of the Manorial-Peasant Relationship in Bohemia, Moravia and Silesia), 1893.

[34] E. G. Bürger, 'Bäuerliche Liegenschaftsübertragung und Vererbung im Gebiet der Tschechoslovakei' (Peasant Transfer of Real Estate and Inheritance in the Czechoslovak Area), in Sering-Dietze, *Die Vererbung des ländlichen Grundbesitzes in der Nachkriegszeit* (Inheritance of Rural Land after the War), Munich-Leipzig, 1930, II, pp. 121ff.

tion and attracted in the decades after peasant liberation an unusually high peasant migration. In the Sudeten German areas on the other hand the surplus rural population after peasant liberation continued to find a living in the varied crafts pursued in villages of their own home region.[35] Both are instances of peasant liberation providing the human wherewithal for the labour requirements of industrialization. It was this which determined the change in social stratification in Bohemia-Moravia in the nineteenth century.

# III

Turning from German or directly German-orientated parts of Central Europe to the Baltic provinces adjacent to the East, the Polish-Lithuanian State and Hungary, the first characteristic of these historical areas from this point of view is their 'inter-European' nature. The lines of German agrarian reform cross the Russian liberation endeavours (Poland-Lithuania) which took effect here half a century later, or reforms adapted to German conditions encountered circumstances of a particular nature, differing essentially from those of the west and centre and bound therefore to provoke different effects (Baltic Provinces, Hungary). This difference took above all two forms:

(1) East Central Europe was essentially an area of a pure agrarian society, with an aristocracy which had largely maintained its marked domination against absolutist endeavours on the part of the State; no precondition appeared to exist for the replacement of this domination by other constitutional forces; there was no evolution of other classes, especially no strong bourgeoisie with a will of its own. Even more exclusively than in the West did the aristocracy determine the agrarian order of a manorial system which tended to persist, in spite of many intrusions of modern methods of agriculture, because socially or economically motivated incentives remained less strong than in the West. The new agrarian movement impinged upon the aristocracy in general at a stage of consciousness which could show little understanding for the political significance, the economic advantage or the human value of reform demands, even though such reforms were taken up and carried in part to conclusion by the more adaptable of aristocratic minorities. Even less than in Germany was the great mass of peasantry ready for what reforms were meant to bestow upon it from above. Dissatisfaction with aristocratic oppression, especially where the régime was modified by arbitrary demands, remained paralysed by a feeling of pre-ordained suffering: a peasant was a drudge, but a protected drudge. Even in the German area peasants had been objects rather than subjects of the reform movement. But the general impression is that pressure for a change in conditions was stronger there and that liberation set free latent energies which tended outwards and prepared the ground for the rise of industrial-

[35] For the particularly favourable conditions turning a village of substantial forest holdings into an industrial village, cf. E. G. Bürger, 'Die Wandlungen des Waldhufendorfes' (Metamorphoses of the Forest Village), *Sudetendeutsches Jahrbuch*, 1928. [Forest Village: farms along one or both sides of the village street, the land belonging to each farm is one long strip radiating out at a right angle.]

ization, whereas pressure in East Central Europe, when released, did not result in action, but passively evaporated.

(2) In the whole area of East Central Europe social order was nowhere based on a single people. Rather did social stratification arise from population belonging to different peoples. Social division coincided widely with separate nationality. To specify, aristocratic domination signified overlordship of German aristocrats over Esthonian and Latvian peasants, overlordship of Polish aristocrats over Polish Lithuanian, White Russian and Ukrainian peasants, and overlordship of Magyar aristocrats over Magyar, German, Slovak, Rumanian and South Slav peasants. Bourgeois functions devolved primarily upon an urban bourgeoisie, German, of German origin, or Jewish, which had penetrated into the towns and dominated the market centres typical of the East. Agrarian reforms in East Central Europe had not only to achieve a transformation of social structure, but along with the old social order to overthrow or undermine national strangleholds. In general they created the pre-conditions for the development of socially stratified nations by loosening domination on the part of aristocrats of foreign nationality and enabling peasants everywhere to enter occupations hitherto closed to them. Peasant liberation opened a path for erstwhile subject peasant nationalities to achieve social satisfaction and degraded traditionally privileged groups within the population to the status of national minorities. This however is a path which even today has not reached its end.

Only with reservations can the Baltic provinces of the Russian Empire be included in this context of East Central Europe. True, they too experienced national division along class lines. But more strongly than in the remainder of the East was their social condition assimilated to Central European evolution through a German pattern of urbanization, and only where such towns had remained dispersed had the 'crochet work' typical of Lithuanian market centres remained in existence. The German aristocracy of the three provinces moreover kept in close contact with general German life and therefore adopted early on its own initiative peasant reform measures in step with events in Central and Western Europe. The agrarian order of aristocratic manorial domination over Esthonian and Latvian peasant subjects widely bore a character appropriate to east German conditions. While the agrarian order of the Baltic peoples even before, and independent of, German domination had strong points of contact with the Germanic economic and social order, this relationship was greatly strengthened by the German hegemony in the history of the territory. Latvian-Esthonian large and medium peasants existed in a manorial subjection similar to conditions east of the Elbe. Labour services on the demesne—here the peasant of the Baltic Provinces differed from his counterpart in the Polish-Lithuanian area—were however rendered chiefly by peasant menials who were members of the peasant household and occupied different social grades, from *Landknecht* [serf] or *Lostreiber* [peripatetic day labourer] up to the *Halbkörner* [sharecropper]. The large-scale peasantry gave scope for earning a living to a large class below, and socially separate from, the peasants. Thus Latvian and Esthonian peasants by inclination and upbringing were related in their way of life to the substantial German peasantry.

Understandably therefore reforms in the Baltic Provinces show many features reminiscent of Prussian development. Here as there, liberation was channelled through the initiative of the aristocracy into paths desirable to owners of large estates. But in Baltic countries the work of reform, in spite of promotion and occasional stimuli on the part of the czar, remained entirely in the hands of the knightly orders, and it is characteristic of the situation, in contrast with developments in Mecklenburg and Pre-Pomerania equally determined entirely by the aristocracy that, beside the naked self-interest of agrarian capitalism, genuine political responsibility concerned with the care for peasant subjects was at work in order to secure eventually in the teeth of strong reaction from its own ranks reforms of a kind tolerable also for the peasants. The route led from traditional measures of peasant protection via personal freedom, freedom of mobility and consequent lack of peasant protection, temporarily retaining old servile obligations, to the introduction of tenancy agreements based on a cash nexus and beyond to the actual acquisition of property. This process dragged on throughout the nineteenth century and entailed substantial loss of peasant land due to cessation of the 'proportion' and purchase of peasant land by estate owners.

Simultaneously with reforms in the course of peasant liberation, enclosure took place, indispensable to the upswing of agriculture. It mostly implied transfer of farms hitherto grouped in widespread hamlets to a central position within consolidated lands, giving more scope for the expression of isolation, self-sufficiency and progressiveness on the part of substantial Esthonian and Latvian peasants.

As in Prussia, reform resulted in the establishment of large estates pursuing husbandry on modern lines, but not developing a rational capitalist economy to the Prussian degree. Even after the liberal reforms the Baltic German aristocracy, in contrast to the narrower world within which the Prussian nobility moved, retained a style of living more open-handed and generous, contemptuous of strict accountancy appropriate to a mere agricultural *entrepreneur*.

In spite of loss of substance during the period of liberty without protection between 1817–9 and the forties, the final reforms around the middle of the century succeeded in creating an independent substantial Esthonian and Latvian peasantry which, similar to East German 'proprietors', copied the example of large estates as regards modern agricultural techniques, achieved great progress and preserved and consolidated in the new environment the characteristics of the substantial peasant class.

The typical nucleus of peasant holdings was of a size between 50 and 150 acres. This was not infrequently exceeded, whereas medium and small peasant holdings below 50 acres hardly existed. The preservation of a substantial peasant proprietorship satisfied the class-conscious intentions of the Esthonian-Latvian peasantry, but had also been provided for by reform legislation when it fixed a size limit below which no division was to take place (particularly high in Livonia at 80 acres). Aristocratic estate ownership and substantial peasantry joined forces in the conservative desire for maintenance of the existing level of proprietorship. Strict observance of primogeniture, even after liberation, had a conservative effect, preventing social mobility downwards, and laid the basis for the evolution of a Latvian and Esthonian bourgeoisie recruited from all occupations, particularly from the professions, from the middle of the nineteenth century onwards.

The new class of agricultural labourers developed in principle in a manner similar to that in Prussia's eastern provinces in the direction of an increasing prevalence of deputies. Side by side with them up to the world war, types evolved from a non-monetary economy like *Halbkörner* or *Landknechte* survived—liable to render labour services for a fixed number of days only in return for the use of an allotment. Adjustment to a new working régime caused no great difficulties because plenty of agricultural labour was always available among the rural proletariat. Even before reform, the peasant had no longer been the real renderer of labour dues. From this same group, rather than from peasants grown landless, was recruited the class of agricultural labourers. This group of allotment holders and landless people, numerically the largest in the rural population, played an intrinsic part in the economy of the manor as well as of the substantial peasant holding both before and after the reforms, except that before liberation the manor had held peasants responsible for procuring the labour services.

The problem of the change-over in the working régime had probably hardly ever been lack of labour, but rather how to accommodate with opportunities for work all the people available, as the more rationally operated system of wage labour could not everywhere make full use of the many peasant workers formerly engaged in labour services. The absorption of a 'proportion' of peasant lands by the aristocracy had been designed to make available to this surplus small holdings to rent. However, in many cases the 'proportion' had in the end been unconditionally incorporated in manorial estates. By and large the overweening and unresigned energy of the rural proletariat, marked after the dissolution of the old agrarian order by pronounced social ambitions and land hunger, remained an unsolved problem and caused continuous pressure in spite of emigration opportunities taken by some—pressure undermining the newly consolidated order of large estates and substantial peasants.

From an early date and apparently without connection with the reforms, these stable conditions co-existed with a remarkably low birth-rate. The population surge experienced east of the Elbe as a consequence of reforms found no counterpart. The excess population, small among peasants, larger among the class below the peasants, mainly moved out, partly to Russia, but above all to towns in their own country which offered new opportunities in crafts and industry. Thus liberal agrarian reform initiated movements for the formation of separate Latvian and Esthonian nations, for the dissolution of a social stratification from the aristocracy downwards and the country's administration by Baltic Germans.[36]

In spite of many regional differences in detail, the area of the Polish-Lithuanian *Rzeczpospolita*, excluding the later Prussian eastern provinces which we have already discussed, formed to a large extent a single area with a consistent agrarian order. In contrast to the course of events in the Baltic provinces, the instinctive readiness of the peasantry to accept German-Central European forms of rural order had from the outset been more feebly developed. A system of substantial farms, it is true, had covered the major part of Poland in the late Middle Ages and of the Chief Principality of Lithuania in the sixteenth century. Nevertheless a substantial

[36] A. v. Tobien, *Die Agrargesetzgebung Livlands im 19. Jahrhundert* (The Agrarian Legislation of Livonia in the Nineteenth Century), Riga, 1899–1911 (2 vols.). A. Agthe, *Ursprung und Lage der Landarbeiter in Livland* (Origin and Situation of Agricultural Labourers in Livonia), Tübingen, 1909. *Handwörterbuch des Grenz- und Auslandsdeutschtums*, II, pp. 183ff., with references to further literature.

peasantry on the German model of full or double holdings had not come into being, because the Slav peasant had in general evaded the demands on him which constituted the debit side of such holdings. The constant struggle between peasant desires and the interests of feudal and manorial systems had mostly led to a type of half-size farmer, restricting himself to a proportion of the holding sufficient to cover subsistence and at best renting from his lord additional land which was less heavily burdened. Thus holdings in lands under the Polish crown before the nineteenth century typically covered 20 to 25 acres, in the Chief Principality of Lithuania approximately 37 acres.[37] This had produced a medium peasantry standardized in type and size of holdings, with a propensity towards reducing holdings which was suppressed by manorial lords concerned to retain substantial subjects.

Differences in the size of peasant holdings remaining in general insignificant, it was a further characteristic of the uniformity of a medium peasantry inclining towards smallness that a numerically significant agrarian proletariat did not exist. Smallholders and landless people over wide parts of the area accounted for no more than ten per cent of rural population. Their proportion rose wherever a larger peasantry had been preserved or established, thereby providing a means of livelihood. This for instance was the case in parts of western Lithuania. Where on the other hand the peasantry had decayed already before the reforms as the result of physical division of land (for instance in the Mozyr District), smallholders increased owing to the obliteration of the boundary line between small peasants and cottars.[38] Lack of development and poor definition of social divisions was a general characteristic of the agrarian order throughout the area of the Polish-Lithuanian State.

That peasants of Lithuanian origin made moves towards more pronounced adoption and preservation of a system of substantial holdings, suggests a long-standing affinity with the Baltic character. Thus they constituted in many respects a transitional zone between Polish-White Russian conditions and the agrarian order of the Baltic Provinces. But common historical fate assigned the major portion of them to the Slav type of peasantry in the Polish-Lithuanian aristocratic republic.

This uniform mass of peasantry faced a numerous Polish aristocracy more strongly stratified: magnates with vast expanses of manors and estates, partly only feebly organized along manorial lines, especially where in the east they were a long way from markets; medium and smaller gentry; finally a large number of small *Szlachta*, wielding no manorial or feudal powers, whom neither size of holding nor method of husbandry distinguished from servile peasants, but merely that aristocratic liberty which had led to physical land division and impoverishment. These latter were the real military and political standard bearers of the idea of a Polish State.

After the partitions of Poland, the agrarian reform of the three partitioning

---

[37] For a comprehensive discussion of the order of holdings, cf. W. Conze, *Agrarverfassung und Bevölkerung in Litauen und Weissrussland, 1. Teil: Die Hufenverfassung im ehemaligen Grossfürstentum Litauen* (Agrarian Order and Population in Lithuania and White Russia, Pt. 1: the Order of Holdings in the Former Chief Principality of Lithuania), Leipzig, 1940.

[38] *Ibid.*, pp. 191ff.

powers had very different effects on the wide region between the Vistula and the Dnieper. Changes in the agrarian order of Congress Poland before the beginning of Russian peasant liberation bore the direct stamp of Prussian developments. The interaction has as yet been the subject of little research. Polish literature so far offers comparatively few clues. The movement gathered force during the New East Prussian and South Prussian period between 1795 and 1807, because the Prussian State began to establish on a larger scale hereditary tenancies and enclosures.[39] The interrupted measures were continued after 1820 by the Russian government and after approximately 1830 by aristocratic estate owners. The lord-peasant labour relation was gradually eliminated by transformation into a terminable tenancy. By the end of the fifties this change had been almost completed on publicly owned estates, whereas on the aristocratic estates only a quarter of peasant holdings had been entirely, another two-fifths partly converted to terminable tenancies.[40] The incentive, as in Prussia, came through estate owners' conversion to agrarian capitalism, whereas for the Russian government political antagonism to the Polish aristocracy played a part. Especially the favourable development of agrarian conditions in the Province of Poznan had its repercussions.

In Congress Poland too, predominantly apparently in areas along the Prussian frontier, peasant clearances demanded many victims, creating an agricultural labourer class on expanding estates. While the medium and small peasant structure of Congress Poland characterized at the beginning of the nineteenth century had still typically included an agrarian proletariat accounting for no more than ten to 20 per cent of the rural population, by 1846 of barely three million rural inhabitants of the Kingdom of Poland around 1·2 million or 40 per cent were landless[41]— a development due exclusively to the expansion of large estates and the partial freeing of the peasant class.

Logically derived from these 'East Elbian' tendencies in many instances enclosure was carried through, in parts combined, as in the New East Prussian period, with the introduction of new German and Polish settlers, as for instance in the region of the Vistula and especially thoroughly in the Lithuanian 'Western Memel' region between the elbow of the Memel river and the frontier of east Prussia.[42] This explains why counties bordering on Prussia (Kalisch, Warsaw, Plock, Lomscha, Suwalki) participated fully in the 'East Elbian' increase in population in the first half of the nineteenth century, whereas southern and eastern regions less affected by liberal reforms lagged behind.[43]

[39] W. Conze, 'Die Separation in der preussischen Landeskulturarbeit in Neuostpreussen von 1795–1807' (Enclosure in the Prussian Work of Land Improvement in New East Prussia, 1795–1807), *Altpreussische Forschungen*, xiv (1937), pp. 268ff.
[40] A. J. F. C. Graf v. Rostworowski, *Die Entwicklung der bäuerlichen Verhältnisse im Königreich Polen im 19. Jahrhundert* (Development of Peasant Conditions in the Kingdom of Poland in the Nineteenth Century), Jena, 1896, p. 34.
[41] C. W. v. Gasczynski, *Die Entwicklung der bäuerlichen Selbständigkeit im Königreich Polen* (The Development of Peasant Independence in the Kingdom of Poland), Munich, 1905, p. 50.
[42] H. Mortensen, *Litauen, Grundzüge einer Landeskunde* (Lithuania, Outlines of a Geography), Hamburg, 1926, pp. 239ff,, and W. Essen, *Die ländlichen Siedlungen in Litauen* (Rural Settlements in Lithuania), Leipzig, 1931, pp. 76ff.
[43] H. Haufe, *loc. cit.*

In the context of assimilation to conditions east of the Elbe, it is striking that, in contrast with the Polish east and south, primogeniture prevailed in the northern parts of the *Wojewodschaft* of Warsaw and Lodz and the western and northern districts of the *Wojewodschaft* of Bialystok.[44] Here too there appears to subsist an affinity with the area east of the Elbe—compare developments in Poznan—strong enough to prevent the recoil of Russian peasant liberation from having its full effect.

A similar development, derived from events in eastern Germany, was lacking in Habsburg Galicia. Reform here took place at the same time as in the remainder of Austria. Nowhere was the soil prepared for effects of the north east German type. Especially agrarian capitalist incentives for estate owners remained far in the background. Large-scale enclosures did not take place. As the change in proportions between lords' and peasants' possessions remained in general apparently insignificant, it was above all the abolition of former peasant obligations which shaped the agrarian system, and no new constructive forces emerged which might have strengthened the peasantry and led it in a particular direction.

The reaction of Polish and Ukrainian peasants to the gift of free land disposal was uniform. In spite of almost unchanging traditional agricultural techniques physical division supervened everywhere. In a liberal agrarian order free divisibility of land was an individualistic feature, just as in a former feudal order, in lieu of a peasant family group existing in a genuine state of primogeniture and giving preference to the heir of the blood, there had existed a tendency towards equalization arising from a consciousness of a quasi-extended family to which all active members belonged. Comparing it to the older custom of physical division within the feudal system, Bürger hits the nail on the head in describing the new custom of division after peasant liberation as 'typical of the contemporary lack of a sense of proportion'.[45] This movement, begun in Galicia with the Josephine reforms, but reaching its full extent only after 1848, led in the second half of the nineteenth century to a strong decline of the medium and an ever-increasing decay of the small peasantry in the face of rigid preservation of large estates. Unlike in the Prussian east or in the Baltic provinces, reforms here did not create a type of medium or substantial peasant acquiring economic strength and competitiveness. Rather did the peasantry, continuing widely to farm for subsistence, decay rapidly into smallholders living poorly, oppressed and dominated by capital from the village usurer's pocket in spite, or perhaps because, of its persistence in backward economic methods dating from feudal and manorial days. The consequence was rural overpopulation—much discussed in the period 1920–39—in regions of an agrarian society of long standing, hardly touched by industrialization—a dynamic development defying all half-hearted attempts at solution which dared not touch at the root of the evil, the physical division of land.

The most impressive description of this tendency towards rural overpopulation is given by Stys, who investigated a representative sample of 26 Galician villages, calculating that the period 1787–1931 saw an increase of 126 per cent in popula-

[44] K. Ballerstedt, *Erbrecht, Erbsitte und Grundbesitzzersplitterung in Polen* (Law and Customs of Inheritance and Fragmentation of Landed Estates in Poland), Stuttgart-Berlin, 1939, p. 112.
[45] E. G. Bürger, 'Bäuerliche Liegenschaftsübertragung . . .', *loc. cit.*, p. 126.

tion, of 190 per cent in the number of separate economic units, but of only 27 per cent in surface area under agricultural cultivation. The proportion of establishments remaining below 13 acres in that period increased from *ca.* 14 per cent to *ca.* 62 per cent, whereas holdings over 25 acres fell from *ca.* 60 per cent to *ca.* 9 per cent.[46] This movement persisted longest in Galicia and has led there to the most pronounced impoverishment of a rural population of small peasants hardly any longer socially stratified at all. But in principle the tendency of the movement was similar in the entire remaining East of Central Europe.

This is also the general context of Hungary where the agrarian order after peasant liberation from 1848 onwards is characterized by an unchanging high manorial share (approximately one half) of total surface, with small peasants crowded into the remaining space and declining through physical division of land.[47] Similar to Poland, the numerous, politically decisive nobles stratified into a high aristocracy,[48] possessing not only manorially organized estates, but other extensive latifundia largely opened up only in the eighteenth and nineteenth centuries by German and Magyar settlers, and the great mass of the gentry, subdivided into squires of medium and smaller estates and an independent ennobled free peasantry. For the peasantry an estate of a size of around 37 acres of full and half 'sessions' [standard size holdings] was widely customary, preserved and buttressed by a state of manorial subjection or feudal dependence.

What inspired reform was hardly the incentive of agrarian capitalism as practised east of the Elbe. Alongside a rather passive yielding to necessity as determined by the spirit of the times, national revolutionary motives springing from the 1848 movement played an important part among the gentry, the nucleus of the 'political nation'.[49] Thus there were no peasant clearances because economic temptation to enlarge estates did not exist. Reform further lost much of its sharp edge because enclosure either did not take place at all or only late and in individual instances. The exceptions were 'segregations' between manorial and peasant land achieving a separation of the demesne from the open field system in which peasant lands continued to be cultivated.

The aristocracy emerged generally with undiminished power from the change and turned a cold shoulder to all further suggestions of agrarian reform.[50] However, some of it fell victim to the land market. Hand in hand with an outflow of estate owners from the medium gentry into professions, above all the civil service,

[46] W. Stys, *Rozdrabnianie gruntów chłopskich w byłym zaborze austrjackim* (Fragmentation of Peasant Lands in the formerly Austrian Part of Poland), Lvov, 1934. Cf. also Ballerstedt, *loc. cit.*, pp. 29ff.

[47] For property distribution in Hungary, cf. A. Winkler, *Ungarns landwirtschaftsgeographische Gestaltung* (The Shaping of Hungary's Agricultural Geography), Berlin, 1938, pp. 45ff. Especially significant impressions of Hungary's agrarian constitution in H. Klocke, *Deutsches und madjarisches Dorf in Ungarn* (German and Magyar Village in Hungary), Leipzig, 1937.

[48] H. Klocke, 'Die Stellung des Hochadels in der Grundbesitzstruktur und im politischen Aufbau der Länder der Stephanskrone' (The Position of the High Aristocracy in the Structure of Landed Property and in the Political Structure of the Lands under the crown of St. Stephen), *Ungarische Jahrbücher*, xv (1935), pp. 296ff.

[49] L. Spohr, *Die geistigen Grundlagen des Nationalismus in Ungarn* (The Intellectual Foundations of Nationalism in Hungary), Berlin and Leipzig, 1936, pp. 47ff.

[50] For the aristocratic view on the agrarian question in Hungary, cf. D. von Sebess, *Die Agrarreform in Ungarn* (The Agrarian Reform in Hungary), Berlin, 1921.

there was a filtering of Jews into landed proprietorship on a scale typical only of Hungary.[51]

Estate owners created an agricultural labouring class apparently mainly from the already existing and numerous population of smallholders who were sharply distinct from the peasantry in terms of class.[52] The existence of this numerically obviously prevalent class of cottars, which even before reform had its established place within the working system of aristocratic manors, constitutes apparently an essential difference from the agrarian order of Polish Lithuania where the corresponding 'gardeners' (ogródnicy) had never developed into a group of any importance.

On the peasant sector of land, development was similar to that already indicated for Galicia, owing to physical separation of land setting in after reform and engulfing all nationalities with the exception of the larger part of German peasants, In the South Slav region of the crown of St. Stephen this process was accompanied by the beginning of the disintegration of zadruga.[53] The consequence was the decline of the medium peasantry into smallholders and the breakdown of class barriers between peasants and cottars. The pressure of a constantly increasing class of smallholders, recruited partly from cottars, but largely from decayed peasants, remained up to the World War and thereafter in the smaller Hungary after 1920 the most urgent unsolved problem of Hungarian life in general. German settlements, having overwhelmingly maintained primogeniture, did not participate in this general tendency. They retained the class stratification of a medium and substantial peasantry. Where physical division of land became customary, as in the Batschka, the declivity of the movement was moderated by a fall in the birth-rate which, to begin with, affected only German settlements.[54]

Common meadows which continued to exist owing to the absence of enclosure through the co-operative fixing of stints even after the reforms and in the face of the individualist trend towards dissolution, held village inhabitants fast in the grip of old co-operative ties, partly also maintaining a measure of old class divisions, because stints for a long time continued to reflect original shares in the land: in some parts separate pasture co-operatives continued to exist for peasants and cottars.[55]

Much more than for the 'historical' Magyar population whose bourgeois middle class was recruited above all from the small and medium gentry, from Jews and magyarized Germans, did peasant liberation signify for Rumanian and Slav nationalities within Hungary the beginnings of creating a bourgeoisie of their own, though as yet a weak one, and an intelligentsia capable of giving a national lead; thus the soil was prepared for the formation of separate nationalities ripening towards new political solutions.[56] Though even after reform the Magyar aristocracy managed to maintain or even to strengthen its dominant position by new econo-

[51] H. Klocke, Deutsches und madjarisches Dorf . . . , p. 21.

[52] Ibid., p. 28. I cannot judge how far this state of affairs applies to the whole area under the crown of St. Stephen.

[53] G. Harms, Bevölkerungsstruktur und Agrarverfassung Slawoniens (Social Structure and Agrarian Order in Slavonia), Leipzig, 1942, p. 28.

[54] Articles on Banat, Batschka and Danubian Swabia in Handwörterbuch des Grenz- und Auslandsdeutschtums. H. Klocke, loc. cit.

[55] H. Klocke, Deutsches und madjarisches Dorf . . . , p. 31.

[56] For the important event of the formation of a modern Rumanian nation beyond the Carpathians through the opening up of the steppe and peasant liberation, which lies outside

mic measures and Hungary remained a country of a markedly feudal way of life, agrarian reform after 1848 constituted a decisive breach in this feudal stronghold through increase and threatened proletarianization of large sections of the liberated rural population and through the formation of new national forces ready to blast apart the old supra-national State edifice.

# IV

While these revolutions of rural structure happened from the beginning or the middle of the nineteenth century in the Baltic provinces, western Poland and Hungary, the wide regions of the largest part of the old Polish-Lithuanian State, especially the 'Ruthenian' east, remained tied to prevailing conditions of agrarian society and stationary population. The reform of 1864, decreeing the personal liberation of, and the transfer of land to, peasants against a quit-rent, bore a special character in these 'western' areas of the Russian Empire, differing from that in Russia proper, because in contrast to the Russian system of open fields it encountered here an agrarian order conceived on Central European lines. In addition, between the manifesto of peasant liberation of 1861 and the beginning of reform in 1864, there had occurred the Polish rising of 1863, furnishing the desired pretext for combining a weakening of noble Polish estate owners with the carrying out of the reform law. Not only were there large-scale expropriations to replace Polish by Russian estate owners, but beyond that, Russian agrarian policy throughout this whole area took a markedly pro-peasant line, even towards national Polish peasants in Congress Poland. State credits assisted peasants in overcoming redemption difficulties; in the face of such peasant protection on the part of the State, manorial lords found it impossible to exploit reform for purposes of agrarian capitalism.

In Congress Poland the movement stood on its head. Instead of wider expansion of large estates at the peasants' expense, the peasants' share of land increased substantially after reform, especially after the Peasant Bank had extended its activities in 1894 to Congress Poland. Between 1894 and 1909 about $2\frac{3}{4}$ million acres passed from estate to peasant ownership in that area.[57] Alongside this, enclosure occurred, though not on a significant scale, and for its part helped further to enlarge peasant living space. This peasant expansion, the repercussion of tendencies from east of the Elbe and the Russian government's policy of peasant protection all combined to produce a relatively favourable development for the Polish peasantry. Between 1868 and 1904 the number of establishments increased by 31 per cent, the surface under peasant cultivation by 11 per cent, while the average size of peasant holdings fell by only 16 per cent.[58] This suggests that physical division of land when it occurred after the reforms did not take the agrarian order and population by storm, as it had done in Galicia, and genial conditions preserved a nucleus of medium peasants which declined only slowly. The picture darkens however considerably if we compare with this development of

the scope of this article, cf. H. Haufe, *Die Wandlung der Volksordnung im rumänischen Altreich* (The Metamorphosis of Social Structure in the Old Rumanian Reich), Stuttgart, 1939.
[57] Ballerstedt, *loc. cit.*, p. 28.      [58] *Ibid.*, p. 23.

holdings that of population. Those 'gaining a living in agriculture' in Congress
Poland between 1857 and 1906 increased from 3·4 million to 6·9 million, i.e. by
more than 100 per cent.[59] This population increase, far in excess of the increase in
holdings, indicates the growth of a mass of landless people who could find only
insufficient means of livelihood on large estates and among peasants who had
little use for them; increasingly they sought to redress the balance by permanent
emigration to America or seasonal migration to central and eastern Germany.
To illustrate events even more clearly, one would need to break down the total
statistics for Congress Poland according to districts or at least counties. This
would show a further division, admittedly with a fluid boundary line, between the
west and north as delimited above and the south and east: i.e. in the north and
west partial maintenance of primogeniture, slowing down of population increase,
that is attenuated conformity with the movements of the north-east German
population after the foundation of the Reich[60] and limited repercussions of the
Russian peasant liberation; but in the south and east a sudden rush from standstill
into movement of the type described in the case of Galicia.

The area of Lithuanian population participated in this rush only to a limited
extent, as shown by Lithuanian agrarian structure and the population figures
quoted by Haufe. The liberated rural excess population apparently sought refuge
in emigration to a particularly substantial extent. Detailed research on these inter-
relationships still remains to be done. The intermediate position of this area,
originally and substantially related to the Latvian structure, but consigned by
history to the Slav agrarian order, remained clearly marked even in the period
after 1864.

Much greater was the violence when the wide White Russian-Ukrainian regions
of the former Chief Principality of Lithuania broke their fetters after 1864. This
development lagged behind the Galician in time, but not in intensity, and only
because of the time lag had not yet at the period of the World War reached that
degree of overpopulation which represented the lowest limit of viability and thereby constituted the transition from movement to conditions prevailing in Galicia.
Typical of the area in general are events in the county of Vilna, where between
1858 and 1897 population increased from 840,000 to 1,770,000 (110 per cent), the
number of peasant holdings in the period 1864 to 1909 from 80,000 to 175,000
(120 per cent), while at the same time the average size of the peasant holding fel
from about 37 to just over 18 acres, that is by one half.[61]

In this area of Russian reform too, enclosure remained by and large in abeyance for the time being and gained momentum only in the course of Stolypin's
agrarian reforms after 1906. Even more firmly than in the Central European South
East did the peasantry persist in traditional three-field cultivation using outdated
techniques of agriculture and drifting into that 'degeneration of agrarian structure'
which, especially well-known through Poniatowski's book,[62] dominated public
discussion in Poland before 1939.

---

[59] *Ibid.*, p. 25.          [60] H. Haufe, *loc. cit.*
[61] *Krestjanskoje Zemlevladenije Vilenskoj gubernii* (Peasant Agriculture in the Government of
Vilna), Vilna, 1909.
[62] J. Poniatowski, *Przeludnienie wsi i rolnictwa* (The Overpopulation of the Village and
Agriculture), Warsaw, 1936.

Whereas peasant liberation in west and south east Germany and Bohemia to a large extent resulted directly in urbanization and industrialization, and the north east German movement, one or two generations after its tempestuous beginning, found itself absorbed by central and west German industrialization, the East Central European movement led overwhelmingly to rural overpopulation unrelieved up to the present day and raising for the countries and peoples of the Central European East the same ominous question, in reverse order, about the preservation of the social structure as the 'flight from the land' in Germany. Liberal agrarian reform proved a blessing wherever either its extreme *laissez faire* implications were impeded and its consequences controlled by responsible public and social policy, or where other modern economic and social developments combined with it to establish a sound equilibrium. This is largely true of north-west Germany. Where its effect remained uninhibited, it largely took place at the expense of healthy social stratification, be it through overwhelming expansion of large estates as in the German north east, be it through excessive fragmentation of peasant holdings as in eastern central Germany. Between them lie regions where the incidence of liberal agrarian reform did not change the social structure essentially, because of 'ossification' of conditions or anticipation of parts of peasant liberation even before the epoch of reforms in the first half of the nineteenth century, as in the south west and in parts of south east Germany. The companion piece and logical complement of liberal agrarian reforms consisted in the rise of an industrial system. Where this remained in abeyance and peasants were torn from the soil while remaining in a persistently rural, technically backward economic and agrarian order, generating no new economic opportunities nor socially constructive forces, liberal agrarian reforms drove towards a steep slope, provoking subsequent agrarian revolutions and, in spite of these, leaving behind them a question still open in the present day.

# Structural Change
# in the Rhenish Linen
# and Cotton Trades at the
# Outset of Industrialization[1]

GERHARD ADELMANN

Translated by George Hammersley

Agreement on the meaning to be attributed to 'industry' and 'industrialization' ought to precede an attempt to describe and discuss structural changes during the process of industrialization either in the whole economy or in any group of trades.[2] The intrinsic significance and the chronology of the historical phenomenon called 'industrialization' both depend on its definition, whether industry be taken to refer to any economic activity, at least if oriented towards the market, especially an export market, or to modern forms of production and enterprise most fully represented by the mechanized factory equipped with machinery.

The latter is the definition of industry adopted in the present paper. 'Industrialization' therefore here refers to any event bearing on the origins of, and the eventual achievement of predominance by, the factory system. This definition bears upon a whole range of technical economic and social factors which belong to two fields, one wider, the other more restricted. In the more restricted sense it demands investigation of the development and growth of trades and of industry itself. Walther G. Hoffmann traced these qualitative and especially quantitative changes in industry in his *Stages and Types of Industrialization*.[3] In the wider sense the notion embraces changes in the whole economy and in society in so far as industry bears responsibility for them. W. W. Rostow's investigation into *The Stage-*

[1] This is a version of a paper read to a conference of Belgian, Dutch and German historians at Heverlee near Louvain, 30 April to 2 May 1964, to which references have been added.

[2] Cf. the etymological discussion in W. Fischer, *Der Staat und die Anfänge der Industrialisierung in Baden, 1800–1850* (The State and the Beginnings of Industrialization in Baden, 1800–50), I, 'Die staatliche Gewerbepolitik', Berlin, 1962, pp. 27–33.

[3] W. G. Hoffmann, *Stadien und Typen der Industrialisierung*, (Stages and Types of Industrialization), Jena, 1931, p. 1 (English edition: *The Growth of Industrial Economies*, Manchester, 1958).

*of Economic Growth* largely addressed itself to that end, albeit concerned mainly with economic aspects.[4] Both enquiries are couched in economic and statistical terms and attempt necessarily to offer general statements and insights, to formulate laws, as far as possible establishing what is typical of the process of industrialization.

Historical investigation too concerns itself with the recognition of changes in kind and even in quantity. Beyond this however it concentrates for preference on particular instances of industrialization and enquires into specific formative causes and forces. In this paper I should like to attempt a review of factors promoting industrialization as they become apparent in the actual historical unfolding of the process; finally I want to refer by way of example to the foundation of a major cotton spinning and weaving firm to act as a focal point for the most important structural questions.

I should like to begin with the structure of the Rhenish linen and cotton trades on the eve of industrialization, i.e. immediately before their move into factories.[5]

Towards the end of the eighteenth century the principal textile districts of the Rhineland were the following:[6]

1 Along the entire left bank of the Lower Rhine, with major centres at Krefeld, Viersen, Gladbach, Rheydt and the Jülich district as far as Aachen, to say nothing of Monschau and Cologne.

2 On the right bank of the Rhine, above all the Berg district and to the north the region around Duisburg, Mülheim on the Ruhr and Kettwig.

These worked on all textile fibres then in common use: silk, flax, cotton and wool. The major concentrations of the linen and cotton trades lay in the Berg[7] and Gladbach-Rheydt districts.[8] I want to deal first with the manufacture of flax into linen which, in the second half of the eighteenth century, remained the older and more important trade. Flax spinning and linen weaving were widespread in Berg and on the left bank of the Lower Rhine where they were produced for the market. We may here disregard the peasants' domestic production of textiles for their own use. Berg, especially in the Wuppertal, was the most advanced district in which the earliest stage of linen manufacture, spinning, occupied only a subsidiary position.

---

[4] W. W. Rostow, *The Stages of Economic Growth*, Cambridge, 1960.

[5] The footnotes refer only to a selection of the more important published work on the economic history of the Rhineland. In the present paper I have had to omit almost all references to works on local or business history.

[6] Cf. H. Aubin and others, *Geschichte des Rheinlandes von der ältesten Zeit bis zur Gegenwart* (History of the Rhineland from Earliest Times to the Present), II, *Kulturgeschichte*, Essen, 1922, pp. 151ff; O. Most, B. Kuske, H. Weber, *Wirtschaftskunde von Rheinland und Westfalen* (Economics of Rhineland and Westphalia), 2 vols., Berlin, 1931; W. Zorn, 'Die Struktur der rheinischen Wirtschaft in der Neuzeit' (The Structure of the Rhineland Economy in Modern Times), *Rheinische Vierteljahrsblätter*, XXVIII, 1963, pp. 37ff.

[7] E. Strutz, *Bergische Wirtschaftsgeschichte* (Economic History of Berg), Remscheid-Lennep, 1958, pp. 71ff.; offprint from *Bergische Geschichte* (History of Berg), by K. J. Narr, J. Hashagen, W. Rees, E. Strutz; W. Dietz, *Die Wuppertaler Garnnahrung* (Wuppertal Yarn Supply); *Geschichte der Industrie und des Handels von Elberfeld und Barmen*, Neustadt a.d. Aisch, 1957; *Industrie und Handelskammer Wuppertal, 1831–1956* (Industry and Wuppertal Chamber of Commerce, 1831–1956), pub. by Industrie und Handelskammer Wuppertal and Dr Wolfgang Köllmann, Wuppertal-Elberfeld, 1956.

[8] A. Thun, *Die Industrie am Niederrhein und ihre Arbeiter* (Industry on the Lower Rhine and its Workers), Leipzig, 1879; F. O. Dilthey, *Die Geschichte der Niederrheinischen Baumwollindustrie* (History of the Lower Rhine Cotton Industry), Jena, 1908.

The Wuppertal worked up and manufactured yarn spun in other regions of Germany, and its prosperity was founded on commerce. The finishing processes, bleaching, dyeing, weaving and finally dressing were most highly developed here with specialization far advanced. This paper can only indicate the specialties which distinguished Wuppertal textile trades.[9] At that time in western Germany ribbon weaving and the turning of straps were practised only in the Wuppertal and neighbouring Schwelm. In the context of the international textile market they were not altogether without competition, but their process of industrialization was subject to special conditions; they cannot unequivocally be compared with the textile trades of the rest of the Rhineland, Belgium and Holland. On the other hand the weaving of linen cloth in the Berg district fits into our category: it shared the exceptional progress of the other Wuppertal textile trades in the second half of the eighteenth century.[10]

Flax spinning and linen weaving similarly prevailed on the left bank of the Lower Rhine, in a triangular area with the line Cologne-Aachen as its base and Gladbach its apex. The manual flax spinning usual in this district was primarily a by-employment, evidence of the area's predominantly agricultural character, interspersed with some craft elements.[11] Mention of by-employment suggests the question: what was the organization of the Rhenish linen trade, what kinds of enterprise or types of firm organized spinning and weaving before industrialization changed their structure? For rural flax spinning and weaving the answer is relatively straightforward; essentially they were peasants' by-employment. During the winter they spun their own flax, wove it into linen and sold it to middlemen or to merchants in the towns. Between merchants and rural part-time spinners and weavers of the Lower Rhineland the relationship was one of simple direct purchase. The same applied to a large proportion of urban spinners and weavers of Mönchen-Gladbach and places near it, but for them linen manufacture more and more became their principal occupation. In these towns too, however, linen weavers were as yet independent masters, working up on their own looms yarn which they might have spun themselves, though they had more often bought it; they sold the cloths to linen dealers or their factors.[12]

Linen weavers of the Wuppertal on the other hand were mostly organized by the Elberfeld and Barmen merchants in a putting-out system.[13] They too had their own domestic looms, apparently no more than five per master,[14] but they often worked up yarn 'put out'—i.e. supplied—to them by the merchant; payment by the piece had previously been agreed and the completed piece was delivered back

[9] Cf. Thun, *op. cit., passim*; J. V. Bredt, *Die Lohnindustrie, dargestellt an der Garn- und Textilindustrie von Barmen* (Working for Wages, illustrated by the Barmen Yarn and Textile Industry), Berlin, 1905; *Geschichte der Bergischen Bandindustrie* (History of the Ribbon Industry of Berg), Ronsdorf, 1920, published by Verein ehemaliger Textilfachschueler zu Ronsdorf e.V.; K. Wuelfrath, *Bänder aus Ronsdorf. 150 Jahre J. H. vom Baur Sohn* (Ribbons from Ronsdorf. 150 years of J. H. vom Baur Sohn), Essen, 1955.

[10] Dietz, *op. cit.*, pp. 113ff.; Thun, *op. cit.*, p. 184.

[11] Dilthey, *op. cit.*, pp. 1ff.

[12] F. Hassler, 'Aus der Geschichte der Textil- und Bekleidungsindustrie im Mönchen-Gladbach-Rheydter Industriegebiet' (From the History of the Cloth and Clothing Industry in the Mönchen-Gladbach-Rheydt Industrial Area), *Melliand-Textilberichte*, XXXVII, Heidelberg, 1965, p. 1126.

[13] Cf. note 10 above.　　　　　　[14] Cf. Thun, *op. cit.*, p. 182.

to the putter-out. Though formally an independent 'master weaver' the producer in the putting-out system then depended much on the merchant; the social implications of this need not be discussed here.

As far as the type of enterprise or firm is concerned, the putting-out system in essence 'comprises only the commercial aspects of the organization of production'.[15] The putter-out, generally a merchant, purchases raw materials and sells finished goods, combining these two functions. Production proper however is parcelled out into the homes of individual weavers. Frequently one clothier employed hundreds of domestic weavers; it is possible to consider this as a large-scale decentralized works or, more accurately, enterprise. By their drive, commercial skill and, not least, planning and co-ordination of the different stages of production clothiers maintained these large putting-out arrangements also known as domestic industry. Looking towards world-wide exports these decisively affected the economic strength of whole regions and the employment of their growing industrial population.

Cotton manufacture in Berg as well as on the left bank of the Lower Rhine from the outset organized on the putting-out system because it relied on foreign raw materials which the merchants imported from Holland and England. In earlier decades of the eighteenth century merchants and clothiers had mainly imported cotton yarn for distribution to domestic weavers; during the 1730s they began increasingly to arrange for raw cotton to be spun in their own country: the invention of the fly shuttle (1733) had created a rapidly mounting, almost insatiable demand for yarn from weavers of cottons and fustians. In places and villages in Berg, even outside the Wuppertal in Upper Berg,[16] thousands of part-time hand spinners who had formerly worked on linen and wool now turned to the cotton put out by the Wuppertal clothiers. In Berg in the second half of the eighteenth century spinning and weaving of cotton increasingly replaced the exclusive linen manufacture. Not merely was cotton cheaper than the homegrown materials, but the demand for cotton cloths was stimulated by their 'varied patterns, *inter alia* made possible by printing'.[17]

Around mid-century the Gladbach-Rheydt district drew its cotton partly from the Netherlands, partly from Berg.[18] Thus as early as 1747 the Elberfeld 'manufacturer', i.e. putter-out, Ullenberg constantly employed 100 cotton spinners and 200 handloom weavers there to take advantage of the lower wages.[19] He and other putters-out not known to us by name employed agents, called factors, to distribute mainly yarn and some raw cotton and bring back the completed cloths into Berg for dyeing, finishing and sale. Thus occurred the transition to the putting-out system on the left bank of the Lower Rhine as well.

In the Rhineland and other textile districts on the Continent of Europe attempts were made to overcome the shortage of yarn by drawing a growing army of hand spinners into the putting-out system. Meanwhile the first spinning machines were

[15] W. Fischer, 'Ansätze zur Industrialisierung in Baden 1770–1870' (Tendencies towards Industrialization in Baden, 1770–1870), *Vierteljahrschrift für Sozial- und Wirtschaftsgeschichte*, XLVII, 1960, p. 187, n. 2.
[16] Cf. Thun, *op. cit.*, p. 188; Dietz, *op. cit.*, p. 116.
[17] Dietz, *op. cit.*, p. 116.    [18] Dilthey, *op. cit.*, p. 3.
[19] E. Brasse, *Geschichte der Stadt und Abtei Gladbach* (History of Gladbach Town and Abbey), II, *Neuzeit* (Modern Times), M. Gladbach, 1922, pp. 509f.

constructed in England. The stages in their development are well known. In 1764 James Hargreaves built his jenny, still driven by hand; in 1769 Richard Arkwright patented his frame, at first based on water power. In 1779 Samuel Crompton combined the roller drawing mechanism of Arkwright's machine with his own improved version of the jenny to make the mule, hand-driven at first, though power was soon applied to part of the process. In 1786 Cartwright invented the power loom. These inventions 'profoundly changed the whole basis of production in the textile trades' and in addition the application of Watt's steam engine to drive them 'facilitated increased production on a very large scale'.[20] From the combination of mechanized production with a mechanical source of power in England there emerged, for the first time, a new pattern of industrial enterprise in the integrated factory system, the modern factory in which 'goods are produced by a larger number of employees working under an organized division of labour and performing prearranged processes helped by these new machines.'[21]

As one of the consequences of mechanization of cotton spinning in England, European markets were flooded with cheaper and better English yarn. Thus on the Continent hand spinners of linen as well as of cotton began to feel English competition many years before the Napoleonic wars. How did the Rhenish textile trade react to this stimulus, to this challenge from the rival products of English industry? This also poses the question of the impetus to industrialization in the Rhineland and thus touches upon a problem common to countries which were then, compared to England, industrially underdeveloped. Two effects can unmistakably be recognized by the end of the eighteenth century, although their further progress was slowed down and temporarily reversed in war time, especially by the Continental Blockade and prohibitive French duties. However, these effects reasserted themselves all the more vigorously after 1814: there was on the one hand a regression in, and decline of, certain craft-based trades unless they evaded competition by shifting into different lines, and on the other hand pressure to develop native industrial production.

The second theme opens up our real subject: it confronts us with the pioneering achievement of Johann Gottfried Bruegelmann, merchant and putter-out of Elberfeld.[22] He was the first entrepreneur in the Rhineland to make use of English inventions; in 1783-4 he set up the first mechanized cotton spinning works in Germany at Ratingen near Düsseldorf at a cost of some 25,000 imperial Taler. The mill was called Cromford in celebration of the English exemplar; the building, on five floors, contained 1,600 fine spindles driven by water, employed between 70 and 80 workers and began operations in 1784.[23] According to the inventory of 31 January 1798 there were then 62 manual or water-powered machines with about 5,200 spindles. As noted by F. J. Gemmert in his monograph, the oldest cotton spinning mill in the Rhineland was therefore, 'during its first decades, simultaneously manufactory and factory, that is to say, had spinning machinery partly powered by hand and partly by energy derived from water'.[24] In the terms

[20] W. Köllmann, *Sozialgeschichte der Stadt Barmen im 19. Jahrhundert* (Social History of the Town of Barmen in the Nineteenth Century), Tübingen, 1960, p. 14.
[21] Fischer, 'Ansätze . . .', p. 187.
[22] F. J. Gemmert, *Die Entwicklung der ältesten kontinentalen Spinnerei* (The Development of the Oldest Continental Spinning Mill), Leipzig, 1927; Dietz, *op. cit.*, pp. 115–9.
[23] Gemmert, *op. cit.*, p. 52.          [24] Gemmert, *op. cit.*, p. 50.

of the definition of a factory here preferred, Bruegelmann's foundation undoubtedly satisfies the criteria of 'the larger number of employees', the 'organized division of labour' and 'mechanized production'. But that leaves open the question whether water power is the equivalent of a 'mechanical source of power' or whether only a permanently operating engine such as represented first by Watt's steam engine can be properly so regarded. 'Regularity of production' at any rate could demonstrably not always be guaranteed, with water power affected by seasonal changes in water supply.

If Bruegelmann's establishment were to be accepted as a proper factory, it would have to be emphasized all the more that in the Rhineland and especially on the Lower Rhine watercourses possessed too gentle a gradient to provide continuous power even for small spinning mills. At least in the plains, continuous development of such embryonic factories was inconceivable without the installation of steam engines. In their absence the industrialization of the Rhenish textile trades lagged. Despite such reservations Bruegelmann's undertaking substantially stimulated other similar enterprises.[25] In fact this was the time when, on the right bank of the Rhine, there 'came into being the leading textile district of Germany which was then severely stricken and almost destroyed by the Continental Blockade.'[26]

We are familiar with the contrasting experiences of the textile trades on either bank of the Rhine during the French period. Decline in Berg confronted striking progress on the left bank of the Lower Rhine. Indeed some observers incline to exaggerate the remarkable extent of the advance because they view it in isolation. This was the period when cotton manufacture on the left bank of the Rhine emerged into independent significance. In some measure however it was merely a stage in the migration of the cotton spinning and cloth weaving of the Wuppertal to a district of lower wages. This move began with the employment of spinners and weavers in Gladbach by putters-out from Berg in 1750 to which reference has been made earlier; it attained a spectacular peak around 1800 when Wuppertal firms established temporary branches on the left bank of the Rhine and even transferred physically. It did not end with the French occupation. Between the 1820s and the 1840s Wuppertal cotton firms continued similarly to emigrate to the industrial region of Gladbach, Rheydt and Odenkirchen on the left bank of the Rhine as well as to Upper Berg.[27]

The rise of cotton manufacture on the left bank of the Rhine cannot be explained simply by the arrival of entrepreneurs and workers from Berg. Linen manufacture with a skilled labour force and its own entrepreneurs had been long established on the left bank of the Lower Rhine. Quite a few of the local linen manufacturers converted to cotton early on; they were among the founders, in the decades around the turn of the century, of small so-called spinning factories, really spinning mills using water-driven mules. One may justifiably single out the achievement of Johann Peter Boelling as representative of immigrant entrepreneurs from Berg[28]

---

[25] Cf. note 22 above.
[26] Cf. Motteck, Blumberg, Wutzmer, Becker, *Studien zur Geschichte der industriellen Revolution in Deutschland* (Studies for the History of the Industrial Revolution in Germany), Berlin, 1960, pp. 18f. [27] Cf. Strutz, *op. cit.*, pp. 94f. and 104f.
[28] Cf. *inter alia* Industrie- und Handelskammer Gladbach-Rheydt-Neuss (pub.), *Werden und Wachsen eines Wirtschaftsgebietes am linken Niederrhein* (Birth and Growth of an Economic Region on the Left Bank of the Lower Rhine), M. Gladbach, 1937, p. 12.

but, as representing local enterprise, Johann Lenssen deserves to stand alongside him.

I do not here want to describe the slow, laborious and varied development of the Rhenish cotton trades after 1814. The superior British competition whose in-dustrialization had advanced still further in the meantime exerted a powerful influence on it, especially as it had taken to export dumping in times of crisis. This is shown by the extent to which Rhenish cotton firms of the first rank suffered collapse and closure after 1814 and more so after 1818 when the Prussian protective duty on British yarn was much reduced.[29] This episode is mentioned even today as a classic example in support of the argument for protective tariffs behind which native industry may develop. On the other hand I should like to draw attention to another feature of the progress of industrialization in Rhenish cotton spinning. Surely the excessive slowness with which mechanization of cotton spinning spread during the Continental Blockade can be explained precisely by the exclusion of those stimuli supplied by the rapid mechanization of the British competitors? The impregnable shelter of protection had permitted establishment of many spinning works with inadequate resources of capital which did not really qualify as factories in the modern sense at all. Given these consequences of the Blockade, it no longer seems extraordinary that most of these establishments could not long survive the end of Napoleonic domination. At the end of the eighteenth century the time lag in mechanization between Rhenish and British cotton spinning had been about ten years, in the first half of the nineteenth century this had deteriorated to about thirty years: undeniably the Rhineland could no longer withstand the over-whelming superiority of British mechanized competition without protection.

The general economic development of the textile trades and especially the in-dustrialization of cotton manufacture during the nineteenth century were in addition much affected by changes in internal and external commercial and customs policies[30] and by economic fluctuations.[31] A survey of international economic relations shows Germany's western neighbours to have taken a signifi-cant portion of Rhenish textiles until the end of the eighteenth century. Except for the special lines produced in the Wuppertal, this market largely disappeared in the first half of the nineteenth century, partly owing to French, Dutch and later also Belgian protective duties. Intensification of the nation State or rather of the nation-al economies becomes apparent also from the way in which sources of capital for the textile industry of the Lower Rhine changed. The account books of Gladbach firms show[32] that, in the early nineteenth century, as in the eighteenth, standing overdrafts at such Dutch banks and exporters as P. J. Berger & Co. of Venlo,

[29] Dilthey, *op. cit.*, pp. 11ff.; *Werden und Wachsen*, pp. 33ff. On the development of duties on textiles in general, cf. G. Jacobs, *Die deutschen Textilzölle im 19. Jahrhundert* (German Textile Tariffs in the Nineteenth Century), Brunswick, 1907.

[30] Cf. note 29 and A. Zimmermann, *Geschichte der preussisch-deutschen Handelspolitik akten-mässig dargestellt* (History of Prussian-German Commercial Policy illustrated by Official Records), Oldenburg & Leipzig, 1892.

[31] Cf. note 29 and W. Köllmann, *op. cit.*, pp. 37ff., 279ff. and appendix 2, 'Konjunkturen und Krisen, 1808–1914' (Business Cycles and Crises, 1808–1914).

[32] At present unpublished and in private hands. More details will appear in my planned publication, 'Interrelations and topographical differentiation in the origins of the cotton and linen industries in north-western Germany and its western neighbours, with a con-tribution on structural change in a craft economy at the start of industrialization'.

Brunge of Amsterdam and Rotterdam and F. C. Ouien of Amsterdam helped to finance them. In the 1830s local banks, Molenaar Brothers of Krefeld and Abraham Schaafhausen of Cologne, began to compete with Dutch firms; by 1850 they had almost completely replaced them. As far as national economic policy was concerned, two features were significant for the Rhenish linen and cotton trades. One was the creation of a home market, first in Prussia, then in the German Customs Union, the other the Prussian and Customs Union duties on textiles. The larger market of the Customs Union provided welcome compensation for the fall in exports, though simultaneously it introduced competition from Saxon and south German textile districts.

The rate of duty on yarn especially served repeatedly to inflame controversies between spinners on the one side and yarn dealers, dyers and weavers on the other. Overall, duties on imported yarn remained too low in the first half of the century to be regarded as really protective. They favoured particularly the later stages of Rhenish production; as duty was charged by weight, it served to restrain foreign imports of only the coarsest yarn. Production of this yarn then was to some extent protected, but its production offered an uncertain return only for the old hand-driven spinning machines. Given such conditions, it would have been highly unprofitable to set up new and extremely expensive mechanized spinning works without adequate protection against the enormously superior British competition. Until the beginning of the 1840s it seemed as if 'cotton spinning, limping along as a manual occupation, was doomed to certain extinction'.[33]

In contrast, on the left bank of the Rhine problems of transition in cotton weaving had been successfully overcome by the end of the 1820s. For a time at least even foreign markets had been regained successfully and the trade maintained its competitive position in the face of lower wages paid in Silesia, Saxony and south Germany. The putting-out system continued to operate in handloom weaving on the left bank of the Lower Rhine; its entrepreneurs shared two advantages characteristic of manufacture of specialties in the Wuppertal: they knew how to gauge the moment at which to drop an unprofitable line and, helped by an adaptable working population, they easily turned to new and more profitable products.[34] This adaptability facilitated a smooth transition from linen to cotton weaving which was virtually complete by 1840 (in diametric contrast to Silesian developments) and later on enabled them to take up the weaving of cotton-wool mixtures and of silk.

This adaptability of the weavers to new lines resulted early in the 1840s in the adoption of beaverteen production; this in turn provided the final impetus for the industrialization first of cotton spinning and then, ten years later, of cotton weaving in the Gladbach-Rheydt district.

The manufacture of beaverteen, a material with a fine, firmly twisted warp and a very thick, loosely spun weft, succeeded beyond all expectation. In consequence hand spinning in those antiquated, inadequately mechanized and water-driven 'spinning factories' (so-called) could no longer keep up with the demand for yarn. Like Richard Arkwright in Cromford sixty years before, industry on the Lower Rhine reacted to the acute shortage of yarn: hesitantly and slowly it converted itself to mechanized steam-powered spinning; at Bruegelmann's works in Ratingen

[33] Dilthey, *op. cit.*, p. 33.      [34] Dilthey, *op. cit.*, pp. 16f.

D

indeed the response came at about the same time.[35] True, the Rheydt firm of Lenssen & Beckenbach had installed a steam engine in its cotton spinning department as early as 1827, but had found no imitators in the Gladbach district. In the final analysis, though, the Rheydt enterprise remained a hand spinning works despite its steam engine: in my view this was employed solely in preparatory processing or even for entirely non-textile purposes. In 1847 it had to close down because of its inability to compete with recently mechanized modern local works.[36] Gradually modern Swiss and from 1850 on the most recent British equipment replaced ancient French machinery in Rhenish cotton spinning. General transition to properly mechanized spinning was a feature of the economic expansion only in the 1850s. By 1860 hand cotton spinning in the district encompassed by the Gladbach Chamber of Commerce was virtually extinct. Since 1857 the fall in prices accompanying depression had accelerated the decline of manual spinning where costs were near the margin. Different wage rates were paid in different branches of the industry operating in close physical proximity: this phenomenon, typical of the textile industry on the Lower Rhine, helped to promote mechanization in textiles. It has been demonstrated that introduction of the industrialized factory in cotton manufacture, i.e. replacement of labour by capital, was hastened by the drift of workers into the better paid trades of velvet and silk weaving. More vigorous implementation of legislation for the protection of juvenile labour reinforced this movement.

In the Rhineland, as in Germany generally, mechanization of cotton weaving and of mixtures began in the mid-1850s. Of course there had been a few isolated forerunners also in this field in the 1840s; by the middle or the end of the 1860s mechanization had generally taken over and, at least in the Rhineland, displaced handloom weaving except for a few insignificant remnants. Finally we ought to refer briefly to the mechanization of flax spinning and weaving in the Rhineland during the 1850s or 1860s. Unlike in cotton there is no gradual transition from manual to mechanized production in the Rhenish flax trade. Flax spinning at least had become extinct when in 1851, 1853 and 1864 three mechanized flax spinning works were founded in Düren, Dülken and Viersen in the Rhineland.[37] Linen weaving, of great importance towards the end of the eighteenth century, had survived only in a few places in the Rhineland (e.g. Burgwaldniel) into the age of mechanization.

A few figures will demonstrate the order of magnitude involved in structural change in cotton spinning and weaving during the crucial years 1834, 1846 and 1861. The data[38] all refer to the local government district of Düsseldorf which covered almost three quarters of the Rhenish cotton manufacture.

---

[35] Gemmert, *op. cit.*, p. 64.
[36] *Werden und Wachsen*, pp. 43, 82.
[37] Schöller, Bücklers & Co.; Niederrheinische Flachsspinnerei A.G.; Viersener A.G. für Spinnerei und Weberei.
[38] Compiled from J. G. von Viehbahn, *Statistik und Topographie des Regierungsbezirks Düsseldorf* (Statistics and Topography for the Düsseldorf Local Government District), Düsseldorf, 1836, pp. 168, 159f. (for 1836); F. W. von Reden, *Erwerbs- und Verkehrsstatistik des Königsstaats Preussen* (Statistics of Trade and Transport of the Kingdom of Prussia), 2 vols., Darmstadt, 1853, p. 1148 (for 1846) and O. von Mülmann, *Statistik des Regierungs-Bezirkes Düsseldorf* (Statistics of the Düsseldorf Local Government District), II, part 2, Iserlohn, 1867, pp. 555ff. (for 1861).

COTTON SPINNING

| Date | Works Mechanized Manual | | Spindles | Total | Workers Male | Female |
|---|---|---|---|---|---|---|
| 1834 | 19 (10 water, 9 steam) | 31 | 57,642 | — | — | — |
| 1846 | 33 | — | 77,801 | 2,392 | 1,244 | 1,148 |
| 1861 | 27[39] | — | 165,151 | 3,265 | 1,742 | 1,523 |

COTTON WEAVING

| 1834 | 8,398 | handlooms | |
|---|---|---|---|
| 1846 | 10,932 | handlooms and 12,469 workers | |
| 1861 | 11,084 | handlooms | 2,704 power looms |

No published figures exist for the 1860s when mechanization fully established itself.

So far I have deliberately concentrated on a full discussion of the objective economic factors in this development in order to demonstrate the structural changes in the economy rather than in society. Nevertheless I hope that, as the economy acted upon them, so the share of man, acting in the capacity of entrepreneur as well as of worker, will have become apparent. But if objective economic factors seemed inexorably to force structural changes upon the Rhenish textile trades I should like to show, by means of a typical case history, the foundation of a fully mechanized textile enterprise, that evidently these factors in the last analysis acted as a challenge to men engaged in economic activity. Industrialization of the Rhenish textile trades in the last resort depended on human attitudes, on the actions and omissions of people.

My example for the impact of the entrepreneur's personality on the process of industrialization is the foundation of the *Gladbacher Spinnerei und Weberei* joint-stock company in 1853.[40] In the contemporary judgment of the Gladbach Chamber of Commerce this introduced 'a new era for the district's industry' 'with independence from the English market in yarn and the creation of an integrated independent form of manufacture which was sought with visible success'.[41] In 1861 there were 165,000 cotton spindles in the local government district of Düsseldorf, 40,000 of them in the *Gladbacher Spinnerei und Weberei A.G.* which installed a further 10,000 in the same year. The acute shortage of yarn for beaverteen weaving on the Lower Rhine, already referred to, gave the external impulse for the foundation of this enterprise. Closer examination of the project to set up a large-scale mechanized spinning and weaving enterprise however reveals something about its originators. The outstanding representatives at least of the existing putting-out 'industry' and of the small, barely mechanized 'factories' had understood the signs of the times and, more important, were prepared to act. They

---

[39] 24 of them on the left bank of the Rhine and 3 on the right (Duisburg 2, Mettmann 1).

[40] For the detail which follows I refer to my contribution to *Spiegel der Geschichte, Festgabe für Max Braubach zum 10. April 1964* (The Mirror of History: Festschrift for Max Braubach for 10 April 1964), Eds. Konrad Repgen and Stephan Skalweit, Münster (Westphalia), 1964, pp. 727–51.

[41] *Jahresbericht der Handelskammer zu Gladbach für 1858* (Annual Report for 1858 of the Gladbach Chamber of Commerce), pp. 15f.

realized that 'wherever the hand of man can be replaced by machinery, there manual labour must lose to its competition; the manufacture concerned therefore must no longer fight shy of the introduction of mechanical power'.[42]

Who then were these founders, appealing to the public by this crucial phrase in their founders' prospectus for subscriptions to their shares? Their appeal was especially addressed to their colleagues, the entrepreneurs in the textile district of the Lower Rhine; they recommended to them for emulation the example of the successful large-scale enterprises of Britain and Belgium.

The prospectus is signed by Quirin Croon and Anton Lamberts Christians Sohn, authorized to represent the association because, among the eleven founders, theirs were the two highest subscriptions for shares. Quirin Croon may be regarded as the real originator of the plan and the driving force behind the founders' whole enterprise.[43] He had not remained content with merely making his firm, Croon Brothers, the greatest textile undertaking in Gladbach, but had always concerned himself with the common interest of cotton spinners and weavers of the Gladbach-Rheydt region. Several visits to Manchester had familiarized Croon with progress in the British cotton and textile machinery industry; its vast superiority, as he clearly recognized, constituted a growing threat to the backward native industry, and he had already drawn the obvious conclusions for his own works. To be properly competitive, he realized, would however require a large mechanized cotton spinning and weaving works with all the most advanced technical equipment; this was far in excess of the financial resources of any one individual. This was not his first venture into the founding of a joint-stock company. The setting up of a cloth-finishing establishment for the district of Gladbach in 1839 had demanded only a comparatively small amount of capital ($30,566\frac{2}{3}$ Reichsthalers).[44] Quirin Croon had also agreed to subscribe to Gustav Mevissen's project for a mechanized flax spinning works at Dülken in 1838; this did not succeed because the number of other entrepreneurs prepared to participate turned out to be too small[45] and also because the government refused its consent for a joint-stock scheme.[46] The project was bound to fail in any case because the economic outlook for German flax spinning was at that time highly unpropitious.

In 1853 on the other hand conditions appeared much more hopeful: the period was one of economic expansion, the project concerned cotton spinning. The share prospectus of the *Gladbacher Spinnerei und Weberei A.G.* was submitted to the public by Croon and Lamberts in May 1853; they did not omit to draw proper attention to the favourable general atmosphere prevailing in the industrial region of Gladbach-Rheydt. They dwelt fully on local conditions facilitating optimum use of factors of production, labour, land and capital. They laid special stress on the knowledge and experience accumulated by local entrepreneurs since the beginning of the century in the foundation and conduct of 'mechanical' spinning and weaving works. 'A

---

[42] Founders' prospectus in Hauptstaatsarchiv Düsseldorf, Reg. Düsseldorf (henceforth cited as HStAD, RD), No. 13,315, folio 2.

[43] Cf. K. Apelt, 'Quirin Croon (1788–1854)', *Rheinisch-Westfälische Wirtschaftsbiographien*, IV, Münster, 1941, p. 62.

[44] HStAD, RD, No. 2,140, folios 85a, 86.

[45] Apelt, *op. cit.*, p. 62.

[46] J. Hansen, *Gustav von Mevissen. Ein rheinisches Lebensbild 1815–1899* (Gustav von Mevissen: a Rhenish Biography, 1815–99), I, Berlin, 1906, pp. 157ff.

capable working class' favoured 'the setting up of ambitious large-scale factories' as much as did moderate wage rates in a still rural region with low costs of living, land and building. The site was similarly favoured by good railway connections to Aachen, the Rhine and to the right bank of the Rhine, permitting easy procurement and disposal, with special emphasis on direct access to the Ruhr and the Wurm coalfields. Existing customs duties on foreign cotton yarn guaranteed profitability; moreover the anticipated expansion of the Customs Union to the sea would stimulate the favourable development of industrial and commercial conditions in general.

Their arguments were convincing. The capital was to be three million thalers of which the first issue was to be one million; this was subscribed within three weeks. The eleven founders between them invested altogether 400,000 thalers in the company, as follows:[47]

|  |  | *Thalers* |
|---|---|---|
| 1 | Friedrich Diergardt, *Geheimer Kommerzienrat*, Viersen, manufacturer of velvet and silk | 60,000 |
| 2 | Paul Jacob Preyer, judge in the commercial court, Viersen, dealer in English yarn and silk manufacturer | 25,000 |
| 3 | Quirin Croon, *Kommerzienrat*, president of the commercial court, Gladbach, firm of Croon Brothers, dealers, cotton weavers and hand-powered machine spinners | 105,000 |
| 4 | Wilhelm Prinzen, Gladbach, of the firm of that name, manufacturer of silk fustians and cottons, grocer | 55,000 |
| 5 | Anton Lamberts Christians Sohn, deputy mayor, Gladbach, of the firm of that name, cotton spinner | 75,000 |
| 6 | Heinrich Pferdmenges, judge in the commercial court, Gladbach firm of Pferdmenges Brothers, merchants, manufacturers of silk fustians and cottons | 30,000 |
| 7 | Carl Schmölder, Rheydt, firm of Wiedemann, Pferdmenges & Schmölder, merchants, mechanized cotton spinners at Elsen Mühle near Grevenbroich | 5,000 |
| 8 | Wilhelm Specken, Dülken, firm of Specken & Weyermann, merchants, manufacturers of velvet and silk | 15,000 |
| 9 | Franz Wilhelm Koenigs, Dülken, brother-in-law of Gustav Mevissen, firm of G. Mevissen, merchants, machine flax spinners, linen twisters, dyers, dressers | 10,000 |
| 10 | Wilhelm Diedrich Lenssen, Rheydt, owner of the now defunct firm of Lenssen & Beckenbach | 10,000 |
| 11 | Johann Wilhelm Brinck sen., Gladbach, dyers and yarn dealers | 10,000 |

This list of the founder members of the *Gladbacher Spinnerei und Weberei A.G.* and of their firms conveys one impression immediately: they were exclusively textile entrepreneurs, indeed the most prominent 'industrialists' from all different branches of the textile trades to be found in the district covered by the Gladbach Chamber of Commerce. These origins correspond entirely with the express inten-

[47] HStAD, Rep. 1,775, No. 11,641, folios 1–14, the notarial articles of association of 12 May 1853.

tion of engaging in integrated spinning and weaving of all kinds of textiles; true, the first object was cotton manufacture, but other fibres were not for the time being excluded. In the absence of adequate records however we can no longer unequivocally explain why or how in particular just these eleven men came to be associated. The region of course was neither extensive nor yet thickly industrialized; therefore they, as leading entrepreneurs, certainly knew one another through professional and personal intercourse. Last but not least, their family connections deserve some attention; though not always immediately apparent, they were in fact of much importance throughout the Rhenish textile industry.

The list of founders is remarkable for another characteristic: the complete absence of bankers. This may be contrasted with the list of founders' names for the *Kölnische Baumwollspinnerei und -weberei*, printed by Hansen.[48] This too had been founded in 1853 on the initiative of Gustav Mevissen; amongst the participants the majority of bankers and the leading role of their subscriptions are striking. In the *Gladbacher Spinnerei und Weberei A.G.* on the other hand businessmen themselves engaged in textile manufacture had joined in a common enterprise, not merely subscribing the capital but wanting above all to become active owners and directors of the joint-stock company. The value of the limited liability joint-stock company for them consisted in the possibility of raising additional capital and in limiting their risk to their share holding. Almost all the founders continued to conduct their own private businesses even after the company had been established. All the founders came from families in the textile business which had acquired a large part of their wealth in the pre-industrial age and had continued to invest in the same trade. The Cologne company was dominated by the investment of bankers who either had never been, or were no longer, primarily specialists in textiles.

Apart from founders' shares the *Gladbacher Spinnerei und Weberei* issued 600,000 thalers of capital; the subscribers are listed,[49] and here too bankers whether acting on their own or clients' behalf occupy only a minor position. 63 of the 85 subscribers taking up shares after foundation lived on the left bank of the Lower Rhine north of the line Cologne-Aachen and mostly were active in the textile trade. The remainder came also from the Rhineland except for some from the western textile districts of Westphalia; some of them were related to the founders. In no sense can the *Gladbacher Spinnerei und Weberei* be described as an 'anonymous society', meaning a vast aggregate of shareholders without other contact with the industry; the founders indeed expressly reserved the right to accept or reject applications to subscribe.

The founders retained a strong personal interest in the direction of the company and the management of the works. This becomes evident in negotiations, protracted for months with official quarters over the terms of the government concession. Discussions involved disputes over a number of sections in the articles of association but only one of them can be singled out here,[50] and this one Croon and Lamberts tried their utmost, but ultimately failed, to retain. The founders tried to establish their right to purchase at nominal value all or part of the balance of the

---

[48] Hansen, *op. cit.*, I, p. 632, n. 1.
[49] HStAD, RD, No. 13,315; HStAD, Rep. 1,175, Nos. 11,680, 11,701, 11,704. A more detailed analysis of these data is planned.
[50] For details cf. n. 40 above.

two million thalers of capital originally issued if there should be a further issue of shares, so as to preserve their decisive influence in any eventuality. To justify their argument for retention of this clause the entrepreneurs presented a classic analysis of the conditions for the successful conduct of an enterprise, drawing a clear distinction between the functions of entrepreneur and of owner of capital: some of their statement is therefore given *verbatim*.

In the personalities of the founders resides the principal guarantee of a prosperous future for the projected spinning and weaving works. It is not just their general standing in the world of business but above all their technical knowledge and experience in the special field with which the enterprise is concerned that offers to all participants the security they require. They are familiar with recent developments in spinning and weaving and this, combined with experience matured in their own businesses over many years, has suggested to each of them independently the idea that a co-operative effort could achieve what none of them could successfully complete on his own. The originators of the company therefore are evidently not people who met accidentally and decided in a burst of speculative enthusiasm to float a limited joint-stock undertaking but they are founders in the only proper sense of the term: they are best qualified to carry to completion most fittingly the project which they designed. Therefore nothing can be more natural or just than that they should be granted preferential treatment over other shareholders. The sort of preference we desire may be rejected as inadmissible in the case of an enterprise which needs nothing more for its existence than the provision of large capital. Here this is not the principal object. In this case it all turns on the need to restore in the fatherland a branch of industry which it had lost owing to the inventive ingenuity of neighbouring countries; this requires expert knowledge to devise methods which will best serve the purpose. If the new establishment is to come up to expectations, this must be the result of ideas rather than of financial strength. Obviously those who have brought the project into being by their intellectual effort, their industry and their knowledge should be allowed to occupy quite a different sort of position in the enterprise created by them than those who merely advance their money in the expectation of a share in profits produced by the endeavour of others. They will clearly have to be given the option of remaining masters in their works, thereby affording them an opportunity of guiding them to the highest state of perfection, for their own and the general advantage. Take away the privilege claimed by the originators and you reduce their enthusiasm which necessarily presupposes privileges in participation and in claims in the enterprises.[51]

The concession for the *Gladbacher Spinnerei und Weberei A.G.* was confirmed on 31 October 1853. Like the cloth-finishing establishment for the Gladbach district it was a kind of co-operative of independent entrepreneurs of the same trade and status. It was founded with the intention of performing for the textile trade of the whole district important functions which exceeded the capacity of individuals. It was this purpose which had persuaded so many of the individualistic entrepreneurs of the Lower Rhineland to co-operate.

Only a small number of new joint-stock companies was founded subsequently in the Rhenish textile industry. The textile industrialist of the Rhineland thus expressed his preference for his own separate sole-owner enterprise which, in independence, he could best maintain despite the uncommonly severe fluctuations and changes affecting his industry.

Finally I must attempt to distinguish the major stages of industrialization in the Rhenish linen and cotton industries and round off with a few hints concerning the development of woollen and silk manufactures. In its stricter definition industrial-

[51] HStAD, RD, No. 13,135, folios 26–8, Croon and Lamberts to the local government of Düsseldorf, 20 July 1853.

ization means the emergence and eventual preponderance of the fully mechanized factory system. This implies assigning the vigorous expansion of the Rhenish textile trades during the eighteenth century unequivocally to the pre-history of industrialization. Nevertheless the first traces of industrialization can be discovered in Rhenish cotton and carded woollen yarn spinning during the 1780s and 1790s. Some relief of manual labour, some lessening of the strain on workers, was offered by water-driven spinning machinery, however simply constructed as yet. True, what was then introduced was mostly hand-driven spinning machinery which only made manual labour more efficient: it merely extended and improved the working hand of man; it was a tool but not yet a machine which manufactures more or less automatically and which at most needs servicing by man's hand. The first traces of industrialization came rather early to the Rhineland; it then stagnated as a result of the Napoleonic wars and their aftermath. Mechanization spread gradually nevertheless, but did not, until the fourth decade of the nineteenth century, significantly exceed the scale attained in the earlier tentative beginnings. Around 1836 on the other hand steam engines began to be employed more widely in the Rhenish textile industry, in the woollen industry around Aachen and especially in spinning. Unmistakably this was due to the example of the neighbouring and more highly advanced Belgian industry and above all to Cockerill's immediate influence.[52] Modern mechanized cotton spinning powered by steam began to come in during the 1840s, a movement reinforced by the economic expansion of the 1850s and thus achieving predominance. The transition to mechanized wool spinning occurred at roughly the same time.

In flax spinning and in cotton and linen weaving the mechanized factory first arrived in the 1850s but came in decisively only in the 1860s. In parts of woollen weaving in the Rhineland the introduction of the power loom took even longer. For silk manufacture this did not start until the 1880s and only attained genuine significance by the turn of the century. The process of industrialization in the textile industries then was lengthily drawn out over a hundred years; it might therefore be more appropriately described by the term 'industrialization' rather than as an 'industrial revolution'.[53]

Concerning types of works and enterprises it should be stressed that transition from domestic manufacture to labour in integrated works occurred first of all in cotton and woollen spinning. However in these trades even some of the works employing handpowered spinning machines and some of the so-called 'spinning factories' emerged immediately as integrated factories and only exceptionally as manufactories. In weaving in the Rhineland, except for the production of woollen cloth in manufactories, mechanization always implied direct transition from a domestic putting-out system to work in the entrepreneur's factory. A revolution in entrepreneurial organization and in techniques was the corollary of industrialization, but without much effect on the type of enterprise prevalent in Rhenish*r*

[52] Cf. my review of source material, published as *Der gewerblich-industrielle Zustand de Rheinprovinz im Jahre 1836* (The State of Crafts and Industry in the Province of the Rhine in the Year 1836), Bonn, Institut f. geschichtliche Landeskunde der Rheinlande, 1967.

[53] This is true of the entire progress of industrialization in Rhineland-Westphalia: F. Steinbach, 'Bürger und Bauer im Zeitalter der Industrie. Studien zur Geschichte des Bürgertums' (Bourgeois and Peasant in the Industrial Era: Studies for a History of the Bourgeoisie), III, *Rheinische Vierteljahresblätter*, XXVIII, 1963, p. 23.

spinning and weaving.[54] Despite the change from putting-out to factory system the industry continued to be dominated by independent firms in single ownership. Corporatively organized enterprises remained the exception, nor were they regarded and conducted as anonymous associations of capital but rather as co-operatives of collaborating and jointly responsible entrepreneurs.

The personalities of Rhenish textile entrepreneurs demonstrate continuity even more strikingly than does the direct transition from pre-industrial to industrial enterprises. Almost all the new industrialists owning factories had been former commercial putters-out and manufacturers. The great importance of Rhenish families of entrepreneurs and the close-knit connections amongst them express this continuity which transcended the person of the individual entrepreneur. But the absence of a break in the transformation of Rhenish textiles from trades into industry owes at least as much to the continuity of an experienced and technically competent labour force, accustomed to wage labour through the putting-out system.

My final point is disguised as a question to which I shall endeavour to supply a brief answer, in the hope of stimulating further discussion.[55] Compared to other trades in the Rhineland, textiles underwent industrialization early; they were in fact first. Did this give the decisive impulse to the whole process of industrialization in the Rhineland or in the whole West Germany economy? I would say, either not at all or only a to very limited degree. The textile industry created too slight a demand for capital equipment to justify this; indeed it imported from abroad the machines it needed. Neither was productivity in the nascent textile industry sufficient to create excess capital for investment in other sectors of the economy. In addition mechanization in textiles did not even create that demand for more labour which could have produced a realignment of population. The process of self-supporting and self-sustaining industrialization in the West German economy was set in motion by the development of heavy industry in the course of railway construction; admittedly some Rhenish textile industrialists helped to promote and finance this. The distinction of chronological priority however belongs to the Rhenish textile trades.

[54] Cf. F. Kreutzberg, *Die Entwicklung der M. Gladbacher Baumwollindustrie* (The Development of the M. Gladbach Cotton Industry), dissertation, Göttingen, 1925 (typescript), p. 56.

[55] For the time being cf. *Anfänge der technisch-industriellen Revolution in Belgien, den Niederlanden und Westdeutschland* (Beginnings of a Technical Industrial Revolution in Belgium, the Netherlands and Western Germany): Report of a conference of Belgian, Dutch and German historians at Louvain, Belgium, 30 April–2 May 1964 (cyclostyled), Bonn, 1965, especially the contributions to the discussion, pp. 37f. I shall reserve for my paper, referred to in n. 32 above, more detailed discussion of arguments for and against 'the textile industry as the leading sector'.

D 2

# The Railway Policy
# of the Second Empire

M. BLANCHARD

Translated by John Godfrey

It has often been said that men are blind to their own times. To be generous, let us say that they are merely very short-sighted. Throughout history, there are many examples of individuals and of groups of people who totally failed to perceive the great events which were unfolding before their eyes. This phenomenon has become a commonplace. But perhaps we can define the process more clearly by noting that among the whole range of human activity there are certain areas in which blindness or myopia of contemporaries is particularly noticeable: at the head of the list come economic events.

Stop the average Frenchman and ask him the most notable thing which has occurred within the last fifteen years in our national life. As far as politics go, our Everyman, generally speaking, will have few relevant ideas, but at least he will have a vague notion of the way the system works, its component parts, its major trends and oscillations, the difference in the positions taken by leading personalities. But should you move to another sphere and ask him to discuss the basic structure of our economic life, you will quickly observe a total lack of comprehension. And if you tell him that one of the essential facts of our economic existence is that France, upon becoming the largest producer of steel in Europe, experienced the creation of a great export industry, and that this fact alone profoundly modified the political position of our country, he will laugh in your face. Little does it signify if our everyday life is immediately and directly conditioned, sometimes ferociously disturbed, by the occurrence of such developments; we live —and suffer—in a total state of ignorance of such matters, just as a savage might suffer from migraine, colic, or fever, without having the faintest idea that he possessed a brain, an intestine, or a circulatory system.

Let us consider a precise example: the impressive and altogether recent development of a French electrical industry. It is no longer possible to visit a mountainous region without stumbling upon some dam or factory; we cannot walk outside our own front doors without noticing the metal skeletons of sub-stations, the mighty pylons, themselves constructions of expressive geometry, and long processions of concrete poles modifying the traditional landscape of our French countryside. Elsewhere, our big cities have become dazzling at night, and our contemporary life has been improved in a thousand ways through the flexible and multiform intervention of this new form of energy. At the same time, a veritable 'politics of electricity' has emerged. How many Frenchmen are even faintly aware of it, and

ave taken even a few minutes off to check on a map the principal lines of the
lectrical network which is being designed at the moment? It would be extremely
resumptuous to claim to have penetrated completely the intentions of some cap-
ain of industry, and it would be possible only at a much later date, if ever, to be
xplicit about the exact nature of his machinations; but even for a non-specialist
quipped only with the facts accessible to the general public, it is not too difficult
ɔ discern some general trends of these politics: a preoccupation with decentraliz-
ıg economic growth and diffusing it more harmoniously throughout the country;
 concern to make up for the deficiencies of our coal industry; the desire, through
lectrical exploitation of the Rhine and the Rhône, to become exporters of energy
nd to control certain sectors of European industry, indeed even to modify pro-
ɔundly certain currents of trade and transportation; of all this, even the en-
ghtened sector of public opinion remains ignorant.

A few decades ago a phenomenon similar in kind but with far graver conse-
uences took place without apparently attracting the attention of contemporaries:
ıe birth and construction of the railway network. I say with far greater conse-
uences because in France this phenomenon coincided with the industrial revolu-
on itself. In England, on the other hand, the elements of the industrial revolution
ere clear already in the eighteenth century, and the revolution was well under
ay at the beginning of the railway age. In France, the construction and develop-
ıent of railways, on the contrary, provoked and accompanied industrial growth:
ıe extension of mines, the renovation and increasing ascendancy of metallurgy,
ıe transformation of old textile industries; so much so that the link between the
xtension of the railway network and the industrialization of France was very close.
es, our grandfathers saw with their own eyes, between 1850 and 1880, this great
ansformation—by far the most portentous economically, and with political im-
lications as important as any political revolution, including 1789 and 1848—our
randfathers saw with their own eyes the end of old France, rural, land-based and
ɔlidly founded, a France of timeless sleepy villages nestling along main routes, a
rance of tracks and rivers, of innkeepers, of waggoners, of tramping artisans,
ıe France, in short, of the novels of Balzac and Georges Sand and of Stendhal's
avels—an old land-based France whose final liquidation one could say was
rought about by the great agrarian crisis of 1880 and subsequent years; they
ıw the obliteration of the old features, the modification of the old design, and
ıe substitution at the same time of the outline of a new country, with new wealth
nd numerous new businesses, giving rise to a new and remarkable equilibrium of
roperty in France's old capitals, now rejuvenated and reinvigorated by industry,
er lands now farmed more efficiently; all this was hardly noticed. More precisely,
ıey did not believe that such developments, integrated with and transforming their
aily lives, were worth taking note of. With all his powerful confused talent, Zola
as barely given us a few literary descriptions, often romantically interpreted in
 sense conflicting with reality. Above all, they did not attempt to discern the deep
auses of this change in order to define its aspects. During the very beginnings of
rench railways, there was a great argument between Arago and Émile Péreire:
rago denied that 'two parallel iron rods could ever give a new face to the moors

of Gascony', Émile Péreire won the argument by using the 'iron rods' to create a
new and magnificent region on French soil; some twenty years later, Arcachon,
created out of nothing, with splendid pine forests extending to the horizon, underlined triumphantly the reality of the financier's vision. This is an individual
instance illustrating a general point. It is the railways which, in France, deserve
the honour and responsibility for the most decisive transformation in the country's
history. However, open the most authoritative histories: emulating the limitations
of contemporaries of the period, their authors devote only a few pages to the railway revolution, without ever appearing to ask themselves whether, in this history,
apparently so technical and specialized, they might not encounter, in the search
for the most vital elements of national life and general history, some truths of the
highest and most urgent significance.

Suffice it to say that the history of French railways remains unwritten; a few
short and limited monographs; collections of administrative acts; a number of
general books, by nature vague, superficial, and unbalanced—this is all there is.
Nevertheless, a few general features have been delineated. In particular, Saint-
Simonian historiography contains a number of ideas which can be considered
capital. In the light of these ideas, I have attempted to distill a synthesized view, of
necessity insufficient and deliberately premature, of the twenty vital years in the
establishment of the railway network.

# I

There is no possible argument about the Second Empire being the vital period
as far as railways are concerned. The unequalled importance of the imperial
period emerges with blinding clarity from the comparison of two sets of figures.
At the beginning of 1852, some three thousand kilometers of line were in use on
French soil, discontinuous sections, incoherent, divided among many companies.
When the Empire collapsed eighteen years later, it left behind nearly twenty
thousand kilometers, organically grouped in a few coherent units, and ever
since, rail transport has dominated French communications; railways have dis-
ciplined transportation, created its essential stages, determined its vital connecting
links, oriented and governed it over long decades in a relatively stable pattern;
railways have ignored some built-up areas, and made the fortune of others. In
short, the physiognomy of the French network for the entire railway era was very
clearly established during this period.

That such a development could have happened without the application of
deliberate policy cannot be believed. The Second Empire had the luck, or the
merit, to combine, at the right time and in an exceptional organization, first-rate
technicians and outstanding financiers as well as politicians guided by clear thinking and firm intentions. Among those who devoted themselves to the task of establishing this network can be found Émile and Isaac Péreire, Rothschild, Bartholony,
Surell, Le Châtelier, Talabot, Franqueville, Magne and Rouher, to name only the
most eminent of the engineers, bankers, civil servants and ministers involved. Men
dissimilar in character and temperament, often driven by conflicting ambitions
and interests which diverged in innumerable ways, but all capable of relentless

activity and gifted with sharp intelligence: they found themselves working together on an enormous project, some of them dragged and borne along, almost in spite of themselves, by a mighty current of collective achievement which was greater than the sum of the parts.

It is impossible to understand and retrace the essential characteristics of their work without examining the situation in which they found French railway construction in 1852.

For nearly twenty years the problem had occupied the attention of technicians and politicians. Many times, more particularly in 1838 and 1842, memorable debates on this subject had taken place in the French Chambers. Despite appearances, neither a clear view of the problem nor a firm overall plan nor a coherent system of ways and means had emerged.

Undecided for a long time on the question whether the new mode of transport should be a public service or whether the risks and uncertainties, but also the profits should be left to private initiative, the July Monarchy, hesitating finally in view of the hazards of the venture, had entrusted, under a variety of arrangements, the construction of lines to associations of capitalists acting, with some guarantees given to them, at their own peril and risk. The public authorities, equipped with an admirable body of civil engineers, had foreseen and outlined the essential plan for an organic network, with all the tracks radiating out like spokes of a wheel from a central point, Paris—with the single exception of a line to connect Bordeaux to Marseilles. But in practice, having handed over the construction of lines to private financiers while not wishing to allow them to dominate national life too completely, the government never freed itself from a narrow conception of lines, seeing them as sections of rail from one town to another, built by different companies to which all forms of combination would be forbidden. From Paris to Marseilles, for example, no less than four or five companies were planned: Marseilles-Avignon, Avignon-Lyons, Lyons-Chalon, and so on. The new mode of transportation was still to be characterized by a strictly local structure. Hence the surprising bitterness of the polemics between towns, hence the furious battles in planning lines, hence, finally, the unhealthy influence of parliamentary coteries working almost exclusively on behalf of narrow combinations of local interests.

Nor did the financiers succeed in having the formula defined which would establish financial foundations for these enormous construction projects. Even at the level of the local railway sections, it was thought sufficient for these suppliers of capital, the members of the *Haute Banque*, to risk their own property, their own capital, while bringing into the enterprise their own immediate clients and their family or business associates. All capital was considered as stock liable to all risks. This basis was by definition too narrow, but it resulted in the unleashing, from 1843 onwards, of a tremendous spate of speculation.

Two quotations are worth noting in this context. Duvergier de Hauranne, who was very well informed on all matters concerning railways, wrote several years afterwards:

If Monsieur de Rothschild had kept all the letters sent to him at the time the concession for the Northern Railway was being allotted, letters sent not only by deputies and civil

servants, but by leading society women, he would have a priceless autograph collection
a minister of the king was never so sought after or fawned upon.

And, in 1844, Bonnardel, from Lyons, noted for his disparaging comments about
railways, wrote in his famous brief to the *Académie des Belles-Lettres et Sciences de
Lyon*:

To find money and create a company, the method is simple enough. Take two or three
deputies, two or three peers of the realm; these are absolutely indispensable, since the best
way to make sure of operating within the law is to enlist the support of those who make it. Add
to these about fifteen administrators, preferably titled, because the nobility has never enjoyed so much prestige as it has since it lost its privileges; take an advertisement somewhere
on the fourth page of various newspapers, since the fourth page is always devoted to financial
news, which is read by everyone, and which best sums up the spirit of the age—and you
will have as much money as you want.

Eventually, flow was followed by ebb; from 1845 the tide of speculation receded.
Hence the beginning of the stock market crisis which, aggravated by the disastrous floods of 1846 and by the bad harvests and near-famine conditions of 1847,
constituted the real prologue to the catastrophes of 1848.

In the same vein, the slowness of parliamentary discussions, the bitterness of
local rivalries and the furious speculation which sent prices rocketing up and down
within a stock market too narrowly based, had brought to a grinding halt the
growth of French lines which seemed to have started so well in 1843. Moreover,
and for this it must receive some credit, the government of Louis-Philippe had not
wished to surrender the construction of French lines to British capitalists, despite
great pressure exerted upon it to do so. In short, the establishment of the French
railway system had barely begun when the régime was swept from power.

The Second Republic brought no solution to the problem. The economic crisis
which accompanied its début rocked the already shaky companies; it soon became
apparent that policy debates concerning the methods of construction and exploitation were a waste of time, nor is it altogether impossible that there may have been
some obscure but very direct connection between the threatened nationalization
of the railways and the explosion of the June days.[1] In brief, all major projects remained stagnant for four years. But throughout these four years, in contrast with
the lack of actual activity, there was a vigorous revival of discussions on the subject.
When construction had begun, a few railway specialists had emerged from the
mass of public works engineers; these specialists began an agitation in various
articles which they wrote or caused to be written, insisting on the absolute necessity
of resuming as quickly as possible the construction of a rail network. They compared the ludicrous state of development of French lines with the situation in
England, Belgium, and the German Rhineland. They underlined the aggravating
truth that France had been left far behind. As a result, France was in danger of
being left out of a general European transportation system: the natural north-
south diagonal for Continental travel, which should have been Calais-Marseilles,
would be bypassed in favour of a more easterly route based on the Antwerp-
Trieste axis. At the same time they emphasized the absolute necessity of getting rid

[1] See, in this context, the very curious article by Matagrin in *Revue socialiste*, 1904.

of the system of fragmented lines; from now on, much larger units were needed.

At the same time as these technicians were becoming impatient, financiers arrived on the scene with proposals whose far-sighted clarity was only to emerge through the passage of time. It was the Péreire brothers who so admirably resolved the problem. They propounded the axiom that the magnitude of the expenses involved in constructing a national network greatly exceeded the potential total capital which those who were thus far associated with the projects were able to provide. What was needed were the savings kept under the mattresses of thousands of people of modest circumstances, a fearful and timid multitude, frightened of high risks and tempted only by the prospect of collecting large dividends or gaining by substantial capital appreciation. Large-scale financing could only be achieved by the participation of innumerable small investors avid for security, which implied giving them various guarantees. From this stemmed the essential and revolutionary distinction between equities liable to every risk and debentures with a lower yield but also bearing fewer risks. The State, if it really wished to promote individual initiative, would no longer intervene, as it had done during the July Monarchy, by means of various expedients, but rather by associating, in favour of bondholders only, its own limitless credit with that of the companies.

Thus, the technical and financial solutions proposed showed great perspicacity and foresight. At the same time, the discovery of gold in California and Australia stabilized the European monetary situation, which had been dangerously extended during the years preceding the cataclysms of 1848. What, therefore, was still required before the building of railways could recommence? Political security and general stability. The Prince President had the great luck of appearing to be the only person capable first of creating, then of maintaining, this security and stability. To the business world, impatient to reopen a new period of profitable activity, but worried about the future and frustrated by the Byzantine delays of the legislature in discussing urgent laws pertaining to business, he appeared as a kind of saviour. The *coup d'État* was the result of this intense expectation. Karl Marx, an irreconcilable adversary of dictatorships, but rendered clairvoyant by his hatred, was not mistaken in pointing to the impatience of capitalists who wished to see the reactivation of railway construction in France as one of the chief factors in the success of the December revolution. In saying this, we have touched on one of the least understood points of internal politics in France; there are many who persist in seeing this return to a personal form of government as merely the traditional appeal to a military strong man, and the Second Empire itself as a Praetorian dictatorship. Who can pretend that this was not to some extent the case? But there was also something completely different: it must not be forgotten that such a government of authority and order had been imperiously demanded by the heads of industry and business, and that some of them had played a very active part in its creation.

So much for the establishment of a régime of personal authority. Decisions began to flow once again and, from January 1852, lines whose construction had been suspended for five years were reactivated: the Avignon-Lyons contract was

awarded on 3 January, the Paris-Lyons contract on 5 January. Such swift proce-
dure was not to stop: during the next few years, while the French rail network
doubled and tripled in size, decisions were arrived at and elaborated by a few
ministers, a few senior technicians and the great financiers. From 1855, in the
middle of the Crimean War, the railway was in complete operation from Paris to
Marseilles; from 1857 from Paris to the German border; even before the war in
Italy had been decided, the railway ran from Lyons through the South Jura,
along the sombre corridor of the Maurienne and on Savoy soil towards the Cenis
pass where the Alps could be crossed; before 1860, the railway wound around
both extremities of the Pyrenees to reach the Spanish border; similarly, attacking
on various fronts, it began to find its way through the valleys of the *Massif Central*.
Meanwhile, the Bordeaux-Sète line linked the Atlantic with the Mediterranean.
In short, the main routes of the French network were established, and from then on,
nothing could modify the basic plan.

The secret behind this rapidity lay in the firmness of decision of an authoritarian
régime combined with the discovery of useful formulae. To begin with, the concept
of networks.

The July government, according to the men of the Second Empire, had seen in
the existence of powerful companies a danger to the State and to public authority.
From this had stemmed the decision to fragment lines and divide their ownership.
An inauspicious decision, for it made any organic conception of rail exploitation
by a system of lines impossible and prevented any truly regional economies of
organization. An entirely different method had to be followed: it was much more
convenient to organize under the same management not only the various sections
of line forming a continuous route, but also and especially the various lines which
served a whole area, an entire region. This was the only way in which to resolve
the problem of lines which were less profitable or even lost money and whose
construction could be demanded as a *quid pro quo* for the profitable routes. Moreover, the imperial government felt strong enough not only not to distrust but
to favour large groupings. It had enough self-confidence to be sure of its power to
impose its arbitration and safeguard the superior interests of the State. Thus was
born, by a systematic process of mergers, the present organization of networks
which divides the territory of France. At the same time, the administrators of the
Empire gave effect to the ideas of Péreire: the vital role of small savings and debentures, the necessity of a State guarantee. It is also worth noting that such a
development could not become current practice until, as a corollary, there had
been a radical transformation of the French banking system.

All this was an immense task, not to be accomplished without opposition and
struggles; these struggles and opposition tell us as much about some aspects of the
task as a direct study.

# II

As a matter of course, railway companies quickly engaged in a severe battle to
defeat all other forms of transport; they had little difficulty in eliminating road

traffic; by greater exertions, but just as effectively, they managed to kill internal navigation. The use of differential rates and steady prices became, in their hands, formidable and effective weapons. Those affected did not fail to register their protests, and the chorus of their complaints and recriminations was heard above the general sound of applause and praise acclaiming the triumph of the railway companies. A book could be filled with these recriminations. Here are a few examples, culled at random:

Railway administrations have interfered with the natural order of things by using methods condemned for a long time by those with interests in agriculture and commerce. Without regard to the terms embodied in their laws of concession the railways, by abuse of preferential rates and individual agreements, have destroyed competition from all other forms of transport and cornered the shipment of merchandise . . . They have even succeeded in sabotaging most transport by river and by sea, and have bought, for considerable sums, the right to transport goods coming from foreign countries, to the detriment of coastal traffic.[2] What we cannot accept is the fact that there are no rules laid down for the conduct of companies and that society finds itself defenceless in the face of an unending range of combinations of speculators. . . . There are no longer any rules about rates, but quite simply offensive and defensive alliances among railway companies, which according to the Criminal Code should be called conspiracies . . . No longer are prices set for goods, but for the people who send them. . . . One is either an ally or a rival, a friend or an enemy of the railways, and that is all there is to it.[3]

Even more vehement were the complaints of the experts and entrepreneurs in inland navigation. I will cite only one, which dates from just after the fall of the imperial régime, formulated at a time when, in the general turmoil of French politics, the moment seemed most appropriate for redressing and avenging long-standing complaints. In 1871, an enthusiast for the old system of navigation on the Rhône explained:

The ministers of the Empire favoured railways beyond measure. They allowed the system of transport by navigable waterways to be destroyed or weakened; they gave aid to the strong to destroy the weak; the result was the establishment of the oppressive monopoly of the great networks. We must hasten to do the opposite of what has been done for the last 22 years and put an end to large-scale administrative and financial corruption.[4]

Though the battle against inland water transport united railway groups in the common cause of putting the opposition out of business, they did not hesitate to fight amongst themselves when it came to delimiting their respective domains. This is one of the most difficult problems on which to obtain information, requiring the most delicate interpretation, but by far the most suggestive.

The networks, or more precisely their senior officers, were essentially and obviously groups of administrators and engineers, financial and technical railway experts. But aside from these duties, nothing prevented them from becoming personally involved in other enterprises. Such businesses might be connected with

[2] Proceedings of the Orléans Chamber of Commerce for 3 November 1855 (*Registre des délibérations de la Chambre*).
[3] Letter to the Minister of Public Works, 25 November 1855.
[4] Maxime Baragnan, *Le monopole du Paris-Lyon et la navigation du Rhône*, Nîmes, 1871.

the railways as both suppliers and clients. They could be singularly aided, not only by the lay-out of a particular track, but by the geographical extension and formation of a network. Access by rail to a market could guarantee domination and victory to an industry which possessed such influence. Hence, to find oneself in the position of deciding on such issues could serve as the basis for the integration of a whole series of interdependent enterprises. The scheming and planning with regard to railways thus became of great importance to a great variety of industries. Added to this was the hidden but extremely powerful influence of the great politicians whose power in Paris was often equalled by the sovereign authority exercised in their native localities. This may give some indication of the severity of the struggles over the most important decisions. The *Grand-Central* affair and the Sète-Marseilles affair can be considered typical examples of the kind of battle which allow us a glimpse into the ante-chambers of big business by casting a vivid light on the side-effects and implications of such events.

The *Grand-Central* affair was simple enough. However strong it considered itself and however much confidence it had in its power to make railway financiers and nabobs dance to its own tune, the imperial government hesitated to confer a transport monopoly between Paris, the Rhône basin and the Mediterranean on a single group of entrepreneurs, believing it desirable and possible, both for its own peace of mind and to reassure the general public, to maintain the traditional rivalry between the Bourbonnais and Burgundy routes. It assigned the latter route to the Paris-Lyons company and planned to award the former route to a special network, the *Grand-Central*, whose territories would separate those of the Orléans company from those of the Paris-Lyons. In addition, this network would be assigned the task of penetrating the *Massif Central*, on the correct assumption that its railway exploitation would tempt few people. To produce the goodwill necessary for such a venture, amalgamation between the *Grand-Central* and the *Midi* companies had been envisaged to provide the latter company with a link to Paris, a link impossible up to that time, owing to the position of its network. It should be noted that there were considerable financial interests involved in the negotiations, since the iron works within the Central area held a far more important position in French industry than they do today. The fate of the *Grand-Central* was quickly decided, despite a certain amount of agitation. The Orléans and Paris-Lyons companies formed an alliance to prevent the *Midi* company grabbing the *Grand-Central* whose lines they divided among themselves. In particular, the Paris-Lyons company gained control of the Bourbonnais line, thus securing for itself an absolute monopoly of transport between Paris and the Rhône basin. This battle had been one between Paulin Talabot, tycoon of the Paris-Lyons company, and the Péreire brothers, dictators of the *Midi* company. Two men, powerful in the régime, both possessed of a stranglehold over the local areas affected by this battle played a major part in deciding the conflict by their intervention: Rouher in the Auvergne and Persigny in the region of St. Étienne. The duel between Talabot and the Péreires was soon to reproduce itself in another area and on a larger scale.

This was the Sète-Marseilles affair, which developed in the years 1860–3, and became, far more than political quarrels or debates, *the* great affair in the Languedoc and Marseilles areas of Southern France. The Péreire brothers, who had relied on the principal line of their network, the Sète-Bordeaux line, becoming the sole means of organizing the traffic of the European isthmus of Aquitaine, had not been slow to realize that, for designs of this sort, Sète was a rather small base of action. If they could reach Marseilles direct, things would be much easier for them. They therefore applied for a concession to build a line from Sète to Marseilles through the region of the salt marshes and the Camargue.

This was a ticklish claim. It posed the question, as yet undefined by law, whether networks were to be homogeneous. Doubtless the line which they desired cut none of the lines of the Paris-Lyons company, but by means of a tangent it entered a domain which the administrators of the Paris-Lyons company considered as being exclusively theirs. Above all, apart from the strictly railway aspect of the question, it involved something else: the exploitation of the enormous business centre which Marseilles had become.

Since railways had been established, by extending its wharves and building more docks, this great Mediterranean port had transformed itself into an immense centre of building speculations and maritime enterprises, as well as of commerce and industry. At the head of this formidable consortium was Paulin Talabot, who held control of the city by means of the railways: he was master of the Paris-Lyons company; shipping: he controlled the *Messageries Maritimes*; docks: he was responsible for the Joliette and the Arrenc; coal: he was the magnate behind the Alès and Grand-Combe companies; and iron: he created Mokta-el-Hadid. But the Péreire brothers who wished to reconstruct Marseilles, just as they had transformed Paris during this same period, counted on having their own line to Marseilles in order to do so, and in Marseilles they planned their own railway station, from Marseilles their own maritime routes. The prizes at stake explain the bitterness of the fighting which involved not only the struggle of two competing lines, but also a war of banks: the *Banque de France, the Société Générale* and the House of Rothschild in league with Talabot to crush the *Crédit Mobilier* of the Péreire brothers. The latter were the losers of this fight to the finish, and it has to be asked if this struggle was not, through its antecedents and consequences, through the collusions it produced and the strings it pulled, the most important affair of the Second Empire.

But there is yet another aspect of the railway policy of the régime which must be sketched at least in broad outlines; we must study the attempt to use this new instrument of action and power for purposes of external prestige and foreign policy.


This is not the place to investigate the direction and designs of Napoleon III's foreign policy; let us simply recall the essential plan: to restore in contiguous countries French influence and prestige; to regroup, as far as possible, countries of French language under French sovereignty. In the pursuit of these two ends, imperial policy was prepared to employ economic means. To begin with, the Emperor and his councillors expected the growth of French influence to be greatly advanced by the economic expansion they anticipated from a liberal policy of commercial treaties; but they also wished to reinforce expansion in commerce by that in railways.

In this respect, they reasoned as follows: through the system of networks, France was grouping her lines in organic units. In so doing, not only had she recaptured all the ground lost to her neighbours during the era of the July Monarchy, not only had she given the most vigorous impulse to construction, but she even found herself attracting into her networks various foreign companies less highly organized than her own. French networks made the attempt to absorb these foreign enterprises through mergers or at least to control them through affiliated companies. In this manner, the *Nord-Espagne*, the Ottoman, the Danube and the Rome railways, while giving rise to a remarkable export of capital, engineers, polytechnicians and *centraux*, at the same time reinforced in all these countries the influence of France. But this policy was applied even more effectively at some points, chief of these being the area of the Alps.

It has already been noted above that French railway specialists had become alarmed by 1848 at the advance being made by Belgian and Rhineland railways; they feared that from the North-West of Europe to Northern Italy, because of the lack of French lines, railways would run through the central Alps, thereby neglecting to the detriment of France the western passes through the mountains and making Trieste, at the expense of Marseilles, the major European port for trade with the Levant. At the same time as being preoccupied with starting lines on their own territory, the men of the Second Empire firmly resolved to make the first breach in the mountains for the benefit of France. This decision prompted their first negotiation with Cavour; it was their resolve to make a passage through the mountains at Mont Cenis and to build routes on either side of this first Alpine tunnel that resulted in the creation, in a fashion similar to the French mergers, of the Victor-Emmanuel company whose administrators and capital were to a large extent French. Thus, the Cenis tunnel was destined to play the same part in the development of a unified Italy under French sponsorship as the Gothard tunnel would play for the benefit of Germany thirty years later. But there was something more. Even before the events of 1859–60 gave Lombardy to Piedmont and presaged the control of all Northern Italy by the House of Savoy, imperial diplomats, and French financiers had sought to prepare the way for the creation along French patterns of northern routes towards Lombardy, linked with the group of the Jura and the Swiss plateau railways which were under the domination of their own networks. This gave rise to an extremely significant plan based on the French Jura-Simplon company and in line with French policy, which was to merge Swiss railways and put a second passage at French disposal by opening the Simplon pass across the Alps; this tunnel itself, when it emerged near the lakes which stretch towards Milan, was to link to another French-inspired enterprise, also equipped with French capital and engineers, the Lombardo-Venetian railway. Better still, when in 1860 Austria was holding on to Venice in despair to save the reputation of its dynasty, its diplomats and its army, there appeared a number of French financiers with railway interests, concerned with the development of all Italy, who proposed a very detailed plan to the Court of Vienna: backed by a committee of financiers, international in name but French in fact, Italy would buy Venice from Austria. Italy would then unify her railway system and mortgage it to this consortium of financiers who would join her in elaborating a general plan of development and exploitation of the peninsula. The upshot would have been that, owing principally to railways, Italy would have passed under the economic tutelage of French finance. This plan was at once rejected for reasons of prestige politics by the Vienna Court; it could obviously be characterized as adventurous, even a little extravagant, in view of the internal contradictions of Napoleon III's Italian policy—yet it was a scheme in which one may well discern certain far-sighted elements which were not ill-conceived. Let us not forget, for example, the veritable economic colonization of Italy by Germany from 1880 to 1914. After all, France was only anticipating German ascendency by establishing her own, and if we ask by whom such lofty designs could have been financed, we should not forget that ten years later, without a great deal of difficulty, from her own resources France managed to pay Germany the five billion francs of its ransom.

Thus, in these years of the Second Empire, a great French railway system grew up, oriented towards the Mediterranean area. There was another towards the North-East and the Rhine, whose general outlines are less easily discernible, and whose constituents, caught in the diverse and unpredictable strands of an inconsistent German policy during the period, call for investigation. The most striking incident, although almost totally forgotten today, an episode particularly important because it illuminates the spirit of imprudence and error characteristic of the last days of the Second Empire, was furnished by the Belgian railway affair, an incident which was to make famous a great politician of the neighbouring kingdom, Frère-Orban.

To give a general outline of the negotiations which took place in 1868–9, the French *Compagnie de l'Est* bought several short lines and various precarious and unprofitable systems serving the Grand Duchy of Luxembourg and the eastern part of Belgium, in order to incorporate these lines in its own organization, to integrate them completely into its own network, to establish direct contact between these services and those of the Dutch companies and also to extend a kind of French railway barrier between Belgium and the German Rhineland. By standardizing timetables and rates, the *Compagnie de l'Est* was in a strong position to influence all Belgian railways. On the economic side, two goals seem to have been paramount: first, to join forces with the Dutch lines, thereby controlling access to Rotterdam for all the trade of Eastern France and Switzerland and thus reserving the threat of exerting irresistible pressure on Belgium by directly endangering the prosperity of Antwerp. In the second place, it seems likely that the *Compagnie de l'Est*, apparently under the influence of French ironmasters, planned to control the export of iron ore from Lorraine to Belgian blast furnaces, thereby enabling a close watch to be kept on the entire Belgian iron industry.

From the political point of view was the object above all else to procure revenge, however superficial, for the humiliating defeat of imperial diplomacy in the Luxembourg incident? Was the underhand railway dealing combined with a clearly thought-out project to control Belgium, indeed, to occupy it militarily and annex it? The Belgians believed it to be the case, alerted the English and the Prussians, and sent Frère-Orban to Paris. The project fizzled out. The clearest result seems to have been a considerable increase in the distrust of the Emperor's policies on the part of British statesmen.

\*　　　　\*　　　　\*

Such was the railway policy, domestic and external, of the Second Empire. The outline which has been attempted, however brief and superficial, has merely scratched the surface of an important and interesting topic. To study it more fully would require far more extensive research in order to ascertain the decisive influence of railway policy on the basic economic life of our country, its orientation, development and industrial location. This would be a gigantic task, for this area of research is almost totally unexploited and would require simultaneous attack on the part of numerous associated teams. In any case, such a project may still be worth attempting at a time when the profound changes brought about by the pitched battle between railways and roads seem likely to reduce the physiognomy of an efficient and profitable French network to the limits and level of development which had already been attained by the end of the Second Empire.

BIBLIOGRAPHICAL GUIDE

At the same time two years ago as Louis Jouffroy gave us the first genuinely historical monograph of the construction of a major French line (from Paris to the German frontier),[5] in the form of a remarkable thesis submitted to the Sorbonne, he also devoted his complementary thesis to a study of sources and drew up a general bibliography covering the beginning of French railways. This work is of absolutely vital significance to the topic and should be consulted from the outset by anyone interested in the history of railways.[6]

There exists no single and substantial general account of French railway history. Doubtless, the works of Alfred Picard, *Les chemins de fer français. Étude historique . . . Débats parlementaires, actes législatifs . . .* (Paris, 1884), in six volumes, and *Traité des chemins de fer*, vol. I: *Aperçu historique* (Paris, 1887) are admirable if taken for what they claim to be: a narrative of the administrative vicissitudes encountered in developing our national network; but obviously this limits their scope. One could say the same, both for its positive qualities and for the limitations of the subject-matter, of the work of Kauffman, *La politique française en matière de chemins de fer* (translated from the German, Hamon, Paris, 1900), an account essentially financial in character, containing some of the most suggestive and illuminating points of view ever presented on the subject.

Generally speaking, Saint-Simonian literature remains among the essential sources of information in order to understand the intellectual and economic climate in which the first great projects were elaborated. In this respect, the publication of the works of the Péreire brothers, if continued, should be considered as being of outstanding importance, judging by the first volume: *Oeuvres d'I. et É. Péreire*, series G, *Documents sur l'origine et le développement des chemins de fer (1832–70)*, collected and edited by P. C. de Villedeuil. At the same time, attention should be directed to Michel Chevalier, the best informed and most convincing of the specialists who acted as a link between the pure technicians and the general public. The essential books on this theme should be quoted: *Politique industrielle et Système de la Méditer-*

---

[5] See *Annales*, vol. VI, 1934, p. 173. On the creation of the Paris-Strasbourg line see also Félix Ponteil, *L'opposition politique à Strasbourg sous la Monarchie de Juillet*, Paris, 1932. Chapter 6 of the second part is entitled 'Les réalités économiques et l'opposition; la satisfaction des intérêts matériels'.

[6] Louis Jouffroy, *Recherches sur les sources de la création d'une grande ligne de chemin de fer au XIXe siècle*, Paris, 1932.

*ranée* (1832), *Des intérêts matériels en France* (1838), *Statistique des travaux publics sous la Monarchie de 1830* (1848); as well as his contributions during the period to the *Journal des Débats*. The role of the followers of Saint-Simon has been diligently studied by Maurice Wallon, *Les Saint-Simoniens et les chemins de fer* (Paris, 1908). Among more recent accounts, part of the story has been clearly, precisely, and pertinently told by E. Lefranc in several articles, the most significant of which was published in 1930 in the *Revue d'histoire moderne et contemporaine* ('Les chemins de fer devant le Parlement français, 1835–42'). Gras has written a very carefully documented monograph on the lines of the Loire: *Histoire des premiers chemins de fer français (Saint-Étienne à Andrézieux, Lyon, Roanne)*, 1924. In several short studies the present writer has sketched out the beginnings of various lines of the South-Eastern region (*Bulletin de la Société de Géographie Languedocienne*, 1923 and 1924; *Études rhodaniennes*, volume II; *Revue de géographie alpine*, 1932).

The history of the constitution of the networks under the Second Empire remains to be written and as yet has not given rise to any really serious study, with one contemporary and intelligent exception: Audiganne, *Les chemins de fer aujourd'hui et dans 100 ans* (two volumes, Paris, 1858).

In addition to the Péreire brothers, the work of two other major figures should be considered; Paulin Talabot, founder of the P.L.M. company, and Franqueville, Director of Railways at the Ministry of Public Works. Only inadequate biographies exist for them. Source material for a general view of the question is unpublished and hard to come by. Printed literature is scattered and voluminous. One aspect which is perhaps easier to gauge is public reaction to the policy of merging companies, a reaction which became particularly vocal during the 1863 elections and in the years that followed in the debates on the law regarding departmental railways. The *Grand-Central* and Bordeaux-Sète affairs gave rise to an extraordinarily abundant proliferation of polemical pamphlets which sometimes contain documents of great importance, such as the anonymous booklet published in 1862 and inspired by the Péreire brothers, *La vraie question*. Isaac Péreire published in 1879 another pamphlet entitled *La question des chemins de fer*, a retrospective view of the history of mergers which contains a great deal of useful information.

The policy of the Second Empire with regard to European lines is even less explored. It would require nothing less than a search throughout all the diplomatic archives of the period, not forgetting those relating to commercial treaties. Naturally, other sources of information must not be overlooked. One particular source should be pointed out: copious literature of protests originating in Switzerland against various French projects for absorbing the lines of the Swiss plateau.

Of this policy, only one episode has really been studied: the affair of the various Luxembourg lines. Once again it should be noted that this information has been presented only unilaterally by the Belgians: Paul Hymans, *Frère-Orban* (vol. II), and de Beyens, *Le Second Empire vu par un diplomate belge* (vol. II). On the French side, the only published material consists of documents relating to the conflict with Belgium (in the collection *Origines diplomatiques de la guerre de 1870*).

# The Old Bank and the New: The Financial Revolution of the Nineteenth Century

## D. LANDES

Translated by Max A. Lehmann

Among the great innovators in the world of business during the Second Empire, those who made the most impact were the Péreire brothers, founders of the *Crédit Mobilier* and precursors of a banking revolution which made itself felt throughout Europe. Their work is too well-known for a detailed account of it to be necessary.[1] The two brothers, Émile as well as Isaac, had in their youth had some contact with the Saint-Simonians. From this experience they retained not the religious fervour and social aberrations of the community of the faithful, but the more practical doctrines of the importance of industry and the possibilities inherent in a system of credit. Émile was the first to abandon the faith and its polemics and turn to the world of business. With the financial support of James de Rothschild, the richest banker in France, he built in 1837 the railway from Paris to Saint-Germain, the first line to catch the imagination of the French public. This alliance was to be extremely fruitful: Péreire supplied inspiration and Rothschild capital and contacts. The line from Paris to Saint-Germain was followed by one from Paris to Versailles (on the right bank) and then one from Paris-Nord. At the end of the 1840s these two men were the most powerful combination in French railways.

[1] A biography of the Péreire brothers is yet to be written. However, those who are interested in them will find a number of works which deal either directly or indirectly with their financial activities: M. Wallon, *Les Saint-Simoniens et les chemins de fer*, Paris, 1908; J. Plenge, *Gründung und Geschichte des Crédit Mobilier* (Foundation and History of the Crédit Mobilier), Tübingen, 1903, still the most useful work; J.-B. Vergeot, *Le crédit comme stimulant et régulateur de l'industrie*, Paris, 1918, of unique interest because of the Péreire archives he uses; P. Dupont-Ferrier, *Le marché financier sous le Second Empire*, Paris, 1935; two recent works are more important: L. Girard, *La politique des travaux publics du Second Empire*, Paris, 1951; B. Gille, 'La fondation du Crédit Mobilier et les idées financières des frères Péreire, *Bull. du Centre de recherches sur l'histoire des entreprises* (referred to hereafter as *Bull. C.R.H.E.*), No. 3, June 1954, pp. 10–28.

The 'archives' of the Péreire brothers, collected by L. de Villedeuil (in 28 volumes, of which 4 have appeared), are simply miscellaneous publications by the two men, together with other relevant publications of the period. The personal manuscript archives are dispersed and in the hands of several descendants of the Péreire brothers.

With the Revolution of 1848 and the Second Republic the two men separated. The details of the break are not known, but the fundamental reasons for it are clear: Rothschild, the hard, solid banker, with a very conservative outlook, looked upon railways as an opportunity for profitable loans and other financial gains; Péreire, the romantic businessman, envisaged a better world at the end of his rails. Where Péreire was eager to rush ahead, spend, build and enlarge the scope of his undertakings, Rothschild proceeded cautiously and never became impatient; where the one wanted to leave a monument, the other wanted to leave a fortune. Besides, Péreire was too strong a personality to be content with a subordinate role, and Rothschild was not the man to tolerate equals. Their separation marked the beginning of a keen rivalry.

The occasion of the opening of the conflict was the creation in 1852 of the *Société Générale du Crédit Mobilier*, an investment bank[2] which closely resembled the *institution centrale du crédit* advocated by the Saint-Simonians. The *Crédit Mobilier*, as it was called, specialized in the first place in the establishment and development of joint-stock companies, but without neglecting the issue of government stocks In fact, the promised intervention of the bank in this field was a principal reason for the favour accorded to it by Louis-Napoleon, who was looking for a counterweight to the ascendancy of Rothschild over French finances.[3] The future emperor found that he had, in the *Crédit Mobilier*, a sufficiently strong instrument for projects of this sort; its capital of sixty millions put the *Crédit Mobilier* in second place among French banking houses, surpassed only by the *Banque de France*.

For Rothschild, of course, the establishment of the *Crédit Mobilier* was a personal affront. In his eyes the Péreire brothers were intruders, not so much because they were newcomers—there was always room for prudent firms, so long as they were prepared to play the game according to the rules—but because they were undermining his personal hegemony. His resentment was exacerbated by the insolence of Émile Péreire; this ex-subordinate, this man whom he had created, had the impertinence to offer him, as a favour, a tiny share in the new business.[4] And what was even more serious was that, given the almost unlimited possibilities of joint-stock companies, the Péreires might even achieve their aims. Under normal circumstances the accumulated wealth of the Rothschild dynasty would be more than adequate to discourage the slightest inclination to compete with them. But even the Rothschild fortune could scarcely rival the savings of the whole of France. The struggle which followed was without parallel in the annals of banking. Rothschild reacted vigorously. At the court, he denounced the new concern as an encouragement to speculation and gambling on margins. At the *Bourse* he made attacks on the activities of the *Mobilier*, manœuvring to undermine its prestige and frighten off investors. When these efforts failed, he organized in 1855 a syndicate of bankers with the aim of competing with the Péreires in the formation of

---

[2] The French words *banque d'affaires* mean 'investment bank' in English, that is to say, banks whose principal activity consisted in operations involving the immobilization of capital for a certain length of time: security issues, direct investments, long-term credit. Unfortunately, there is no simple French equivalent for the English term 'investment bank' to designate the category of operations so defined and the professional group, that is to say, the corpus of banking institutions, which is involved in it.

[3] C. J. Mirès, *A mes juges*, Paris, 1861, p. 21.

[4] Plenge, *op. cit.*, p. 81.

companies. From the start France was not large enough for two protagonists of such stature. During 1854–5 the *Crédit Mobilier* expanded into Austria, for long the territory of the Rothschilds, and founded the Austrian State Railway Company, undertaking to buy, complete and exploit the State-owned railways; the Rothschilds replied by creating the Lombardo-Venetian Railway Company, responsible for the railway network of southern Austria and northern Italy. In March 1856 Péreire organized a *Crédit Mobilier* in Spain; a week later the Rothschilds announced the establihment of the *Sociedad espanola mercantil e industrial*. In the same year the Péreires proposed to the Austrian authorities the creation of a similar company; but the Rothschilds succeeded not only in persuading the imperial government to impose conditions unacceptable to their opponents, but also in getting hold of the project themselves.[5] The result was the *Credit-Anstalt* which was to dominate Austrian banking right into the twentieth century. Before long, the two giants found themselves locked in conflict from the plains of Castile to the valley of the Danube, from London to Constantinople and from Moscow to Trieste.[6]

The epic character of the struggle made a great impression on contemporaries and on succeeding generations and left a considerable mark on historical literature. In fact, the traditional interpretation sees this rivalry as a conflict between old and new banks—between the established system: private banks, personal relations, confidential transactions, traditional investments—and the new system: joint-stock companies, functional and impersonal organization, industrial businesses started more or less hastily—in short, the financial *status quo versus* the progressive financial organization of the future. This interpretation no doubt has its source in the content of the attacks made on the *Crédit Mobilier* by James de Rothschild himself,[7] perhaps also in the account of the struggle left by Mirès, the speculator, promoter and financial adventurer *par excellence* of the Second Empire.[8] Whatever the source of this tradition, it has since then been the object of a detailed development in a classic monograph by Dupont-Ferrier, and it is further sanctified in Sée's general treatment;[9] it reappears from time to time in more recent studies, original as well as secondary.[10]

\*            \*            \*

[5] The government demanded that the board be composed entirely of Austrian citizens: the Rothschilds, who had one of their houses in Vienna, could satisfy this condition; the Péreires could not.

[6] The best discussion of this is to be found in R. E. Cameron, 'The *Crédit Mobilier* and the Economic Development of Europe', *Journ. of Pol. Econ.*, LXI, 1953, pp. 461–88; see also P. Cousteix, 'Les financiers sous le Second Empire', *1848, Rev. des Révol. Contemp.*, XLIII, 1950, pp. 105–25.

[7] At the time of the creation of the *Crédit Mobilier*, James de Rothschild sent a note to the Prince-President explaining his reservations. The note was sent on 15 November 1852; the decree of authorization had just been signed. Extracts from this memorandum are to be found in the article by Gille quoted in n. 1, pp. 17–18.

[8] *A mes juges*, pp. 91–7.

[9] Dupont-Ferrier, *Marché financier*, pp. 77–9; Henri Sée, *Hist. écon. de la France*, II, Paris, 1943, p. 256.

[10] For example, the important thesis of L. Girard, *La politique des travaux publics*, p. 109. Cf. A. Gerschenkron, 'Economic Backwardness in Historical Perspective', in B. Hoselitz, re-ed., *The Progress of Underdeveloped Areas*, Chicago, 1952, where he refers to the conflict between 'Old Wealth and New'.

The title of this article: The Old Bank and the New, rather than: The Old Bank *versus* the New, is deliberate. It seems to me that the traditional conception of a conscious conflict between two banking systems is inexact: it rests on the one hand on a confusion between the personal rivalry between two men and the alleged conflict of the financial techniques with which historians have identified them; and on the other, on a fundamental misunderstanding of the nature of private—or rather 'merchant'—banking and the place it occupied in the rapidly developing economy of the mid-nineteenth century.[11]

In the financial world of the nineteenth century, merchant bankers were a race apart. As the name indicates, most of them, in this as in earlier periods, had entered banking from trade and still concerned themselves with transactions of a purely commercial nature. This was true even of a house like that of the Rothschilds whose income from financial operations would have seemed to make commercial enterprises unnecessary. Indeed many of them, whether from a spirit of conservatism or from snobbery, still called themselves 'merchants' and nothing more.[12]

Nevertheless, their activities as financiers went far beyond their trading interests. They constituted the cadres of the commercial credit of the age. Their principal instrument was the bill of exchange, the concrete expression of short-term credit. They discounted negotiable instruments, issued bankers' drafts, accepted the bills of clients and cashed these for them, at the same time advancing the necessary funds to back their associates from the beginning of transactions to the point where revenue began to flow. In a word, merchant bankers fulfilled all

[11] Once again, problems arise in translation. There are no precise French equivalents for the English terms 'merchant banking' and 'merchant banker'. The former designates the institution: a group or category of financial activities which we shall define in the text; it also means the occupation associated with this. The latter designates the agents who carry out these operations; in French they are called *banquiers-négociants*, for want of a better word.
The origin of the English terms lies in the necessity of distinguishing between these bankers whose financial operations arose out of commercial transactions and who had mostly themselves begun their careers in commerce, and the 'pure' bankers, whose *raison d'être* was the administration of deposits, normally in connection with the issue of notes. These latter were generally called 'bankers', the former were normally known as 'merchants'. Furthermore, the word 'private' was added to the title 'banker' to distinguish between the various houses in question, limited partnerships and joint-stock companies. (It goes without saying that bankers and merchants often overstepped the demarcation line we have just established for purposes of definition. 'Pure' bankers invested their capital in commercial ventures and even took part in enterprises which in the long term were fundamentally incompatible with the administration of deposits; merchants sometimes, though not often, accepted deposits.)
It is obvious that the English banker had no counterpart in France, where note issue was never allowed without the permission of the State, a permission rarely granted. The French banker was essentially a merchant banker in the English sense. The only distinction drawn was between those who, above all in the provinces, were involved solely in domestic transactions and those who financed international operations. In England the same distinction was often made by calling houses, especially in London, which financed overseas trade 'foreign banks', and the bankers who took part in this 'foreign bankers'.
[12] In the middle of the nineteenth century—and up until the twentieth—the foreign bankers who constituted the Court of the Bank of England always called themselves 'merchants'. See also the advertisements of the financial journals of the period; for example, in *The Economist*, 12 March 1864, p. 348, the advertisement of the North British and Mercantile Insurance Co.

the functions necessary to make regular transactions possible between widely distant places.[13] Nevertheless, in the nineteenth century, pure commerce and commercial credit between them represented only part of the activities of merchant bankers. Fortunes made in this traditional sphere were looking for new outlets; and when they were not, they were sought after. Some of these supplementary outlets were the natural complement of commercial credit; for example, insurance. Others, investment operations for example, constituted a new departure.

In each case the additional activity had to find its place in the ranks of existing interests and had to be subordinated to the characteristic limitations of the system of family banking, with its well-defined and restricted resources and its select

[13] The evolution, functions and techniques of international merchant banking in the eighteenth and nineteenth centuries are best studied in the histories of Anglo-American trade. The best work here is A. H. Cole, 'Evolution of the Foreign Exchange Market of the United States', *Journ. of Econ. and Business History*, I, 1929, pp. 384–421. See also N. S. Buck, *The Development of the Organization of Anglo-American Trade, 1800–1850*, New Haven, 1925, especially chapters V and VI; R. W. Hidy, *The House of Baring in American Trade and Finance*, Cambridge, Mass., 1949.

On Holland: Ch. Wilson, *Anglo-Dutch Commerce and Finance in the Eighteenth Century*, Cambridge, 1941; J. B. Manger, Jr., *Recherches sur les relations économiques entre la France et la Hollande pendant la Révolution française, 1785–1795*, Paris, 1923, pp. 42–9; Van Dillen, 'De Beurscrisis te Amsterdam van 1763' (Stock Exchange Crisis of 1763 in Amsterdam), *Tijdschrift voor Geschiedenis*, XXXVI, 1922.

We are less well informed for France, where eighteenth-century merchant banking is perhaps better known than its successor in the first half of the nineteenth century. Worth mentioning for the *Ancien Régime*, apart from the works of Sayous, Bouchary and Bigo, is the article by H. Lüthy, 'La République de Calvin et l'essor de la banque protestante en France de la Révocation de l'Édit de Nantes à la Révolution', *Bull. C.R.H.E.*, No. 1, 1953, pp. 1–35 also published in *Schweizer Beiträge zur allgemeinen Geschichte*, XI, 1953. On the subject of commercial history, see also e.g. L. Dermigny, 'Circuits d'argent et milieux d'affaires au XVIIIe siècle', *Rev. Hist.*, Oct-Dec. 1954, pp. 239-78. For the nineteenth century, see the bibliography of R. Bigo, *Les Banques Françaises au cours du XIXe siècle*, Paris, 1947, pp. 287–95; also 'Notes sur un plan de recherches sur l'histoire des banques', *Bull. C.R.H.E.*, I, 1953, pp. 42–50; 'Bibliographie bancaire', *ibid.*, II, 1953, pp. 32–4. This literature, though at first sight abundant, unfortunately contains only scattered fragments of information on merchant banking in the proper sense of the term.

On German banks, see A. Dietz, *Frankfurter Handelsgeschichte* (History of Commerce at Frankfurt), vols. 4 & 5, Frankfurt, 1925; A. Krüger, *Das Kölner Bankiergewerbe* (The Trade of Banking at Cologne), Essen, 1925; R. Ehrenberg, *Grosse Vermögen*, Vol. II: *Das Haus Parish in Hamburg* (Large Fortunes, Vol. 2: The House of Parish at Hamburg), Jena, 1905; H. Rachel and P. Wallich, *Berliner Grosskaufleute und Kapitalisten* (Berlin Large-scale Merchants and Capitalists), Vols. 2 & 3, Berlin, 1938-9; E. Korach, *Das deutsche Privatbankgeschäft* (The German Private Banking Business), Berlin, 1910. As for France, there is little information on merchant banking; on the other hand there is more on particular enterprises; see for example the classic bibliography in H. Corsten, *Hundert Jahre deutscher Wirtschaft in Fest- und Denkschriften* (A Hundred Years of German Economy in Festschriften and Memoranda), Cologne, 1937, and F. Redlich, *The Beginnings and Development of German Business History* (supplement in *Bulletin of the Business History Society*), Cambridge, Mass., 1952. The autobiography of V. Nolte, *Fünfzig Jahre in beiden Hemisphären* (Fifty Years in Both Hemispheres), 2 vols., Hamburg, 1854, should also be mentioned; Nolte did business with merchant bankers from all countries of Western Europe and from the United States.

An excellent description of this sort of finance, though in a different setting, will be found in M. Greenberg, *British Trade and the Opening of China, 1800–42*, Cambridge, 1951, ch. 6. On the technique of foreign exchange, J. Bouchary, *Le marché des changes de Paris à la fin du XVIIIe siècle*, Paris, 1937; G. J. Goschen, *The Theory of the Foreign Exchanges*, London, 1861, is the classic theoretical discussion.

clientele of merchants and wealthy capitalists. When a field of action, even a very profitable one, would have extended the financial means of private banks too far, or proved incompatible with their confidential character, banking houses were always sufficiently wise to leave it to other enterprises of a new type. Their contribution to the establishment of central discount banks[14] and joint-stock insurance companies[15] bears witness to this.

In the nineteenth century, the future of finance lay in long-term ventures; firstly, in the promotion and negotiation of government stocks, and secondly, in the promotion and support of private enterprise. Already in the eighteenth century, the great merchant houses of Amsterdam, London and Frankfurt were paying increasing attention to investment: Russian and English loans, French bonds,[16] etc. In the following century such operations were to become more and more frequent and important; the years after 1815 were the great age of the Barings and the Rothschilds, of the loans connected with the liberation of France after the 1815

[14] The French and English cases are too well known to require illustration. On the Bank of Frankfurt, K. Jackel, *Gründung und Entwicklung der Frankfurter Bank von 1854–1900* (Foundation and Development of the Bank of Frankfurt, 1854–1929), Borna-Leipzig, 1905 pp., 1–21; R. Winterwerb, *Die Frankfurter Bank 1854–1929* (The Frankfurt Bank, 1854–1,299) s.l., n.d., pp. 13–34; Dietz, *Frankfurter Handelgeschichte* (Commercial History of Frankfurt), v, p. 658; Handelskammer zu Frankfurt-am-Main, *Geschichte der Handelskammer zu Frankfurt-am-Main, 1707–1908* (History of the Frankfurt-am-Main Chamber of Commerce), 1707–1908), Frankfurt, 1908, pp. 654–70; H. Pallmann, *Simon Moritz v. Bethmann*, Frankfurt, 1898.

[15] Here the circumstances are less clear than in the case of the discount banks. It is certain that from the beginning of the nineteenth century there were other considerations as important as the need for an institution to undertake operations incompatible with the character of private banks. For example, there was the desire, especially in France, to create institutions which by investment would furnish outlets for new issues and support for existing securities. Among the insurance companies in whose establishment merchant bankers were involved in the nineteenth century, we find the *Alliance* in England, the *Royale* (later the *Nationale*) and the *Union* in France, and the *Rheinschiffahrts Assecuranz Gesellschaft*, the *Aachen-Münchener* and the *Colonia* in Germany. These considerations were probably least important in England, where Lloyd's was ready to insure almost anything. However, even in England the merchant banker often had to cover his overseas deals with Lloyd's; obviously it was thought advantageous to avoid this aspect of business, remunerative though it could be. Cf. C. Wright and C. E. Fayle, *A History of Lloyd's from the Founding of Lloyd's Coffee House to the Present Day*, London, 1928, pp. 240–60, 307–17; R. Straus, *Lloyd's: a Historical Sketch*, London, 1937, pp. 147–62, 190–3; V. Barbour, 'Marine Risks and Insurance in the Seventeenth Century', *Journ. of Econ. and Business Hist.*, I, 1929, pp. 561–96; L. A. Boiteux, *L'assurance maritime à Paris sous le règne de Louis XIV*, Paris, 1945, pp. 11–20; W. R. Dawson, *Marine Underwriting at Rouen, 1727–1742*, London, 1931, pp. xvii–xx; V. Senès, *Les origines des companies d'assurances*, Paris, 1900; *1828–1928: Un siècle d'assurances; l'Union—Incendie; notice historique et statistique*, Paris, 1928; *Le centenaire de la Nationale, ancienne Compagnie royale d'assurances sur la vie, 1830–1930*, Paris, 1930; Kähler (re-ed. J. Hansen), *Die Rheinprovinz, 1815–1915* (The Rhine Province), 2 vols., Bonn, 1917, I, pp. 547–55; Hansen, *op. cit.*, 148–9; R. Bergmann, *Das rheinische Versicherungswesen bis Mitte des 19. Jahrhunderts* (The Rhineland Insurance Business until the Middle of the Nineteenth Century), Essen, 1929; F. Plass and F. R. Ehlers, *Geschichte der Assecuranz und der hanseatischen Seeversicherungs-Börsen: Hamburg, Bremen, Lübeck* (History of Insurance and Hanseatic Maritime Insurance Exchanges: Hamburg, Bremen and Lübeck), Hamburg, 1902. See also J. Halphen, *Les assurances en Suisse et dans le monde; leur rôle dans l'évolution économique et sociale*, Neuchâtel, 1946.

[16] On Amsterdam see E. Baasch, *Holländische Wirtschaftsgeschichte* (Dutch Economic History), Jena, 1927, p. 225; Ch. Wilson, *Anglo-Dutch Commerce and Finance*, esp. ch. 3; A. C. Carter, 'Dutch Foreign Investment in the Light of the Amsterdam "Collateral Succession" Inventories', *Tijdschrift voor Geschiedenis*, LXVI, 1952, pp. 27–38. On London, see E. T. Powell,

occupation, of the German and Austrian loan issues, of the entry of far-off, exotic countries into the European financial market.[17] In the process the entire field of investment in joint-stock companies was added to the raising of loans; central banks, public works programmes, and, above all, railways were developing their hitherto undreamed-of need for capital. Of course merchant bankers of various countries responded in different ways to these opportunities. In England, the great London houses took relatively long to enter the field of business promotion;[18] by contrast, on the Continent there was hardly a joint-stock company of any importance which did not number among its founders one or more merchant bankers from Paris, Frankfurt, Cologne, Geneva and . . . London.[19] For if the English at home were a little slow to get interested in the game, they were sufficiently skilful and strong to play a role of the first importance on the Continent after 1840.

In fact, co-operation—national and international—was the distinctive mark of investment banking. Its success depended on teamwork. In the first place, transactions were often negotiated at a distance, and skilful and powerful collaborators on the spot were indispensable. But even more important, investment operations tied the merchant banker to capital markets and to the stock exchange, institutions which had their own methods of operation. He had to sell something—railway shares, government stock—to a difficult and versatile public. He had opportunities of making a fortune, but equally he might lose his shirt. If his appetite was too keen and he tried to corner an issue, his colleagues could easily spoil the market. On the other hand, the judicious allocation of a promotion could open the door to several markets instead of only one, and at the same time ensure the goodwill of other houses.

*Evolution of the Money Market, 1385–1915*, London, 1915, pp. 148–62; A. H. John, 'Insurance Investment and the London Money Market of the Eighteenth Century', *Economica*, n.s., xx, 1953, pp. 137–58; S. R. Cope, 'The Goldsmids and the Development of the London Money Market during the Napoleonic Wars', *Economica*, n.s., ix, 1942, pp. 180–206; R. H. Mottram, *A History of Financial Speculation*, London, 1929, pp. 146–55. In the eighteenth century London was always behind Amsterdam and even Frankfurt as a financial centre. On Frankfurt, see Dietz, *op. cit.*, v, pp. 28–30, 753–79; C. W. Berghoeffer, *Meyer Amschel Rothschild*, (Frankfurt, 1922, pp. 29–44; R. Ehrenberg, *Grosse Vermögen, I, Die Fugger-Rothschild-Krupp* (Great Fortunes, I: Fuggers, Rothschilds, Krupps), Jena, 1925, pp. 49–57. See also on Geneva, A. Sayous, 'La banque à Genève pendant les 16e, 17e, et 18e siècles', *Rev. écon. internat.*, xxvi, 1934, iii, pp. 437–74; *idem*, 'Les placements de fortune à Genève depuis le XVe siècle usqu'à la fin du XVIIIe', *ibid.*, xxvii, 1935, ii, pp. 257–88.

[17] The best discussion is found in L. H. Jenks, *Migration of British Capital to 1875*, New York, 1937, ch. ii.

[18] Cf. the passage in Disraeli's *Endymion*, cited by Jenks, *Migration*, p. 130. By an irony of fate it was not a merchant banker who showed the other London bankers the way in financing joint-stock companies; it was one of those whom the English call 'private bankers', that is to say, a banker dealing with traditional deposits, George C. Glyn, who set the example. J. Francis, *A History of the English Railway*, 2 vols., London, 1851, ii, pp. 3–9; R. S. Lambert, *The Railway King, 1800–1871: A Study of George Hudson and the Business Morals of his Time*, London, 1934, index (Glyn); R. Fulford, *Glyn's 1753–1953: Six Generations in Lombard Street*, London, 1953, ch. vii; E. Cleveland-Stevens, *English Railways*, London, 1915, pp. 51–6.

[19] For France, see the lists of founders and officers published with the decrees authorising joint-stock companies in the *Bulletin des Lois*; also the information furnished by shareholders' manuals, for example that by A. Courtois fils, *Des opérations de Bourse; manuel des fonds publics et des sociétés par actions*, Paris, 1857; or A. Vitu, *Guide financier*, Paris, 1864.

In this way merchant bankers learned to moderate their ambitions and divide their projects. Financial groupings and syndicates began to appear. The composition of the latter was to a certain extent dictated by personal and social relationships; however, the dominant factor was the contribution each member could make to the success of the operation. There was too much at stake to allow subjective considerations to intervene. So, although merchant bankers had their preferences and their dislikes (however they might appear to their clients and debtors, they were still human), even the proudest of them, for example James de Rothschild, learned to subordinate their emotions to their profits.[20]

In the same way that investment syndicates represented common interests, the capital market, taken as a whole, was characterized by the tolerance and cooperation of the various syndicates active in it. Small discounts, habitually reserved for friendly but non-participant houses, were more than courtesy gifts; they were a sign of the mutual *laissez-faire* and benevolent neutrality of the market. Naturally there were exceptions to this rule of which the conflict between the Rothschilds and the Péreires is the most spectacular example. But on the whole the tendency was always towards maintenance of equilibrium between the few privileged groups. There was neither contract nor formal code, and it was exceptional for the agreement to be reduced to writing.[21] But it was none the less real for that. In this respect the situation has not changed much in the meantime, as the recent literature on the subject of Wall Street monopolists shows.

Of course, the system was not proof against everything. Cracks appeared from time to time in the shape of intruders into the established network of business re-

[20] There were exceptions: for example, Labouchère, of the house of Hope, who had, it would seem, an 'invincible prejudice' against the Rothschilds (R. Ehrenberg, *op. cit.*, I, p. 112). And the Rothschilds would have nothing to do with the Erlangers, for a multitude of personal reasons. Cf. L. D. Steefel, 'The Rothschilds and the Austrian Loan of 1865', *Journ. Mod. Hist.*, VIII, 1936, p. 29, n. 6.
Nevertheless, such dislikes and irrational reactions were rare. In this context, the case of the Rothschilds is instructive. In 1851 James de Rothschild, enraged by Cavour's decision to contract a loan with Hambro, did everything he could to make Sardinian stocks fall in London and Paris; the loan nearly failed. However, as soon as it was clear that his campaign had failed, James sent his son hurrying to Turin to suggest a new loan, at a record price, to Cavour. E. Corti, *Rise of the House of Rothschild*, New York, 1928, pp. 281–9. It would seem that this experience was sufficient. Thus, in 1852, when Bechet-Dethomas et Cie. of Paris, with the help of Mirès and Ch. Devaux and Co. of London, won the contract for a Turkish loan, every one recognized it as a defeat for the Rothschilds. One of the principal bankers on the spot wrote to an associate: 'M. Hottinguer told me about the Turkish loan and we laughed to think of Rothschild's annoyance at seeing the account go to M. Bechet . . . Mirès will bang the big drum and the public will decide the matter. To prevent this, Rothschild would have to be angry enough to unload and upset the market. But this is highly unlikely. His own interests come before everything else, even his pride.' *Correspondence Demachy-Seillière*, letter of 31-1-1852. (In fact, the public did not get the chance to decide the matter. When the contract was presented to the Turkish government for ratification, it was rejected. The adjudicators were reimbursed for their expenses and received an award of 2,000,000 F, about 4 per cent of the nominal value of the loan.) A. Du Velay, *Essai sur l'histoire financière de la Turquie*, Paris, 1903, pp. 139–40.
[21] Cf. for example the contractual agreements between the houses of the *Haute Banque* of Paris during the 1830s, which allocated various prospective issues in advance. *Archives De Neuflize, Schlumberger et Cie.*, nos. 148, 150, 151. The facsimile of one of these undertakings, that of January 1833, is reproduced in the commemorative volume, *De Neuflize et Cie.*; *notice historique publiée à l'occasion du 125e anniversaire de l'établissement à Paris de leur maison de banque*, Paris, 1926.

lations. But they soon learned to play the game according to the rules, or else . . .
For, in spite of its consideration for those who were more or less its equals, the
*Haute Banque* knew how to be totally ruthless towards newcomers and weaker
houses when the situation demanded it.[22] On the other hand, once these less substantial houses were established, they were treated in the normal way. They became integrated, and indeed they had good reasons to want to be.[23] However
incredible it might have seemed in 1850, only one generation earlier the Rothschilds had been poachers in the territory of the established interests.

To sum up, the so-called 'Old Bank', that is to say, the corpus of merchant
banks not only in Paris but in all the commercial centres of Europe was, in spite of
its reputation for conservatism, a malleable and supple institution. Its abilities and
imagination had been amply demonstrated even before it promoted and upheld
the railway boom of the 1840s. The profession had its laggards, but equally it had
its intelligent innovators.

At the same time, the 'Old Bank' had developed an unwritten code of conduct,
intended to give operations the maximum of security and limit the destructive
effects of conflict. And although this euphoric state was constantly troubled by
change, means existed to reduce these troubles to a minimum. The majority of the
disruptive elements could be suppressed; those which could not could always be
disarmed.

The *Crédit Mobilier* must be seen against this background of banking flexibility
and ingenuity if its role in the economic development of Europe is to be understood. This new house represented a spectacular departure; but it was not founded
with the intention of turning finance upside down, and it came as no surprise to the
'Old Bank'.

On the contrary, the joint-stock investment bank had been developing for
several decades. As early as 1825, a group comprising most of the houses of the
Parisian *Haute Banque* and including a few foreign houses of major importance,
had proposed the formation of a *Société commanditaire de l'Industrie*, with the then

---

[22] The careers of Ouvrard and Mirès furnish examples of this; both were received with
hostility by the established financial powers. On Ouvrard see his *Mémoires*, 2nd ed., 3 vols.,
Paris, 1826–7; O. Wolff, *Die Geschäfte des Herrn Ouvrard* (Mr Ouvrard's transactions),
Frankfurt, 1933, ch. XII; A. Liesse, *Portraits de financiers*, Paris, 1908, pp. 1–67; G. Weill,
'Le financier Ouvrard', *Rev. Hist.*, CXXVII, 1918, pp. 31–61; M. J. Savant, *Tel fut Ouvrard*,
Paris, 1954. On Mirès, see *A mes juges*; Girard, *Politique des travaux publics*, pp. 267–9; *idem*,
*Bull. de la Soc. d'hist. mod.*, 10e série, No. 22, Jan.–Feb. 1951, which points out that the dos-
siers on the Mirès affair have been plundered. The efforts of Mirès in 1864, after the disaster
of 1861, to conciliate the *Haute Banque*, which he had criticized so bitterly before, are pitiful.
Cf. the prospectus for his project for a *Banque des États* in the *Journal des chemins de fer*, XXIII
(1864), p. 819: 'This company would not involve any incursions into the domain of other
financial establishments.'

[23] In this respect George Peabody is an excellent example of professional adaptation; he
passed from the boldness of the merchant to the traditional prudence of the merchant
banker, applying to good advantage the rules he had formerly ignored; see the typewritten
manuscript by Muriel Hidy, *George Peabody, Merchant and Financier, 1795–1869*, Cambridge,
Mass., 1949, ch. XI–XII. I would like to thank Mrs Hidy for allowing me to see this work
before its publication.

fabulous capital of a hundred million francs. The project had to be abandoned when the *Conseil d'État* of the Restoration, dominated by landowners who were afraid of the growing influence of fortunes other than those in real estate, refused to authorize it.[24] During the next 25 years, every effort to organize investment banks took the form of limited partnership which did not need authorization by the State. These were the so-called *Caisses*, one of the first of which was founded by Jacques Laffitte in 1837, most of the rest came into existence during the railway boom of the 1840s.[25]

In the meantime, true joint-stock banks made their appearance in Belgium and flourished there. The *Société Générale de Bruxelles* was founded in 1822, and after the Revolution of 1830 became the principal promoter and support of Belgian industry, especially heavy industry.[26] Then, in 1835, the *Banque de Belgique* was established to operate on the same principles. Of these two, the *Société Générale* in particular became an example to the whole world of the scope for this kind of activity. And in fact, when the *Crédit Mobilier*, later on, became notorious for playing the stock exchange, the *Société Générale* by comparison seemed to be the model of a solid and serious investment bank. For example, in 1863 Achille Fould, then Finance Minister, explicitly made this comparison in the report he presented to the Minister of Commerce on the statutes submitted for authorization by the French *Société Générale*.[28]

Without belittling the originality of the Péreires, it is only fair to point out that they themselves described the *Crédit Mobilier* as the realization of the underlying conceptions of the ephemeral *Société commanditaire de l'Industrie* of the previous generation.[29] The *Crédit Mobilier* was effectively the product of 20 years of effort in the sphere of industrial credit, stimulated by railway speculations; the *Caisses* provided a foretaste of the fruits of an Empire which was far more tolerant in this field than its predecessors.

Similarly in Prussia, Mevissen, supposed to be an imitator of the Péreires, had tried as early as 1845 to form a joint-stock bank at Cologne to help, among other things, the development of industry in Rhineland-Westphalia and Prussia. When in 1852 he took up the project again, he found himself compelled to establish his headquarters at Darmstadt, because he was unable to get authorization

[24] Mongéry, 'Réflections sur quelques institutions . . .', *Rev. encyclopédique*, 7e année, 2, série, xxvii, 1825, pp. 625–47; J.-J. Baude, 'Notice sur la Société commanditaire', *ibid.* xxxix, 1828, pp. 28–41.

[25] A. Courtois fils, *Histoire des banques en France*, pp. 155–8; E. Kaufman, *La banque en France*, pp. 11–2; Bigo, *Les banques françaises*, pp. 138–45.

[26] J. Malou, *Notice historique sur la Société générale pour favoriser l'industrie nationale, établie à Bruxelles, 1823–1862*, Brussels, 1863; *Le centenaire de la Société générale de Belgique*, Brussels, s.d., 1922, pp. 49–61; Schöller, 'La transformation économique de la Belgique de 1832 à 1844', *Bull. de l'Inst. de recherches écon. et soc.*, Louvain, xiv, 1948, pp. 566–8, 572–85. R. Liefmann, *Beteiligungs- und Finanzierungsgesellschaften* (Companies for Participation and Finance), 2nd ed., Jena, 1913, pp. 111–33, offers useful information, taken principally from Malou.

[27] E. van Elewyck, *La Banque nationale de Belgique; les théories et les faits*, 2 vols., Brussels, 1913, I, pp. 20–6; B. S. Chlepner, *La banque en Belgique*, pp. 68–74, 85–95. In fact, the *Société Générale's* policy of large scale-investment in industry dates only from 1835; it was to some extent a reply to the competition of the National Bank.

[28] *Arch. nat.* (Paris) F¹² 6776, letter of 8 June 1863.

[29] *Société Générale du Crédit Mobilier, Rapport présenté par le Conseil d'administration*, 29 April 1854, p. 2.

in Cologne or Frankfurt for a concession he assumed to date from 1846: the Habers, court bankers of Hesse, had already put forward their own joint-stock company which was destined to take part in, among other things, industrial credit operations. Here too, railways were demanding new financial institutions; and here also the crisis of the later years of the 1840s had led to a setback which lasted for several years. It is true that the *Darmstädter Bank* gained considerable impetus from the success of the Péreires in Paris; the creation of the *Crédit Mobilier* acted as a stimulus for Mevissen and his allies in the house of Oppenheim at Cologne. But even so, Mevissen took great care, right from the beginning, to draw a clear distinction between his own sound and constructive interest in industrial credit and the speculations of the Péreires.[30]

It is, however, only part of the story that the *Crédit Mobilier* was neither a complete novelty (I will not go as far as one writer in particular, who treats it as a copy —*Abklatsch*—of the *Société Générale*)[31] nor a surprise for the 'Old Bank'. The essential point is that the *Crédit Mobilier* and other organizations like it were very largely established with funds advanced by existing merchant banks; and furthermore, the old so-called conservative banks were well represented on the boards of the new concerns and often dominated them.

The principal shareholder of the *Crédit Mobilier*, apart from the Péreires themselves, was the Paris house of Fould and Fould-Oppenheim; and it would be interesting to know, in this context, whether the total cost of the stock subscribed by the Péreires was covered by their own personal resources. As well as Benoît Fould, the board of directors of the *Mobilier* included Charles Mallet, Ernest André, Baron Seillière and Gédéon des Arts, all of them eminently respectable members of the *Haute Banque*.[32]

Later investment banks, in France as elsewhere, were formed in a similar way. In France, Rothschild and a group of merchant bankers tried in 1856 to set up a *Comptoir impérial des Travaux Publics, du Commerce et de l'Industrie*, without doubt intended in part to act as a counterweight to the *Crédit Mobilier*; the project never came to anything.[33] In 1864, almost the same group, though without Rothschild, succeeded in founding the *Société Générale pour le Développement du Commerce et de l'Industrie*.[34] In Germany, established houses like the Oppenheims of Cologne, the Heines of Hamburg, the Mendelssohns, the Bleichröders, the Warschauers and Gebrüder Schickler of Berlin were among the first to promote investment banks.[35] And in England there were Heath, Huth, Stern Brothers, George Peabody and

---

[30] J. Hansen, *Gustav von Mevissen; ein rheinisches Lebensbild* (Gustav von Mevissen: a Rhenish Biography), 2 vols., Berlin, 1906, I, pp. 380, 648–53, 655 n. 1, 655–6.

[31] H. Sattler, *Die Effektenbanken* (Banks for Securities), Leipzig, 1890, p. 69, cited by Liefmann, *op. cit.*, p. 133.

[32] The statutes, the names of the founders and the lists of subscribers and officers are to be found in the *Bull. des Lois*, 10e série, supp., x, 1852, pp. 781–96.

[33] *Arch. nat.* F12 6776, letter of 4 Dec. 1856. Without precise information, it seems likely that the project failed because the time was badly chosen; it was planned on the eve of the financial and commercial crisis of 1857.

[34] *Bull des Lois*, 11e série, supp., xxiii, 1864, pp. 1357–75.

[35] W. Däbritz, *Gründung und Anfänge der Disconto-Gesellschaft in Berlin* (Establishment and Beginnings of the Disconto-Gesellschaft, Berlin), Munich and Leipzig, 1831, pp. 36, 46, 48, 64 *et passim*: *Darmstädter Bank, Preussische Credit-Gesellschaft* (failed), *Disconto-Gesellschaft* (reorganized), *Berliner Handelsgesellschaft*. See also A. Krüger, *op. cit.*, pp. 182–8.

Co., Ch. Devaux and Co. among others.[36] And it was the same throughout Europe.[37]

Briefly, then, the houses of the 'Old Bank' were from the beginning involved in the creation of the 'New'. They did so, not because they were obliged to act in this way to defeat the Rothschilds or Péreires, as the case might be, but because investment banks promised to be profitable enterprises which—and here is the essential point—far from conflicting with their normal activities seemed to be in perfect accord with them.

The nature of the private banking house was in itself an obstacle to participation in large-scale promotions and loan issues. First of all, its clientele was limited, and the growing scale of investment operations demanded new sources of wealth. Whereas the merchant banker did business—and preferred to do business—only with established businessmen and a few rich capitalists who put their fortunes in his hands, the big company, less discriminating and choosy, was well designed to draw on the savings of lesser capitalists who were often not in commerce and who, as a rule, were too small to be of interest to the 'Old Bank'. Furthermore, private houses traditionally felt a certain responsibility towards their clients when recommending investments—in effect, the name of the promoting bank mattered much more to those who lent their capital than the credit of the borrower.[38] The impersonal joint-stock companies, on the other hand, had no need to restrict themselves in this way.[39] This was an advantage; for, with profits from industrial credit growing, they were able to take part in a whole range of investments which merchant bankers preferred not to submit to their private clients, but which were ideally designed for promotion in the public sphere.

The attitude of the old houses on this subject was without doubt influenced to a

[36] See the prospectus of the *International Financial Society* in the *Money Market Review*, VI, 1863, p. 467; *Bankers' Magazine*, London, XXIII, 1863, pp. 518–9; and the prospectus of the *General Credit and Finance Company*, founded in conjunction with the French *Société Générale*, *ibid.*, pp. 476–7.

[37] For example, the role of Dutch houses in the creation of the *Crédit Néerlandais*; of Italian houses in that of the *Credito mobiliare italiano* and the *Banca di credito italiano*; of houses like Stieglitz and Gunzberg in the development of finance in Russia, etc. H. Hirschfeld, *Het Ontstaan van het moderne Bankwezen in Nederland* (The Genesis of Modern Banking in the Netherlands), Rotterdam, 1922, ch. III; *Journal des chemins de fer*, XXII, 1863, pp. 308f.; R. E. Cameron, 'The *Crédit Mobilier*', pp. 476 n. 62, 480; *La Semaine financière*, VIII, 1863, pp. 90, 100, 309; the articles on Gunzburg in the *Universal Jewish Encyclopaedia* and the *Encyclopaedia Judaica*.

[38] Cf., for example, the *standesherrliche Schuldschreibungen*, loans floated above all at Frankfurt by the magnates and nobles of Central Europe and known usually by the names of the issuing banks. The way in which they were assessed at the Frankfurt Stock Exchange is revealing; see the *Frankfurter Zeitung* of this period. In the same way, Brazilian government stock enjoyed exceptional prestige at the London Stock Exchange because of its long and unbroken association with the Rothschilds: A. K. Cairncross, *Home and Foreign Investment, 1870–1913*, Cambridge, 1953, p. 90.

[39] There was a time, at the beginning, when new companies declared their intention to pass proposed projects through a sieve and to underwrite their issues in the best banking tradition; at least some newcomers, like Laing, the English counterpart of the Péreires, and Talabot in France, were rash enough to make this promise. Laing was forced to give it up when first brought into contact with reality; a large joint-stock company could not act in the same way as a small private bank, even when it wanted to do so. Cf. Laing's communications with the shareholders of the *General Credit and Finance Company* over a Venezuelan loan that turned out badly. 'The General Credit Co. was free from responsibility in the matter, and the public invested their money at 10 or 11 per cent with their eyes open.' Capitalists too were slow to recognize the distinction between new and traditional finance.

considerable extent by the experience of the 1840s, when they had succeeded in launching the railways only at the price of abandoning some of their traditional habits. In this period, dozens of banking syndicates, competing for railway concessions, had been obliged to show evidence of *bona fide* subscriptions covering the entire capital of the projected companies. The traditional method of investment on the basis of personal recommendation showed itself to be inadequate; only a handful of houses, notably the Rothschilds, had a sufficient number of connections and clients to risk subscribing large sums in their name in the expectation of an eventual distribution of profits.

The rest were forced to fall back on advertising, a practice which was distasteful to them when it did not seem totally out of keeping with their character.[40] It was certainly not a coincidence that the merchant bankers who took the initiative in creating the new investment banks after 1850 (the Foulds of Paris and the Oppenheims of Cologne, for example) were precisely those houses whose financial ambitions—which went as far as attempting to rival the Rothschilds—surpassed their resources as private businesses. In contrast, even the Rothschilds, who were never forced to resort to advertising to raise funds, had cause to tremble when they remembered the piles of useless paper left on their hands as a result of the crisis of 1848. Merchant banks, great and small, could well afford the luxury of sharing this sort of business with helpers in the shape of joint-stock companies.

In this discussion of the role of the 'Old Bank' in the formation of new banks, it is not maintained that these innovations were the work of established houses alone. In each case, new forms and methods were suggested in part by new men; and the period of transition and competition offered exceptional opportunities to newcomers. Even taking into account the increasingly pressing need for new credit institutions, it must be recognized that the Péreires (above all), Mevissen, Hansemann and others deserve credit for having seen the possibilities of the situation, for having aroused the interest and gained the support of some of the most powerful houses, and for having got the new techniques under way.

At the same time, it would be equally far from the truth to see the 'Old Bank' as being unanimously in favour of the new methods. Some houses were interested; others wanted nothing to do with joint-stock companies; and a few, faithful to commercial credit, had never wanted to be involved in industrial credit in any form. Centres of conservative bankers, for example in Frankfurt, still existed as a proof of unshakable resistance to financial companies.[41] Family groups like the Rothschilds were divided on the question. Even teams as close as that of Baring, Hope and Hottinguer, inseparable when it came to commercial transactions and usually associated in raising loans, found themselves split: Baring and Hottinguer

See the letters from disillusioned shareholders in the financial journals, for example, the *Money Market Review*, IX, 1864, p. 375.
[40] For France, see in particular the *Journal des chemins de fer*.
[41] Even in 1863, a project to create a *Crédit mobilier* at Frankfurt was stifled by the protests of 125 of the principal houses of the town (London *Times*, 19 May 1863, p. 12). No official of a credit company could be a member of the board of directors of the *Frankfurter Bank*; *ibid.*, 8 May 1863, p. 10. Cf. Hansen, *Gustav von Mevissen*, I, pp. 648–9; P. Emden,

were ready to take part in joint-stock companies, while Hope remained completely indifferent to them. Perhaps the most striking example of all was the division in the Fould family on the subject of the *Crédit Mobilier*. On one side, the family bank, led by Benoît Fould, made a considerable contribution to the capital of the company and recommended its authorization; on the other, Benoît's brother Achille, formerly his associate and still one of his shareholders, and Minister of Finance throughout almost the whole of the Empire, was hostile to the project from the beginning, and did his best to limit the activities of the bank once it had been established.[42]

There is nothing surprising about such a division of opinion. Merchant bankers were never unanimous on the subject of the advisability and usefulness of the new activities. The essential point is that *merchant banking as an institution* always showed itself open to change and skilful in adapting to newcomers and their methods, even while assimilating them. In spite of the revolutionary possibilities of joint-stock banking—and the long-term consequences were to surpass by far the expectations of their promoters in the 'Old Bank'—their introduction was no exception to this rule.[43]

It goes without saying that the private houses which had promoted companies were ready to collaborate with them. But even houses which had been indifferent, if not hostile, to the 'New Bank' soon learned to work with it. The Rothschilds of Frankfurt, for instance, made peace with the *Disconto-Gesellschaft* after some pre-

*Money Powers of Europe in the Nineteenth and Twentieth Centuries*, New York, 1938, pp. 265–9; Korach, *Das deutsche Privatbankgeschäft* (German Private Banking Business), p. 28 *et passim*; O. Wormser, *Die Frankfurter Börse: ihre Besonderheiten und ihre Bedeutung* (The Frankfurt Stock Exchange: its Peculiarities and Significance), Tübingen, 1919, pp. 20–1.

[42] *Arch. nat.* F¹² 6776, letter 8 June 1863 to the Ministers of Agriculture, Commerce and Public Works. Cf. L. Véron, *Quatre ans de règne; où en sommes-nous?*, Paris, 1857, pp. 345–6; Plenge, *op. cit.*, p. 81. Girard is wrong in assuming that Fould supported the *Crédit Mobilier* because of his family's role in its foundation: *Politique des travaux publics*, p. 109.

[43] Thus Kahler, in Hansen, *Rheinprovinz*, I, p. 529: 'The contrast between private banks and joint-stock banks is not an absolute one. Private bankers participate in the establishment of foreign and domestic joint-stock banks, feeling that above all in the business of shares, perhaps also in that of loans, their resources no longer suffice; though the former difficulties of money transfers no longer present a problem, they still find scope for profitable activities in traditional banking activities in providing credits for industrial clients, in discounting bills and keeping current accounts and in the administration of clients' investments. With the growing importance of capital investment and speculation in securities and funds, they open up new fields of business by acting as intermediaries for their clients' buying and selling orders in stock exchange speculation. Thus even in this period an indirect connection subsists between the business of private bankers and joint-stock banks.' See also A. Weber, *Depositenbanken und Spekulationsbanken* (Deposit Banks and Banks for Speculation), 2nd rev. ed., Munich and Leipzig, 1915, pp. 63ff.

In this context Émile Péreire was convinced that his *Crédit Mobilier* would not compete with the private banks, because each had his own sphere, credit companies providing industry with capital, while the *Haute Banque* provided it for certain special borrowers, governments in particular. As Péreire said: '*Je ne suis pas banquier*'. H. Hirschfeld, 'Der Crédit-mobilier Gedanke mit besonderer Berücksichtigung seines Einflusses in den Niederlanden' (The *Crédit Mobilier* Idea with special reference to its influence in the Netherlands), *Zeits. f. Volkswirtschaft u. Sozialpolitik*, n.s., III, 1923, p. 443; Plenge, *op. cit.*, p. 85.

liminary skirmishing and in the sequel were associated with it in almost all the loan issues for Central Europe.[44]

In fact, it could be said that the idea of conflict, based on the error of interpretation symbolized by the expression 'Old Bank *versus* New Bank', has been greatly exaggerated by historians. In spite of his resentment, James de Rothschild did not shut the door in Émile Péreire's face immediately; for several years after the establishment of the *Crédit Mobilier* he continued to hope that his protégé would see reason; Émile did not leave the board of directors of the *Nord* Railway (a Rothschild fief) until 1855.[45] In the same year James formed his *Syndicat des Banquiers* to compete with the *Crédit Mobilier* in raising loans and constructing railways.[46] And while after this date rivalry was keen, he did not lose his head to the extent of sacrificing his material interests; and when circumstances demanded it, as in Spain during the 1860s and '70s, the two groups united to achieve common aims.[47]

And furthermore, the practice which was exceptional and only temporary for these two protagonists was a common occurrence among their allies. Sal. Oppenheim jun. and Co. could collaborate with the Rothschilds in the formation of the *Kölnische Rückversicherungsgesellschaft*, at the same time as they were joining Fould to finance the *Crédit Mobilier*.[48] Marcuard and Co. were among the founders of the *Crédit Mobilier*; they were represented on its board and took part with it in a number of transactions during the whole of its existence; this did not prevent them from joining the *Syndicat des Banquiers* of 1855. Erlanger was at one point Frankfurt agent of the *Crédit Mobilier*, at another an associate of the *Credit-Anstalt*, and thus obedient to Rothschild.[49] These examples could be multiplied *ad nauseam*.

Here, too, however, it is not my intention to play down the importance of the

In fact, there were frequent encroachments on both sides of the line of demarcation laid down by Péreire, especially at the beginning. For joint-stock bankers this expansion of their field of action—which was inevitable—was often unexpected. Thus the *Comptoir d'escompte* of Paris was founded to help Parisian trade; this did not prevent it from lending to the Viceroy of Egypt, or from participating in the establishment of the *Société Générale*. M. Sabry, *Épisode de la question d'Afrique: l'Empire égyptien sous Ismaïl et l'ingérence anglo-française, 1863–1879*, Paris, 1933, pp. 89–90; *Bull. des Lois*, 11e série, supp. xxiii, 1864, first part, pp. 1358, 1361–75. For the analagous case of the Berlin *Discontogesellschaft*, cf. O. Lindenberg, *Fünfzig Jahre Geschichte einer Spekulationsbank* (Fifty years in the History of a Bank for Speculation), Berlin, 1903, pp. 6–7.

[44] See H. Münch, *Adolph von Hansemann*, Munich and Berlin, 1952, pp. 79–84.

[45] Cf. *Journal des chemins de fer*, xii, 1853, p. 384; xiii, 1854, p. 386.

[46] *Ibid.*, xv, 1856, pp. 194–5, 986–7; M. Aycard, *Histoire du Crédit Mobilier, 1852–1867* Paris, 1867, pp. 200–1.

[47] *Arch. nat.* F[30] 280, Minister of Foreign Affairs to Madrid Ambassador, telegramme 21 Dec. 1866. This collaboration in Spain, where the two groups had important and long-standing common interests, was not simply a passing affair. In 1875, on the occasion of an agreement between the Péreires' Spanish Northern Railway and the Rothschild-dominated Madrid-Saragossa-Alicante line, the annual report of the latter declared: '*Etrangers à toutes les rivalités, et ennemis de l'esprit de lutte, nous avons toujours accueilli toutes les mesures qui conciliaient les intérêts de notre Cie. avec la marche et les désirs des autres entreprises.*' I would like to thank Professor Rondo E. Cameron of the University of Wisconsin, the author of a doctoral thesis on *French Foreign Investment, 1850–1880* (available on microfilm in the University of Chicago Library), who drew my attention to this quotation.

[48] Krüger, *op. cit.*, p. 149; Hansen, *Gustav von Mevissen*, i, p. 621.

[49] *Bankers' Magazine*, London, xxv, 1865, p. 782. In this operation, an Ottoman loan of £3,636,363, the Erlangers appeared to have taken, one would say, exactly the place that the

conflicts which broke out on the subject of the new investment banks (of which that between the Péreires and the Rothschilds is only the most spectacular example). In the past, innovations in banking had never failed to shake the fabric of existing relations and the equilibrium of the market in one way or another. But these earlier disturbances were only minor upsets by comparison with the world-shaking changes wrought by the joint-stock company.

I have tried to show here that these world-shaking changes have hitherto been described in a misleading fashion, and that in reality events were more complex and relations between men and institutions involved far more subtle than they are usually represented as being; and that the traditional interpretation scarcely does justice to the so-called 'Old Bank', an institution whose role in the economic development of modern Europe deserves a deeper and more careful examination on the part of historians.

Rothschilds should have had. Cf. also the *Moniteur des intérêts*, Brussels, 1865, pp. 36, 186. On the hostility between the Rothschilds and the Erlangers, see above, p. 119.

# Economic Fluctuations
# in the Netherlands
# in the Nineteenth Century

I. J. BRUGMANS

Translated by Alice C. Carter and Sytha Hart

# I

That economic life under modern capitalism does not proceed without friction, shock and even rupture, was already known when those symptoms usually called a crisis began to impress themselves on observers. Later, when these crises occurred repeatedly, the impression grew that they should not be regarded as more or less accidental symptoms of social ill-health, but rather as a rhythmical movement in economic life. The crises were soon understood to be purely periodic disturbances, manifestations merely of a cyclical movement governing economic development.[1] Thus the problem of crises became the problem of economic cycles, the crisis theory developed into the trade cycle theory.

We need not consider here the causes of the ups and downs of economic life today. We should remember, however, how cyclical wave movements manifest themselves. If we start our examination of these movements from the end of a depression and the beginning of upward movement, we can see a transition from falling to rising prices on the commercial market; supplies diminished during depression begin to be replenished, a process facilitated by low interest rates in the capital and money markets. At first, only a few industries show this revival, but it gradually spreads throughout the economy not only because of an increasing spirit of enterprise, but also because the industries which showed this revival first cause a decrease in unemployment because wages usually rise, thus increasing the spending power of the masses. At this stage of the upward trend we also see a rising tendency on the stock market and the money market, easy at first, gradually tightens up.

The upward movement sketched here cannot continue *ad infinitum*. The absorptive capacity of the commercial market appears not to be unlimited, contrary to the expectation of many an optimistic entrepreneur. Interest on loans, and the interest rate which rises as a result of the increasing demand for credit, reach

---

[1] J. Schumpeter, 'Die Wellenbewegung des Wirtschaftslebens' (Cyclical Fluctuations in Economic Life), *Archiv für Sozialwiss. und Sozialpol.*, xxxix, 1915, pp. 1ff.

such a height that many producers produce less, order less, pay lower wages and run down stocks. Banks begin to apply credit restrictions. Prices of commodities decline, those of securities fall rapidly, and a minor cause may start a panic, thus inaugurating an ensuing period of depression which consists of stagnation following the crisis.

Where the crisis is signalled by decreasing commodity prices, a rapid fall in securities, falling incomes, an increase in unemployment and a considerable decline in production, depression brings little change in prices, but falling production, lower incomes, a minimal spirit of enterprise and an easy money market. From this situation there evolves a new move through the forces already described which completes the economic cycle.

From this simplified description of an economic cycle we can conclude that we have here phenomena inconceivable without the modern capitalist structure of national economy. Good and bad times can, it is true, be found in older economic structures; but such periods are then the result of chance factors such as poor harvests, measures of commercial policy, wars, etc.; the modern cyclical rhythm is, however, the result of a dynamism inherent in society itself.

Writings on the subject do not give a unanimous answer to the question when this regular movement of the economy first appeared. According to Tugan-Baranovsky, the periodic interchange of boom and slump began with the crisis of 1825; Bouniatian considers the great crisis of 1793 as the point of origin.[2] However, it is certain that rhythmical movement first showed itself in Britain, the country where the so-called Industrial Revolution began and where modern capitalism first appeared. Other countries followed as they were absorbed into the modern capitalist system.[3] Hence we can conclude that it is of great interest to find out where in a country like the Netherlands the first business cycle phenomena can be discerned, and especially how the Dutch national economy reacted to the rhythm shown in the economic life of surrounding countries in the nineteenth century.

So long as the Netherlands in the last century was still in an early phase of capitalism, mainly characterised by agriculture and small rather than large-scale industrial enterprise, mechanization and a credit system, the fluctuations in its economy will be seen to produce no more than a ripple. It is only when the country has arrived at the period of modern capitalism (Sombart talks of *Hochkapitalismus*) that economic fluctuations confront society as a whole in all walks of life.

The lapse of time between two economic cycles cannot be specified with any certainty. Roughly one can say that one crisis is followed[4] by another at an interval of seven to eleven years. It is impossible to be more precise because economic cycles do not manifest themselves in the same way in every country. Each country has its own economic structure and fluctuations occur simultaneously as well as consecutively. Moreover, it appears that fluctuations, while becoming less violent in

---

[2] E. Wagemann, *Konjunkturlehre* (Theory of Cyclical Fluctuations), 1928, pp. 77–8.
[3] According to N. W. Posthumus, *Geschiedenis van de Leidsche lakenindustrie* (History of the Leyden Cloth Industry), II, 1939, pp. 1124ff., the cyclical movement began some centuries earlier, even in the Middle Ages, at least in the cloth industry. This opinion is shared by F. Ph. Groeneveld, *De economische crises van het jaar 1720* (The Economic Crisis of the Year 1720), but does not seem tenable. We hope to revert to this question later.
[4] It might be better to say: was followed. After the crisis of 1929 economic life has been subject to so much direction from above that free play of social forces is impossible.

E 2

the nineteenth century, recur more frequently. One cannot speak with absolute certainty here because each country shows its own symptoms and because the problem occurs of drawing the boundary between a local more or less incidental disturbance and a deviation determined by the rhythm of the general trade cycle.

The most characteristic and remarkable part of the cyclical wave is naturally the period of crisis which marks the transition from boom to slump. It is therefore convenient to identify the successive cycles by their crisis year occurring at the crest of the wave. In that sense we can still speak of crises and by giving a survey of the crises of the nineteenth century we can gain insight into the rhythm of economic life in that period.

Since the crises of 1815 and 1818 can be regarded as an aftermath of the Napoleonic period, the crisis of 1825 is the first which can undoubtedly be considered as a symptom of an economic cycle.[5] The crisis raged mainly in Britain. The British public had become financially involved on a large scale in the new investment opportunities presenting themselves everywhere. Construction of harbours and waterways, exploitation of minerals and construction of factories at home, also Mexican silver mines and South America had attracted the attention of capitalists. Where opportunities for making profits appeared to have been over-estimated, an appreciable drop in prices set in, accompanied by a stock exchange crisis and the ruin of a great number of banks. Unemployment and falling wages afflicted the workers.

By 1830 the crisis of 1825 had been almost completely liquidated. New opportunities to expand were opening everywhere. This was the time when the railway began its triumphal march and when the steam engine began to appear in industry. Again Britain led the way, but this time followed by the United States. Speculation was so widespread and affected so large a section of the British people that shares were issued in denominations as low as £10 and £5. Repercussions were first felt in 1836 when a number of banks failed in the United States, causing an appreciable fall in exports to that country from Britain followed by falling prices and other after-effects; some Irish banks were also obliged to stop payment. This crisis did not work itself out completely so that as early as 1839 there was a new crash, first in the United States, then in London. The British working class was again the victim of such misery that it gave impetus to the growing Chartist movement.

New forces tending towards revival soon occured. Railway operation expanded widely after 1843; not only in Britain but also in France many new lines were being constructed, benefiting also the iron industry. Moreover, prices rose as the result of bad harvests in 1845 and 1846. During the year 1847 a French railway company suddenly had to stop construction; there followed a panic on the stock exchange which carried other railway shares with it. This temporarily stopped further expansion of railway networks; the metal and mining industries felt a severe reaction. This started the crisis of 1847 which raged not only in France but in Britain, where the Bank of England had to be given permission to exceed the fiduciary issue. This collapse of economic life together with unemployment and poverty for the working class gave new life to ideas of social reform. Chartism

[5] Details about this and the following crises in J. Lescure, *Des crises générales et périodiques de surproduction* (On general and periodical crises of overproduction), 1923.

revived in Britain while France resorted to the co-operatives. These events form the historical background to the revolutionary movement of 1848.

The economic cycle went on. By about 1850, Lescure writes, all conditions for a new boom were present.

Prices have fallen a great deal; production has reduced its overhead costs, improved its methods, speeded up the substitution of coke for charcoal in smelting and thrown overboard a whole host of small enterprises whose cost of production was too high to survive the depression. Capital is abundant and cheap, and there is plenty of labour. All conditions are present for a new upswing.[6]

The boom did come, stimulated by discoveries of gold in California and Australia which led to a rise in the general price level. Otherwise the revival of 1850 shows the same aspects as the last boom: prosperity of shipbuilding, expansion of railways, mining and metal industries. The French *Crédit Mobilier*, which was copied in other countries, provided the credit necessary for the reviving spirit of enterprise until the tide turned in 1857. There had already been signs of tension similar to those of earlier crises when facts proved trade prosperity to be on the wane: the crash, heralded by the loss of a ship loaded with gold, came first in the United States where more than a hundred banks stopped payment, then in England where the Bank of England had to exceed the fiduciary issue. The end of the Crimean War made things more difficult; Russian grain, which Western Europe had had to do without for two years, appeared again on the world market in 1857 and caused a considerable drop in grain prices.

The period following the crisis of 1857 presents a blurred picture since the American Civil War disturbed the regularity of the cyclical pattern. Since trade relations with the United States were disturbed, and especially since the supply of American cotton was stopped—these were the years of cotton famine—there were signs shortly after 1860 similar to crisis symptoms which however can not really be regarded as such. It would be better not to consider 1861 and 1864 as peak years, showing however a certain relapse, but a downswing followed by a new upward movement, not by a crisis and then a depression.[7] It is not 1861 or 1864 but 1866 which should be considered the crisis year following that of 1857.

In 1866 we see the usual symptoms: lower production, stock exchange crisis, drop in profits and wages. It was now mainly industries carried on in countries like Russia, Austria, Italy and Spain which caused disappointment to French and British investors and turned earlier optimism to distrust. The fall on the American stock exchange, where Black Friday caused another panic in 1869, was the final flare up of this crisis.

Economically the period after 1866 is characterized by the cycle affecting Britain and France less than it did economically less developed countries like Germany, Austria and the United States. France and Britain had been through the Industrial Revolution and had reached a certain saturation point. It was in other countries still in full swing. In the United States, the end of the Civil War freed energy and released a spirit of enterprise while in Germany the war indemnity of 1871 had artificially stimulated a boom. Stock speculation in Vienna reached such proportions that it was compared to the well-known Dutch tulip mania. As well as in mining, metal industries and railways, owners of capital were now also interested

[6] *Ibid.*, p. 42.    [7] *Ibid.*, pp. 6off.

in the building industry. Big cities now began to expand. On this occasion 1873 was the year in which the tide turned, sparked off by a crash on the Vienna stock exchange and the fall of the great American house of Jay Cooke & Co. That production had outrun demand appeared most clearly from the fact that the more recent undertakings were the first to go down. Railways, building, metal production and the textile industry felt the influence of the crisis the most. It should further be noted that prices dropped farther in 1873 than in the crisis before, a fall which went on till about 1895.

It was only between 1877 and 1879 that the depression consequent on the crisis of 1873 seemed to have come to an end. Reviving activity was as usual stimulated by low wages and low interest rates. The revival was mainly in France and the United States as was the following unavoidable relapse. In France the revived spirit of enterprise was mainly directed towards the provision of utilities such as railways and tramways, gas and waterworks, activities from which mining and metal industries again profited. There was a similar development in the United States. In 1882 the fall of a finance house, the *Union Générale*, heralded the beginning of a crisis. The pace of the economy in the United States began to slacken, but the panic came only in 1884. Unlike in France, it was accompanied by a serious credit crisis. Germany and England felt these events only indirectly through the repercussions on their foreign trade.

Like that of 1882, the crisis of 1890 was preceded by only a few boom years. While France and the United States were the countries mainly involved in the crisis of 1882, in 1890 and 1893 Britain and the United States felt its effect most. France, still suffering from the depression of 1882 and subsequent years, was not involved. In these years Britain made large-scale investments in Australia, Canada and South America in which the house of Baring Brothers played an important part; Britain's foreign trade increased so considerably that she had to enlarge her merchant fleet. Under the influence of her prevailing protectionist ideas, Germany developed into an industrial state with a large metal industry. In the United States agriculture, especially cotton-growing, shared in the revival which expressed itself in rising prices. The crisis of 1890 which put an end to the upward movement is often called the Baring crisis, because the fall of Baring Brothers was the alarm signal and thereby many hopes of gain were thwarted. It appeared that enterprises established in the Argentine and elsewhere abroad were not as profitable as had been hoped. Britain's exports declined, necessitating a contraction of her trade and industrial activity. In Germany the crisis was felt mainly at home; industrial activity was reduced but there was no panic. The United States managed to avoid a crisis, thanks to her extensive home market and to strong protectionist measures. This turned out to be only a delay. The reversal came in 1893. In the same year crisis also affected Australia where the building industry declined because it had built on land purchased at too high a price in the course of speculation. The stock exchange crisis which Britain suffered in 1890 occurred in the United States in 1893.

The last years of the nineteenth century, from 1895 onwards, show an upward trend in which Germany above all became remarkably prosperous; this time there were developments not only in railway construction, in mining and in the building industries, but also in a new branch of production, the electrical industry. The crisis of 1900 which put an end to this boom affected Germany most severely. In the United States the reversal did not set in until 1903, so that it would be best to consider the turning point around the turn of the century to belong to the twentieth century.

In the twentieth century, which falls beyond our scope, the cyclical movement in the economy at first continued. The year 1905 clearly shows transition from depression to boom, to end in a further crisis in 1907. Several years later the slump begun in 1907 was replaced by a boom which in its turn reached a climax in 1913. In the second half of 1913 and the first half of 1914 there were clear signs of economic tension which point to the turning of the tide. The World War prevented this economic blizzard from discharging itself in the accustomed manner.

# II

The rhythm of modern economic life is not fully reflected in the cyclical movements just sketched out. It is only recently that we have perceived that besides the short cycles of seven to eleven years, easily visible to the outsider, there are also long-term movements of approximately 50 years. These long-term movements lack the dramatic convulsive character of the short waves. They are indicative of changes in the tempo of modern economic development. The rising curve of the long cycle, lasting for around 25 years, is characterized by rising prices; the declining curve shows a period in which price levels go down, often accompanied by agricultural depression. The short waves referred to earlier should therefore be regarded as fluctuations around a base line which rises in some periods and falls in others. During an overall rise, recovery from a depression is rapid and booms prevail. During a period of decline, slump conditions last longer and intervening periods of prosperity are shorter.[8]

Western European prices in the nineteenth century do indeed indicate the existence of long cycles, i.e. of around 50 years. Between 1809 and 1850 the overall trend was falling; the price rise which began about the middle of the century lasted till the crisis year of 1873. The fall which then began lasted until around 1895, to be replaced by a new rise which continued until the World War.[9] These developments are usually explained in monetary terms; the rise in the middle of the century results from gold strikes in California and Australia. The post-1873 fall is attributed to a flight from silver in most countries, resulting in a relative shortage of gold. The rise after 1895 was caused by the discovery of gold in South Africa.[10] If this is true one cannot speak here of automatic cyclical movements unless discoveries of gold are considered not to have been accidental but determined by general developments in the economy, as indeed some scholars do.[11]

[8] Information as to researchers who first observed these long cycles in S. de Wolff, *Het economisch getij* (Economic Fluctuations), 1929, pp. 49ff.

[9] Walter T. Layton and G. Crowther, *An Introduction to the Study of Prices, with Special Reference to the History of the Nineteenth Century*, 1922, p. 22.

[10] A. L. B[owley], in *Encycl. Britannica*, 14th ed., XIX, pp. 470ff., *sub* prices (statistics of).

[11] N. D. Kondratieff in the article referred to below. Cf. also J. Tinbergen, *Economische bewegingsleer* (Theory of Dynamic Economics), 1943, pp. 163ff.

How long cycles are caused is a theoretical question which does not concern us here. We would first have to study the facts in the light of the theory of the Russian scholar N. D. Kondratieff. In an important article[12] he collected material for Britain, France and the United States on commodity prices, interest rates, wages, foreign trade and the consumption of raw materials such as coal, iron and lead. From this he concluded that a long-term cyclical movement is unmistakable. It may therefore be of some interest to enquire into this economic ebb-and-flow in the Netherlands.

# III

So far, little has been done to investigate historically cyclical fluctuations in the Netherlands. The *Business Annals* published by Thorp and Mitchell, which give the cyclical pattern year by year in the leading countries of the world from the onset of cyclical fluctuations, start in the year 1890 as far as the Netherlands is concerned.[13] J. Ridder, in a dissertation published in Rotterdam in 1935 which dealt with cyclical fluctuations in the Netherlands between 1848 and 1860,[14] produced much valuable data, but the time span is too short to give an impression of Dutch economic development during the last century. This research, the results of which are considered below, must therefore be considered as a cursory reconnaissance in largely unexplored territory.

The sources for studying the history of the economic cycle are twofold. Firstly, we can use contemporary descriptions of different branches of industry or industrial centres, annual reports of firms, chambers of commerce, public bodies and other material of this kind. In the work published in collaboration with Mitchell, Thorp based his picture of each country's trading, industrial, financial and agricultural position on just such material. He added a few words on social, political or other events affecting economic life and summed up each year's developments as favourable or unfavourable, as a change for the better or for the worse.

Secondly, statistical material can be used. This is of course of value only if long runs of figures for the same commodities are available. Where these statistical records are obtainable, their value is much greater than descriptions because of their objectivity. A combination of both methods will yield best results, but statistics must act as the foundation, while descriptions complement and explain the figures. Since our research is of a preliminary nature, we will restrict ourselves to such statistical material as is available. Available data can be grouped as follows: figures of (1) exports and imports, (2) shipping, (3) capital and money market, (4) prices, mainly of agricultural products.

[12] N. D. Kondratieff, 'Die langen Wellen der Konjunktur' (Long Business Cycles), *Archiv für Sozialwissenschaft*, LVI, 1926, pp. 573ff.
[13] Willard Long Thorp and Wesley C. Mitchell, *Business Annals*, 1926; for the Netherlands, cf. pp. 255ff.
[14] J. Ridder, *Een conjunctuur-analyse van Nederland 1848-1860* (An Analysis of Cyclical Fluctuations in the Netherlands, 1848–1860), 1935.

# IV

Statistics of Dutch import, export and transit trade have appeared regularly since 1846. Their many defects were summarized by the Government committee of 1895[15]: inaccurate registration of duty-free goods, especially for export; inadequate distinction between imports for domestic use and goods in transit; lack of detail in specification of goods; unsystematic valuation of goods; insufficient identification of countries of origin and destination. Nevertheless, from these figures we can collect data which provide a picture of economic fluctuations in the Netherlands.

The amount of raw and ancillary materials consumed by industry is of great importance in discerning the course of economic fluctuations. If we focus on raw materials which cannot be supplied from, or obtained within, the home country, then the amount of imports, net of later re-exports, gives a valuable picture of later consumption. This is above all the case with metals; import and export figures give us the consumption of iron, steel, lead, copper and tin.

Of these metals, iron is undoubtedly the most important. The consumption of iron—a raw material so important in economic life that Sombart called modern capitalism the 'iron age' in contrast to the preceding age of wood—is an important index of economic activity. Spiethoff[16] even regarded the curve of pig-iron consumption as an index of cyclical fluctuations. What can Dutch statistics tell us about this? Until 1869 iron ore and pig-iron[17] were shown as one item, so that separate figures for pig-iron can be obtained only from that year. This is not a serious disadvantage since the figures show that not much iron ore was used in the Netherlands; blast furnaces were almost unknown, entirely so until 1885, and the number of iron foundries was not great. Imported iron ore was destined for re-export, though not necessarily at once. This explains the remarkable fact that more than once in the nineteenth century the Netherlands showed an export surplus of iron. As for pig-iron there was, of course, an import surplus of this raw material, since it could be used here. As for the consumption of pig-iron since 1872,[18] this shows clearly the effects of the 1873 crisis. The import surplus fell from 72,000,000 kg. in 1873 to 22,000,000 kg. in 1874 and to 16,000,000 kg. in 1875. For the following cycle the turning point comes after 1883; the import surplus of that year amounted to 44,000,000 kg., but in the following year it was only 19,000,000 kg., and in 1885 18,000,000 kg. Also, during the next downswing the crisis made itself felt here a year later than in other countries; the fall begins after 1891 and continues, with an interruption in 1893, to 1894. It should be noted though that the consumption of pig-iron did not increase after 1872. During the years 1872–5 it averaged 42,000,000 kg. a year, and from 1897–1900 about 31,000,000 kg. a year.[19]

[15] Cf. *Staatscourant*, 1896, No. 164.
[16] In *Handwörterbuch der Staatswiss.*, vi, 4th ed., 1925, pp. 8ff., *sub* Krisen.
[17] Iron cast in rough blocks or pieces, among which are the so-called 'boats for ballast'.
[18] The figures begin in 1869, but do not specify for that and the following year volume, but value of imports and exports.
[19] A graph of iron consumption in the Netherlands can be found in the original Dutch publication of this essay. There are also included graphs of other statistical matter given in this essay.

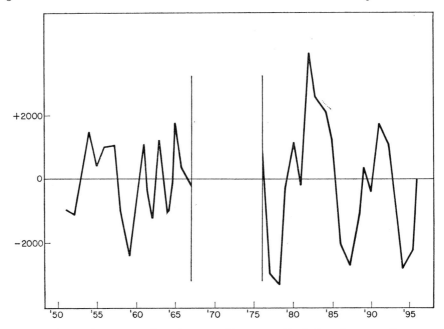

FIG. 1   Import surplus of processed iron, etc. (deviations from trend)

This certainly does not justify the conclusion that there was no economic expansion in the Netherlands after 1872. Rather was the need for iron being increasingly met by partially finished products like forged and sheet iron.[20] But from 1872 to 1900 the import surplus of pig-iron decreased from 57,000,000 to 15,000,000 kg., while the import surplus of processed forge iron, sheet iron, (iron rails, etc.) increased in the same period from 30,000,000 to 132, 000,000 kg.

The consumption of processed iron shows a continuing rise between 1847 and 1900. It is perhaps possible to obtain a more detailed picture by making use of modern statistical methods. One can, for instance, eliminate the short waves by means of so-called moving averages, which in this case in the consideration of average duration of the cycle should be nine-year averages. In this way we get two curves. The first indicates the average of the surrounding nine years year by year, showing the general direction of the economic movement, not the short cycles. The second illustrates year-by-year deviations from annual averages, thus affording a clear picture of the short-wave movement unconnected with possible long waves and with the so-called secular trend, that is the non-cyclical movement. If we apply this method to processed iron (see fig. 1), it appears that in short-cycle terms the Netherlands undoubtedly felt the rhythm of the capitalist movement. We see clearly the wave of which 1857 is the peak. The peaks of 1882 and 1891 (*sic*) are pronounced, that of 1866 is less so, while material concerning the crisis of 1873 is lacking. The other curve in which the short waves have been eliminated (fig. 2) is even more remarkable. It shows a regular rise for the period 1851–67, but quite a different picture for 1876–96; a rise up to 1883, a turning-

[20] Shown in the statistics as forge, bar, rod, hoop and sheet iron.

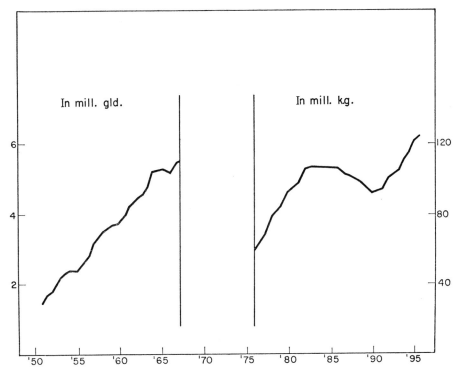

FIG. 2    Import surplus of processed iron, etc. (nine-year averages)

point between 1883 and 1890, a renewed rise after 1890. With a product so subject to cyclical movement as is processed iron, the ebb which various researchers observe for the period 1873–95 thus becomes clearly perceptible. This period of ebb is of shorter duration in the Netherlands than elsewhere, as it is confined to the 1880s here. We will give further attention to this phenomenon later.

After iron, the consumption of steel requires our attention. The import surplus of this material, very small for a long time, began to rise rapidly after 1874. Among other things this is connected with the replacement of iron by steel rails on the permanent way. In 1878 consumption reached a maximum of 46,000,000 kg. There was then a considerable drop which continued till 1887, followed by a new rise. If we compute the trade movement as we did before, eliminating short cycles, we discern here also a recession in the eighties. This begins earlier than with pig-iron, that is to say in 1879, and it is already over by 1883. Once again, we see traces here of the falling curve of the long wave which elsewhere covers the period 1873–95. We can say that the Dutch economy already felt the influence of cyclical fluctuations, but less deeply and drastically than other countries, a conclusion which will become more evident later on.

The other metals, copper, lead and tin, are of less significance for our economic structure, though not without importance as an index of economic development. The ores, just as in the case of iron ore can be disregarded since they are mainly articles in transit. As a result our country sometimes shows an export surplus for these ores. As to raw materials in the first stage of manufacture (red copper, lead in the pig and tin), we may observe that though short-wave movements are noticeable, special circumstances had apparently a greater influence than cyclical fluctuations. This is especially true for copper, which shows movements that only an exhaustive study of the metal market could explain, for instance, the deep decline in the year 1898. This also applies to copper ore. There are no signs of a decrease in tempo in the last quarter of the century.

Besides metals there are other industrial raw materials which are almost entirely imported, the movements of which could thus also be studied in import/export statistics. Among them are wood, coal and cotton. Among many different kinds of wood enumerated in the import/export figures, the most important are unsawn timber for shipbuilding and carpentry.[21] To calculate the import surplus here is impossible, as export figures cannot be compared with those for imports. This is not a great handicap because of the small amount of export. If we apply this method of calculation to the item unsawn shipbuilding and carpenters' timber, we get a somewhat erratic picture from which we can draw the same conclusion as for metals, copper, lead and tin. The cyclical influence is perceptible but can be modified and sometimes overshadowed by special factors. The revival after 1852 and the crisis of 1857 are easily recognizable. The crisis year 1866 also appears to have affected timber consumption. The crisis of 1873 left little trace since before then imports were never very large. The years 1883 and 1892 mark the peaks in the cycle which might indicate that the change in economic conditions came later here than elsewhere, a phenomenon we have already observed with regard to consumption of pig-iron.

When we take into account the nine-year averages for the supply of timber, in order to obtain an insight into the long-term cyclical movement, we see a decline between 1880 and 1889; the rise which was slow previously, is accelerated after 1889—the slowing down of the pace of development during the eighties, already shown in figures for iron and steel, appears also in those for material for carpentry and shipbuilding.

An important raw material in modern economic life is coal. Wherever man-, water- and wind-power are replaced by the steam engine there comes an increase in coal consumption. The consumption of coal is thus an important measure of capital development in years before competition from electrical, turbine and diesel motors. One problem is that coal is not used in industry only as such; according to a statement of the year 1854,[22] 29 per cent of the coal used in the Netherlands was for the generation of gas, 9 per cent was used by the railways, and the remaining 62 per cent in factories and for domestic fuel.[23] Figures now available show that coal presents a regular cyclical fluctuation but that other factors exerted considerably more influence; we observed the same for metal and wood. It is at once obvious that 1857 did not usher in a fall but a rise, continuous till 1860. As will appear, this last year can be considered as one of reversal, also for other

[21] Timber for shipbuilding and carpentry in complete or mixed cargoes is shown as a single item. As imports of the first were given in weight and of the second in value, weight figures had to be converted to money values in accordance with the value statements given in the statistics.

[22] Quoted by Ridder, *op. cit.*, p. 141.

[23] According to Sombart, *Der moderne Kapitalismus* (Modern Capitalism), III, 1927, p. 100.

products; the American cotton crisis is undoubtedly responsible for this. The movements, of which the years 1866, 1873 and 1882 constitute the crisis points, also appear clearly; the situation in the last decade of the century is, however, somewhat erratic, since 1888 and 1891 are peak years, but 1895 is a nadir. The figures for coal do not provide any guide to long-term cyclical fluctuations. The nine-year averages show a regular and uninterrupted rise. The year 1850 shows an import surplus of less than 5,000,000 guilders, but 1896 an import surplus of almost 44,000,000 guilders.

Until in modern times chemical and electrical industries have come to take the lead, textile manufacture was the most important of all industrial activities, especially in the middle nineteenth century. The consumption of raw material for the textile industry is therefore of special importance in evaluating any country's economic condition. Import and export figures give a decisive answer here in case this material is unobtainable from domestic sources. This is the case with cotton. The annual import surplus for this raw material was relatively low before the end of the 1860s, owing to the fact that several years (1850, 1855, 1856, 1858, 1861, 1862, 1865) showed an export surplus. After 1870, when textiles revived with the introduction of free trade in this field, the consumption of raw cotton increased; export surpluses disappear, and consumption, which before 1870 was rarely more than 4,000,000 kg. a year, increased to between 10 and 20,000,000 kg. On closer inspection it appears that the international repercussions of economic fluctuations certainly did not leave consumption unaffected, but that other factors also exercised some influence. The trend line which indicates the course of the nine-year averages is moreover of particular interest because here too we can see a recession in the eighties; after an almost uninterrupted rise to 1882 there ensued a fall to 1890. Consumption subsequently rose more rapidly than it had fallen before 1890—movements which we have already observed in the consumption of wood.

One reason for the erratic course in the consumption of cotton can be given at once. Domestic production of cotton yarn was insufficient for the needs of the textile industry; in 1873 half the necessary cotton yarn had to be supplied from abroad.[24] Alongside the import of raw cotton, we have therefore to consider the import of cotton yarn. We cannot compute an import or export surplus here, as the export of domestically spun yarn and transit of yarn have to be taken into account.[25] Yet import figures are good for something. They bear out the observations made for raw cotton, that here also the influence of random factors was far greater than those of periodical cyclical fluctuations. An example: the crisis of 1873 caused only a slight reduction in yarn imports, and this was connected with the abolition of differential duties in the Dutch Indies in 1872. The cotton crisis in the United States, to which reference has been made, caused on the contrary a tremendous drop in imports: from more than 16,000,000 kg. in 1861, they fell to less than 4,000,000 kg. in 1863. The figures for the years after 1880 are likewise remarkable. From 1881 the import of yarn increased, a rise which continued till 1884 and is not affected by the crisis of 1882. The fall after 1884 can be explained by special con-

[24] J. A. P. G. Boot, *De Twentsche katoennijverheid 1830–1873* (The Cotton Industry of Twente, 1830–1873), 1935, p. 154; P. J. Bouman, *Rotterdam en het Duitsche achterland* (Rotterdam and the German Hinterland), 1931, p. 157.     [25] Boot, *ibid.*

ditions in Indonesia, where the sugar crisis of 1884 had caused a recession and decreased the demand for cotton goods. The special relation of our cotton industry in Twente to the Indies caused colonial factors to be much more decisive in creating ups and downs in this branch of industry than was the rhythm of economic life in Western Europe and America.

Up till now we have considered various raw materials, but import-export and transit trade figures can also yield insights into exports of industrial products. We have chosen three products: cordage, cotton goods and madder.

Until about 1875 the Netherlands was a country which exported a considerable amount of cordage. The products of rope walks and cordage works which existed here of old not only served to supply the needs of shipbuilding at home, but were also exported.[26] Imports of cordage were small. After 1875 this changed to such a degree that rising exports of cordage were overtaken by increased imports so that from then on the Netherlands imported more cordage than it exported. Therefore the picture presented by the pre-1875 data is the more trustworthy. These figures do not suggest that cordage exports felt the influence of cyclical fluctuations to any appreciable extent. There is some falling away between 1847 and 1857, though this is often greater in other years. Moreover the crisis of 1866 leaves no trace; on the contrary, the export of cordage even shows a rise after 1866, which continues till 1869. The same phenomenon occurs in 1882; the export of cordage does not fall after that year as might be expected, but rises with little interruption till 1890. An explanation of this unexpected situation will be given below.

Cotton goods were an important export product since King William I promoted the calico industry in Twente and elsewhere, in order to replace Southern Netherlands exports to the colonies. The larger part of these exports was manufactured in the Netherlands, so the figures for the export of 'manufactures, linens, and cotton goods, reflect reasonably accurately activity in the Dutch cotton industry. Figures for 1872 and the following years are not entirely comparable to those before 1872, since from that year on exports of cotton cloth are given in kilogrammes instead of in guilders. In spite of this difficulty the trend of development is clear enough. It seems indeed that there can be no question here of normal development—sales expansion in boom periods, restriction of exports in times of depression. Quite the contrary, as a rule, we see a rise in exports after a crisis year. Crisis years 1847, 1857, 1873 and 1883 mark, not the peaks, but the troughs of the curve. Only 1866 is a peak year, but this exception must be seen in connection with the cotton crisis which had abnormally reduced exports in preceding years.

Similar to cordage exports, the exports of cotton goods show a movement more or less contrary to the course of the economic cycle. That this is not accidental appears from the export pattern of quite a different product, madder. Until around 1870, when a chemical product was found to replace the red vegetable dye, madder cultivation was very extensive, especially in Zeeland, which had a great number of small factories ('madder stoves') where madder was dried, crushed and pulverized. Export figures (madder 'powdered, common and loose', show that the years 1857, 1866, 1873 and 1883 marked not peaks but troughs, thus starting points of a new upward movement, not depressions. Around the middle

---

[26] In the statistics shown as 'cable or netting, rigging and all other kinds of cordage' after 1863 with the addition 'and also cable and coiled rope'.

of the nineteenth century dyes began to be liberated from the madder root by means of sulphuric acid. This product was called garancine.[27] The export of garancine soon grew to be of some importance; its value amounted to about 3,000,000 guilders annually in the good years after 1855. The export surplus after 1846 shows no diminution at any time after crisis years; the years 1866 and 1872 do indeed show a minimum, but the recession of 1858 was completely reversed in the following year.

Now it is well known that imports of any given country are more susceptible to cyclical influence than are exports.[28] Exports depend upon the economic situation abroad, where the market is much wider and much less uniform than at home, with a territorially more restricted market. In times of slump there is always an urge to find new foreign markets where recessions are less violent than at home. This does not however sufficiently explain the phenomenon that Dutch industrial products profited from depression. For that we need a closer analysis of crisis phenomena in connection with the Dutch economic structure, along the lines given in Ridder's dissertation, of which mention has already been made, which makes valuable observations on this point.

Modern capitalist undertakings, characterized by mechanical power and other forms of large-scale production, feel the unfavourable influence of the depression in that the relation between the fixed and variable costs becomes more unfavourable. The greater the market, the smaller the fixed costs per production unit, so that contraction of the market causes a rise in fixed unit costs. This factor does not appear in undertakings not organized capitalistically, such as small-scale industry. Overhead expenses are small here, so it is only the difference between the selling price and the cost of the raw and auxiliary material and wages which is decisive. As a result small-scale industry can expand its market in times of slump. Having low fixed costs, it can sometimes offer its output advantageously during depression. An example of this state of affairs is supplied by the Schiedam distilleries which did not complain in the depression year of 1858, but profited from low corn prices.[29] Ridder's proposition that highly capitalized industry could profit from a boom while the pre- and early-capitalist industries fell into depression because of it[30] appears to be confirmed by the particulars given above. Closer research on a broader and more solid basis is much to be desired, especially since this export rise in periods of depression is typical of industrial organization which has not yet been modernized.

We can find a good indication of industrial development in the Netherlands, and of the cyclical changes occurring therein, in the import statistics of machinery and steam engines. Since the Dutch machine industry also exported its products, it would be misleading to calculate an import-export balance. The import figures possibly also include goods in transit, but notwithstanding this lack of precision the figures of imports remain of some interest. If we isolate the short cycles from the trend movement and the long-term fluctuations in the manner sketched in figure 3,

[27] Cf. the article by Miss B. W. van der Kloot Meyburg in *Econ. Hist. Jaarboek*, xviii, 1934, pp. 59ff.; P. J. Bouman, *Geschiedenis van den Zeeuwschen landbouw in de 19e en 20e eeuw* (History of Agriculture in Zeeland in the Nineteenth and Twentieth Centuries), 1946, pp. 23ff., 108.

[28] Cf. Wagemann, *op. cit.*, p. 154.

[29] Ridder, *op. cit.*, p. 160.          [30] *Ibid.*, p. 163.

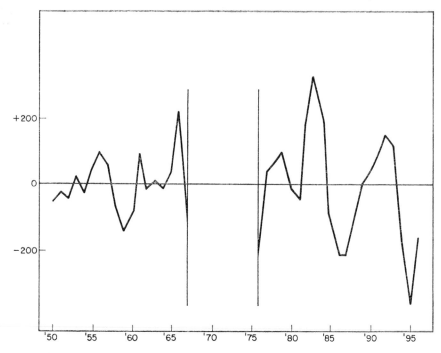

FIG. 3    Imports of machinery and steam engines (deviations from trend)

the seven-to-eleven-year cycle movement is clearly evident; a rising line from 1850 to 1856, a fall from that year to 1859, then a rise from 1859 to 1866. Because of the changes made in the official figures in 1872,[31] figures for 1868–75 are lacking. The year 1876 appears to be one of depression, the rise which then begins, continues until 1883, reversing to fall until 1886. The new rise is also clearly evident; it lasts till 1892, after which the depression begins till it reaches its lowest point in 1895.

If we take the line of nine-year averages from which the short waves have been eliminated (fig. 4), we get a picture which agrees with our own observations: uninterrupted rise with a reaction in the eighties, 1881–9. Thus it can be taken for certain that the development in the economic life of the Netherlands was retarded between 1880 and 1890.

To summarize, Dutch industry shows the following characteristics in the second half of the nineteenth century. The influence of international cyclical fluctuations was felt, though frequently overshadowed by special factors such as war, market opportunities in the Indies and the like. Cyclical fluctuations appear most clearly in the modern capitalistically organized industries according to figures for the import of machinery and steam engines or the consumption of iron. Small industries which still existed in great numbers reacted negatively to the economic cycle, since they exported their products and could quite often expand their

[31] From 1872 onwards, figures refer not to imports generally, but to retained imports. It is known that goods intended for transit were not thereafter declared as such; this is true above all for duty-free commodities, thus not for machines which paid a tariff of 1 per cent *ad valorem*.

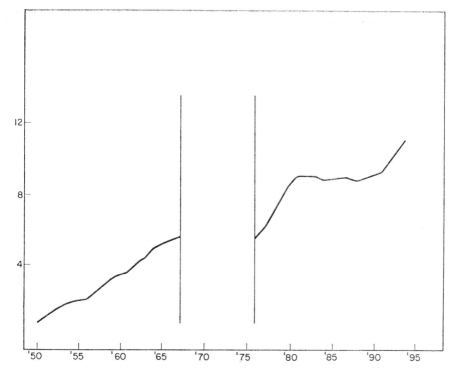

FIG. 4   Imports of machinery and steam engines (nine-year averages in million guilders)

market in times of depression, while it had decreased in boom years. Whether the same holds good for small-scale industry working for the home market, we cannot determine through lack of data. Figures available for canvas production in Krommenie[32] point in that direction; 1825 and 1826 are depression years, while 1857 is no more than a point on a curve moving downwards from 1854 onwards. These figures do not go beyond 1861. This field of research remains still unexplored.

# V

Import and export figures supply valuable information about industrial activity, and also contain data about the shipping industry from 1824 onwards.[33] To obtain reliable information we must of course consider not only the number of ships cleared, but also their constantly increasing carrying capacity. Tonnage figures of cargoes discharged show a continuous increase.[34]

[32] J. Zeeman, 'Statistiek van de zeildoekfabricage in Krommenie' (Statistics of Sail Cloth Manufacture in Krommenie), *Staatk. en Staathuisk. Jaarboekje*, 1863, p. 418. That the toy manufacturers of the Thüringer Wald came through the crisis of 1873 unharmed is apparent from K. Bücher, *Die Entstehung der Volkswirtschaft* (The Genesis of National Economy), II, 3rd ed., 1920, p. 166.
[33] Figures for trade and shipping in 1846 contain a retrospective survey from 1824.
[34] From 1876 onwards cubic metres must be converted into tons by dividing them by 2,214 (cf. *Voorbericht statistiek In-, Uit- en Doorvoer*, 1876, Pt. II, p. xiv).

When we once again divide short- from long-term fluctuations, we find that short cyclical waves are not everywhere in evidence and that here also special circumstances are of considerable significance. This is understandable. Dutch shipping was in contact with the whole world, which in the nature of things does not come under the influence of cyclical movements simultaneously or in the same way; some parts may even remain exempted. We note immediately that there is no trace of the crisis of 1836. On the contrary, the years 1837–9 show an increase, although this period is recognized as one of depression in Britain, France and the United States. But Germany, which like the Netherlands had not then reached the modern capitalist phase, did not experience a recession;[35] Dutch shipping to the Indies was even active. During this period cultivation[36] was determined by the government and, not being subject to cyclical influence, began to yield its first considerable profits. Also in this period exports of cotton goods to the Netherlands Indies increased considerably.[37] The boom beginning in 1845 was also noticeable in shipping, but the recession after 1847 was replaced by an upward movement in the very next year, so that a peak is visible in 1852, between the peaks of 1847 and 1857. Looking at short cycles we observe that the crisis of 1873 was more pronounced than that of 1866. Moreover, shipping seems thereafter to be less susceptible than industry to cyclical influence; whereas the depression begun in 1873 lasts till 1879 in most countries, Dutch shipping shows an important increase between 1875 and 1877. The depression after 1882 lasts till 1886. However, the picture during the last two decades is somewhat obscure.

By eliminating short-term movements, however, the course of development in shipping becomes clear: an uninterrupted rise without any more question of recession. We notice that the rise accelerates all the time. Between 1828 and 1850, the increase in cleared tonnage is 80 per cent. Between 1850 and 1873 it reaches 163 per cent, between 1873 and 1895 it is 224 per cent. There is thus no question of deceleration in the pace of development after 1880 and even less of any ebb in the period 1873 to 1895. There are many reasons why Dutch overseas shipping in the nineteenth century should be reinvestigated.

Another aspect of economic life that was clearly subject to cyclical rhythm is money and banking. Banking developed late in this country. Until the mid-nineteenth century there was in the Netherlands only the *Nederlandsche Bank*, being the bank of issue, but no bank which accepted deposits and made loans. There was hardly any large-scale industry seeking loan capital; banking thus had no occasion to provide industrial finance. Smaller concerns also stood in little need of organized credit machinery. Trading on borrowed money was treated as gambling. A merchant needing money would borrow it from other trading houses or from retired merchants, since prevailing rates of interest did not attract much capital from outside lenders. Most loans were negotiated outside the public money market.[38] It was only after 1860 that modern banking developed.[39] Figures for the *Nederlandsche Bank*, now well-known thanks to the excellent work of Mr A. M. de

---

[35] Cf. Spiethoff, *op. cit.*, p. 48.
[36] In the Netherlands Indies [Transl.].
[37] Figures in Boot, *op. cit.*, p. 72.          [38] Ridder, *op. cit.*, p. 62.
[39] I. J. Brugmans, *De arbeidende klasse in Nederland in de 19e eeuw* (The Working Class in the Netherlands in the Nineteenth Century), 2nd ed., 1967, pp. 79–80.

Jong,[40] do not accurately reflect economic life in the Netherlands in the earlier years. It is for example to be noted that banks played no part in the economic upsurge which took place here after 1850.[41] This is why we do not draw on *Nederlandsche Bank* material for our investigations.

A single remark on the rate of interest. As is well known, this rises in times of boom, to fall again in times of depression, with the proviso that interest rates react more slowly than other factors to cyclical changes. Nineteenth-century changes in interest rates in this country represent the economic situation less well than they would do today. They reflect the foreign rather than the domestic business cycle and are a barometer rather of capitalist prosperity than of industrial development. With this restriction in mind it is worth while to examine changes in the prices of our government stocks in the nineteenth century. Figures for these are available from 1844 onwards, the year of our financial reconstruction.[42] If we take the highest annual prices for Netherlands 2½ per cent irredeemable stock and from these compute nine-year averages, we see from the short fluctuations (deviations from the nine-year averages) that rates are determined by two factors: the relation between demand for, and supply of, capital, and the confidence of investors in government credit. This explains the abnormally strong fluctuations of around 1850. Investors' confidence had been shaken in the days of revolutions and caused low prices of government bonds in 1848 and 1849, notwithstanding the crisis of 1847. Only in 1850-2 does a rise of interest in the price of bonds reflect abundance in the capital market. Ridder's remark that the stock exchange was hardly influenced by economic events,[43] is valid for the following years. This was to be expected: there was as yet no link between industry and the capital market to cause cyclical fluctuations therein. We do not observe in the figures any reflection of the crisis of 1857. But things are different for the following crisis: prices show a hardening tendency after 1867 as well as after 1873. In the crisis which began for most countries in 1882, it is again apparent that confidence plays an important part: that the fall continues till 1885 may perhaps be connected with the shock to the whole credit system from the credit stringency of 1884 in America. Interest rates became more regular after 1890. Around 1891 we observe rises in 2½ per cent Netherlands government irredeemable stock. It should be borne in mind that these figures represent the highest prices in any one year, so that a single day of panic can change the picture for the whole year.

The influence of long cycles is clearly manifest in the rate of interest and is represented in day-to-day prices of 2½ per cent Netherlands irredeemable stock. Between 1856 and 1870 there is a continuous clearly marked fall. The rise beginning after that year continues till about 1895. The reaction which set in during the last years of the nineteenth century is visible in falling security prices; the rising tendency of the years 1848-56 could be an offshoot of the slower pace of the years 1820-48. In any case a fall in security prices means rising interest rates and *vice versa*, so that the long cycle manifests itself here with undeniable clarity in the shape

---

[40] A. M. de Jong, *Geschiedenis van de Nederlandsche Bank* (History of the Netherlands Bank), I, 1930, reprinted 1967.
[41] Ridder, *op. cit.*, p. 75.
[42] Published as an appendix to National Income Statistics in 1912, p. 113.
[43] Ridder, *op. cit.*, p. 90.

of rising interest rates between 1850 and 1870, and falling interest rates between 1870 and 1895. We can assume that the remarkable revival of Dutch economic life[44] since 1870 has profited from this low rate of interest. In other countries whose industrial revolution had been largely completed, low interest rates were symptomatic of a certain degree of saturation—evidence therefore of slackening progress. In the Netherlands where the impetus of modern capitalism came late, low interest rates facilitated modern industrial development. Here we have a phenomenon analogous to that observed for small-scale industries, where the fall in prices accompanying the depression not seldom appeared advantageous.

# VI

Prices are important as an index of economic prosperity. On the upswing prices tend to rise, while they fall in a period of depression. Prices of agricultural products provide about the only consecutive series for the whole (or a large part) of the nineteenth century; we have no figures for clothing and housing. Here we are faced with the special difficulty that prices of agricultural products are determined by harvest results which are beyond human influence. Yet there is a connection between prices of agricultural products and the business cycle, since what is influenced by the expectation of prices is not the volume of crop yield, but that of crop planted; the demand for agricultural products is also greater in good times than in times of depression, while a good crop increases farmers' ability to purchase commodities. Thus a bad crop can mean the end of a boom period while a good crop increases the farmers' purchasing power. Spiethoff[45] rightly concludes that it most certainly will not do to rule out crops as being without historical significance. A weakness in Ridder's dissertation to which reference has already been made, is that agriculture is ruled out systematically on theoretical grounds.[46]

The sources for agricultural prices are the following: in the first place there are a couple of publications by the Central Office for Statistics from the beginning of this century. One surveys market prices for grain at Arnhem from 1544 to 1901;[47] the other, market prices of grain at Middelburg, and rentals of farms in Walcheren in the years 1801–1900.[48] The Arnhem figures do not explain how the yearly prices are arrived at; for Middelburg the yearly averages of the weekly price quotations were taken from the *Middelburgsche Courant* newspaper. Secondly, we have agricultural reports which generally contain much material important for economic history. From these can be obtained the following data. First, highest and lowest prices of agricultural products at the public markets in Leiden in 1824–50.[49]

[44] I. J. Brugmans, *op. cit.*, pp. 220ff.

[45] Spiethoff, *op. cit.*, p. 21. The quotation in the original text is given in German [Eds.].

[46] On the connection between industrial and agricultural cycles, cf. Wagemann, *op. cit.*, pp. 146ff.

[47] 'Bijdragen tot de statistiek van Nederland' (Contributions to Netherlands Statistics), *Nieuwe Volgreeks*, XXVI, 1903. Cf. also fig. 5.

[48] *Loc. cit.*, XLVI, 1904.

[49] *Landbouwverslag*, 1847, supplement N (for the years 1824–47), continued in 1848, supplement F, 1849, supplement B, 1850, supplement D.

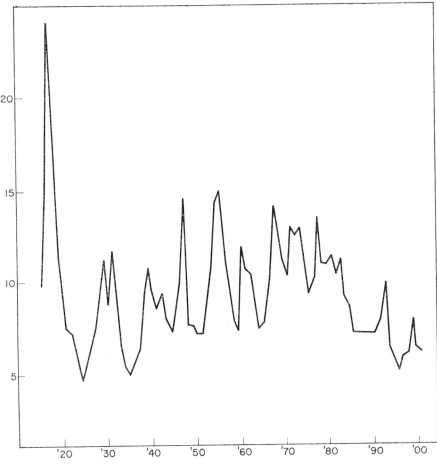

FIG. 5 Wheat prices at Arnhem (guilders per hectolitre)

Second, highest average prices of butter on the market at Leeuwarden from 1832 onwards.[50] Highest daily prices were added together and divided by the number of market days. Thirdly, annual price averages in the Netherlands for some agricultural products, 1851–1900.[51] These figures were only roughly calculated: the total value of the crop given in the old agricultural reports was divided by the amount harvested. Such a method yields only approximate results.

Other sources to be considered are: fourthly, a list of prices charged for food, etc. furnished to the Institution at Meerenberg.[52] Fifthly, a list of market prices at Utrecht published in the *Oud Utrecht* Yearbook of 1933.[53] As his sources were only

[50] *Loc. cit.*, 1908, p. 101.
[51] *Loc. cit.*, 1900, I, p. 525.
[52] *Jaarcijfers* (Statistical Yearbook), 1891, p. 47, j⁰. 1900, p. 73.
[53] W. H. Vertmooten, 'Schets van de geschiedenis van het Utrechtsche markwezen in de 19e eeuw' (Outline History of Market Regulations at Utrecht in the Nineteenth Century), *Oud Utrecht*, 1933, pp. 157ff.

of weekly prices, the writer of this article took the quotations for about 16 April every year, which greatly increases the random factor. Sixthly, the Government Gazette, which has never been used as a source for our price history, contains among other things a 'three-monthly price-list of the amount for which some articles taxed by value could be declared'. These price lists were drawn up by sworn Amsterdam brokers[54] and are important because they refer not only to agricultural products but also to spices and groceries, drugs, paints and whalebone. The value of official lists is of course dubious,[55] but we can assume that the brokers concerned recorded price changes with approximate accuracy. Seventhly, some years ago a publication began to appear which attempted to survey available price material for the first time. We refer to the work of N. W. Posthumus, the *Netherlands Price History*, of which the first, and so far the only volume appeared in 1943 [second volume 1964, published in Leiden. Transl.]. Besides exchange rates this first volume surveys prices of commodities on the Amsterdam produce exchange from 1585 to 1914. Grain prices play an important part, but also others, for instance prices of colonial wares, textiles and metals are given. When we first published our study of the Dutch cyclical pattern in the nineteenth century (1936), the definitive work of Posthumus had not yet been published, and we have to admit that we did not use this almost overwhelming body of facts to the full. For the time being we must be content to remark that the conclusions drawn from the scanty material then available are confirmed by statistics in the *Netherlands Price History*.

Our examination of prices in the Netherlands in the nineteenth century must begin with grain, for there is no group of commodities about which figures are available in so continuous a series, even after Posthumus' publication.

After the Netherlands had regained its freedom (1813), the high grain prices of the French period, with its abnormal conditions, did not at once decline. Only gradually could the normal course of business be restored; moreover harvests in the immediately succeeding years were not very good. Thus, 1817 was a peak year with a price level higher than had ever been reached before. But after 1817 the fall in prices was greater than at any time later in the nineteenth century.[56] This fall lasted till about 1825, but was at its most rapid between 1817 and 1820. The price of wheat at Arnhem per hectolitre was fl. 19·66 in 1817, fl. 8·10 in 1820 and fl. 4·27 in 1826, the lowest point. This fall was due in great part to protective measures taken by other countries against our grain exports. After 1818 our grain was everywhere prohibited, in Britain, France, Spain, Russia and Prussia.[57] On the other hand, the Netherlands did not prohibit the import of foreign grain. This was especially important to Russia which began to be a grain exporter around this time.

It is no wonder that the demand for protection became stronger and stronger. It was responded to in 1825: import duties which had afforded some small measure

[54] In pursuance of art. 49 of the order of 12 May 1819, *Stbl.* (Official Gazette), No. 20, j⁰; art. 123 of the order of 26 Aug. 1822, *Stbl.*, No. 38.
[55] Somewhat analogous are the Swedish *markegangstaxor*; cf. G. Myrdal, *The Cost of Living in Sweden 1830–1930*, 1933, pp. 25ff.
[56] Blink is mistaken in writing that grain prices began to fall about 1820; by 1820 this fall was almost completed. H. Blink, *Geschiedenis van den boerenstand en den landbouw in Nederland* (History of the Peasant Class and of Agriculture in the Netherlands), II, 1904, p. 295.
[57] *Ibid.*

of protection from 1822 were considerably increased. This brought the desired rise in prices; from 1824 till 1829–31 grain prices rose, but the old high level was far from being regained.

The secession of protectionist-inclined Belgium forced the government to a new course. Considering that the unusual economic circumstances in which this country found itself ought not to be aggravated by high food prices, the king decided upon a reduction of import duties on grain in 1830. The result was indeed a fall in grain prices which lasted until 1835, but not to as low a point as in 1825.

In 1835 there was a further move towards protection. Agriculture had once more to be supported, and by a new system, that of the so-called sliding scale of duties, which moved in accordance with domestic prices.[58] Thanks to these regulations, grain prices again rose after 1835, a rise which lasted till 1839.

1839–44 was a period of falling grain prices. This fall was not connected with tariff regulations but must be attributed to declining domestic consumption: these are the years in which the Netherlands almost succumbed to the heavy financial burdens of war with Belgium, until Van Hall in 1844 was able to restore health to the Dutch economy.

In 1845 a beginning was made towards freeing the grain trade, in accordance with the prevailing tendency throughout Europe—Britain's famous repeal of the corn laws was in 1846. Sliding scale duties were suspended in 1845 and 1846 and abolished in 1847, to be replaced by a fixed import duty. This was lowered in 1853 and finally abolished in 1877.[59] That this policy of freeing the trade was accompanied by rising grain prices in 1844–7, is due to special circumstances, there being poor harvests in these years. After our country had been afflicted by potato blight in 1845, 1846 yielded slender crops, so that 1847, the year of crisis in the business cycle, was also a year of high prices of agricultural products. It was only in 1848–53 that prices really began to decline. The Crimean War, which had stopped Russian exports, caused a temporary abnormal rise in grain prices, so that a fall became inevitable, lasting till 1859. Thereafter prices tended to rise, a tendency sometimes interrupted by depressions, until the beginning of the great agricultural depression caused, as is well known, by the influx of grain from America.

According to Blink, who bases his opinion on a statement of D. R. Mansholt, the great fall set in 1877.[60] The material described above gives a slightly different picture. At Middelburg the price of wheat reached its peak in 1877. But at Arnhem (see fig. 5.) this had already appeared in 1874, while 1873 is the peak for average prices throughout the Netherlands, if the returns can be trusted. The price of rye was at its maximum at Middelburg as well as at Arnhem in 1874, while 1874 also appears a peak point for the average over the Netherlands as a whole. Noting further that the price of barley reached its peak at Arnhem in 1875, and at Middelburg in 1874, and that the price of oats reached a peak in 1875 at Arnhem and buckwheat in 1874, it appears that Blink postdated the beginning of the agricultural crisis by several years. In any case the great fall began in the seventies, and continued till 1895, after which a new upward movement began.

The movement sketched here is valid not only for such grains as wheat, rye,

---

[58] Z. W. Sneller, *Geschiedenis van den Nederlandschen landbouw 1795–1904* (History of Netherlands Agriculture 1795–1904), 1943, p. 50.
[59] *Ibid.*, p. 51.   [60] Blink, *op. cit.*, pp. 311–2.

barley and oats, but also for an agricultural product such as buckwheat. That the movement differs from that presented by some other products such as green peas, white beans, horse beans and cole-seed, may be ignored, for the main course of development can be seen here also. Only cole-seed shows fluctuations that do not occur in other agricultural products, possibly due to the fact that the province of Groningen, the centre of cole-seed farming, exported elsewhere and also imported from East Friesland.[61] The cultivation of cole-seed was considered a risky business, both because prices fluctuated wildly and because this crop was particularly liable to disease.[62]

In general, fluctuations in prices of wheat are regarded as the best indication of price levels as a whole.[63] It is possible in some measure to verify this opinion by comparing fluctuations in wheat prices with those of potatoes, the main national food for the greater part of the nineteenth century, and of butter and meat. Price lists available for potatoes in the first half of the century, at Leiden and Utrecht, show that the movement in prices of potatoes runs fully parallel with those of wheat: a rise between 1824, 1827 and 1830, a fall from 1830 to 1833, a rise from 1833 to 1839,[64] a fall from 1839 to 1844, a rise from 1844 to 1847, a fall from 1847 to 1850. This parallel between potato and wheat prices remains till after the middle of the century, with the exception only that the fall after the seventies was less perceptible here than in the wheat prices, this appearing most clearly from the prices made under contract for the Meerenberg Institution. It should be noted further that potato prices follow those for barley even more closely than they do the wheat prices; this of course is due to the fact that potatoes, like barley, are usually grown on sandy soil.

A single remark will suffice on the subject of butter prices, since these also move similarly to wheat. The agricultural crisis can be seen here to occur after the peak year of 1876. Prices of beef and mutton at Leiden to 1850 show the same fluctuations as we observed for wheat. For the period after 1850 we know only the prices of the beef contract for the Meerenberg Institution, which on the whole are only a damped-down version of prices on the free market and should therefore be used with reservation. It is especially to be noted that there is scarcely any trace here of an agricultural crisis, for only after 1844 does there appear a falling tendency, lasting beyond 1885.

From the foregoing we can conclude that at least as far as food prices are concerned, wheat prices give a fairly good indication of fluctuations of the price level in general; it must also be borne in mind that grain is used not only as food for man and beast, but also as a raw material in industry (distilleries, breweries).

The question now arising is as follows: what was the relation between the movement in prices of agricultural products, as sketched above, and the movement of long and short cycles? If we take as our measure the prices of wheat which sufficiently represent agricultural price levels, it seems that prices of agricultural products react to short cycles in the second half of the nineteenth century, but not

[61] *Ibid.*, p. 306.
[62] P. J. Bouman, *Zeeuwsche landbouw* (Agriculture in Zeeland), p. 102 (for full reference, cf. n. 27).
[63] A. L. B[owley], *op. cit.*, (cf. n. 10), p. 473: 'On a broad view it is seen that the price of wheat has moved with the price of things in general.'
[64] The Leiden figures only go back to averages for the years 1824–7.

in the first. 1825, the year of the first economic crisis, is also the year which sees the end of the tremendous fall in prices of agricultural products, that which set in after 1817. Moreover, 1836 was not a crisis year for the Dutch farmer because, as already indicated, the period 1835–9 was one of rising prices for agricultural products. 1839 showed a crisis in industry in Western Europe which was an offshoot of that of 1836. That prices of wheat fell here after 1839 was the result of the end of the war with Belgium rather than evidence of cyclical influence. This is also true of 1847, when grain prices show a peak as a result of harvest failure.

We mentioned earlier that the Crimean War caused a considerable rise in grain prices, due to lack of Russian grain. The peak came in 1855. At the coming of the downturn in 1857, grain prices were therefore already falling fast, a fall which continued to 1858 or 1859, but had been more or less completed by 1857. The continuing relative prosperity of the farmers mitigated the effect of the 1857 crisis on the industrial economy. It is said that brickmaking continued to profit from the expansion of sheds and barns after 1857 and that the woollen cloth industry continued to prosper because of continuing demand from agricultural areas.[65] Nor can we say of the year 1866 that the industrial and agricultural crises proceeded side by side. Grain prices, which had reached their lowest level in 1864–5, rose again in 1867–8. So there can be no question of a relapse in 1866.

After this year the relationship began to change. 1873 and 1874 are years in which grain reached a very high price; the fall thereafter thus proceeded in absolute conformity with the downturn of the cyclical curve from its zenith in 1873. It was no different in 1882; the fall in grain prices of 1874 continued without interruption until 1895, but was steepest after 1882. Around 1890 we see the economic development of agriculture and industry following the same course. Only in the years 1888–91 is there a temporary reaction from the continuing drop in prices, in the shape of a price rise reverting to a drop after 1891.

We can indicate three causes for the fact that grain prices show no connection with the cyclical rhythm until after the middle of the nineteenth century, but do so later on. In the first place the prevailing agricultural protectionism of the first half of the century caused an artificial rise in prices; price fluctuations represented the differential pressures of protection, and influences operating on the free market could be neutralized by protectionist regulations. When protection ended—the last remnant disappeared in 1877—grain prices more accurately reflected the state of economic life. In addition, we can suggest secondly that the farming class increasingly lost its self-sufficiency, especially after the great agricultural crisis in the seventies, and began to produce for the world market instead of growing crops for home consumption. The farmer became more and more of an agricultural entrepreneur and this increased his dependence upon the state of the world market. In modern times the farmer cuts down his demands upon productive resources, and for commodities, during periods of depression, in line with the town-dweller.[66] As a third factor we could indicate that the non-agricultural part of the Dutch economy also felt the full impact of the cyclical influence rather late. Special circumstances exercised more influence on the course of affairs in trade and industry

[65] Ridder, *op. cit.*, pp. 162, 169.
[66] Cf. F. Beckmann, 'Der deutsche Bauer im Zeitalter des Kapitalismus' (The German Peasant in the Age of Capitalism), in *Schmollers Jahrbuch*, L, 1926, pp. 719ff.

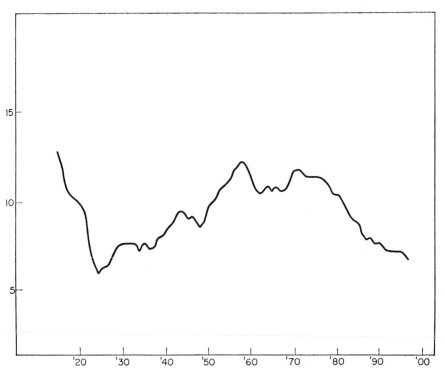

FIG. 6   Wheat prices at Arnhem (guilders per hectolitre, nine-year averages)

than did periodic fluctuations, which is why agriculture can hardly be expected to be highly susceptible to cyclical influences.

We should now examine the relation between the prices of agricultural products and the long cyclical waves. If we observe the line indicating nine-year average-of prices of wheat at Arnhem (fig. 6), we see at once how different were Nethers lands circumstances from those in surrounding countries. There is the same fall between 1870 and 1895 as elsewhere, but before that the picture is quite different. After the tremendous price fall up to 1825, we see a rise in Netherlands prices that continues with minor fluctuations to the end of the fifties. In the sixties there is a certain hesitation which after 1870 is replaced by a constant fall. In Britain, however, the price-line for agricultural products is totally different: fall, 1810–40; rise, 1848–70. In the United States there is the same tendency: fall, 1817–43 (here the decline lasts for a rather shorter time than elsewhere); rise, 1843–74.[67]

This state of affairs requires special comment. That the Netherlands between 1825 and 1850 had continually rising grain prices when these were falling else-where, certainly increased considerably the stagnation of our contemporary econo-mic life. High taxes, and especially the duty on milling, must also bear some responsibility. The complaint that the Netherlands could not compete with

[67] N. D. Kondratieff, 'Die Preisdynamik der industriellen und landwirtschaftlichen Waren' (The Dynamics of Prices of Industrial and Agricultural Commodities), *Archiv für Sozialwiss. und Sozialpol.*, LX, 1928, pp. 31, 33.

foreigners because of high taxation and high food prices is only too just. The further complaint, that the labouring class got poorer since wages were not adjusted to higher costs of living is likewise confirmed by figures referred to here.[68] On the other hand Dutch economic life must have profited from the fact that between 1860 and 1870 our prices did not rise, while elsewhere the price rise begun in 1850 lasted to 1870. The period 1850–70 is indeed the period of transition into modern capitalistic structure[69] in the Netherlands' economy, so that after 1870 our country no longer occupied its former backward position among other Western European nations.

We do not have enough figures to answer the question whether the price movement of non-agricultural products followed a similar course. The quarterly price quotations previously referred to, given in the Government Gazette, refer mainly to goods of little importance for daily life; this list also gets shorter and shorter and disappears almost completely with the tariff law of 1862. Moreover, the figures collected by Posthumus about prices on the Amsterdam produce exchange are not such as to allow positive conclusions, partly because consecutive series of figures covering the whole century are far less frequent than one might have hoped, but also because several of the articles dealt with there show a movement of their own, which is apparently influenced less by cyclical than by special causes. More intensive research into these matters is required.

# VII

The economy of the Netherlands in the nineteenth century was in transition from early to modern capitalism. The influence of cyclical fluctuations, which by then were part of the economic life of the more advanced countries of Western Europe and the United States, was not deeply felt in the Netherlands. This can be explained partly in psychological terms; the Dutch nature appears not to have been easily tempted to sanguine expectations about possible developments at home and in the colonies, and to have had a certain immunity to foreign speculative fevers But above all, at least until 1870, the conditions for a strong cyclical rhythm had not yet been created: we had neither power-operated large-scale industry nor a banking system in overall control. According to the figures for imports of iron, machinery and steam engines, it was the up-to-date industries organized on modern lines which felt most strongly the influence of cyclical fluctuations, though here also special circumstances such as the cotton crisis and market possibilities in the Indies often had an even greater influence. Small-scale industry often reacted negatively to the economic cycle, taking advantage of the low prices of raw materials in time of depression; thus the presence of small-scale industry mitigated the influence of cyclical fluctuations. The fact that the crisis sometimes appeared later here than elsewhere seems to indicate that the cyclical fluctuations met with some resistance in the Netherlands; in particular the crises of 1882 and 1890 seem to manifest themselves here only in 1883 and 1891.

The industrial revolution came late in the Netherlands, later than in the

[68] I. J. Brugmans, *op. cit.*, pp. 134ff.    [69] *Ibid.*, pp. 21ff.

F

surrounding countries. That is why the slowing down of the pace of development, perceptible in other countries between 1873 and 1895, appeared here in the eighties only in a moderate form. That is also why until 1866 prices of agriculturas products could move in a way completely different from that of the general cycle; thus besides small-scale industry, agriculture helped to neutralize cyclical influences. The fact that prices of agricultural products in the Netherlands in the first half of the century moved in a direction quite contrary to that in other countries contributed more than anything else to keeping the economy stagnant and backward.

# Industrial Crises

# in Russia 1847-67

S. STRUMILIN

Translated by Malcolm E. Falkus

An important study of international economic crises has recently been published by a body of Soviet economists.[1] From the first page, however, one is struck by a glaring omission—Russia. Why, in this monumental enquiry into the history of capitalist nations, has no place been found for capitalist Russia?

The various industrial crises embraced by the study are listed in the first table. They cover the period 1825 to 1929, and all major countries are included, even Japan. Yet Russia is ignored.

Why should the authors of *World Economic Crises* neglect Russia in this way? Perhaps they would rank Russia as only a second-class power, equivalent to, say, Belgium, Denmark or Holland, which had little 'international' significance. Perhaps the authors considered Russia to have been free from capitalist crises. Perhaps these 'internationalists' lacked sufficient interest in the past of their own country. Such explanations should not surprise us. Regrettably, Russia's history attracts very little attention from her own economists.

The authors of *World Economic Crises* have not omitted all reference to Russia. In this massive work of over 800 pages the reader can indeed find about 30 lines dealing with Russian crises. But for the period up to 1900 (that is, the period of development of industrial capitalism) there is no word about Russia. For the subsequent period (monopolistic capitalism) we find some 'enlightening' comments on the crises of 1900, when it is claimed that, in this year, 'for the first time a clearly marked cyclical pattern appeared in Japan's industrial development' and 'the first crisis occurred in Russia'. The authors continue: 'in this study we will not give an exhaustive analysis of industrial cycles in Tsarist Russia because they started comparatively late and had already finished by 1913.' Instead of any further clarification or analysis, the authors merely note that their diagrams 'to a certain extent illustrate the cyclical nature of industrial production in Russia'.

Unfortunately however, these diagrams do not provide the slightest confirmation of a 'comparatively late' starting date (1900) for the Russian crises, nor of the suggested finishing date of 1913. It is well known that the year 1913 was not one of economic crisis, either in Europe or in the United States. Consequently, 1907

[1] *World Economic Crises* (*1848–1935*), Vol. 1, Moscow 1937, p. 4 (in Russian). *Editors' note:* subsequent source references in the original article have been omitted.

should be taken as the year of Russia's last industrial crisis. With regard to the beginning of these industrial cycles, the authors of *World Economic Crises* have taken a big step backwards even by comparison with the outdated study by Tugan-Baranovsky. Thus, Tugan-Baranovsky was aware not only of the 1900 crisis, but of the 'hesitation' and 'depression' of the early 1890s, the 'stagnation' and 'crisis of heavy industry' during the 1880s, the 'crisis and bankruptcy' at the beginning of the 1870s, and even the 'general industrial and commercial stagnation' of 1857.

The year 1857 marked the first international crisis, according to *World Economic Crises*. In what sense, therefore, can it be maintained that Russia, which experienced crises in 1857 and in subsequent years, 'began comparatively late'? Compared with what? Compared with world crises in the nineteenth century? If the authors seriously consider 1900 to have seen the initial capitalist crisis in Russia, then a number of errors follow. For example, is it possible that throughout the entire period of Russia's industrial capitalism there were no industrial crises? After about 1900 Russia entered the stage of imperialism. The logical conclusions from *World Economic Crises* would therefore have to be either the anti-Marxist proposition that capitalism could develop without industrial crises, or that Russia was not in fact a capitalist country in the second half of the nineteenth century— a position held by the *Narodniki*[2] but refuted by Lenin. Further, if the nineteenth century saw no industrial crises in Russia, then Russia must have by-passed capitalism altogether, proceeding directly from the feudal to the imperialistic stage of development. Is it plausible to believe in such an extravagant historical jump? The answer must of course be 'no'. There are many reasons for studying the economic development of one's own country, and one of these must be to avoid the type of historical errors we have been discussing, which run counter to Marxist analysis. Russia's economists have neglected the history of their country, as mentioned before, but it is worth adding that existing materials for such research are more than adequate.

Tugan-Baranovsky was able to discover only three crises in Russia prior to 1900. It is now possible to say with certainty that none of the international cyclical crises up to 1907 failed to influence Russian industries to some extent. There is nothing surprising in this. No matter what stage of industrial development a country had reached, once drawn into the orbit of world trade it was unable to escape the pervasive and elemental impact of world crises. Upheaval could not be avoided in the absence of a foreign trade monopoly utilized by a socialist society in the conscious planning of its economy.

The origin of these industrial crises has been explained by Marx, who pointed to the basic contradictions of capitalism. The private capitalist, in his unbridled pursuit of profits, blindly increases production until output reaches the low ceiling of effective demand. As output grows and profits increase, so the means of production grow disproportionately to the means of consumption. Ultimately, when production outstrips the limited purchasing power of the working masses, a crisis inevitably follows. Succeeding the crisis comes a new, though temporary, possibility to renew investment and once more to raise production, until again the dis-

---

[2] *Translator's note*: A movement which developed among intellectuals from the 1870s, advocating agriculture as the basis of a revolutionized society.

proportion between profits and wages leads to another of the periodic depressions. The Marxist theory of industrial crises is too familiar to require further elaboration here.

It is important to emphasize, however, that the organization of industrial production meant inevitably that a crisis in one industry spread as a chain-reaction throughout the economy. For example, greater production of printed cotton goods would not be possible without a corresponding increase of yarn and woven cloth. Similarly, a curtailing of printed goods production would lead to a decline in the output of calico and, consequently, of yarn. As specialization and division of labour developed, so the chain-reaction linking industrial production throughout the economy accelerated. Also, after each crisis had spent its force, there followed a period of renewal and expansion of industrial investment.

An industrial crisis entailed declining production and a lower standard of living of the working classes. As a consequence, the import and export capability of the country would be reduced. In this way, under capitalism, a crisis in one country would spread to others through the mechanism of foreign trade and the corresponding network of international credit and world prices. A national crisis thus becomes a world crisis.

In such an international crisis, the victims are not only the advanced capitalist nations, but also backward colonial and semi-colonial countries which have been drawn into world trade. Moreover, historical experience shows that even the most backward countries, once brought within the international economy, are by no means always the last to feel the influence of world crises. On the contrary, being the weakest links in the capitalist chain, they frequently suffer earlier than advanced countries, and in this way they sometimes signal the starting-point for the development of a general crisis. Examples of such starting-points were Australia, Java and Brazil for the international crisis of the 1850s, and Argentina, Transvaal, Uruguay, Mexico, and other similar backward countries for the crisis of 1890.

Even during Russia's feudal period large quantities of foodstuffs and raw materials were exported in exchange for the surplus industrial products of capitalist nations. By 1860 Russian foreign trade amounted to over 340 million roubles, which was nearly twice the value of total factory production at that date. Statistics of foreign trade show that in each world crisis, accompanied as it was by a lowering of prices and effective demand, there was a decline in Russia's total external trade. I have estimated that the extent of this decline during the six crises following the emancipation of the serfs in 1861, that is from 1867 to 1908, amounted to not less than 2,000 million roubles, of which the drop in exports alone was more than 1,112 million roubles. Falling prices for the products of Russian agriculture, such as grain, butter, eggs, flax and hides, were responsible for much of this large decline in export values. Clearly such a decrease in rural earnings, effectively sacrificing many millions of Russian workers to the Moloch of world capitalism, would not be without consequence for Russia's internal market. In a world depression, the peasants were unable to sell a significant part of their marketable produce and what they could sell fetched miserably low prices. As a result, the Russian village reduced its demand for domestic industrial products such as textiles, sugar, kerosene and metal manufactures. If we remember also the direct dependence of many of Russia's industries on imported goods (machinery, raw cotton, paints, chemicals, etc.), then the impact of a world slump on Russian industry can be clearly appreciated.

In considering the effect of a world cyclical depression on a backward country, we must distinguish between a country experiencing limited periodic misfortunes and one experiencing a genuine industrial crisis. For the latter to occur, the country must necessarily have developed a certain minimum scale of industrial activity organized on a capitalist basis. Industry itself must also have reached a certain level of technological development. For example, it is well known that until the Industrial Revolution at the end of the eighteenth century, Britain, despite the existence of capitalist production, did not experience industrial crises. In the following epoch, however, the introduction of mechanization led to frequent crises as production quickly outstripped the effective demand of the population. Earlier, apparently, such a growth rate had not been possible within the confines of handicraft technology.

By the middle of the nineteenth century Russian industry, organized as it was in a feudal manner, lagged considerably by comparison with industry in Britain,[3] or even in post-revolutionary France. The lag was not so great, however, between Russia and Central European countries such as Austria and Prussia. Up to the 1848 revolutions these countries had not completely ended the old forms of feudal serfdom, and handicraft production still dominated their industries. At that time the basis of modern industry everywhere was mechanized cotton spinning and the manufacture of machinery. Russia, for example, had a total of only twenty-five mechanized factories in 1850. All the more significant was the large share of Britain's exports of machinery taken by Russia. In 1848, out of total British exports of £817,000, Russia, according to British data, took no less than 26 per cent. Thus it is evident that Russia was far from being the least important country in this branch of trade. Russian statistics show that, between 1820 and 1840, the import of machinery rose ninefold and in 1850 the value of such imports reached 2,315,000 roubles; the total value of machinery imported over the period 1824–47 amounted to at least 17·4 million roubles.

Cotton spinning was the most important branch of mechanized industry in Russia in this period, and its development can be gauged by the imports of raw cotton. In 1820 Russia imported about 1,000 metric tons, in 1830 2,500, in 1840 6,500, by 1850 as much as 20,000 tons. Over the same period Russia's population grew by some 41 per cent and the number of factory workers by 180 per cent. This demonstrates the magnitude of Russia's progress, so that by the mid-nineteenth century Russia was by no means the most backward of European countries in the manufacture of cotton textiles. The Zollverein had a total consumption of not more than 17,800 tons of raw cotton in 1850. Judging by the number of spindles employed, Prussia could not have consumed more than a quarter of this total. Before the 1848 revolution there were about 150,000 spindles in Prussia, whereas Russian industries at this date had between 600,000 and 700,000.

By the mid-nineteenth century the old handicraft form of production based on the cottage had already declined to a significant extent in Russia. The next stage,

---

[3] *Editors' note*: The author uses 'England' and 'English' throughout. 'Britain' and 'British' have been substituted in translation.

machine industry, was being approached. The number of possessional factories[4] fell rapidly after 1840, and by 1860 the proportion of serfs in the total of permanently employed factory workers was under 13 per cent.[5] It is clear therefore that by the end of the feudal epoch Russian industry had reached the level necessary for participation in the industrial cycles of the capitalist world. And Russia certainly entered upon these cyclical crises no later than the majority of other countries on the European Continent.

It must not be forgotten that Russia, prior to the emancipation of 1861, was still in the feudal epoch; industrial capitalism was as yet only in its initial stage of development within the womb of feudalism. The Russian crises of this period must therefore be viewed as a response to the crises of the capitalist West, and the nature of this response was that of a backward semi-colonial nation. But it should be emphasized at once that even these very early crises in Russia were not simply superficial reflections of foreign influence, reflections caused by the response of world prices to changes in international trade and credit. The Russian crises exhibit the more fundamental feature inherent in all genuine industrial crises, fluctuations in production.

The authors of *World Economic Crises* have failed to bring out the international character of the 1837 crisis. They mention only the slumps experienced at this time by Britain (in 1836) and the U.S.A. (in 1837). But crises also occurred in both France and Germany. According to de Laveleye this crisis began in November 1836, reaching its climax in the U.S.A. only in 1839 when no less than 959 banks suspended payments. But already in 1837 and 1838 there were 3300 recorded bankruptcies in the United States, with total liabilities of some 440 million dollars. Britain also experienced a serious crisis in 1837, with many bankruptcies, and the connections with America led to a further financial panic. Industries curtailed production and there was much suffering among industrial workers who, in the words of de Laveleye, 'began to listen to the Chartists'. France did not escape the crisis. Between January and June 1839 there were 600 bankruptcies in Paris, 93 of them among joint-stock companies; the total liabilities of these firms amounted to 148 million francs. 1839 also saw the peak of the crisis in Hamburg, where numerous bankruptcies occurred and interest rates were raised to the 'unprecedented' level of 7 per cent.

Not only is the international crisis of the 1830s overlooked in *World Economic Crises*, but unfortunately that of 1847–8 is also neglected. The authors justify the omission by 'the insufficiency of statistical data' and, not very convincingly, conclude that 1857 saw 'the first international crisis'. This is puzzling, for how should the crisis of 1847–8, which was certainly international, be described? How does the 'international' nature of the 1857 crisis differ from that of 1847? Both crises were industrial, both dominated by the same countries, Britain, the United States, Germany and France. If these are not enough to mark 1847 as a world crisis, then this should also apply to 1857. Another perplexing passage in the book reads: 'In

[4] *Translator's note*: The 'possessional factory' was a form of industrial enterprise in which the labourers, their village, as well as the enterprise itself, formed one inseparable unit. The owner was usually a merchant and the operations of these 'factories' were strictly controlled by the State. See P. Lyashchenko, *History of the National Economy of Russia*, New York, 1949, pp. 293–4.

[5] In the case of mining enterprises however, the liquidation of these concerns did not begin until 1861.

the mid-nineteenth century the stage of capitalist development had been reached by a number of countries other than Britain. In this sense 1857 can be described as the first international crisis.' Now such an argument is neither clear nor convincing. 1848 is no less 'mid-nineteenth century' than 1857. Also, international and even world significance can hardly be denied to the economic crisis of 1847, particularly since it was intimately connected with the series of bourgeois revolutions which followed in 1848. It is unnecessary to prove that capitalism had developed on a sufficiently wide scale by this time to engender international capitalist crises— the revolutions of 1848 themselves are proof enough. We may therefore conclude that 1847 was the true beginning date of world cyclical crises.

## THE CRISIS OF 1847

In Britain the climax of this crisis came in November 1847 when the panic brought many bankruptcies and Bank rate reached a peak of 9½ per cent. In the United States, however, the severest point of the crisis was reached only in 1848. The crisis itself had in fact been building up gradually over a long period. Its origin can be seen as early as 1846 in Britain, when there is evidence of some decline in production and sales. In that year, as is well known, there were extremely poor harvests in Britain, France and Germany, and these countries were obliged to import large quantities of grain from Russia and the United States. The corresponding outflow of gold from countries which suffered from bad harvests caused great difficulties. Bullion reserves held by the Bank of England dwindled from £15 million to £9 million as early as December 1846. Bank rate was raised quickly from 3 to 9½ per cent and in September 1847 the Bank even announced that it would make no further advances on Exchequer bills. According to de Laveleye 'the origin of the British depression lay in the grain trade'; subsequently other factors deepened the crisis. As a result 'many factories were shut' and 'more than 100,000 workers were fed at the workhouses under the Poor Law system'. The first wave of the industrial crisis in Britain was felt as early as the spring of 1847, the second, of greater force, came in the following autumn. And so de Laveleye is able to say that in 1847 'there were two crises—in April and October'. Important sectors of British industry suffered, such as cotton textiles, iron, coal and railway construction. So acute was the crisis that in 1848 a protest march of over 50,000 starving workers took place.

France did not escape the crisis. The gold reserve of the Bank of France fell from 252 to 59 million francs between July 1846 and 15 January 1847. In order to avoid financial disaster the Bank, according to de Laveleye, bought gold in small quantities to the value of 25 million francs from British banks, and also purchased 50 million francs worth from the Russian Emperor to be repaid in the form of an annuity. But even the feudal gold of Tsar Nicholas I, who was thus not only the gendarme of reactionary Europe but also the generous banker to monarchical France, failed to save France from either the capitalist crisis or the bourgeois revolution of 1848. The financial crisis, which developed around intense speculation in railway building, led to bankruptcies, unemployment and similar phenomena throughout France. And it is well known that Germany also could not escape the blast from the same economic hurricane.

The close interconnection between national economies at this period is demonstrated by Anglo-Russian relations. Britain's share in Russian foreign trade amounted to one-third of Russia's imports from Europe and one half of total Russian exports; Britain was thus able, in case of need, to draw from Russia not only supplies of raw materials but also gold reserves. In particular, at the time of the 1847 panic, a significant quantity of gold arrived in London from Russia. This gold was now the property of British capitalists who had long since penetrated Russia and who were able to draw it out to save themselves from financial crisis.

Noting the bad harvests of 1846, de Laveleye rather naïvely explains the world crisis of 1847–8 by 'bad weather' in the preceding season. Bad weather, he says, resulted in a bad harvest; a bad harvest led to an outflow of gold, and from this sprang a monetary crisis, bankruptcies, and all the other consequences. This does not prevent him, however, from attributing the following world crisis of 1857, not to an outflow but to an enormous influx of gold from Australia and California to Europe, amounting to over four thousand million francs from 1848 to 1856. Additionally, it may be pointed out that not all countries experienced bad weather on the eve of 1847 and a subsequent outflow of gold. Specifically, the U.S.A. was able to sell surplus grain to famished Europe at very high prices and therefore achieved an inflow of gold from Europe. This, however, failed to save the United States from the crisis. It is evident that the crux of the matter is not the outflow or influx of gold. These were only symptoms of fundamental anarchy in world capitalism, and this anarchy, regardless of the contradictory gold movements foreshadowed only one ominous end—world crisis.

How then did this first world-wide industrial crisis affect Russia? The most direct and obvious influence from abroad on the domestic economy is through foreign trade. Figures for 1845–9 show that, already by 1847, Russia played a significant part in world commerce:

RUSSIA'S FOREIGN TRADE (IN MILLION SILVER ROUBLES)

| Year | Exports | Imports | Total |
|------|---------|---------|-------|
| 1845 | 92·6 | 83·2 | 175·8 |
| 1846 | 102·7 | 87·0 | 189·7 |
| 1847 | 148·6 | 89·2 | 237·8 |
| 1848 | 88·3 | 90·8 | 179·1 |
| 1849 | 96·1 | 96·2 | 192·3 |

Russia's turnover of foreign trade lagged behind that of Britain, France, the U.S.A. and the German Zollverein, but considerably exceeded that of Austria (amounting to approximately 144 million roubles) and Prussia.

As a result of the crisis, however, world demand for Russian exports fell sharply, by 60 million roubles (or 40 per cent); such a blow could not but leave its mark on Russian industry, the total production of which in 1847 barely amounted to 105 million roubles. Further, the reduction of 60 million roubles in the earnings of agricultural (mainly grain) exporters caused a large fall in effective demand within Russia for the products of domestic industry. The capitalist countries lessened demand for Russian goods not only by their own reduced purchases but by withdrawing gold from Russian circulation. In particular, 1848 saw a net outflow of gold and silver from Russia amounting to 6,780,000 roubles, whereas there was normally a net inflow of gold. This drain alone could initiate bankruptcies and upheavals, leading to disruption of credit and finance.

Owing to an exceptionally bad harvest in Western Europe in 1846 and to the subsequent rise in grain prices, Russia exported 11·5 million chetverts[6] of grain valued at 71 million roubles to these areas in 1847; but the grain market collapsed in the second half of that year.[7] According to the official *Review of Foreign Trade*, a 'commercial crisis' developed in the West and consequently in Russia 'many trading houses suffered big losses'. But this was not all. In its review of 1848, the same journal offered the following explanation for the sharp fall in Russian exports:

the effects of the commercial crisis which had dislocated transactions on the European stock exchanges in early 1847 were still being felt at the beginning of 1848 when political unrest swept over Western Europe; the February revolution in France and the uneasiness that followed in Germany and Italy disrupted the trade and industry and in fact the whole economic systems of these countries. The intense financial and commercial crisis which beset those countries troubled by riots could not but prove detrimental to general foreign trade which in turn affected all nations.

The 'intense crisis' must, however, have been more severely felt in Russia than in any other country. A devastating outbreak of cholera swept Russia in 1848. The epidemic and consequent quarantine measures adopted by western countries forced whole factories to close down. Added to this was the bad Russian harvest of autumn 1848. Thus the cost to Russia of the disastrous international crisis, coupled with cholera and starvation at home, was enormous; it led to the loss of perhaps a million people in that single year.[8]

Although total exports reached their low point in Russia in 1848, the slump in export prices (of grain, flax and other goods) was felt already in the second half o 1847. Equally for certain commodities, exports began to fall off earlier, in 1847 for leather, 1846 for iron and raw hides, and even 1845 in the case of flax and wool.

The state of the domestic market can be adequately judged from the activity at the great annual Fair at Nijhni-Novgorod.[9] The table on p. 164 shows the general transactions at the Fair (in million roubles).

The domestic market is shown to have reacted earlier than foreign commerce to the world crisis since both 1847 and 1848 saw a decline in goods marketed and in actual sales at the Fair. The decline of 13 per cent in total sales over the two years and the simultaneous rise in unsold stocks from 12·1 to 15·3 per cent of total marketed goods are evidence of an overproduction crisis in the country.

Closer analysis of the statistics, broken down by commodities, reveals that this crisis had developed over a period of time. Difficulties in selling cotton and leather

---

[6] *Translator's note*: A chetvert: a capacity measure equivalent to about 8 bushels of grain.

[7] The price of wheat in St. Petersburg in August was 7r. 50k. a chetvert; in June 1847 it was 11r. 71k. and in June 1848, 7r. a chetvert.

[8] During the average harvest year of 1847 the number of recorded deaths was 1,877,000; in 1848 the figure was 2,840,000. It should be added that this increase in mortality of fully one million people could hardly result solely from a single bad harvest in 1848; the effect of the bad harvest would probably have been still stronger in 1849, yet in 1849 there were 1,876,000 deaths, no more than in 1847. It is likely that cholera and scurvy, themselves products of famine and malnutrition and only worsening the deep crisis, should be blamed.

[9] *Translator's note*: The largest and most important of Russia's many great trading fairs, held for 6 to 8 weeks each year at Nijhni-Novgorod.

TABLE 1
PRODUCTION OF LEADING INDUSTRIES IN RUSSIA,
1845–50 (EXCLUDING POLAND AND FINLAND)

| Year | Woollen cloth and materials | Flax and linen products | Cotton spinning and weaving | Wrought metals | Printing, dyeing and bleaching | Silk and brocade | Stationery and paper | Glass and crystal | Chemicals, dyestuffs, and acids | Miscell-aneous | Total | Pig-iron | Coal (Donetz) |
|---|---|---|---|---|---|---|---|---|---|---|---|---|---|
| | | | | | *million roubles* | | | | | | | *million poods* | |
| 1845 | 25·1 | 4·4 | 27·7 | 11·3 | 10·3 | 6·2 | 2·9 | 2·1 | 1·4 | 4·3 | 95·7 | 11·4 | 1·69 |
| 1846 | 24·1 | 2·4 | 29·3 | 17·8 | 15·3 | 6·4 | 3·1 | 3·0 | 1·5 | 5·0 | 107·9 | 13·1 | 1·45 |
| 1847 | 21·0 | 2·0 | 27·3 | 18·3 | 15·5 | 6·8 | 3·2 | 3·1 | 2·2 | 5·6 | 105·0 | 11·7 | 1·45 |
| 1848 | 27·3 | 2·7 | 30·4 | 15·9 | 12·0 | 4·2 | 2·9 | 2·8 | 1·6 | 4·9 | 104·7 | 12·1 | 2·18 |
| 1849 | 22·6 | 3·1 | 30·7 | 17·5 | 12·6 | 7·9 | 2·9 | 2·7 | 1·7 | 4·4 | 106·1 | 11·6 | 2·53 |
| 1850 | 25·1 | 2·8 | 28·7 | 17·2 | 16·2 | 6·7 | 3·5 | 3·0 | 2·2 | 5·5 | 110·9 | 13·2 | 3·54 |

| Year | Goods brought | Sales | Difference |
|------|------|------|------|
| 1843 | 47·9 | 39·1 | 8·8 |
| 1844 | 50·4 | 42·7 | 7·7 |
| 1845 | 55·8 | 48·7 | 7·1 |
| 1846 | 57·2 | 50·3 | 6·9 |
| 1847 | 56·0 | 48·7 | 7·3 |
| 1848 | 51·7 | 43·8 | 7·9 |
| 1849 | 55·5 | 45·5 | 10·0 |

goods as well as metal work began as early as 1846. The fall in cotton and silk manufactures marketed at the Fair occurred in 1847 and 1848 while, on the other hand, marketing of sugar fell sharply only in 1848 and 1849. Also, prices of textiles began to decline as early as 1845 and fell by 24 per cent over the three years. The price of pig-iron dropped by 14·5 per cent during 1847–8, while in the same period calico prices fell by 10 per cent.

As early as the 1846 Nijhni-Novgorod Fair, commentators noted a reduction in the prices of a number of goods and the lengthening of sales credit from six to eighteen months. In 1847, the international crisis and 'foreign bankruptcies' were blamed for causing the tightening of credit, large losses and problems of solvency for many Russian firms. Still worse, of course, was the Fair of 1848. But most indicative are the actual figures of production and employment. The Department of Manufactures gave the following figures for all Russia (except Poland and Finland):

| Year | Enterprises | Workers |
|------|------|------|
| 1841 | 6,831 | 429,638 |
| 1842 | 6,939 | 455,827 |
| 1843 | 6,813 | 466,579 |
| 1844 | 7,399 | 469,211 |
| 1845 | 8,302 | 507,577 |
| 1846 | 8,333 | 508,607 |
| 1847 | 9,029 | 532,056 |
| 1848 | 8,928 | 483,542 |
| 1849 | 9,172 | 495,364 |
| 1850 | 9,843 | 501,639 |

It can be seen from these official statistics that in only one year, 1848, did the number of enterprises and workers fall. Unfortunately no data are available for the total value of production in the same years, but we do have reasonably detailed summary statistics for the main branches of industry for 1845–50 (table 1). Thirty-eight products were included for the compilation of the above table by the Department of Manufactures. They covered not only dutiable goods, such as wine, tobacco and sugar, but also the products of peasant kustarny[10] industries, mainly the processing of foodstuffs and animal products. Until 1851 the Department of Manufactures included in the totals the products of a number of iron works in the province of Perm; these were excluded as from that year so that the figures before and after 1851 are not truly comparable.

As can be seen from the above table, the reduced output in certain branches of

[10] Translator's note: A general name covering domestic peasant handicraft industries.

Russian industry began as early as 1846, although a large fall in total production was not recorded until 1847–8. The extent of the reduction varied as between different branches of industry, from 6·8 per cent in cotton spinning to 16·3 per cent in cotton piece-goods, 22·6 per cent in printed calicoes, 27·3 per cent in chemicals, 38·4 per cent in silk and 54·5 per cent in linen production. On average, the falls recorded in the above table amounted to 17 per cent, but as they did not occur simultaneously the total reduction, between 1846 and 1848, was only about 3 per cent. Such an aggregate is thus misleading. The uneven development of the different branches of industrial production and the divergence between the high and low levels of these branches during a crisis make the use of an aggregate index most unreliable. For example, it is possible to quote several instances of crises where the general indices of annual industrial production show no decline at all.[11] Moreover, for the period 1845–50 industrial production in Russia is seen to have risen by 16 per cent; at a steady rate of growth, production for 1847 and 1848 would therefore have increased by 6 per cent; thus the observed aggregate fall of 3 per cent is to be considered a true fall of not less than 9 per cent.

The crisis of 1847 was no less apparent in other branches than in manufacturing industries. For example, iron smelting, amounting to 11·4 million poods[12] in 1845 and 13·1 million poods in 1846, fell back in 1847 to 11·7 million poods, a drop of 10·7 per cent. Coal-mining in the Donetz Basin, which reached 1·69 million poods in 1845, declined in the following two years to 1·45 million poods, a reduction of 14 per cent. Evidence of crisis is provided also by railway construction in Russia: 134 kilometres of new track were opened to traffic in 1846, 90 kilometres in 1847 and only 14 in 1848. And we have omitted discussion of many further signs of the crisis, such as falling prices.[13]

Can all these phenomena be considered accidental? Can it be pure coincidence that the fall in production and employment in Russia occurred in the same years as the industrial crises in Britain, France, Germany and the United States? Of course not. The laws of probability would indicate that the chances of such a coincidence of 'accidental' events is insignificant. In all these countries we observe common consequences, for common causes gave them birth.

That the world capitalist crisis could have such a marked impact on the still feudal serf society of Russia should perhaps provoke reflection. But a fact remains a fact. It goes without saying that feudalism dominated the Russia of Tsar Nicholas I. But although this dominance was complete in agriculture, by this time vigorous seeds of capitalism were already sprouting in the field of large-scale industry. We may take cotton textiles as an example of an advanced industrial sector. This industry had always employed freely hired labour, and by the late 1840s the transition from capitalist cottage industry to capitalist factory was progressing rapidly. It may be recalled that as early as 1839 the textile industry had experienced a feverish re-equipment boom based on British machinery. The boom was pioneered in Moscow by Ludwig Knoop, the famous representative of the Manchester firm of D. Jersey. Knoop himself re-equipped no less than 122 of Russia's cotton textile

[11] For example, the crises of 1866, 1883 and 1900 in Germany.
[12] *Translator's note*: 1 pood = 36 lbs English.
[13] We could note, for example, the failure of the Russian Government to float a foreign loan due to the 'political incidents' at the beginning of 1848; or the record number of dishonoured bills held by the State Commercial Bank, and so on.

enterprises. And many other branches of Russian industry did not lag behind cotton spinning.

It is a commonplace that the rise of new methods of production and the corresponding new forms of organization do not occur in isolation from the old system, nor after the latter has disappeared. The new occurs within the womb of the old. More particularly, as Lenin has noted in the case of Russia, 'the capitalistic organization of the textile industry took place prior to the ending of serfdom'. Now, if it is accepted that within the womb of feudal Russia capitalist industry had already made its appearance, why should not genuine industrial crisis also occur? Similar causes always bring forth similar consequences.

## THE CRISIS OF 1857

The world crisis of 1857 was foreshadowed by several ominous harbingers. Most relevant was the crisis at the close of 1853 in Australia where a whole series of bankruptcies occurred, particularly among importers. In 1854 and 1855 a significant decline began in British exports, leading to depression in a number of important industrial sectors, notably textiles. And in the autumn of 1856 there was a violent stock market panic in France.

The real crisis, however, broke only at the end of August 1857, in the United States. It began with intense panic and numerous bankruptcies which followed in the wake of fierce speculation in railway securities. On 3 September 175 banks closed their doors and discount rates reached 30 to 40 per cent. Industries immediately shut down, throwing their workers out of employment. In the United States and Canada there were no fewer than 5,722 bankruptcies with liabilities totalling 1,500 million francs.

From America the crisis quickly spread to Europe. From the end of October there were bankruptcies among British banks and industrial firms having business dealings with the United States. Then the crisis spread to the Continent, to the major centres of Germany, Austria, Denmark, Sweden and France. Its impact was even felt beyond the Equator, in Java and Brazil. So widespread was the crisis in Europe that, at the end of November 1857, Marx could write that 'on the Continent of Europe the infection has spread from Sweden to Italy in one direction and from Madrid to Budapest in the other'.

The actual duration of the 1857 crisis was not extensive, however. After the intensity of the first months the crisis moderated to only a mild depression, and in Britain the symptoms of the crisis had passed altogether by 1859. 1858 saw the worst of the crisis in the majority of Western countries, with the maximum number of bankruptcies and highest rate of unemployment coinciding with the lowest point of production. In some branches of industry however, for example in production and consumption of iron, the low point was reached as late as 1859 in France and 1860 in Germany.

Russia did not remain immune from the 'infection' of the world crisis. In Russia also ominous harbingers of crisis can be found as far back as 1852, while the effects of the crisis did not pass completely in some branches of industry until 1860. But the main blast was felt in 1857, and in that year Russia experienced those characteristics fundamental to every industrial crisis. According to Tugan-Baranovsky 'the usual symptoms of an industrial crisis appeared in Russia at the end of the 1850s:

the failure of banks, joint-stock companies, trading houses and factories in Russia, a stagnation of trade, and falling production'.

Foreign trade statistics show a decline of 2·3 million roubles in Russia's imports for the year 1858, but that year also saw a fall in exports by 17 million roubles. Although Russia's balance of trade was positive, there was a net outflow of gold amounting to 14·9 million roubles as early as 1857, 24·2 million roubles in 1858, and 25·8 million in 1859.[14] Thus during the three years of crisis foreign capitalists extracted from Russia gold bullion and coin to the value of about 65 million roubles. These withdrawals could not, of course, save the capitalist West from the crisis. But in poverty-stricken Russia the outflow of gold significantly hastened the beginning of general bankruptcy and stagnation of trade. Contemporary discussions of the situation by the committee on political economy of the Russian Geographic Society emphasized the financial problems: 'The shortage of money is a burden experienced throughout our commercial activities'; 'the discounting of trade bills is difficult beyond belief'; and 'vendors, almost without exception, are obliged to wait from six to nine months before finding a market for their goods'. At the same time, the committee noted that the nation's reserves had declined from 164 million roubles on 1 January 1855 to 84 million roubles by the beginning of 1860, while the foreign debt had risen by 162 million roubles. In view of this, when the problem of the economic crisis was discussed, the view was put that 'we have gone too far . . . there is no money now to pay us with', and 'the possibility of national bankruptcy' was even mooted.

Difficulties in the internal market were not experienced until the end of 1857. The Nijhni-Novgorod Fair, which ran from 15 June to 1 September that year, apparently finished before the onset of the crisis in Russia, since an observer described the Fair as 'unusually successful'. High prices for cotton textiles continued until the end of 1857, when news was received of falling cotton prices in Britain and the beginning of a trade recession there. Prices of woollen textiles also were well maintained until late 1857 when falling overseas demand led to a price decline of 10–15 per cent; declining foreign purchases were also responsible for a sharp fall in the price of leather soles. The latter fetched 1400 roubles per hundred in the province of Kaluga in the spring of 1857, but towards the end of the season the collapse of foreign sales resulted in a drop to 800 roubles. This price was well below cost, the raw leather alone costing up to 700 roubles per hundred. At the close of 1857 the price of sugar also fell some 15–20 per cent, and by then the influence of speculative activity on the St. Petersburg market was being felt. The existence of internal causes for Russia's economic difficulties were underlined by a government official, V. Tatarin, who wrote at the beginning of the following year, 1858: 'Due in part to the general depressed condition of European trade, in part also to an over-rapid pace of activity during the preceding two years, a stagnation of sales has been experienced.'

This second influence on the 'stagnation' of 1858 and 1859, when 'even the soundest enterprise was unable to escape the crisis', was further emphasized in 1860 by the same government official. Referring to his 1858 article, where he had

---

[14] The value of payments abroad in 1859 amounted to 50 to 60 million roubles, of which 13m. r. went on servicing foreign loans, 5.4m. r. on interest to foreign shareholders of railway stock, and 5.2m. r. in various payments to foreign governments.

warned that the approaching crisis would threaten joint-stock enterprises, he argued that Russia's manufacturers, 'tempted by the increased demand of the preceding years . . . extended their production out of all proportion'. In this connection we may note that although sales at the Nijhni-Novgorod Fair were declining, products brought for sale showed no falling off in 1858 and 1859. As a result traders were obliged to sell their goods on extended credit, even though previous debts remained unsettled. A marked reduction in the number of transactions at the Fair only became apparent in 1860 and 1861.[15]

A contemporary observer, S. Serafin, said of the 1860 Nijhni-Novgorod Fair that 'under the influence of a general trade stagnation, shortage of money, and intolerably hot weather it was extremely sluggish'. Early on the Fair was disrupted by an outbreak of cholera, and in general it 'must be considered one of the least successful ever'. Yet the Fair of 1861 went no better, 'with disastrous price reductions . . . the great bulk of goods were sold on credit of six to 12 and even 24 months', and at the same time the majority of old debts were not paid. The same commentator also considered the causes of the crisis to be 'general and complete lack of money', overproduction, and 'the trade crisis', which extended 'a universal misfortune to our industrial classes'.

In this way, the impact of the world crisis of 1857-8 lasted significantly longer in some branches of Russia's economy than it did in the West, thus linking up with the general disruption of Russia's feudal society in 1861.

The early stages of the 1857 crisis in Russia are somewhat obscured by the Crimean War, which lasted from March 1853 to February 1856. This three-year war inflicted severe damage on the whole economy. In particular, it led to cessation of railway construction, and for a time it resulted not only in a stagnation of production but even in an absolute fall, reaching its lowest point in 1854. For certain industries the decline lasted until 1855, but in general a distinct improvement was evident before this in spite or in view of war deliveries, perhaps because of hostilities.

A contemporary wrote that

a distinct acceleration of industrial and commercial activity took place in Russia between 1854 and 1857, beginning even before the conclusion of peace. It was shown in a remarkable expansion of factory production, particularly in the northern industrial region . . . and in a quite unusual buoyancy at all internal fairs where there was a rapid rise in sales of both domestic and foreign manufactures. . . . The climax of the boom came in 1855 and 1856, a period which all Russia's industrialists and merchants remember as a golden age. Ordinary workers and factory workers as well as manufacturers and merchants said of this time 'how prosperous we were'. Factories were unable to turn out sufficient goods to satisfy the demand. New factories were built, old ones extended. Working time was doubled and night work was general. All prices of commodities as well as wages rose immeasurably.

The peak of company flotations came, apparently, at the end of 1856 and beginning of 1857. The capital of new joint-stock enterprises founded in 1855 totalled 750,000 roubles; in 1856 it climbed to 15,500,000 roubles, and in 1857 advanced enormously to 300 million roubles. But in 1858 it fell back to 51 million roubles. Describing stock market activity, a contemporary wrote that

[15] The total value of goods brought to the Nijhni-Novgorod Fair was 94·9m. r. in 1858, 103·3m. r. in 1859, 102·3m. r. in 1860, and 96·8m. r. in 1861.

TABLE 2

PRODUCTION OF LEADING INDUSTRIES IN RUSSIA, 1851–60 (EXCLUDING POLAND AND FINLAND)

| Year | million roubles | | | | | | | | | | | million poods | |
| | Cotton spinning | Printing, dyeing and finishing | Linen and flax products | Woollens and worsteds | Silk and ribbons | Cotton weaving | Wrought metals | Leather products | Chemicals and dyestuffs | Glass, china and pottery | Total | pig-iron | Coal (Donetz) |
|---|---|---|---|---|---|---|---|---|---|---|---|---|---|
| 1851 | 13·5 | 15·7 | 3·2 | 23·6 | 6·2 | 12·2 | 10·7 | 9·6 | 2·2 | 3·7 | 100·6 | 12·6 | 3·31 |
| 1852 | 15·6 | 16·3 | 2·2 | 24·4 | 5·7 | 14·2 | 11·9 | 9·2 | 2·4 | 4·0 | 105·9 | 13·2 | 4·00 |
| 1853 | 17·3 | 16·8 | 2·5 | 22·5 | 5·5 | 15·9 | 12·7 | 10·0 | 2·6 | 3·8 | 109·6 | 14·5 | 3·84 |
| 1854 | 15·6 | 14·3 | 2·9 | 23·3 | 4·9 | 11·9 | 13·4 | 9·1 | 2·9 | 3·6 | 101·9 | 14·2 | 3·75 |
| 1855 | 15·2 | 12·1 | 3·3 | 25·4 | 4·9 | 13·5 | 15·0 | 9·6 | 3·4 | 3·4 | 105·8 | 15·3 | 4·50 |
| 1856 | 18·5 | 16·5 | 2·9 | 32·4 | 6·4 | 15·6 | 15·6 | 10·0 | 3·9 | 4·0 | 125·8 | 15·8 | 3·80 |
| 1857 | 21·9 | 19·2 | 4·0 | 28·9 | 5·8 | 13·4 | 15·2 | 9·4 | 3·4 | 4·1 | 125·3 | 13·1 | 4·50 |
| 1858 | 23·6 | 22·3 | 4·0 | 31·9 | 6·7 | 18·7 | 17·8 | 11·1 | 4·4 | 4·1 | 144·6 | 16·9 | 4·50 |
| 1859 | 31·3 | 20·0 | 4·3 | 32·6 | 7·9 | 21·5 | 22·8 | 14·0 | 4·7 | 4·7 | 163·8 | 16·5 | 2·80 |
| 1860 | 28·7 | 23·6 | 6·1 | 35·4 | 7·1 | 19·3 | 23·4 | 16·6 | 4·1 | 5·1 | 169·4 | 20·5 | 6·01 |

it seemed at first as though share transactions were progressing very satisfactorily, and the public evidently regarded shares with unusual confidence. They could be easily resold on the exchanges and were frequently used in place of cash or bonds. But all this suddenly changed. The unfavourable balance (of payments) led to a falling exchange rate and there was a large demand for coin. Banks no longer granted mortgages. The value of shares dropped, and they could no longer serve instead of money . . . the shortage of money became general. The effect of all this spread throughout the economy, particularly in manufacturing industry, and resulted in a universal stagnation of trade in Russia.

Another contemporary, V. Bezobrazov, also commented on the situation.

After the industrial boom came a period in reverse; general industrial and commercial stagnation produced a crisis in 1858 and 1859. From 1858 one can discern a faltering in certain branches of internal trade and production which in 1859 was transformed into definite crisis . . . It is unnecessary to describe the failure of the joint-stock companies; this is only too familiar . . . The limitless demand for shares gave way to either frenzied panic or complete apathy.

This mood was further strengthened by a sharp fall in prices which began from 1857–8. For example, the price of raw sugar fell from 8 roubles 78 kopeks gold per pood to 6r. 24k. between 1857 and 1859, that is by almost 29 per cent; Russian wool prices declined from 6r. 26k. per pood in 1857 to 4r. 77k. in 1859, or 24 per cent; the price of American raw cotton sold in Moscow declined over the same period from 7r. 67k. per pood to 6r. 61k., or 14 per cent; cotton yarn similarly fell from 21r. to 17r. 12k. a pood, or 18·5 per cent; prices for sheet iron slumped during 1859 alone from 1r. 45k. to 1r. 29k. per pood in St. Petersburg, a fall of 11 per cent, and so on. Another source gives the price of cotton yarn (counts of 30–40) in the town of Shuya: from 24r. 50k. silver a pood in 1856 and 1857, the price dropped to 18r. 50k. in 1858, to 18 roubles in 1859 and to 16 roubles in 1860, thus falling by 33 per cent over the three years.

We do not have completely comparable data for all branches of industrial production during this period. The range of products covered by the statistics of a province all too often varied; frequently also the number of items grouped under one classification was altered. On occasions, gaps in the data for some provinces were filled by figures for adjacent years; sometimes the official publications simply note that the statistics are 'incomplete'. However, by confining ourselves to the major branches of industrial production, it is possible to obtain reasonably detailed and comparable statistics for the entire period under review. The statistical picture for the 1850s is shown in table 2.

If we ignore the somewhat remote precursors of the crisis, such as the reduced output of the calico, linen, silk, leather, and sugar industries which occurred as far back as 1852, then it might be possible to attribute the rather marked falls of production during the war years (the minimum output was in 1854 at the height of the hostilities) entirely to war-time dislocation. The fall in total production evident in the table, however, is more than accounted for simply by the decline in cotton textiles. General output fell by 7·7 million roubles, or 7 per cent, between 1853 and 1854, from a total of 109·6 to 101·9 million roubles. Cotton textiles alone declined by 8·2m. r., or 16·4 per cent, from 50 to 41·8m. r. and the fall continued into the following year. Moreover, it is known that a decline analogous to that of Russian textiles took place in 1854 and 1855 also in Britain, France, Germany, and even in the United States, that is including countries not caught up in any war. The international character of the decline does not allow us to attribute it solely to the Crimean War as far as Russia is concerned.

After the low point of 1854 in Russia, and the subsequent boom conditions of 1855 and 1856, the statistics reveal a period of renewed decline in production corresponding to the world crisis of 1857. This year saw a new fall in the output of seven out of the thirteen groups in the table, and three more followed in 1858. Of the remainder, linen manufacture had already reached its minimum in 1856, and cotton textile production, recovering from the difficulties of 1854–5, did not reach a new minimum until 1859 and 1860. For sugar, the lowest point occurred in 1856, and coal-mining production was at a minimum in 1859. The low points for the various branches of production thus diverge considerably, and consequently the general totals given in the table show only a cessation of growth in 1857, not an absolute fall. Since, however, the average annual growth rate had been up to 7 per cent, a cessation is also extremely important. If we look at the several branches of production individually, the absolute decline of output in certain crisis years reaches a much more significant level. In cotton spinning, for example, falls of 8·5 per cent and 12 per cent took place at different times; in silk, woollen, piece-goods, and chemical manufacture the declines ranged from 9 per cent to 13 per cent, for flax and cotton weaving 12 per cent to 14 per cent, and for pig-iron and coal up to 17 per cent and 38 per cent respectively.

A fundamental feature of these fluctuations is the complementary movement of such competitive goods as linen and cottons. It is noticeable that each decline in cotton processing is matched by an increase in flax manufacture; in reverse, each fall in flax output brings a corresponding rise in the cotton industry. This was not accidental. The prospects of the Russian flax industry would always rise as the sales of cotton textiles slumped. And this partly explains that divergence in time between the high and low points of different industries which is so noticeable in the table.

As a general rule, the lowest level of production coincides with the maximum of unemployment and *vice versa*. However, there was also another marked feature observed during the late 1850s. This was that the greatest fall in employment actually took place after the low point of the 1857 crisis. We give below statistics for all manufacturing industry (except for dutiable commodities which were excluded on the eve of the emancipation) taken from the Department of Manufactures:

| Year | Number of 'factories' | Number of workers (thousands) | Production (million roubles) |
|---|---|---|---|
| 1856 | 10,011 | 432·1 | 166·0 |
| 1857 | 10,152 | 445·9 | 173·0 |
| 1858 | 11,456 | 530·6 | 195·5 |
| 1859 | 12,242 | 503·5 | 221·1 |
| 1860 | 13,325 | 468·6 | 234·5 |

The year 1858 saw a rise in all three indices. The value of production and the number of enterprises continued to grow during the following years, yet the number of workers employed fell by 11·6 per cent in the two years. Again, this is not accidental, and in the official report of the Department of Manufactures for 1861 we find the explanation: 'Such a reduction in factory employment results in part from the declining output of possessional factories, and in part from the mechanization of industry which is reflected in the continuous growth of the manufacture of machinery in Russia.'

The development of the machine industry can be seen from the following statistics:

| Year | Number of Enterprises | Workers | Production (thousand roubles) |
|------|------|------|------|
| 1850 | 25 | 1,475 | 423 |
| 1856 | 31 | 6,604 | 3,865 |
| 1857 | 43 | 7,032 | 4,015 |
| 1858 | 47 | 7,602 | 4,199 |
| 1859 | 85 | 8,526 | 5,260 |
| 1860 | 99 | 11,600 | 7,954 |

Over the years 1856–60, despite the crisis in other sectors of industry, machine building doubled. For that period of time the growth rate was remarkable, particularly after 1858 when production rose by 90 per cent in two years. Yet this should not surprise us. Each capitalist crisis gives way to a period when basic capital must be renewed on a large scale. This renewal, intensified under a competitive system, naturally leads to a new upsurge in machine building. In the years under consideration, the post-crisis renewal of basic capital coincided with the transformation of cottage industry into factory industry. This latter process, which involved replacing manual labour with machinery, could only result in a reduction of the total labour force even if production increased. There still remained in this pre-reform period numerous possessional industries using unpaid serf labour. These enterprises found it difficult to compete successfully with factories employing the more productive free labour. During the economic crisis these difficulties were aggravated; in the succeeding reconstruction boom, associated as it was with the adoption of advanced techniques in capitalist factories, competition became quite impossible. Possessional enterprises, unable to compete, were forced to close. And in this way the 1857 industrial crisis, which developed within 'Serf' Russia, and which led to crisis throughout the entire declining feudal system, without doubt accelerated the inevitable collapse of feudalism.

THE CRISIS OF 1866

Preceding the world crisis of 1866 were the American Civil War of 1861–5 and the consequent cotton famine. The latter led, as early as 1861, to severe stagnation and unemployment in the textile industries of Britain and several other countries. The industrial crisis in the U.S.A., however, flared up earlier than in other countries due to the ending of military expenditure; its harbinger can be found in the New York stock market panic which broke out in April 1864. The American industrial crisis followed soon after the cessation of hostilities in 1865, but although pig-iron production dropped to its lowest point in that year, other branches of industry fell to their minimum levels only in 1867.

In Britain the difficulties began when one of London's biggest banking houses crashed on 10 May 1866. By the evening of 11 May six more bankruptcies had taken place, involving a total of £21m. sterling. On the 17th 'the panic had apparently eased', but bankruptcies were reported in Vienna, Stockholm, Le Havre, Schaffhausen, Barcelona, etc. Production in different branches of British industry reached its low points in the years 1866, 1867 and 1868. In France, on the other hand, there was a period of recovery after the stagnation of 1861–4, and the real crisis exploded only in 1867 with the failure of the largest French bank, the *Crédit Mobilier*. Industrial production thus did not reach a minimum in France before 1867 and 1868.

In Russia during the 1860s there was one notable factor other than the cotton famine and the world crisis which retarded the development of certain branches of industry. We refer to the crisis in the country's social structure leading to the abolition of serfdom with the reform of 19 February 1861. Those sections of industry still relying heavily on unfree labour were most severely hit by the change and production actually fell in the next two or three years. There was considerable delay in introducing the new regulations into the manufacturing establishments, but nevertheless the former system of production was rapidly destroyed as liberated workers left to seek better conditions elsewhere. In a number of cases, especially in the mining, sugar and cloth industries, enterprises worked only intermittently for several years after the reform.

Emancipation had innumerable social, political and economic consequences throughout society, most notably in agriculture. This is a topic which deserves special treatment, but we cannot leave this subject without touching on matters which affected the industrial crisis. Emancipation gave an enormous boost to both existing and new sectors of economic activity, industry in particular. But the great upheaval necessary everywhere in order to adjust to the new economic conditions required immediately considerable expenditure and also considerable time. In general the old landed classes were unable to cope with the changes. Rather than face the unpleasantness of associating with former serfs who had been 'private property', these landlords, until they were replaced by the avaricious kulaks,[16] often withdrew from their estates. They sought the solace of Russia's great cities or of foreign resorts, and to this end they sold their redemption bonds[17] and subsequently their hereditary possessions. The novelist Shchedrin has indelibly portrayed these landowners, likening them to butterflies flitting abroad to Paris or Monaco. He describes how they conduct their business affairs, sending urgent telegrams to their agents in Russia ordering the sales of their estates, which had now become a burden, in order to raise money. '*Vendez Russie vite, envoyez argent.*'[18] How glittering these beautiful and remote places sound in Shchedrin's writings by comparison with Russia!

Turning from literary to statistical evidence, we can see how the situation led to an unparalleled outflow of gold after emancipation. For greater clarity we show only the imports and exports of gold in bars and coin across Russia's European borders for the years 1860–7 (in thousands of roubles).

---

[16] Wealthy peasants, or the so-called 'village bourgeoisie'.
[17] *Translator's note*: Bonds received by former serf-owners from the State by way of compensation.     [18] 'Sell Russia quickly, send money!'

| Year | Exports | Imports | Balance |
|------|---------|---------|---------|
| 1860 | 6,546 | 7,065 | +519 |
| 1861 | 11,752 | 6,968 | −4,784 |
| 1862 | 32,206 | 4,838 | −27,368 |
| 1863 | 59,921 | 4,990 | −54,931 |
| 1864 | 21,938 | 5,048 | −16,890 |
| 1865 | 18,924 | 3,021 | −15,903 |
| 1866 | 25,827 | 2,373 | −23,454 |
| Total (1861–6) | 170,568 | 27,238 | −143,330 |
| 1867 | 12,131 | 33,229 | +21,098 |

Thus for six years in succession following the emancipation of 1861 an uninterrupted stream of gold flowed abroad. And this despite foreign loans amounting to £15m. sterling or 96m. gold roubles in 1862, and an Anglo-Dutch loan of 38m. roubles in 1864. If the contraction of these loans had been impossible, the gold outflow during the six years under consideration would have reached 277m. r.[19] But this was not all. The slogan 'starve, yet export' which was voiced throughout Russia's countryside from 1861 to 1866 was based on reality, for imports exceeded exports (across European borders) in these years by at least 178m. r. Thus total liabilities payable in gold by Tsarist Russia to the other capitalist Western countries from 1861 to 1866 amounted to no less than 455m. r. Certainly part of this total was interest on foreign government loans and foreign capital investment. But the scale of payments in 1861–6 compared with earlier and succeeding years was without precedent. Even the most intense industrial crisis could not have caused such an outflow, and it is evident that this was in fact a crisis embracing the entire economic system. It extended beyond industry, and, among others, the landowning classes—the rulers of the declining feudal system—participated by sending gold flowing out of their own bankrupt society.

The total sum of Russia's foreign liabilities, discussed above, was in fact considerably greater than the gold reserve held by the State Bank.[20] We can conclude, therefore, that feudal Russia after the Crimean War was already 'doomed'. Russia could not meet her obligations. And even if abolition of serfdom had been delayed for a few years, internal crisis and drain of wealth would have led inescapably to total national bankruptcy.

The cotton famine in Russia, a consequence of the American Civil War, reached its peak in 1862. The imports of cotton across Russia's European and Asiatic frontiers separately are shown on p. 175 (in thousand poods). It can be seen that the cotton famine in Russia did not end until 1866 and that in 1862 imports hardly reached 30 per cent of their 1860 level. The decline in the number of workers engaged in cotton spinning mills however was somewhat less, from 41,300 in 1860 to 22,400 in 1862, that is, to 54 per cent of the 1860 figure. Due to a rise in prices, the reduction in the value of production was still smaller, standing at 92 per cent of the 1860 level in 1862. The figures for the imports of cotton do not,

[19] Incidentally, we see an inflow of gold into Russia in 1867 of 21m. r., explicable only by a new Anglo-Dutch loan of 4 Nov. 1866 for 38m. r. gold. Without this there would have been still a net outflow of gold of 17m. r.

[20] By 1861 this stood at no more than 60m. r.

COTTON IMPORTS THROUGH EUROPEAN AND
ASIATIC FRONTIERS

| | | | |
|---|---|---|---|
| 1860 | 2,611 + 229 | = | 2,840 |
| 1861 | 2,491 + 152 | = | 2,643 |
| 1862 | 445 + 405 | = | 850 |
| 1863 | 587 + 495 | = | 1,082 |
| 1864 | 933 + 704 | = | 1,637 |
| 1865 | 1,125 + 466 | = | 1,591 |
| 1866 | 2,372 + 580 | = | 2,952 |

of course, correspond to total processing in the same year; thus, judging by the number of workers employed, manufacturing reached its minimum only in 1864, a year of excellent prospects for selling cotton goods when prices for yarn were $2\frac{1}{2}$ to 3 times greater than in 1861.[21] It is therefore clear that not all declines in output can be attributed to overproduction crises.

Other causes must be found to explain reduction and stagnation of production in various industries after 1866. From 1864 to 1866 there was a noticeable expansion of Russian industry, both in the number of workers employed and in total output. But the trend altered sharply at the end of 1866. Prices of raw cotton and cotton yarn and cloth, after rising rapidly, fell equally abruptly. Thus, for example, the Moscow price of cotton yarn (of counts of 38–40) which in 1864 had reached 46 credit roubles,[22] or 35r. 50k. gold a pood, stood at 17r. 28k. in 1867 and 16r. 54k. in 1868.

Due to the poor harvests of 1864 and 1865 there was also a drop in the financial resources of the agricultural sector. This was shown most clearly by the fall, in 1865, in the Treasury's revenue from all indirect taxes, including such a major item as the spirit duty. In 1864 these taxes yielded 191·2 million roubles, in 1865, 188·8m. r., and in 1866, 181·7m. r. During the same years there was an equally significant withdrawal of deposits from savings banks in towns, especially in the larger capital cities. Thus, for example, in Moscow and St. Petersburg new deposits in savings banks amounted to 1,006,000 roubles in 1865, 852,000r. in 1866, and 790,000r. in 1867; withdrawals from the banks in those years were, respectively, 1,691,000r., 896,000r. and 817,000r. Thus, on average over the three years, withdrawals exceeded new deposits by 28·6 per cent.

The 1866 world crisis had the further effect of reducing the exchange rate. On the London market the silver rouble fell from $32\frac{7}{8}$d. on 12 March 1865 to $25\frac{3}{4}$d. on 14 June 1866, a reduction of almost 22 per cent. Internal monetary difficulties compelled the State Bank to raise the discount rate from 5 per cent to 8 per cent over the period 18 June 1866 to 16 June 1867; the rate then remained at this level for over nine months, until 28 March 1868, when it was again lowered, returning to 5 per cent only in February 1868. This period also witnessed a falling off in trade which reached its nadir in 1868. The value of goods brought to the Nijhni-

[21] The price of yarn (of counts of 38–40) was 10r. 50k. gold per pood in 1861 and fluctuated from 62r. 40k. to 35r. 50k. in 1864.

[22] *Translator's note*: During the Crimean War convertibility of the paper credit rouble ceased. In terms of the nominal silver and gold rouble the credit rouble depreciated, and until the gold standard was adopted in 1897 the credit rouble was the *de facto* currency in circulation.

Novgorod Fair fell from 128m. r. in 1867 to 126m. r. in 1868, while the turnover of foreign trade dropped from 510m. r. in 1867 to 487m. r. in 1868.

We turn, finally, to manufacturing industry. Production figures are available for 34 commodities in the 50 provinces of European Russia:[23]

| Year | Number of Enterprises | Workers (thousands) | Production (million roubles) |
|------|------|------|------|
| 1864 | 5,782 | 272 | 201 |
| 1865 | 6,175 | 290 | 211 |
| 1866 | 5,775 | 311 | 239 |
| 1867 | 6,934 | 314 | 236 |
| 1868 | 7,091 | 329 | 249 |
| 1869 | 7,325 | 341 | 283 |
| 1870 | 7,691 | 354 | 314 |

It can be seen that although the number of establishments and workers included in the table rose in 1867, production definitely fell in that year.

This fall appears even more clearly in figures given by V. I. Lenin which cover all manufactured goods. The decline is shown to have begun in 1866, reaching nadir in 1867, and to have affected both total production and the number of workers employed. Unfortunately these more comprehensive totals do not provide a series of truly comparable data, and are, furthermore, not broken down into the different branches of industry. Therefore, in order to obtain a more detailed picture, we give another table which covers a narrower selection of the major industries but provides a series of comparable data for the entire decade (see table 3).

The three years following the completion of the reform, 1863 to 1866,[24] witnessed a growth of 42 per cent in the production of the ten branches of industry quoted in the table. It is true that in some cases, for example in the production of pig-iron, paper and silk goods, the stagnation caused by the reform persisted throughout the decade. All the more significant therefore is the growth in the remaining branches. For them, the effects of the cotton famine and the disruption of the reform were evidently matters of the past by the mid-1860s. Nevertheless, due to the world crisis of 1866–7, a new fall in production occurred in 1867, followed by a period of stagnation. The average annual growth rate for the decade was 6 per cent to 7 per cent; production fell in 1867 by 2 per cent, rising thereafter in 1868 to a level 4 per cent above that of 1866. The crisis in 1867 and 1868 thus caused production to grow by at least 10 per cent less than would otherwise have been the case.

The effect of the world crisis was more marked in some branches of Russian industry than in others. Already in the first year of the U.S.A. crisis, 1865, paper and glass production fell noticeably; in the same year sugar production dropped by 23 per cent and machine building by 30 per cent. In 1866 machine building and

[23] *Translator's note*: That is European Russia excluding Finland and the Polish and Caucasian provinces.

[24] *Translator's note*: There was a two-year transition period during which the reform of 1861 was put into effect.

TABLE 3

PRODUCTION OF LEADING INDUSTRIES IN RUSSIA, 1860–70 (EXCLUDING POLAND AND FINLAND)

| Year | Chemicals and dyestuffs | Machinery and foundry products | Glass and china | Cotton spinning and weaving | Printing, dyeing and finishing | Silk and ribbons | Leather products | Paper products | Linen and flax products | Woollens and worsteds | Total | Pig-iron (Empire) | Coal (Donetz) | Granulated sugar |
|---|---|---|---|---|---|---|---|---|---|---|---|---|---|---|
| | | | | | *million roubles* | | | | | | | | *million poods* | |
| 1860 | 4·1 | 13·1 | 5·0 | 48·0 | 23·6 | 7·1 | 16·6 | 6·4 | 6·1 | 35·4 | 165·4 | 20·5 | 6·0 | 4·0 |
| 1861 | 4·9 | 12·8 | 5·1 | 49·8 | 29·3 | 7·7 | 19·0 | 6·3 | 7·7 | 32·6 | 175·2 | 19·5 | 10·2 | 2·6 |
| 1862 | 3·5 | 13·0 | 4·6 | 44·9 | 24·5 | 6·6 | 18·1 | 6·3 | 7·1 | 32·9 | 161·5 | 15·3 | 7·1 | 1·9 |
| 1863 | 3·1 | 18·2 | 5·0 | 38·7 | 21·4 | 4·7 | 18·2 | 6·1 | 6·3 | 33·3 | 155·0 | 17·0 | 6·4 | 2·9 |
| 1864 | 2·5 | 20·9 | 5·4 | 52·4 | 23·5 | 3·7 | 17·8 | 5·3 | 7·9 | 42·0 | 181·4 | 18·3 | 7·0 | 3·9 |
| 1865 | 2·8 | 14·6 | 4·9 | 61·8 | 24·6 | 4·4 | 18·4 | 5·2 | 8·4 | 45·6 | 190·7 | 18·3 | 9·8 | 3·0 |
| 1866 | 3·9 | 14·5 | 4·8 | 80·2 | 32·8 | 4·7 | 18·6 | 5·5 | 9·6 | 45·6 | 220·2 | 18·6 | 13·8 | 5·7 |
| 1867 | 4·6 | 17·8 | 4·8 | 72·6 | 32·1 | 4·4 | 16·1 | (5·3) | 10·4 | 51·2 | 216·0 | 17·6 | 9·3 | 6·3 |
| 1868 | 6·3 | 19·2 | 5·5 | 70·8 | 39·0 | 6·3 | 16·9 | 7·0 | 10·3 | 48·8 | 228·0 | 19·8 | 7·9 | 4·1 |
| 1869 | 6·4 | 19·2 | 5·5 | 89·3 | 39·4 | 6·9 | 20·7 | 7·4 | (9·4) | 52·5 | 256·7 | 20·1 | 13·4 | 5·0 |
| 1870 | 6·1 | 28·5 | 6·8 | 95·5 | 40·1 | 7·4 | 25·0 | 8·0 | (11·0) | 54·3 | 283·7 | 21·9 | 15·7 | 6·3 |

figures in brackets are approximate

glass and porcelain production continued to fall, while output of piece goods remained stationary. In 1867 there was a decline in eight of the thirteen branches examined in the table. 1868 saw the continuation of the crisis in the cotton spinning and coal industries, and there was again a fall in cloth production and also in linen and sugar-beet. In 1869 flax weaving declined. Each branch of industry listed in the table thus experienced a fall at some time in the second half of the 1860s, one or more in every year; this included reductions in leather goods and paper manufactures by up to 31 per cent, in sugar production by 35 per cent and in coal output by more than 42 per cent.

Nowhere in the West did such a sharp fall in production occur in any branch of industry during the world crisis of the 1860s.[25] The crisis in Russia in 1866–7 was thus apparently more severe than in the U.S.A., Britain or Germany, and yet this crisis has so far not been mentioned in our economic literature.

In this short review of the crises of 1847, 1857 and 1867 in Russia we have by no means made an exhaustive economic study of this period of the liquidation of feudalism. The role of the industrial cycle in bringing on the crisis in the pre-reform economic structure is still not clear; but there can be no doubt that this role was not a minor one. Each of the industrial crises gave a new impulse to the mechanization of production: in 1845 imports and domestic output of machines totalled 1·25 million roubles and rose after each crisis, to 2·5m. r. in 1850, 16·5m. r. by 1860 (thus increasing 6·6 times in a decade) and to 65m. r. in 1870 (a further fourfold rise). The total therefore increased by 52 times during the 25 years. The total value of machines in use in Russia by 1861 already stood at over 100m. r., and by the end of 1870 had risen to not less than 350m. r. Certainly by present-day Soviet standards this was still a negligible amount, but at that time it represented an enormous step along the road from cottage industry to factory. At any event, a growth of mechanization on such a scale was never again achieved in the capitalist period of Russia's development.

[25] In the U.S.A. declines in certain sectors reached 18%, in Germany 12%, in Britain 8%, and in France 3% to 4%.

# The Coal Age and
# the Rise of Coalfields in
# the North and the Pas-de-Calais

MARCEL GILLET

Translated by Carol H. Kent

The degree of evolution attained in production in prehistoric times, as well as the different stages reached in the social and intellectual evolution of mankind, can be distinguished by the characteristic use of a technique or of a metal.

It obviously cannot be claimed that the 'Coal Age' characterizes in such a sweeping fashion the period of contemporary history which saw the establishment of the decisive role of the coal industry in the economic sphere. This decisive role stems initially from two fundamental technical innovations: on the one hand the progress of coking and, at the beginning of the eighteenth century, the first results of smelting iron by coke and, on the other hand, the development and perfection of the steam engine in the decade 1770–80, a decisive invention since it was first used to secure the pumping out of mines in Cornwall and above all opened up immense outlets for the use of coal. From the time of these two achievements, the importance of coal grew without interruption; it occupied a fundamental and increasing place in the structure of fuel consumption; it seems difficult to make valid estimates on a world scale, but, for comparative size, the conclusions at which P. C. Putnam arrives in his work, *Energy in the Future*, can be upheld[1]: about 1870, solid combustible minerals accounted for one-third of fuel consumption, while wood continued to hold the lead with a percentage of nearly 50 per cent; in 1910, the proportion of solid combustible minerals had risen to nearly two-thirds, while wood did not make up more than 15 per cent and hydro-electricity and oil were only just entering upon the scene. The importance of coal also lies in the fact that, for more than a century, coal production formed an excellent criterion for establishing the hierarchy of nations so far as their economic and even their political power is concerned. Finally, it is shown in the important part played by the coal industry in the location of industrial enterprises and in the

[1] P. C. Putnam, *Energy in the Future* (New York, Van Nostrand Co., 1953); Marcel Sala, 'Caractères historiques de l'économie des substances minérales', *Annales des Mines*, January 1958, p. 33.

movement and distribution of population as in business fluctuations. Industrial investment and profits were then relatively easy in coal-mining which had its Golden Age. Thus, coal played an essential part in industral development, since it was itself the foundation of economic growth. Inevitable differences appeared in the manner in which, and the time when, various countries entered their Coal Age; as is well known, Great Britain played the part of initiator and dominated the world economy and markets for a long time, as a result of the wealth of her resources and her coal output, and, still more, of the benefits which she derived from her means of communication, her position in the world and the distribution of her investments abroad, to such an extent that the Coal Age is mainly identified with British predominance in the world economy, and this predominance was never more striking than during the Victorian era. Keynes emphasized this role of the coal industry in British power in the brilliant formula: 'The Empire was in reality built on coal and iron, rather than on blood and fire.'

The example of Great Britain prompts the attempt to fix the chronological limits of the Coal Age. By the middle of the nineteenth century, the traits by which the period can be characterized are certainly already well defined in the big industrial countries of Europe and to a lesser extent in the United States; the first half of the nineteenth century can be considered as the time when these traits were established, since Britain's progress in the Industrial Revolution and the development of the manufacturing industries was very pronounced by 1815. Britain's crisis in the twentieth century developed from the turn of the century, yet it is the war of 1914–18 which can be taken as the great divide when the decline of coal began apace, both because the threat of competing sources of energy loomed larger and also because internal problems tended to slow down the growth of the coal industry. The crisis of 1929 would perhaps afford a clearer turning point but, at least on a European scale, it seems that the divide of 1914 can be considered valid.

So far as particularly the economy of the North[2] of France and its coalfield are concerned, the war of 1914–8 caused such disaster that it brutally cut short the expansion which coal-mining had experienced before 1914 and which only continued partially when the damage was repaired. Our intention is to confine our analysis primarily to the development of the coalfields in the North and the Pas-de-Calais during the nineteenth and the beginning of the twentieth centuries, in order to isolate, by means of comparison with the development of other great coalfields in the world, some fundamental problems of the world economy and the coal industry during the Coal Age.

# I

In the competition which opposed coalfields in Northern France to French and foreign rivals, it can be held that the North and the Pas-de-Calais enjoyed a certain advantage: the relatively late exploitation of the Pas-de-Calais field. Not before

[2] *Le Nord* in French can be used to denote either the *Département du Nord* or a larger contiguous region (including this *Département*), or of course in a more general sense. 'North' has been used here in both senses. Transl.

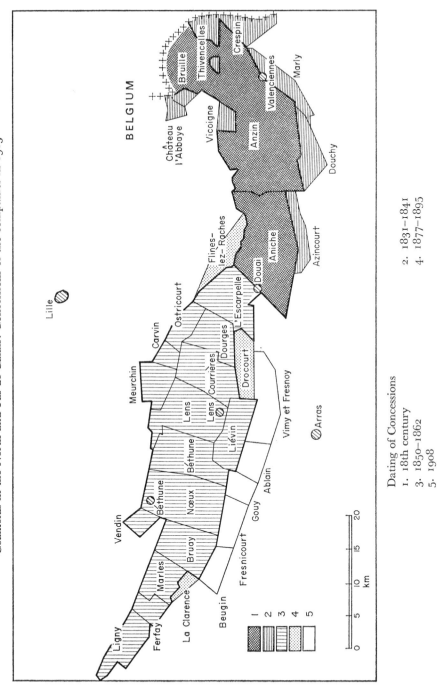

Coalfields in the North and Pas-de-Calais: Concessions of the companies in 1913

Dating of Concessions
1. 18th century
2. 1831–1841
3. 1850–1862
4. 1877–1895
5. 1908

the middle of the nineteenth century were the coal measures, situated to the west of Douai, located and developed, at the very time when industrial development made a rapid increase in the production of coal indispensable. The possibility of suddenly disposing of considerable and completely untouched wealth, capable of systematic exploitation and distribution, gave the North an obvious advantage over its direct rivals in the *Massif Central*, Belgium and Great Britain, and to a lesser extent over the Ruhr, all endowed with seams discovered and mined earlier. This advantage was both diminished and enhanced by the fact that the Valenciennes field had been for its part discovered and mined in the eighteenth century. It was diminished in that methods and traditions established in a century of limited industrial change weighed upon the manner of tackling problems in the nineteenth century; in particular, the Anzin Company, founded in 1757, served for a long time as a model for coal-mining companies established in the nineteenth century which ought perhaps to have adopted other forms. Furthermore, the precedent set by the granting of vast concessions in the eighteenth century was often invoked in the following century. Conversely, however, the experience acquired in the northern coalfield and the existence of a labour force already trained were extremely useful for the exploitation of the Pas-de-Calais field.

The birth of mining in the Valenciennes field illuminates some of the compelling economic and political conditions which favoured the 'take off' of the coal industry. The example of the mining of coal in the fields of Charleroi and of Mons was followed in the North only after a delay of several centuries. This is due, firstly, to geological conditions: contemporaries concluded from observing the east-west direction of the coalfields of Charleroi and of Mons that the coal seams mined by opencast methods in the Borinage would continue towards the west underneath the barren rock. However, it was necessary to abandon the idea, then widespread, that coal occurred everywhere at the same depth, and above all the need for new discoveries had to become imperious. The decisive incentives seem to have been the growing scarcity of wood, the strengthening of the frontier between France and the Netherlands and, finally, the desire on the part of those who exploited the Charleroi field to set up big enterprises on modern lines in unexplored territory: thus the frontier proved equally decisive as an obstacle and as a bond. The prominent part played by the Désandrouin family, a typical family with interests on both sides of the frontier, is characteristic. The discovery of a seam of non-coking coal at Fresnes in 1720, a few kilometres away from the frontier and from Valenciennes and, above all in 1734, the finding of bituminous coal in a pit at Anzin permitted the 'take-off' of mining in the Valenciennes field, a 'take-off' helped by the experience acquired in the Belgian fields. However, accompanying this success, a great threat quickly materialized, showing how premature had been the hopes nurtured by the promoters of prospecting—hopes for the easy establishment of modern enterprises on virgin soil. It concerned the demands of the feudal overlords, upholders of the customs of the Hainaut, according to which only the overlords could concede mining rights. The royal decree of 1744, however precise in its confirmation of State rights over underground mines, did not put an end to the disputes, but favoured the solution advocated by the government and the *Intendants*: on 19 November 1757, the award to the Anzin Company was signed, uniting in the same company landlords and representatives of the first exploiters. The outcome of several decades of efforts was that the Company could from then on develop without hindrance and rapidly became one of the most important coal-mining companies in the world. On the eve of the Revolution, it already employed a personnel of 4,000 workers and produced about 300,000 metric tons, out of a total French output probably of the order of 1,000,000 metric tons. An output of some 10,000,000 metric tons established the British lead, even though the rate of growth of French production was more rapid in the eighteenth century.[3]

The success of the Anzin Company stood in great contrast to the immense difficulties encountered by explorations undertaken farther west in the extension of the field which had been discovered, but also far away, in the region of Lille, Douai, Maubeuge and also in the Artois, in an attempt to establish continuity between the concession of Aniche and the small Boulonnais field discovered at the end of the seventeenth century. On the eve of the Revolution, only two small firms were in existence besides the Anzin Company, those of Aniche and of Saint-Saulve.[4] Concessions for the main part of the northern field had however been awarded, and one of the principal nineteenth-century tasks was the search for the westward continuation of this field.

In the long conquest of the northern coalfield, the period between the Revolution and the end of the Restoration marks relative stagnation. The revolutionary events were the initial cause, in the first place re-opening the whole question of the distribution of property in the field discovered in the eighteenth century and, ultimately, for a time, transforming the coal-mining region into a zone of military operations. When the coming and going of the armies had stopped, the annexation of Belgium seems to have delayed the development of the northern field: free entry of Belgian coal and the certainty of being able to count on the important resources of the Liège, Charleroi and Mons fields did not encourage the development and extension of production of a field only beginning its convalescence. Output at Anzin stagnated under the Empire at between 210,000 and 220,000, and at Aniche at between 15,000 and 25,000 metric tons.

At least this period had defined the rights of the different companies over their concessions. The law of 1791 had already confirmed existing awards for fifty years, and the law of 21 April 1810 reserved to the State alone the right of granting mining concessions in perpetuity. In contrast to Britain, rights of landowners over deposits below ground were not recognized, and in relation to the *Ancien Régime*, the rights of the State were diminished; once a concession had been granted, the latter was entitled only to fiscal demands, supervision of security regulations and very restricted powers of eventual forfeiture in the case of a concession remaining unworked. Article 51 of the law of 1810 stated: 'Grants prior to the present law will, from the day of its publication, cease to be subject to commutation.' The

---

[3] On the Valenciennes field in the eighteenth century: Archives of the Anzin Company, *procès-verbaux* of the meetings of the Board of Directors (*Conseil de Régie*) Arch. dép. du Nord, J. 316 and 317); Edouard Grar, *Histoire de la recherche, de la découverte et de l'exploitation de la houille dans le Hainaut français, dans la Flandre française et dans l'Artois, 1716–1791*, Valenciennes, 1847–51, 3 vols.; Marcel Rouff, *Les mines de charbon en France au XVIIIe siècle (1744–1791)*, Paris, 1922, thèse lettres; A. De Saint-Léger, *Les mines d'Anzin et d'Aniche pendant la Révolution*, Paris, Leroux, 1935–8, 4 vols.

[4] Archives of the Aniche Company: registers of the Board of Directors and Émile Vuillemin, *Les mines de houille d'Aniche*, Paris, Dunod, 1878.

total surface area granted in the North and the smaller field of the Boulonnais rose in 1810 to 44,623 hectares.

The Aniche Company retained close ties with regional finance, but the Anzin Company had been integrated into a national network of capital: after 1795, a large part of its capital had been acquired by important partners belonging to banking, trade and industrial circles; among them, the representatives of the Périer family were not to relinquish their predominant role within the Anzin Company.

During the Restoration, the Aniche Company continued to stagnate; with a low output of 40,000 metric tons, it was unable to distribute a dividend. In contrast, the Anzin Company increased its extraction by 50 per cent, as a result of sinking new shafts, particularly towards the western boundary of its concessions, and in June 1826 Casimir Périer was able to report to the board of directors that the Company now had a precise and reassuring estimate of the wealth which its concessions contained.[5] From that time, the Anzin Company was no longer so anxious to acquire a share in the coal mines of the Charleroi field nor did it envisage prospecting at the periphery of its possessions. The initiative leading to the restarting of prospecting in the North belonged to the Dumas Company, directed by Lille merchants, which in May 1829 sank a successful bore in the region of Denain, to the south of the zone for which concessions had already been awarded. This company evidently encountered competition from the Anzin Company: in June 1831, the latter received a new concession, that of Denain, of 1,344 hectares; the Dumas Company itself obtained in February 1832 further south the concession of Douchy of 3,419 hectares.[6] During the Casimir Périer Government, the interests of the Anzin Company were thus not sacrificed, but the Government had to take into account the desire expressed by the mining engineers and the Chambers of Commerce of the North that competition should be stimulated by the establishment of new companies.

In December 1832, the *Compagnie des Mines de Douchy* was transformed from a coal-prospecting to a coal-mining company, and its success gave an immediate stimulus to a bout of an extraordinary prospecting fever in the northern region which lasted from 1834 until 1839. It sufficed for the Douchy Company to find a seam of coal in its only pit in May 1833 for its shares to make a spectacular leap, their quotation being multiplied by 105 in one year. Though the Douchy Company had established that the zone of coal in the North *Département* extended beyond the boundary of the former concessions, exploitation risked yielding only very limited results. Nevertheless, capitalists looking for profitable investments saw in the Douchy Company proof of the possibility of founding new coal-mining companies in the northern region beside the Anzin Company—companies likely to make spectacular capital gains very quickly for their founders even before serious exploitation had started. This explains the patently speculative character of prospecting then carried out in the North: it was not so much long-term capital investment in serious companies as an attempt to obtain quick results of sufficient promise to permit the resale at a high premium of shares cheaply acquired.

---

[5] Archives of the Anzin Company, Board of Directors, 15 June 1826.
[6] *Arch. dép. du Nord*, S. 8311 and 8312.

Development in mining techniques facilitated serious as well as purely formal explorations: the invention of trepanning went back to 1775 but, according to the mining engineer Bonnard, almost all prospecting carried out in the eighteenth century and under the Empire had been done by sinking shafts which were inevitably very costly;[7] the widespread employment of trepanning required no more than 8,000 to 10,000 francs per bore-hole by about 1830.[8]

Prospecting fever from 1834 to 1839 was not confined to the northern region: M. Bertrand Gille, in his work on *La Banque et le crédit en France de 1815 à 1848*,[9] has emphasized that it also affected the Loire and the Gard fields; Belgium experienced it too. It is one of the symptoms indicating the increasing part played by coal in the economy and the need which each country and each area felt to increase its coal supply.

In 1837, 70 applications for concessions had been transmitted to the *Préfecture* of the North and numerous applications to the *Préfecture* of the Pas-de-Calais. In the North, at the periphery of existing concessions, the attempts came from companies run either by industrialists and businessmen from the northern region or by representatives of Parisian or Belgian banks. Prospecting in the Pas-de-Calais, probably because it appeared to entail greater risk, mobilized much more specifically regional capital; explorations continued to follow the direction of the seams of the northern field, and since the change of direction in the region of Douai was unknown, about 4,000,000 francs were then sunk in vain in these projects alone.[10]

After 1839, prospecting in the North stopped as suddenly as it had begun. The craze could have been maintained only by resounding successes which had not been achieved. Furthermore, the economic crisis of 1839 engendered an atmosphere of pessimism.

To sum up the situation in the northern coalfield, explorations conducted during this period led to the granting of concessions which gave an almost definitive physiognomy to the division of the field. The surface area under concession rose under the July Monarchy from 34,756 to 55,844 hectares, in other words, it grew by 56·89 per cent. However, the increase in the field's real potential was much less important. The vast concessions of Anzin and Aniche were flanked at their periphery by much smaller and considerably less productive concessions, often stretching beyond the boundaries of coal deposits. Six companies divided the new concessions among themselves. Government effort had tended to stimulate competition while avoiding excessive division; thus it had succeeded in combining a dozen enterprises into the companies of Vicoigne, Azincourt and Thivencelles, and the Anzin Company had acquired the possession of a quarter of the Vicoigne Company's capital in 1841.[11] Only this Company and the Douchy Company were to acquire any importance. In 1847, companies formed under the July Monarchy accounted for about only one-third of the production of the northern field, that is

---

[7] De Bonnard, 'Notice sur diverses recherches de houille entreprises dans le département du Pas-de-Calais', *Journal des Mines*, XXVI, 1809, p. 439.
[8] Du Souich, *Essai sur les recherches de houille dans le Nord de la France*, Paris and Arras, 1839, p. 6.                                             [9] Paris, P.U.F., 1959, pp. 334–5.
[10] According to a report from the Inspector General of Mines Dufrénoy, 12 February 1850, in the *Arch. nat.* F[14], 7819.
[11] Archives of the Company of Vicoigne, Nœux, Drocourt.

G

370,000 out of 1,250,000 metric tons. The Anzin Company alone provided half the output.

At the time of the economic crisis of 1846–7, the northern field still accounted for only a quarter of French output; it was the Loire field, exploited very much earlier, which continued to hold the lead among French fields, producing one-third of national output; but it suffered from a decisive handicap: coal from the North and Belgium was to benefit from the expansion of markets in the Paris region at its expense; the Saint-Quentin canal, begun in 1810 and put into service at the beginning of the Restoration, was the highway giving access to Paris. It was the superiority of transport to the main centres of consumption rather than its resources or progress in mining which gave a field its advantage. On a national scale, the northern field enjoyed such an advantage over its principal competitor.

The significance of the northern region in the national and international economy was considerably increased by the discovery and development of the Pas-de-Calais field in the middle of the nineteenth century. A century of effort had not discovered an extension of the Valenciennes field beyond Douai. In contrast, within a few years beginning from 1846 the direction of the coal seams in the Pas-de-Calais was located and the main part of the coal measures found. Once the change in the direction of the coalfield near Douai was realized, rapid advance was bound to follow.

In considering the discovery of the change in direction, excessive importance is too often attached, it seems, to the lucky chance that led to the discovery of coal north-west of Douai. It must not be forgotten, firstly, that the Pas-de-Calais coalfield was discovered and above all developed when changes in industrial structure and the development of railways rendered an increase in French coal production both indispensable and profitable. In addition the long-term cyclical upswing from 1851 onwards was bound to encourage the development of new fields. It is characteristic that the 'take-off' in mining in the Lorraine coalfield and above all the great rise in the output of Ruhr coal similarly date from the middle of the nineteenth century.

The fact is that a prospecting engineer, Georges Mulot, had found a coalfield near Oignies already in June 1842 at a depth of 151 metres in the park of Henriette Declercq, the widow of a Parisian banker, while looking for water, but neither Mulot nor H. Declercq took immediate advantage of that discovery. The decisive strike was made by a company founded by Eugene Soyez, a merchant from Cambrai, which made a successful boring at L'Escarpelle on 20 May 1847, finding a seam of coal at a depth of 158 metres. Although it is denied, Soyez, a man without technical knowledge, was indebted to Élie de Bracquemont, chairman of the Vicoigne Company who, ever since 1845, had in vain asked his board of directors to undertake borings in the Douai area. De Bracquemont was impressed by the lessons of the unproductive borings in the period 1834–9 and also by the theories of Du Souich, engineer of the Pas-de-Calais mines from 1831. Scientific considerations had led Du Souich to suspect in 1844 that the extension of the coal seams in the Pas-de-Calais must be parallel to the line of the primary outcrops of the Artois; this made him realize the change in direction of the coal seams in the Douai region. In any case, this theory guided the explorations towards the west after the successful Escarpelle boring. Thus, the discovery of the Pas-de-Calais field appears, in the context of favourable general economic conditions, to be the result of combining science and technology, from which certain enterprising businessmen knew how to take advantage; the tenacious legend of accidental discovery ought to be abandoned.[12]

At the time when it was resumed and crowned with success, coal prospecting in the North did not, however, provoke a feverish campaign similar to that of the years 1834–9. Memories of previous set-backs had probably left a deep imprint on the state of mind of owners of capital. The stagnation which overtook the coalfield of Valenciennes in 1847, followed by the Revolution of 1848, served only to accentuate this lack of enthusiasm which even the beginnings of the Second Empire did not quickly cure.[13] Finally, the development of railways greatly attracted investments.[14] This results in a very marked contrast between the slow, steady development of the years 1847–54 and the increase in the number of coal-mining companies, the prospecting activity and the rush of capital witnessed in the 1830s and recurring ultimately. This decisive mid-century period saw neither a race nor a rush for coal; the main part of the new field could be located and development started by experienced companies, taking swift action at the right moment, without encountering excessively harsh rivalry.

The companies in the northern coalfield and several business men involved in the prospecting which had already been undertaken in this field played a decisive part. As in the eighteenth century, experience acquired in the field was used when a new pit was opened. However, because of their distance, the role of the Belgian companies this time remained secondary. The policy adopted by the civil service and the government concerning the award of concessions constituted an extremely important element for the future of the new field. The example of Belgium and of Great Britain, often invoked, appeared to argue in favour of small concessions. The period is characterized by the desire to lower prices by stimulating competition rather than to increase production. This encouraged multiplication of concessions, all the more as it was desired to avoid a monopoly such as that of the *Compagnie des mines de la Loire* which the government wanted to break by the decree of 23 October 1852, which prohibited the merging of concessions without authorization. However, new mines had to be enabled to resist the richly endowed Anzin and Aniche Companies. It seems probable that, failing governmental intervention, all the main part of the field would have been divided among a few interconnected companies associated with the Anzin, Vicoigne and Douchy Companies. It was this intervention which undid bonds too quickly tied. From September 1850 to December

---

[12] On the discovery of the Pas-de-Calais field: *Arch. nat.* F.14, 7819 and 7836, *dossier* 17; Archives of the Company of Vicoigne, Nœux, Drocourt: A. De Bracquemont, reports to the directors of the mines of Vicoigne and Nœux from 1844 to 1872, pp. 27–9; Du Souich, 'Notice historique sur la recherche du prolongement du bassin de Valenciennes dans le Pas-de-Calais', *Bulletin de la Société de l'Industrie minérale*, February 1913, pp. 113–60; Émile Vuillemin, *Le bassin houiller du Pas-de-Calais*, Lille, Impr. Danel, 1880–3, III, pp. 109–19; Févre and Cuvelette, *Notice géologique et historique sur les bassins houillers du Pas-de-Calais et du Boulonnais*, Arras, Impr. Repessé-Crépel, 1900, pp. 71–2.

[13] Cf. Marcel Gillet, 'Aspect de la crise de 1846–1851 dans le bassin houiller du Nord', *Revue du Nord*, XXXVIII, No. 149, 1956, pp. 15–27.

[14] Cf. Louis Girard, *La politique des travaux publics du Second Empire*, Paris, A. Colin, 1952, pp. 6–10.

1855, ten new concessions were granted in the new field, endowing ten companies each with a single concession, with the exception of the Vicoigne Company, installed both in the North and in the Pas-de-Calais because of its concessions at Vicoigne and at Nœux. Following the advice of Du Souich, the field had been cut up into fairly large transverse slices, in order to facilitate and diversify marketing for the companies by giving them the possibility of mining coal of low, medium and high volatility, in accordance with the structure of the field.

By the beginning of the Second Empire, most of the Pas-de-Calais field had been discovered and put under concession. New prospecting fevers in 1855, 1873 and at the end of the nineteenth century did indeed permit the location and extension of the northern and southern limits of the field at the price of increasingly costly explorations giving rise to 16 new concessions, but they were usually very limited; alone among those set up after the beginning of the Second Empire, the Liévin Company, founded in 1862, was able to attain an importance comparable to that of companies installed along the axis of the field.

The example of the coalfields of the North and the Pas-de-Calais throws into relief the way in which the French coal industry entered the Coal Age. The long-term evolution of the coal industry perhaps reflects, rather than precedes, the evolution of the economy as a whole. The 'take off' in the Pas-de-Calais field is in this respect particularly significant; but in the short run, delays and difficulties in adjustment appear. There is a pronounced contrast between the extraordinary frenzy of explorations and the easy mobilization of capital which the region knew at the time of the prospecting fever and the relative apathy displayed during the decisive years 1847–54. The stimulus of the early successes was necessary in order to set up a multiplicity of companies, but these worked in a chaotic fashion and often arrived too early or too late. Many disappointments and failures counterbalanced the brilliant successes of companies which had been able to set up at the right time and obtain valuable concessions in the richest parts of the field. Subsequent capable management was obviously essential for the expansion of companies. The Liévin Company is a good example of an enterprise seemingly badly provided for in the beginning, yet obtaining excellent results; but, on the whole, the starting-point and the territory obtained were extremely important for the development of the different companies and their adaptation to the Coal Age.

# II

From the middle of the nineteenth century until 1914, the North and the Pas-de-Calais coalfields continued to account for a growing part of national output, mainly as a result of the rise of the Pas-de-Calais field, a new field with a rate of growth exceeding that of output and consumption for France as a whole. From 1876 onwards, the Pas-de-Calais field accounted for more than half the coal output in the North of France; on the eve of the 1914–8 War, it supplied three-quarters of total production. By the middle of the Second Empire, output from the North and the Pas-de-Calais fields drew level with that of the Loire and regularly exceeded it from 1863. From 1886 onwards, it represents more than half French output and, on the average of the years 1908–12, the North and the Pas-de-Calais fields account for three-quarters of French output, averaging nearly 26,000,000 out of a national output of about 39,000,000 tons; this last period marks the apogee of their relative importance. The second French field, the Loire, supplied only less than one-tenth of national output; it fell considerably behind, completely reversing what had been the situation up to the middle of the nineteenth century.

On an international scale, on the other hand, the importance of the basin in the northern region increased in more modest proportions. This can be gauged by comparing French production with that of the main coal-producing countries. On the eve of the 1914–8 War, France with 41,145,000 metric tons accounted for only 3·3 per cent of world coal production, which reached 1,215,000,000 metric tons. She thus took fourth place in the world among coal-producing countries, a long way behind the U.S.A. (517,000,000 metric tons), Great Britain (292,000,000 metric tons) and Germany (190,000,000 metric tons). France's relatively modest output by comparison with the main producing countries resulted from the inferiority of her resources and from the much higher rates of growth enjoyed by Germany and the U.S.A. during the second half of the nineteenth and the beginning of the twentieth centuries. Even if one takes average annual percentages of *per capita* growth, important differences appear.[15] It is true that a certain parallelism can be observed between the series as far as the different phases of development, themselves reflecting the fundamental pattern of the succession of long-term cyclical movements, are concerned: high rates of growth for the period of take-off 1820–50, maintained during the years 1851–73, slowdown between 1873 and 1896, and a clear upturn during the period 1896–1913. However, German and American rates are much higher: for 1850–73, the German rate is 8·71 per cent against 6·12 per cent for France; the levels are the same for 1873–96, but between 1896 and 1913, the German rate of growth is almost five times that of France: 8·49 per cent against 1·74 per cent. In the middle of the nineteenth century, the coalfields of the French northern region and of the Ruhr had outputs of the same volume, but from 1870, production in the Ruhr with nearly 12,000,000 metric tons was ahead of that of the North and the Pas-de-Calais by 17 per cent and, until the World War, the Ruhr's lead increased: in 1913 its output with 110,000,000 metric tons equalled four times that of the northern region.

On the other hand, British and French graphs are roughly similar for a long time and, around 1900, *per capita* output even tends to decline in Great Britain, an obvious sign of crisis in the British economy. The end of the nineteenth century (to be exact the year 1899) saw American coal output overtake that of Great Britain and in 1913 British production amounted to only 56·4 per cent of U.S. output.

American coalfields on the other hand did not constitute competitors before 1914, since they played hardly any part in French imports. It is important that the rhythms of growth of French and British production were alike; so is the fact that the North and the Pas-de-Calais fields did not cease to grow in importance relative to the Belgian mines. In the middle of the nineteenth century, the difference between the output of the northern field and that of its rivals in the Hainaut

[15] Pierre Léon, 'L'industrialisation en France en tant que facteur de croissance économique du début du XVIIIe siècle à nos jours', *Première conférence internationale d'histoire économique*, Paris and the Hague, Mouton and Co., 1960, pp. 188–9.

and in Liège had been considerable. In the long succession of coalfields stretching from the Ruhr to the northern region of France, it was fields occupying central positions which were still by far the most actively exploited. For the years 1843-7, Belgian output with 4,809,000 metric tons was greater than that of the Anzin field and, at the end of the Second Empire, remained still three times those of the North and of the Pas-de-Calais. However, from 1890 to 1894, the Belgian lead was reduced to 39 per cent and, at the beginning of the twentieth century coal output in the northern region reached the level of Belgian production which it regularly outstripped from 1908, being ahead of it by about 10 per cent on the eve of the War.

The relative importance of the Belgian fields in the heart of the big Ruhr–North of France coal axis was thus completely reversed: the central fields became weaker than their neighbours, particularly to the east, but also those in the west. Compared to their most immediate competitors, the Belgian fields, the importance of the coalfields of the North and the Pas-de-Calais continued to increase, and this development is particularly reflected in the decreasing place occupied by imports of Belgian coal into France. During the years 1843-7, imports of Belgian coal amounted to two-thirds of all French imports. In the years 1908-12, although trebled in absolute terms, they constituted no more than one-fifth of French imports. It seems that the discovery and rise of the Pas-de-Calais field brought about the falling off of the development of the Belgian fields and the decline of Belgian coal imports into France, in proportion as coal from the Pas-de-Calais supplanted competing supplies from the Hainaut.

A comparison between the development of the coalfields of the North and the Pas-de-Calais and that of other big fields in the world throws into relief some of the fundamental problems. An attempt can be made to ascertain whether the rise in coal production was characterized by an exponential growth in the nineteenth and beginning of the twentieth centuries; ignoring short-term cyclical fluctuations, were rates of growth during this period roughly constant and, consequently, can series corresponding to output in the world, in the principal producing countries and in the leading fields be represented on semi-logarithmic graphs by straight lines? In 1865, in his work *The Coal Question*, the English economist Stanley Jevons, applying the celebrated comparison of Malthus to the coal industry, thought that in order to ensure an arithmetical progression of industry and population, a geometrical progression in coal production was necessary, and he was worried by the threat of exhaustion of British coal mines.

Actual developments suggest that in the short term, production was subject to cyclical fluctuations, but if the effects of crises are eliminated, a second fact emerges: the second half of the nineteenth and the beginning of the twentieth centuries were definitely characterized by regular and continuous growth of world coal output, attaining an annual average rate of about 4·1 per cent, which corresponds to a 50 per cent growth every ten years and to a doubling of production every 17 years. On a world basis, therefore, the above-mentioned decrease in growth rates during the last quarter of the nineteenth century in the main producing countries, including Germany and the U.S., was compensated for. So far as the fields of the North and the Pas-de-Calais were concerned, the growth rate was 9·4 per cent during the years 1851–73 at the time of the 'take-off' of the Pas-de-Calais, in a favourable long-term upswing; it halved during the 1874–96 down-

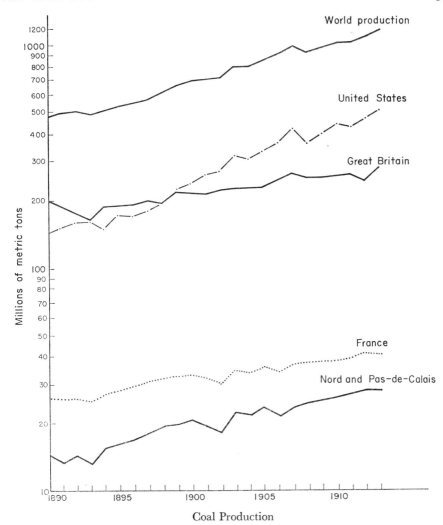

Coal Production

swing, falling to 4·5 per cent. In the North and the Pas-de-Calais fields, the decline even continued into the 1896–1913 period, since annual rate of growth of extraction fell to 2·8 per cent.[16] The high level attained by production, in itself a retarding factor, improvements in the productivity of coal-using equipment, and probably above all growing difficulties of extraction, consequent upon progress in depth, tended to limit the advance of the coal industry in the North and the Pas-de-

---

[16] In order to determine growth rates, we were satisfied with applying the formula of compound interest:

$$r = n \sqrt{\left(\frac{B}{A}\right)} - 1$$

$r$ = rate of growth; $n$ = number of years; $A$ = first term; $B$ = last term; this formula only uses the extreme terms of the series; we know that better approximate rates can be calculated, but by means of calculations which are far too long: cf. our study *Techniques de l'histoire économique*, Paris, C.D.U., 1962, pp. 70–3.

Calais and in certain large producing countries like Great Britain where this took effect even before 1914. Furthermore, in the long run, all growth curves appertaining to a particular economic sector tend to flatten out.

However, it must be emphasized that on a world scale total coal production from the beginning of the twentieth century until 1914 continued to develop at the same rate and continuity as during the second half of the nineteenth century; some producing countries of long standing maintained the speed of their growth, other producers, such as Russia, compensated for the slowdown of production in some of the older fields. The economic situation also favoured continued expansion. In the long run internal problems would probably have tended to slow down the growth of coal output. But, on a world scale, they had not yet appeared, especially as exogenous problems had not yet added their effect to internal ones. Competition from oil, gas and hydro-electricity had shown a tendency to slow down the rise in coal production without as yet, it seems, becoming a decisive factor: in 1910, of all the power developed in the world from coal, lignite, oil, natural gas and hydro-electricity, the first two still account for almost 93 per cent.[17]

It is true that world statistics of power consumption are not very accurate. The value of the series differs according to countries; in order to determine total power consumption, coefficients of equivalence have to be established between different sources of energy, coefficients always a little uncertain and variable for that period. Despite these reservations, world production of energy in the second half of the nineteenth century and up to 1914 can be considered to have developed in a continuous and regular fashion, following a curve which, until the end of the nineteenth century, remained parallel to that of world coal production. However, after 1914 exogenous factors, such as the development of competing sources of energy, caused a considerable slowing down in the development of the coal industry, while at the same time violent short-term cyclical fluctuations led to considerable recessions, in particular as a result of the Great Depression of 1929–33. Moreover, world production of energy as a whole went through a period of considerable fluctuations between the two world wars, and at the same time a tendency towards a general deceleration in the growth of power consumption asserted itself. By comparison, the nineteenth century seems characterized by a straight-line development in coal production and power consumption, and this regular and substantial expansion constitutes an essential characteristic of the Coal Age: it seems that the world experienced a straight-line development in energy again only after 1950, in an age when coal still plays a considerable, but much more limited part than in the nineteenth century.

The evolution of coal production raises, among many others, the problem of the connection between the increase in national incomes and that of the coal output of different countries in the nineteenth century. In our day, increases in national income and standard of living appear to be directly conditioned by those of energy production and consumption. For the period between the two world wars it has been possible to compare some series which show a certain parallelism between the evolution of national income and power consumption. This is particularly the case with France; here we refer to the graph reproduced by M. Jocelyn Moniez

[17] Cf. C. M. Cipolla, 'Sources d'énergie et histoire de l'humanité', *Annales E.S.C.*, XVI, 1961, p. 530.

in his study on the French coal industry since 1946.[18] The graph was plotted from a study by M. Prevot based on a report by M. Dumontier at the *Conseil économique* in 1957, a report which evaluates *per capita* national income in France from 1901 to 1957. The parallelism of the curves for national income and power consumption is marked in the interwar period and continues until 1957.

Had this parallelism existed already in the nineteenth century? This is difficult to ascertain in the absence of national income statistics during the last century, and studies so far undertaken have not yet succeeded in giving sufficiently valid results. From the particularly important work directed by the *Institut de Science Économique Appliquée* and M. François Perroux, it seems that, from 1780 to 1940, French national income doubled every 40 years, rising in terms of constant prices in 1913 from four billion francs in 1780 to 8 billions in 1820, 16 billions in 1860, 32 billions in 1900 and 64 billions in 1940. The average annual rate of growth of national income was thus established at a fairly low level during one and a half centuries, that is at 1·7 per cent per year. It is obvious that in the nineteenth century the progress of production and consumption of energy proceeded at a much quicker rate. Whereas French national income increased by 300 per cent between 1820 and 1900, coal production increased by 2,284 per cent and, what is even more significant, coal consumption in France by 2,620 per cent. In a century in which coal continuously increased its prime role in the structure of power consumption, a clear lag seems to appear between the growth of power, or at least coal consumption and that of national income. However, national income figures represent only an approximation and a very long-term trend. What can tentatively be suggested is that at the beginning of the nineteenth century the development of the coal industry, by favouring industrial growth, permitted national income to escape from its probable stagnation in previous centuries. Nevertheless, remarkable efforts and considerable expansion yielded only a relatively modest result. Industrialization and the growing place of coal in power consumption caused the curves for national income and for coal consumption in France to draw closer together. Between 1896 and 1913, French coal consumption grew on average by 1·8 per cent per year, hence at a rate practically equal to that of the French national income, if we accept the rate of 1·7 per cent as valid for national income growth. It is a striking fact that between 1896 and 1913 production of coal and national income increased at exactly the same rate. At the moment when the Coal Age was beginning to be superseded, a remarkable coincidence in the curves for coal production and national income thus emphasized in a last fling the decisive place which coal had acquired in national life. Hence power consumption and national income have pursued their parallel progress, at least until the last few years. Economists think that today the correlation between power consumption and gross domestic product is less close. Instead of almost 1, we now have an elasticity coefficient equal to 0·9 or even 0·8, power consumption increasing less rapidly than gross domestic product. The present situation, therefore, seems to be the reverse of the nineteenth century when power consumption increased more rapidly than national income.[19]

[18] Jocelyn Moniez, *L'industrie charbonnière française depuis 1946*, 1959, 2 vols., thèse droit Lille, ii, p. 361.
[19] Since the presentation of this study, important research has been done, within the

We hope to have proved that it would be a most fruitful field of research to attempt to compare the growth of national income and coal consumption in the nineteenth century. Comparisons between countries and between continents would probably show clearly how much faster national incomes grew in the main coal producing and coal consuming countries, thus providing additional justification for calling the nineteenth century the 'Coal Age'.

# III

Increase of extraction in the coalfields of the North and the Pas-de-Calais was much faster than in other French and Belgian fields, similar to that of the British fields, but slower than in the Ruhr. It is worth trying to explain these divergent developments.

A first obvious and fundamental factor lies in the distribution, quality and mining conditions of different coal measures. In this respect, the fields of the North and the Pas-de-Calais appeared to be unfavourably situated by comparison with the German, but slightly more favourably than the other French and Belgian fields. The disparity of geological conditions is particularly marked between the Ruhr and the French northern field.

On the eve of the 1914 War, the Ruhr mines covered a proven surface area of 300,000 hectares. 136 coal seams of a total thickness of 108 metres had been discovered. Not counting intermediate barren beds of rock and seams not considered worth mining (less than 65 cm thick), the Westphalian coalfield was reckoned to be 3,000 metres across and to contain 80 metres of marketable coal divided among an almost equal number of exploitable seams which, though undulating and faulted, were much less dislocated than in the Franco-Belgian fields. Exploratory work suggested that the field down to a depth of 1,500 metres contained 54 billions of metric tons, a contribution towards giving Germany the first place in European coal reserves. At a time when cutting remained essentially manual, a comparison of yields gives some idea of the advantages resulting from the structural simplicity of coal measures. Most sources will allow of no better measure of productivity than annual output per worker: for the decade 1861–70, the annual average yield of a miner in the Ruhr exceeded by one-third that of the worker in the Pas-de-Calais (himself superior to that of the North), 188 metric tons against 142. In the decade 1871–80, the difference rose to almost 50 per cent (244 metric tons against 167); it was no more than 11 per cent in the decade 1901–10 (251 metric tons against 225). In addition to number, potential and regularity

framework of an international study advocated by Simon Kuznets, on the comparative evolution of national income, in particular in France by J. Marczewski and T. J. Markovitch who have published several *Cahiers de l'Institut de Science Économique Appliquée*, relative to *l'Histoire quantitative de l'Économie française*. For his part, T. J. Markovitch also concludes, in his work *L'industrie française de 1789 à 1964—Analyse des faits (suite)*, *Cahiers del' Iséa*, June 1966, p. 138, that the rate of growth of sources of energy in France was much quicker than that of global industrial growth. Let us also note that a research team, under the direction of François Crouzet, is working to build up an index of industrial production for France in the nineteenth century.

of its coal seams, the Ruhr enjoyed another essential asset in relation to the Franco-Belgian fields: the abundance of coking coal which was easiest to mine in the middle part of the coal measures in 1913. Out of the Ruhr's total output of 110,000,000 metric tons, the bituminous coal which largely preponderated enabled the making of 20,000,000 metric tons of coke, supplying the regional steel industry and exports.[20]

The coalfields of the North and the Pas-de-Calais display mining conditions which vary greatly in different sectors, but are on the whole fairly difficult, especially because of the very complicated structure of the coal measures which resulted from the coalfields having been affected by a system of very strong folds, the majority sloping towards the north, intersected by a series of big longitudinal inverse faults. In 1913, at the Geology Congress in Toronto, Deflines, chief inspector of mines, estimated the reserves of the field at 3 billion metric tons up to a depth of 1,200 metres, with soft coking coal containing between 18 and 26 per cent of volatile matter accounting for about one-third of these reserves.[21] However, production of coke had begun in the North in 1855 only by the Aniche Company; during the years preceding the War of 1914, it reached only 2,200,000 metric tons, out of a global production of about 26,000,000, despite recent large-scale development of coking by the Lens Company which supplanted the Aniche and Anzin Companies' lead over the companies of the North and the Pas-de-Calais. Coke output in the northern region corresponded roughly to almost half of French coke production, which covered only two-thirds of French consumption.

In comparison with the fields of the North and the Pas-de-Calais, the Ruhr possessed superiority in other ways: geographical position and ease of transport; for long-distance deliveries, producers in the Rhenish-Westphalian field used waterways as much as possible: on the one hand the Rhine which enabled them both to export through Rotterdam and to supply Southern Germany, Alsace-Lorraine, France and Switzerland, on the other hand the Dortmund-Ems canal which facilitated trade with Northern Germany.

As far as geographical position and means of communication go, it has often been emphasized how inconvenient for the French economy was the peripheral position of the fields of the North and the Pas-de-Calais, and also how vulnerable to foreign competition, owing to the proximity of the Belgian fields and the ease of importing English coal across the sea. It is true that the inconvenience of their geographical situation was partly balanced by the great advantage of being in an industrial region possessing very important metallurgical and above all textile industries which from the start ensured easy markets.

Nevertheless the problem of access to markets remained essential. From the middle of the nineteenth century, the question of rail communications with the Paris region was happily resolved, initially just before 1848 for the field of the *Département du Nord*, then in 1860 as a result of the construction of a railway for the collieries of the Pas-de-Calais field; railway construction, in addition to in-

---

[20] E. Gruner and G. Bousquet, *Atlas général des houillères*, Paris, C.C.H.F., 1911, pp. 105–9 and 111; M. Baumont, *La grosse industrie allemande et le charbon*, Paris, thèse lettres, 1928; E. A. Wrigley, *Industrial Growth and Population Change*, Cambridge, 1961, pp. 38–9.

[21] A. Defline, 'Les ressources de la France en combustibles minéraux', *The Coal Resources of the World*, 12th International Geological Congress, Toronto, 1913, vol. II, pp. 649–712.

creasing ease and rapidity of transport, obliged the canals to lower their freights. Water transport remained the basic and also the most advantageous means of transport for the coal mining companies, enabling them to hold their own most effectively against foreign competition. In fact the importance of tariff protection continued to decrease during the course of the nineteenth century. In order not to encroach upon Professor Crouzet's paper,[22] let us mention only that from 1863 French import duties on Belgian coal were reduced to a specific rate of 1·20 francs per metric ton. The protection thus afforded varied according to price fluctuations; it increased in the period 1874–96, when the price of coal at the pit-heads of the North and the Pas-de-Calais went down to 9·03 francs in 1888 (resulting in a customs duty of 12 per cent) and decreased in the period 1897–1914, when coal went up to 15·67 francs in 1909 (making the duty 7 per cent).

The system of canals ensured fairly good protection against the Charleroi coal-field. It is true that the Sambre facilitated colonization of the metallurgical region of Maubeuge by the coal and capital of the Charleroi field. However, the canal from the Sambre to the Oise, designed to carry the coal from Charleroi to Paris, was finished in 1838 only and navigation on it remained difficult, owing to geographical conditions, so that the price of freight to Paris remained higher by the Sambre than by the Escaut. This price difference was further accentuated after the nationalization of the Escaut and Saint-Quentin canals in 1860. The network of the Sambre remained under concession to private companies levying high tolls, nor was nationalization of the canals of the Sambre and from the Sambre to the Oise included in the Freycinet Plan of 1878. The rivalry of the Charleroi field was thus held in check.[23]

The competition of the Borinage field was stronger, owing to the use by Belgian coal of canals from Mons to Condé and from the Escaut to the Saint-Quentin Canal, canals which had been in operation since the beginning of the Restoration and gave easy access to Paris. The rise of the Pas-de-Calais changed the situation by bringing about progressive saturation of the Saint-Quentin Canal and necessitating a new route to the Paris region to assure easier and cheaper access for the coal from the northern region which as a result could meet Belgian and also English competition more effectively. From 1860 the principal companies of the Pas-de-Calais grouped themselves in a *Comité des Houillères du Pas-de-Calais* responsible for coping with transport problems, but it was only after 1878 that the Committee, enlarged into the *Comité des Houillères du Nord et du Pas-de-Calais*, under the presidency of Émile Vuillemin, chairman of the Aniche Company, took major steps with a view to obtaining the development of water connections. It was the projects then elaborated for the improvement of the Seine river bed and the transformation of Paris into a sea port which inspired the coal-mining companies of the North and particularly of the Pas-de-Calais to strive for a fundamental improvement. This led in 1878 to the first studies regarding the *Canal du Nord* by a special commission of the Ministry of Public Works charged with finding out 'suitable means of putting the coal mines in a position to withstand foreign competition'. However, the efforts of the companies in the northern region remained ineffective for a long time. It was

[22] François Crouzet, *Le charbon anglais en France au XIXe siècle, Actes du Colloque Charbon et Sciences Humaines*, Paris, Mouton, 1966, pp. 173–206.
[23] René Gendarme, *La région du Nord, essai d'analyse économique*, Paris, A. Colin, 1954, p. 49.

only on 23 December 1903 that the *Canal du Nord* was officially authorized, for a distance of 93·71 kilometres from Arleux, on the Sensée, to Pont-l'Evêque, near Noyon, at a time when the Saint-Quentin Canal, on its own, accounted for 146 kilometres between these two points. If one establishes the equivalents for the existing or planned locks and tunnels, one arrives at the equivalent of 201 km. for the Saint-Quentin Canal, and the equivalent of 118 km. for the *Canal du Nord*, thus a very important decrease. The canal was to admit coal barges of 300 metric tons and lead to a fall of 30 per cent in freight prices. The coal-mining companies in the northern region had to make a large financial contribution through the intermediary of the Chamber of Commerce of Douai. The work, begun in 1908, was three-quarters completed in 1914, the coal mines having contributed a share of 23 million out of the 72 million francs expenses incurred. The 1914–8 War initiated a long period of renewed lethargy as regards the question of the *Canal du Nord*, by interfering with and stopping the work until its recent resumption. While during the second half of the nineteenth century the coalfields of the North and the Pas-de-Calais had enjoyed important connections by water, they had not then been able to obtain a more adequate canal which would probably have stimulated their expansion.

# IV

The desire to obtain from public authorities the improvement of existing or the creation of new means of communication was one of the principal bonds which led coal-mining companies of the North and the Pas-de-Calais to unite their efforts. All through the nineteenth and at the beginning of the twentieth century, coal companies of the northern region remained in fact much more independent of each other than German or even in certain fields Belgian companies. The decree of 1852 contributed to maintaining this situation by forbidding mergers of concessions without State authorization, whereas the German law of 1865 allowed mergers. Merging of concessions was extremely rare in the North and the Pas-de-Calais and usually only concerned small concessions of bankrupt companies acquired by their more thriving neighbours; it was thus that, after the disappearance of the Douvrin Company in 1869, Lens bought its concession in 1873 and added it to its perimeter in 1875.

Legal or financial connections between different companies were very rare: the most important, already indicated, was the share of the Anzin Company in the Vicoigne-Nœux Company; when in 1873 the Anzin Company distributed to its shareholders the shares of Vicoigne-Nœux which it owned, it kept the right to appoint two of the eight Nœux directors. The Douchy and Courrières Companies often had common directors because of the important part played by Douchy directors and capital in the creation of Courrières. However, it is certainly an established fact that between the Second Empire and 1914, no coal-mining company in the northern region acquired a share large enough to give it control over any of its neighbours. Especially significant is the example of the small Company of Ligny-lez-Aire, founded in 1894 to resume mining at Auchy-au-Bois and Fléchinelle, at the western extremity of the Pas-de-Calais field; the major part of the capital of 2,000,000 francs was subscribed by shareholders of Marles, encouraged by the example of their managing director, Firmin Rainbeaux. But in 1904 the directors representing the Marles interest were eliminated from the business by a Marles ex-engineer, Clément Baily, who had gradually, with relatives and friends, acquired the majority of the shares.[24] The situation in 1914 in the North field was that the Anzin and Aniche Companies went back to the eighteenth century; among the nine companies founded in the nineteenth century, five survived in 1914, among them Douchy and Vicoigne-Nœux; in the Pas-de-Calais, of 22 companies established in the second half of the nineteenth century, 14 were still extant on the eve of the War, all financially independent of each other. Some developments, however, were important: the penetration of the de Wendel Company which had acquired the small concessions of Crespin and La Clarence, and the grant of new concessions south of the Pas-de-Calais field to steel companies of the North and of Meurthe-et-Moselle. Nevertheless, it was still very far removed from the situation in the Ruhr where steel companies were closely associated or integrated.

The companies of the North and the Pas-de-Calais continued to draw the major part of their shareholders and directors from local sources, in particular from the bourgeoisie of the towns of Cambrai, Valenciennes, and Lille-Roubaix-Tourcoing. However, a trend begins which, as at Lens, tends to transfer the reins of power to the engineers who often come from the *Corps des Mines*, whose advice dominates discussions in the boards of directors and for whom the development of their company is the major objective.

The legal status adopted by most coal-mining companies did not facilitate closer relationship or mergers of several companies. In fact, even after the laws of 1867 and 1893, the majority of coal-mining enterprises remained private companies (*sociétés civiles*). When the law of 1893 had made it easier to change the articles of association, several companies, among them Courrières and Douchy, adopted limited liability, but the majority remained private companies, and it was only after the 1914–8 War and the law of 1919 that the adoption of limited liability became general.

The method of financing companies worked in the same direction. What is initially striking is the relative modesty of the capital employed in coal-mining companies in the North and the Pas-de-Calais at the time of their foundation, particularly under the Second Empire. Its inadequacy is sometimes even notorious, as in the case of the Bruay Company, which at the outset only had 1,040,000 francs effectively subscribed. This weakness in share capital can stem from difficulties in finding shareholders, at a time when savings were very much sought after by the railways. The cogency of this explanation is evident for the small companies set up on the northern and southern fringes of the field, but seems to us less obvious for the substantial companies established along the axis of the field; here, the wish to limit the number of associates, to ensure quick appreciation of shares and to obtain high dividends, in short, a spirit of speculation, may well have greatly contributed to limiting the size of share capital. From this sprang the necessity of

[24] Archives of the Ligny-lez-Aire Company.

ploughing back profits on a large scale, an essential source of investment, all the more as the floating of debentures by coal-mining companies of the northern region was relatively rare, at least under the Second Empire. It was only at the beginning of the twentieth century that bond issues increased, at the same time as subdivision of shares into tenths or hundredths multiplied to a greater or lesser extent the number of shareholders in the companies. To take two extreme cases among the big companies: the Anzin Company had only 5,550 shareholders in October 1912, whereas Lens had about 80,000.[25]

Owing to the importance of self-finance, the management of the coal-mining companies closely resembled that of the textile enterprises in the North which, moreover, had procured for them a part of their initial capital; many of the directors of coal mines continued to be recruited from the employers' families of Lille-Roubaix-Tourcoing. Except in particular instances, such as Anzin and Dourges, equal distrust of big Parisian banks and a preference for regional banks, such as the Verley-Decroix and Dupont banks and the *Crédit du Nord*, are to be found both in coal-mining and in textile circles. Perhaps this explains the steady but very deliberate progress of the mines of the North and the Pas-de-Calais.

All these circumstances contributed to limiting the ties, associations and agreements tending to unite companies in the coalfields of the North and the Pas-de-Calais. It was the importance of the transport problem which first brought together the majority of companies in the *Comité des Houillères du Nord et du Pas-de-Calais*, an unofficial organization already mentioned, and this pressure group was very much in evidence after 1876, but chiefly illustrated the ineffectiveness of many entrepreneurial pressure groups in the nineteenth century. In 1886, the problem of participation in an employers' association organized on a national scale for the defence of coal-mining was raised for the companies in the North and the Pas-de-Calais. At the beginning of 1887, the setting up within the framework of the law of March 1884 on trade unions of a permanent employers' committee was envisaged which would concern itself with legislative and economic questions. The secretary of the committee was Edouard Gruner, who spent several months in Germany in 1887 in order to study the working of the German employers' organizations. For their part, with the exception of the Anzin and Dourges Companies, the companies in the northern region held back from the projected organization, probably because they were afraid of being in a minority in an association formed especially to make decisions on freight charges, also because they did not like making use of the law of 1884 against which they had fought, and finally because they probably preferred less formal action. It was only with difficulty that the reserves of the companies in the North and the Pas-de-Calais could be overcome, and the *Comité central des Houillères de France* was officially set up in December 1892.[26]

The existence of the *Comité des Houillères du Nord et du Pas-de-Calais* rendered easier the conclusion, between employers and miners, of the first collective agreement of Arras in 1889, since at the end of their general strike representatives of trade unions recently set up or reconstituted were confronted with an organization which could speak for the majority of the companies in the coalfields and conclude an agree-

---

[25] Archives of the *Comité central des Houillères de France*.
[26] Cf. Marcel Gillet, 'Aux origines de la première convention d'Arras: le bassin houiller du Nord et du Pas-de-Calais de 1880 à 1891', *Revue du Nord*, xxxix, 1957, pp. 111–23.

ment on wages upheld by practically all the companies. However, in March 1891, the companies in the North and the Pas-de-Calais organized a defensive associa-tion against strikes, the *Union des Houillères du Nord et du Pas-de-Calais*, an employers' association governed by the 1884 law; the articles of this association provided for a subsidy to be paid to companies hit by selective strikes, but as later conflicts usually affected the whole of the fields, the association intervened only relatively rarely. However, its example was followed in France as a whole, and in 1907 the *Comité central des Houillères* regrouped under its auspices all regional defensive associations against strikes.[27]

Ultimately in 1893, the *Comité des Houillères du Nord et du Pas-de-Calais* was dis-solved because some companies accused it of having favoured the conclusion of regional collective agreements by its very existence, and it was the *Chambre des Houillères du Nord et du Pas-de-Calais* which from 1898 took over the defence of the coal owners' interests in the transport field. At the end of the strikes, it was the theoretically temporary delegations of mining employers who signed wage agree-ments with trade unions.

In the strictly economic field, it is possible to find traces of temporary limited agreements between some companies about price-fixing or market allocation all through the nineteenth century. However, it was only after the 1880s that attempts at agreements on the scale of entire coalfields were precisely formulated within the framework of the *Comité des Houillères du Nord et du Pas-de-Calais*; and only in 1901, when an economic crisis increased marketing difficulties, did an *Office de Statistique* unite the majority of regional companies. This non-committal title hid a price-fixing cartel: the majority of companies agreed to standardize their selling prices from then on, according to a zoning system which fixed the base price of coal at the pit-head at a level which increased, the nearer to the field it was sold; it was on the regional market that coal sold at the highest price, where transport costs were lowest and industries gained financially from their proximity as regards the price of coal delivered at the factory; the high profits made on the regional market en-abled companies to lower prices in distant markets where competition was more dangerous. It must be emphasized that the Anzin, the Bruay and several of the smaller companies only agreed intermittently to take part in the *Office de Statistique*, and that consequently the latter never had the importance and strength of the Rhine-Westphalian Coal Syndicate set up in 1893.[28]

Summing up, therefore, all through the nineteenth century, it was under the banner of liberalism that the coal-mining companies of the North and the Pas-de-Calais developed, although certain important decisions, in particular about trans-port and wages, were made collectively by all the companies, or by the most power-ful companies, of the fields. The process of integration was much less rapid than in Germany. This seems bound up with less rapid growth, whether it is its cause or its effect.

In order to compare and explain the evolution of the chief coal-mining fields, an analysis of recruitment and employment of personnel in the service of different

---

[27] Archives of the *Comité central des Houillères de France*.

[28] Archives of the *Office de statistique de Douai*; Paul Robinet, *L'Office de statistique des Houillères du Nord et du Pas-de-Calais*, thèse droit, Lille, 1910; Max Heaulme, *L'évolution com-merciale des Houillères du Nord et du Pas-de-Calais*, thèse droit, Lille, 1948.

companies is pertinent. Since special studies have been devoted to the demographic and sociological problems created by the coal-mining industry, we have preferred to omit this part of our study, despite the considerable amount of research we have devoted to them. Let us simply point out that, so far as the coalfields of the North and the Pas-de-Calais are concerned, it was only at the beginning of the twentieth century, when some difficulties appeared in the recruiting of the labour force, that recruitment of Polish workers timidly began, to be considerably increased after the 1914–8 War. As for social conflicts, attention should perhaps be drawn to the speed, compared to the serious conflicts afflicting other fields and industries, with which people in the fields of the North and the Pas-de-Calais settled down to the conclusion of collective agreements after the first big strike of 1889. Even before 1914, these collective agreements seem to have had two effects. In the short run, they could be taken as aggravating conflicts, as wages could no longer be settled flexibly within the framework of each company; the whole field was concerned when short-term fluctuations imposed a wage change. In the long run, on the contrary, the signing of the Arras agreement appears to have led to a relative attenuation of conflicts. In fact, practice of periodic discussions led some companies to look with favour upon the existence of trade unions which they had at first opposed, then tolerated, before accepting them.

Finally, we must emphasize the essential problem which the analysis of the development of the coalfields of the North and the Pas-de-Calais during the nineteenth and beginning of the twentieth centuries raises. Was coal one of the essential factors, or even *the* essential factor, of industrial growth, or was it industrial growth itself which brought with it the rise of the coal industry? Perhaps it is the easy way out to suggest that there was continuous action and reaction, and that coal was only an instrument, although an indispensable one, in the service of the greater or lesser dynamism of different areas and different countries. As regards the northern region, obviously the development of coalfields was both stimulated by the presence of important industries which preceded it, and at the same time it favoured the development of these industries. In the centre and on the periphery, glass-making and metallurgical industries experienced a great expansion, particularly in the *Département du Nord*. In contrast, a coal-based chemical industry developed slowly and late, starting its real rise only at the beginning of the twentieth century, rather as in Great Britain, but very much behind Germany. This delay can be explained firstly by the dependence of coal-based chemistry on progress in the making of coke, itself, as has been mentioned, very backward in relation to the Ruhr: also by the textile industry in the North reaching its apogee at the end of the nineteenth century: in the form of dividends, substantial capital was transferred from the Pas-de-Calais field to the Lille-Roubaix-Tourcoing area in order to relieve the difficulties of the textile industry, but at the expense of investments which ought to have been made in the coalfield in order to shift capital from a primary to a secondary sector of the economy.

On a national scale the problem chiefly resolves itself into an attempt to give an answer, less obvious than was perhaps thought, to the question whether France during the nineteenth century, particularly in relation to the United States, Germany and Great Britain, was characterized by stagnation, due especially to the caution of its entrepreneurial class. An American historian, Professor Rondo

Cameron, thinks the negative aspects of French industrial growth in the nineteenth century have been exaggerated. In an article in *Annales* of 1957 in particular, he estimated that the failure of French heavy industries to maintain themselves at the level of those of Germany and Britain after 1870 was probably, more than any other factor considered in isolation, responsible for the well-known myth of an economically stagnant France. Furthermore, he maintained that heavy industry depends largely on local resources which France does not possess in the same proportions as its neighbours.[29] He would thus principally stress the difference in resources to explain the comparative evolution of different coalfields, without assigning to the French economy a dynamism inferior to that of the big industrial countries of Europe during the nineteenth century which we have designated as the Coal Age. This dynamism would have been sustained at the beginning of the twentieth century, when the internal combustion engine, electricity and a new industrial structure brought about a second industrial revolution.

Thus, among factors which explain the unequal growth of the different coalfields of the world, and, in particular, the rise of coalfields in the North and the Pas-de-Calais, geological conditions evidently played a decisive part, but the use made of means of transport, the legal status adopted by coal-mining companies, the ties which united them within the same industrial region, the methods of finance employed, the recruiting of workers and their personal relationships with management came to react upon the influence of natural factors. In the last resort, it is the dynamism of the different regions and of the different countries which appears to have counted for a great deal in the development of the coalfields during the Coal Age.

[29] Rondo E. Cameron, 'Le développement économique de l'Europe au XIXe siècle; le rôle de la France', *Annales E.S.C.*, xii, 1957, p. 250; cf. also R. E. Cameron, *France and the Economic Development of Europe, 1800–1914*, Princeton, 1961.

# The Italian Economy in the
# First Decade after Unification

## G. LUZZATTO

Translated by Anna Hearder

# I

### CONTRAST BETWEEN HOPES AND REALITIES

Francesco Ferrara, in one of his financial reviews in *Nuova Antologia*, January 1866, comments on the disastrous state of the Italian economy a few months before the declaration that the paper currency was no longer convertible into gold. His sorrowful and stern words echo the deep disillusionment, widespread throughout the country, at the jarring contrast between early hopes and harsh reality which had confronted the new Kingdom in the first five years of its existence.

After mentioning the very unflattering comments which were being made abroad on Italian financial policy—even by the cautious and authoritative *Economist*—and remarking with great bitterness that Italy appeared abroad like a beggar knocking at everybody's door, or a bankrupt who could at any moment drag to ruin those who had been naïve enough to give him credit, the great economist pronounces his indictment against the new Italy which had revealed such an exasperating lack of initiative in economic matters. 'If we did not know', he writes, 'that 22 million people have for some years been united in society and government, there would be very little in the economic order to show the observer that a great nation has been formed, that a great community of civilized men has been united by their own will. What little sporadic industrial movement there is, is nothing but the artificial and ephemeral activity of a government whose only industrial aim is to clothe soldiers and make guns. The nation is tied to its past; the spark of progress has not touched it; it tills the soil as it used to, it plies its ancient crafts; it does not feel the need for great undertakings or cannot find the means of carrying them out . . .; a thoughtless and inept generation succeeds one which was servile and indolent. The world around us moves in feverish strides; new inventions, new methods, the needs of everyday social life help to regenerate all branches of industry; but Italy just looks on and admires, and buys if it can; it neither acts nor is moved by envy . . . Why so much fire in the soul, so much light in the intellect, and such inertia in industry? . . . The reason for all this is the lack of certainty and of confidence in the future; understandably, since the State itself has none, forced as it is to face daily the problem of its very existence, to live on borrowed money, to be devoured by the big usurers.'

This pessimistic and disillusioned diagnosis is all too accurate. As for the causes of this unfortunate situation, Ferrara hits the mark, at least in part, by blaming the lack of private initiative on the State deficit 'which saps the economic strength of the nation'. But his condemnation is too severe when he puts the blame entirely on men—a whole generation, the same which had made Italy—for the hard facts which even the two leading economists of the time—Antonio Scialoja and Ferrara himself—could not overcome when they were unlucky enough to be given the finance ministry.

The prime cause of Italian inferiority during the first decade in the life of the Kingdom was that Italy had achieved unity rapidly at a time when the major Western European States, and some of the minor ones like Belgium and Switzer-land, had made gigantic progress on the way to industrialization and a fast rate of capital accumulation. Italy found itself completely unable to keep pace, not be-cause of the inadequacy of government or of private initiative, but owing to the very conditions of life of the individual regions, called upon almost unexpectedly to unite into one State.

The modest but promising advance made in some regions, not only in the North but also in the South, between 1830 and 1847, had been nullified by the rapid leap forward of the more advanced nations after 1850. The most obvious and probably the most important manifestation of this leap forward was the expansion of the railway network, which between 1848 and 1870 grew in France from 3,083 to 20,189 km., in Germany from 6,044 to 19,575, in the United Kingdom from 10,653 to 24,999, in Belgium from 851 to 2,997. A few isolated lines serving local needs had grown into organic national networks which were soon trans-formed, with the linking up of the French, Belgian and German railways and finally, around 1860, with the first transalpine lines, into a great European net-work.

The economic importance of railways, once completed—integrating into the market economy vast regions in the interior which had hitherto been excluded; contributing to the revolution in maritime transport; accelerating the transition from quality production to mass production; stimulating agricultural production in new directions—was preceded and surpassed, in the construction period and in the first few years of operation, by the powerful stimulus given to industrial pro-duction as a whole and to the movement and accumulation of capital by a policy of large-scale works. These were soon followed by the construction of harbours suited to the new needs of steam navigation, by the building and enlargement of great cities and by the development of public services. It has been calculated, however approximately, that capital employed in Europe in railway building alone rose from 850 million (contemporary) francs in the 1840s to 2,000 million in the 1850s and to 2,400 million in the 1860s.

This formidable demand for capital for undertakings to be completed in a short time gave impetus to a profound transformation of the credit system which was to assume such importance in the great economic development of the second half of the nineteenth and the beginning of the twentieth centuries. It became obvious that the amounts required by such large-scale enterprises were far in excess of the private fortunes available to take the heavy risks involved. It became necessary to dip into the pockets of middle and small savers. This period saw the beginning of the slow but continuous decline of the great private bankers who in France constituted the so-called 'high finance' and who lent their own capital and that of a restricted clientele of relatives and friends. Their place was taken by joint-stock companies, relying on deposits for day-to-day banking operations and on share capital and bonds for long-term loans to finance production.

The example of England, where the creation of great deposit banks in the form of joint-stock companies goes back to 1833, was followed and developed in France under the Second Empire. Favoured by the great influx of gold that the discovery of the rich Californian and Eastern Australian mines released onto the European markets, generating for 25 years a general and almost uninterrupted rise in prices, the savings accumulated, especially by the large land-owning class, in a long period of peace—savings which hitherto had remained almost entirely unproductive—were mobilized to such an extent that France could be hailed as the 'banker of the universe'. Capital which up to 1848 had seemed hardly sufficient for internal needs multiplied after 1852 to such an extent that it provided not only for rapidly expanding railway building, for modernization of the merchant navy and of docks and harbours, and for intensive urban building in all major French cities, but also became a powerful instrument of French world expansion. In 1868 alone, 14 different countries turned to the Paris market for the sale of 2,127 million francs' worth of their government bonds. At the same time French capitalists and technicians had taken a dominant part in building and often in operating railways in Austria, Lombardo-Venetia, Piedmont and the Papal States. The largest international undertaking of the period, the cutting of the Suez Canal, was mainly financed by French capital.

While in France savings were mobilized and capital accumulated through public works and financial operations at home and abroad, in Great Britain, especially after the triumph of free trade, they were employed preferably in the impressive increase in industrial production, shipping and overseas trade. The production of coal rose from 50 to 147 million tons (It.) in the 20 years between 1850 and 1870, that of pig-iron from two to six million tons. The building of steamships in British yards rose from only 14,500 tons in 1850 to 225,000 in 1870. The consumption of raw materials by the two major British textile industries, cotton and wool, doubled in the same period, reaching by 1870 six million quintals of 100 kg. each for cotton and two million for wool; while total overseas trade rose from £177 to £502 million.

# II

## THE CAUSES OF ITALIAN ECONOMIC INFERIORITY IN 1861

In contrast to these countries which were making gigantic strides in all fields of economic life, the structure, the equipment, and to a great extent the mentality of the new Italy belonged to past centuries. The State found itself so narrowly restricted in its economic activities that, apart from the solitary field of railway construction, not only could it not encourage the very urgent task of renewal and transformation, but it was forced to be the greatest obstacle to such a policy of rehabilitation.

In the days of Rome, as in those of the Communes, the greatest economic, social and cultural force in Italian life had been the development of hundreds of towns, major centres of attraction and energy. This development had slowed down after the Renaissance, and with few exceptions had remained stationary for two-and-a-half centuries until two or three decades after unification: a demographic stagnation which in some cases, as at Ferrara, turned into decline. The population of all provincial capitals varied in 1861 between 15,000 and 30,000 inhabitants. Where it is possible to compare it with the sixteenth and seventeenth centuries, in many cases the figures are almost identical: a most significant indication of the stagnation of economic and social life in a great part of Italy. Towns continued to be administrative and ecclesiastical centres of a fairly extensive area; they still provided the sites for weekly markets and for the modest crafts supplying the town itself and its surrounding countryside; but they had lost the attraction which they had exercised up to the sixteenth century. Migration from country to town had practically stopped and the excess, almost always considerable, of births over deaths went almost entirely to fill the gaps caused by pestilence, famine and emigration from minor towns to the few big cities, capitals of the major regional states.

It is impossible to judge and condemn the much lamented slowness and indolence of Italians on the morrow of unification, their inability to wrest from their victory the benefits that had been hoped for, without taking into account this demographic stagnation of the towns in a country which, according to fairly sound estimates, had doubled its total population in 250 years, and without considering that with this stagnation went an acute narrow-mindedness, a limited and monotonous way of life.

The picture changes only in part when restricted to the big cities which had been capitals of the major Italian States before 1861. Naples, whose population had more than doubled between the middle of the sixteenth and the end of the eighteenth centuries, was still the largest Italian town, but its population had remained completely stationary from 1800 to 1861. Palermo, which had reached 202,000 inhabitants in 1800, had only 194,000 in 1861. The exceptions are: Milan which grew in the same 60 years from 135,000 to 242,000 inhabitants; Florence from 81,000 to 143,000; Genoa, though no longer a capital city, from 80,000 to 151,000; and especially Turin, continuing the rapid growth begun at the end of the sixteenth century when it only had 16,000 inhabitants, rose to 78,000 in 1800 and 205,000 in 1861—a significant indication of the rise of Piedmont, which after an initial awakening under Charles Albert became in Cavour's decade the centre of the national political and economic movement.

The slow development of railways, so much less impressive than that of more advanced countries, contributed to the stagnation and isolation of life in the majority of Italian towns. It is true that between 1840 and 1859 attempts had been made everywhere, except in Sicily and Sardinia, to make up for lost time. Piedmont in particular had a dense network, totalling 800 km. in 1859, with four main lines linking Turin to Genoa, to Susa and the French frontier, to the Swiss frontier on Lake Maggiore and to Lombardy and the bridge over the Ticino. In Lombardy the Milan-Venice line had at last been completed. The link-ups between the Austrian lines in Lombardo-Venetia and those being built in the Duchies and Legations, and between the latter and the Tuscan network, had been planned and partly begun. Even in the Papal States there were projects for some important lines and some concessions had been granted. But at the outbreak of war in 1859 such vast plans had been realized only to a very minor extent: Venetia was still without connections to Emilia and Central Italy; the Tuscan network, extending along the coast only from Pisa to Massa and Cecina, and in the interior from Pistoia to Arezzo, remained completely isolated from the railways in Northern Italy.

The traveller from Piedmont or Lombardy to Florence had to cross by sea from Genoa to Leghorn or to use the ancient stagecoach between Bologna and Pistoia. If he then wanted to make his way south of Arezzo or Cecina, unless proceeding by sea, he had no better means of transport than had been available a century earlier.

# III

## FINANCIAL DIFFICULTIES OF THE NEW KINGDOM

An even greater obstacle preventing Italy from emulating countries in the fore-front of economic progress were the financial difficulties facing the new Kingdom and the means taken to overcome them.

According to fairly similar calculations from various sources, the joint revenues of the various States which united to form the new Kingdom amounted, in 1859, to a total varying from 433 to 550 million lire, while expenditure had risen to over 624 million, and the public debt to 2,446 million (1,483 for the Kingdom of Sardinia and 707 for the Kingdom of the Two Sicilies).

The budget deficit grew from year to year at an alarming rate: from 185 million in 1859 to 410 in 1860, to 468 in 1861; it fell slightly to 446 million in 1862, and more considerably in 1863 (382 million), in 1864 (367), and in 1865 (271), but took an alarming jump in 1866, when, with a real revenue of only 617 million, ex-penditure rose to 1,338, leaving a deficit of 721 million. In a mere five years from 1861, a deficit of 2,187 million accumulated, with total effective revenue at only 2,842 million.

The revenue from what was then the major direct tax, the State tax on land and buildings, could be increased only from 115 to 132 million; and even this very small increase (the communal and provincial surtax, still very slight, was no great additional burden) was enough to provoke endless protests. These cannot be attributed solely to the taxpayers' stubbornness, since they are sadly confirmed by the high number of evictions—the most convincing proof of the critical situation in which many landowners found themselves in those years.

In view of the impossibility not only of collecting existing revenues in full, but also of relying on future increases which would have justified the usual Treasury expedients, it became inevitable to cover the deficit by increasing the non-redeem-able public debt. In only four years the public debt, which was 2,449 million in 1861, rose by another 2,660 million; what is worse, only just over 1,800 million of these actually reached the Treasury, since it had been necessary to issue at a 30 per cent discount, which put effective interest rates at seven per cent and in some cases eight per cent rather than the nominal five per cent.

# IV

## INSUFFICIENT DEVELOPMENT OF SAVINGS

A chronic deficit, extreme dependence on credit and the very high interest rates which had to be paid for it, were an even greater evil in a country where accumulation of savings was still extremely slow and the amount of capital available for investments to increase agricultural and industrial production very scarce.

In 1865, more than 40 years after the establishment of the first savings banks which had meanwhile become numerous in all towns of Northern and Central Italy, their deposits reached only a very modest figure. Only in Lombardy, in this as in other fields the most advanced region of Italy, did deposits reach an average of 40 lire per head of population, while for the whole country the average remained a mere 9·79 lire. It is true that the level of deposits was kept artificially low by the structure of savings banks, regarded as benevolent institutions designed to develop the habit of thrift in the working classes. They tried to attract depositors with a very high rate of interest which in some cases reached five per cent.

Statistical data on savings deposits in other banking institutions are lacking for the first ten years of the new Kingdom; but they must have been very modest if in 1872, when figures were first officially collected, the total amount for all ordinary and co-operative banks was a mere 18·8 million, against 446·5 million in savings banks.

The banks' annual reports, it is true, do not make it easy to distinguish between savings accounts and current accounts, and the latter no doubt reached much higher figures. We know for instance that total liabilities of banks of issue for interest-bearing and non-interest-bearing current accounts were 50 million lire at the end of 1866 and touched a maximum of 80 million at the end of 1872. As far as ordinary banking institutions are concerned, we know that the major one, the *Società generale di Credito mobiliare*, had in the first year of its activities, 1863, liabilities of only 13 million lire for current accounts which rose to 24 million in 1866 and 54 million in 1870.

In the absence o fuller and more reliable data, confirmation for the scarcity of savings and the near-impossibility of investment can be found in the high rates of discount and of interest which savings banks had to offer to savers. The official discount rate of the *Banca Nazionale*, which ought to have been kept at around five per cent, often rose to seven per cent and even nine per cent, while the discount rate of ordinary banks rose even higher and in critical moments touched 12 per cent.

This scarcity of money, on which even the healthiest and most promising projects foundered, can be explained not only by the inadequacy of savings, but also by the very high interest offered to investors in government bonds. If, as we have just seen, this interest rate maintained an average of seven per cent even for bonds acquired at the time of issue, it could often go considerably higher for bonds acquired at market prices. On the basis of such prices it has been calculated that the actual yield, maintained at about seven per cent in 1862 and 1863, rose to 7·40 per cent in 1864, 7·67 per cent in 1865, 8·83 per cent in 1866, and 9·38 per cent in 1867.

When one notes that during the same years the actual yield of government

bonds in Britain varied between 3·29 per cent and 3·28 per cent, and the discount rate between 3·50 per cent and 4 per cent, it is evident that the Italian entrepreneur was in a hopelessly inferior, if not impossible, position for obtaining the
minimum capital required for setting up a new enterprise.

# V

## FOREIGN CAPITAL IN ITALY

In its first five years the new Kingdom was largely helped out of this difficulty
by foreign capital, first mainly French, but subsequently also British, and in a
smaller measure Belgian and Swiss, which in a period of plentiful money supply
was ready to move into foreign investments, especially attracted to Italy by the
high rates of interest or by the hope of high profits from shares or from the creation
of new industries.

The major investments between 1861 and 1865 were in the newly issued
government bonds. The only positive indication of the total of these investments is
given by payments of coupons made by the Italian Treasury in foreign markets,
especially in Paris. From 32 million lire in 1861 these payments rose to 52 in 1862,
66 in 1863, 84 in 1864, 85 in 1865, 98 in 1866. In this year, and in 1867, when they
reached and surpassed the amount paid out at home, there is no doubt that the
number of coupons cashed in Paris and London was swollen by those sent from
Italy to take advantage of the difference in the rate of exchange, which reached
over 15 per cent.

According to a French author, Duchêne, who in 1869 wrote a book on the
*Empire industriel*, deploring the excessive liberality with which the Second Empire
had allowed the quotation of foreign securities on the Paris *Bourse*, there were in
France in 1867 about 36 million Italian 100-lire bonds, that is a nominal capital of
3,600 million lire. This figure is obviously exaggerated, since it would represent
more than half of the whole Italian national debt; it was probably based on the
coupons cashed in Paris. It can be calculated with relative certainty that the share
of the Italian national debt in foreign hands rose from 640 to 1,700 million from
1851 to 1865, but after this date, as we shall see, it certainly fell. The contribution
of foreign capital towards covering the issue of loans by a young State, whose
vitality was still a matter of doubt, was on the face of it a great advantage both
from an economic and a political point of view. 'In those days of political uncertainty', wrote Ubaldino Peruzzi fifteen years later, 'Italy tied to her fate the
interests of large and small capitalists in the main nations of Europe.'

But there was also a reverse side to the coin. It was not so much the danger, so
often lamented in more recent times, of making the Italian economy dependent on
foreign countries, but rather that of transforming the financial into a political
problem, of equating a threat of bankruptcy with a threat to the very existence of
the Italian state.

In 1864 an unassuming English observer, in a book about Italy which was in
general sympathetic,[1] wrote discouragingly, at a time when nobody yet dreamt of

---

[1] F. C. Cotte, *Italics* (*sic*) : *Brief Notes on Politics, People and Places*, 2nd edition, London, 1864
(quotation in Italian in the text.)

the necessity of an inconvertible paper currency and when credit was still gener-
ously granted to Italy: 'From a financial point of view it is improbable that the
present course can be pursued without leading to bankruptcy. The annual deficit
is 300 million francs; nor can it be expected to be cured by the sale of the railways
or of crown lands, by the seizure of ecclesiastical property, the general development of national resources or by an increase in taxation. Therefore it is evident that
the struggle will not last long: either Italy can gain her point, organize herself, put
herself on a solid base as a great and free nation, or in a very short time her armies
will be made impotent, her strength will fail and her last state will inevitably be
worse than her first.'

While foreign capitalists until 1865 invested mostly in government bonds with a
guaranteed interest of seven per cent, they also played an important part in the
establishment and operation of public services, primarily railways, and in the
introduction of new industries. Already a few decades before unification foreign
capital, especially from France and Belgium, had taken an interest in the building
and running of water supplies and in the production of gas for lighting. At the same
time German and Swiss finance played a part, albeit small, in setting up spinning
mills and some cotton weaving sheds in Lombardy and around Naples, while
British capital concerned itself with maritime transport, insurance, mining and
the export trade, especially from Sicily and Sardinia.

It has been calculated, as quoted by Lanza in his answer to the commission of
enquiry into the inconvertibility of paper currency, that foreign capital invested in
Italy in transport, industry and commerce amounted altogether to one billion
lire.

After unification, because of the almost total absence in Italy of large joint-stock
companies which could have provided ordinary credit, this had to be created, at
great inconvenience where it was medium or long-term credit, by the banks of
issue. Therefore in this field too it was foreign capital which contributed in part or
entirely to the establishment of the major lending banks.

While up to 1862 there were only three such institutions of any importance, the
*Cassa di sconto* and the *Cassa generale*, both in Genoa, and the *Cassa del commercio e
delle industrie* in Turin, between 1863 and 1866 thirteen new ones were founded.
The most important were the Anglo-Italian Bank, with a capital of one million
sterling entirely raised in Britain, aiming at facilitating Anglo-Italian trade; and
the *Società generale di Credito mobiliare* which was for nearly thirty years the most
important and active lending bank in Italy after the *Banca Nazionale*. Founded on
1 June 1863 with a capital of 50 million (40 paid-up), with half its shares assigned
to the shareholders of Turin's *Cassa del commercio e delle industrie* with which it
amalgamated, it was a direct descendant of the *Société générale de Crédit mobilier* and
was created with direct participation of the founders of the famous French institution who from the start were on the board of directors of the Italian company.

The articles of association of the *Società* were a slightly revised copy of the French
sister institution and numbered among its functions, in addition to the usual
banking operations: participation in underwriting public loans by the State or by
local bodies; the establishment of all kind of enterprises—road and railway building, canals, land improvement, irrigation, factories, mines, docks, street lighting;
reorganization and negotiation of mergers of companies and the issue of their

shares and bonds; farming of taxes and public services; advancing of money on goods.

Apart from public loans, the main French investment in Italy was for the establishment of companies for building and operating railways. A railway network was universally recognized as an urgent necessity for the rapid economic union of the new Kingdom, which had not been achieved by abolishing internal tariffs alone but it came up against an apparently insurmountable difficulty, the ack of large financial resources.

The minimum programme after unification required the construction of at least 6,000 km., in addition to the 2,000 km. already in existence. The average cost at the time for land and fixed plant alone was estimated at about 210,000 lire per km. for a single-track line, to which had to be added about 30,000 lire for rolling stock and buildings. The estimated expenditure was therefore about 1,500 million lire, to be spread over ten years. For a government whose real annual income hardly reached 500 million, barely sufficient to cover normal military expenditure and to service the national debt, an additional expenditure of 150 million (roughly 60 billions of today's lire) for railway construction alone would have seemed folly. To begin with, the attempt had been made to build a few lines by public finance; but even before 1859 it was realized that the target could not be reached in this way. It was preferable to adopt the method already common abroad, of relying on private capital, enticing it with long-term operating concessions, with guarantees of interest on capital advanced for building the line which would eventually revert to State ownership, and of a minimum yearly revenue per operating kilometre.

The majority of these lines were built with foreign capital, with some slight co-operation, in some cases, from a few Italian capitalists. The first place goes to the Austrian company for southern railways (*Südbahn*), which, in spite of its name and headquarters in Vienna, was in fact constituted mainly by French capitalists, headed by the House of Rothschild in Paris.

A long way behind the *Südbahn*, the most important foreign companies holding concessions for building and operating Italian railways were the *Società Vittorio Emanuele* and the *Società delle strade ferrate romane*. Founded entirely on French capital, the *Società Vittorio Emanuele* was in 1857 granted the concession for the railways in Savoy, to which were soon added the Susa-Turin and Turin-Novara-Ticino lines, the company undertaking to share the cost of the Susa-Modane line which would have linked the company's two networks, separated by the Alps, through the Fréjus tunnel. After the cession of Savoy to France the company gave back to the Italian State the two trunk lines it operated on the Italian side of the Alps and obtained in exchange the concession for the Calabro-Sicilian railways whose plans had just been approved.

The *Società delle strade ferrate romane*, also formed mainly with French capital, but with participation by some Spanish capitalists resident in France and a few Italians, obtained from the new government in 1861 the concession for nearly all the lines planned by the Papal government in the territories which it had lost in 1859 and 1860.

Besides these and other minor foreign companies, the only large undertaking which was Italian in name and partly also in substance was the *Società italiana per le strade ferrate meridionali*. The much debated and criticized events which led to this

company obtaining the concession for all the lines planned by the Bourbon government on the eve of its fall are well known. A first agreement, settled with the
French engineer Talabot and ratified by a law of 21 July 1861, was subsequently
annulled because Talabot did not succeed in raising the necessary capital. Negotiations initiated by the government with various Italian capitalists having failed,
it was necessary to turn to the House of Rothschild in Paris, with whom, in association with Talabot, an agreement was negotiated on 15 June 1862, and submitted
to Parliament on the following day. The ministerial proposal met with strong
opposition in the House, led by Susani, whose main argument was that it would
have been a grave political and economic blunder to grant concessions for all
railways south of Ancona to the same foreign company which already controlled
all the lines in Lombardy, in Central Italy, and—under a different name—in
Venetia and Southern Austria. It was Susani who, after a trip to Paris to find
alternatives to Rothschild, urged Bastogi to promote an Italian company.

An officially appointed committee had just begun to discuss the ministerial
proposals when a letter from Bastogi was submitted to it. He asked the ministry to
be given building and operating concessions for the same lines and on the same
conditions agreed with the House of Rothschild, and undertook to transfer the
concession to a company in the process of being formed with a capital of 100
million lire subscribed entirely by Italian banks, financiers and businessmen. The
list of subscribers stressed that the capital had been raised entirely by banks and
bankers from Turin, Milan, Leghorn, Genoa and to a very small extent from other
North Italian towns. The largest subscriber was Bastogi, with 35,000 500-lire
shares.

Serious doubts about the purely Italian source of the capital are raised by the
fact that a few months after the Company's birth, at the directors' meeting of
26 February 1863, Bastogi as chairman read to the board a communication from
Fould, the great Parisian banker, listing banks in Brussels, Amsterdam, Frankfurt,
Paris and London entitled to cash bond and even share coupons payable in Paris
and London. Six years later, at a meeting of 91 shareholders, the biggest shareholders were Armand Charles, Domenico Speers and Massimo Petit, who had not
appeared among the founding shareholders in the company's statutes.

One can also hazard the hypothesis that the *Société générale de Crédit mobilier* was
behind the *Cassa del commercio e delle industrie* in Turin, which had subscribed 21,000
shares, and its representative Balduino. This hypothesis is suggested by the fact that
just at this time the transformation of the *Cassa* into the *Società generale di Credito
mobiliare* was taking place under the auspices of the brothers Péreire; and that
Susani, initiator and champion of the agreement with Bastogi, had previously
negotiated in Paris with men hostile to the Rothschilds—in all probability the
Péreires themselves or members of their entourage.

For the same reason, it is not unlikely that the bitter struggle between the two
major banking and railway groups in France was in some way connected with the
heated campaign waged against the new Company in Italian journalistic and
parliamentary circles. As was shown by the report of the parliamentary commission
of enquiry presented to the House of Deputies on 15 June 1864, the accusations
were not completely unfounded. It was against the constitution for the House to
overrule the government and approve by acclamation a contract with partners

different from those contemplated in the convention approved by the ministry. As for the ethical side of the question, it was ascertained that Susani, member of Parliament and secretary of the parliamentary commission, had received from Bastogi a commission of 1,100,000 lire. Bastogi had in turn extracted from the share subscribers an additional signed declaration which appointed him general contractor for building all lines and fixed plant at a uniform price of 210,000 lire per km., with the option to sub-contract the whole network in separate lots to firms of his choice. This he hastened to do for the whole 1,150 km., divided in three lots sub-contracted respectively to Messrs. Brassey, Parent and Bussington, to Angelo Frascara, and to Vannotti e Finardi Co., for the uniform price of 198,000 lire per km. This would give the general contractor a profit of 14 million lire, of which it seems two-thirds went to Bastogi.

However, although its beginnings had been such as to account for, if not completely to justify, the campaign of suspicion and accusations waged against it, the Company managed to overcome the serious financial difficulties of the first years and thereafter by its conduct dispelled all hostilities and acquired a reputation as one of the most responsible and solid economic bodies of the new Italy. Even in the first few years, in spite of the financial troubles mentioned above and the onerous terms at which its bonds were issued, the Company managed to fulfil its obligations: the Adriatic line from Ancona to Brindisi was already finished in 1865.

All in all, the first six years of the Kingdom added another 2,000 to the existing 2,000 km. of track, so that Naples, Rome and Bari were in 1865 linked with each other and with Bologna, Genoa, Milan and Turin.

# VI

## POOR ECONOMIC RESULTS FROM RAILWAY BUILDING

If the technical and political results of railway expansion were up to, perhaps even above expectation, the financial and economic consequences were unfortunate. The minor companies which had been granted short trunk lines were not viable and in 1865 the whole national network had to be divided between four large companies. Of these, the *Vittorio Emanuele* soon foundered after sustaining heavy losses; the *Meridionali* and the *Romane* carried on amidst serious difficulties and in the end had to borrow from the State; only the *Societa dell'Alta Italia*, financially very strong, was able to prosper.

In this early period railway construction did not have those immediate effects on the Italian economy which could reasonably have been expected. Gross revenue per km., far from rising, showed an almost continuous and discouraging tendency to fall—not only in Central and Southern Italy, but even in the Po Valley. In the northern network, after reaching a maximum of 28,556 lire in 1861, gross revenue per km. remained just above 23,000 lire during 1865–8. On Roman railways it fell from a maximum of 16,679 lire in the same year 1861 to a minimum of 10,871 in 1876 and rose again to 11,215 in 1868. On the southern railways in 1860, with the company not yet formed and the line from Bologna to Ancona the only one in operation, gross revenue had reached the exceptionally high figure of

26,420 lire; in 1867, when construction was almost finished, it tumbled to 8,110.

Clearly the almost universal and constant decline of gross revenue per km. cannot be attributed to a contraction of local traffic, but rather to the fact that the first lines to be built were those linking large ports to major centres of consumption, while later construction was extended to areas where demand was smaller, in the mistaken hope that the railway alone would engender an increase in traffic. This delusion was reflected in a serious strain on State finances, since the government had guaranteed to the contractors a gross revenue per km. which proved a vast overestimate. Thus for instance in the case of the Southern Company guaranteed revenue was 29,000 lire per km., of which in 1867 21,000 had to be shouldered by the taxpayer.

The economic achievement is even more depressing when compared with that of countries which had pioneered railways: in Britain, for instance, gross revenue per km. rose from 27,000 lire in 1861 to 47,500 lire in 1868.

Moreover, Italian industry did not reap from railway building the immediate benefit that had been felt in other countries; that is, the stimulus given to iron and steel production, to engineering and to the production of all the fixed and mobile equipment used by the railways. As far as rolling stock is concerned, we know that the *Società delle strade ferrate dell'Alta Italia*, from its origins to 1878, bought 247 locomotives in Alsace, 25 in Britain, 125 in France (in addition to those bought in Alsace before 1870), 110 in Belgium, 90 in Austria, five in Bavaria: a total of 602 acquired abroad against only 39 acquired in Italy (two from the *Officine ferroviarie* in Verona, and 37 from the *Stabilimento Ansaldo* in Sampierdarena).

The situation was much better with regard to passenger coaches, freight and cattle trucks: taking again the *Società Alta Italia*, against 6,947 imported coaches, 9,859 came from Italian factories of which the best equipped were *Ansaldo*, *Officine nazionali* in Naples, and three Milanese firms, *Elvetica*, *Miani-Venturi* and in particular *Grondona e Comi*, the oldest among them, for which even the directors of the *Alta Italia* had nothing but praise.

But Grondona himself, questioned by the commission of enquiry into the running of the railways, complained that as long as the *Alta Italia* railways were in the hands of a foreign company, they would order all their equipment abroad; and from the Roman *Strade ferrate*, while it was under French management, he could not obtain orders for a single truck. It cannot be denied that there was bias against Italian suppliers, and that this must be considered, at least in part, as a corollary to the influx of foreign capital and foreign technicians who made a valuable contribution, sometimes at a loss, to the creation of the Italian railway network.

However, this bias sprang to some extent from necessity, at least as far as locomotives were concerned: as witness the first order for 24 locomotives, approved by the Italian Company running the southern railways on 28 July 1863, which was placed entirely with a foreign firm. Only in 1865 did the Company, which according to its charter should have opened its own engineering works in Naples, make an agreement with the new *Società nazionale delle industrie meccaniche*, which had taken over the *Pietrarsa* and the *Granili* works, granting it part of the repair contracts and of the orders for rolling stock. But it continued to rely heavily on foreign industry, especially for locomotives.

As regards fixed plant, the position was much worse: especially for rails, the total lack of efficient Italian steelworks made recourse to imports inevitable.

# VII

## INCONVERTIBILITY OF PAPER CURRENCY: CAUSES AND CONSEQUENCES

The very grave difficulties besetting the Italian State in the first five years of its life reached an acute and menacing crisis at the beginning of 1866, when the only remedy to avoid bankruptcy was to declare the inconvertibility of *Banca Nazionale* notes. It was said then by those not fully aware of the gravity of the situation that the measure was taken to save the *Banca Nazionale* and ensure its pre-eminence over other banks of issue. But the truth slowly gained ground and was given its most complete and best documented exposition by Domenico Balduino, director of the *Società generale di Credito mobiliare* and an experienced financier, in his answer to the commission of enquiry into the inconvertibility.

After mentioning the heavy dependence on foreign credit up to the beginning of 1865, Balduino writes that foreign confidence in Italy, kept high in the first three years of the Kingdom,

was seriously shaken towards the end of 1864, and flagged in 1865, in view of the absence of radical measures to eliminate the Italian deficit (and, it must be added, in consequence of the grave financial crisis on the Paris market). It was also feared abroad that a great war was imminent, in which Italy would take an important part.

Hence the deluge of Italian securities pouring back from foreign markets onto the Italian market, selling at ever lower prices. Since they represented a value of billions, it hardly needs pointing out what loss of capital was involved and what were the consequences on metallic currency and on exchange rates of the flight of specie and the influx of bonds. As the crisis continued, not only public and private securities, but also bills of exchange drawn on our markets and held by foreign capitalists poured back into Italy.

It was not long before the idea took hold, both at home and especially abroad, that extreme need and the lack of alternative solutions would inexorably drive the government to adopt the inconvertibility of bank notes. This realization pervaded the market long before it became an issue for the government; it expressed the pressures and dangers of a crisis which was at first financial and political, then monetary. . . . As can be expected, the expectation of inconvertibility affected first holders of current accounts, who were induced to withdraw their capital from the banks and convert it into metal coin. Gold became the only currency in demand, the only investment, the only object of speculation.

The depositors besieging their banks for 20-lire gold pieces (*marenghi*) sounded the alarm. What had started as the effect of panic became a new cause of intensified crisis.

Francesco Ferrara himself, who a few days after the decree establishing inconvertibility had severely criticized it by the well-known argument that it merely aimed at ensuring the monopoly of the *Banca Nazionale*—which was anathema to an ardent believer in the freedom of banks—when he became aware of the real situation, admitted his error with rare honesty. He gave Scialoja his due and recognized the necessity of his measures when he told the House on 2 March 1867:

At that time a banking crisis and extreme penury in the Treasury fatally coincided . . . facts then not known, at least not to me, have now been confirmed: in Genoa, in Turin, in Milan, even in Naples, merchant credit was daily ebbing away. Bank deposits were withdrawn in haste, our bonds from abroad flooded our stock exchanges. Everybody asked for cash, and no sooner were they given bank notes than they rushed to the cash desk to exchange them for coin . . .; scores of bankruptcies were declared everywhere, casting doubt even on the solidity of the most reliable firms.

In my opinion, let me repeat, the State should remain aloof from a banking crisis which it has not caused and which it cannot cure without making matters worse; but the banking crisis in the spring of 1866 immediately turned into a national crisis, since it precluded recourse to any purely financial device. Therefore inconvertibility was not only a legitimate, but the only possible remedy, answering both to the needs of commerce and of the impoverished Treasury. Similar circumstances imposed it on Britain in 1797, on France in 1848, even recently on America.

In effect, looking at it from a distance, inconvertibility not only meant the end of the exchange of bank notes for gold, but also and more especially the substitution of a fiduciary issue for the metallic currency hitherto prevalent. The fiduciary issue, which had not been at all popular before 1866 and was only grudgingly accepted afterwards, accounted in 1865 for only a quarter of the value of the metallic currency in the hands of individuals. Therefore the introduction of inconvertibility, while it supplied an urgent need of public finance which could no longer rely on foreign credit, was above all the instrument which accustomed the Italian population to the fiduciary issue which slowly even the most reluctant came to accept. With the balance of payments in the state it was, rapid expansion of paper money coupled with continued free convertibility of bank notes would have been utterly utopian.

A supposed consequence of the introduction of inconvertibility, long vaunted by industrialists and businessmen engaged in exports, especially by producers and merchants of raw silk, was the stimulus it gave to exports, while putting a brake on imports, because of the deterioration in the exchange rate with countries with harder currency (with France it soon rose to 115).

There was indeed an improvement in our trade balance in the five years which followed the introduction of inconvertibility. The deficit in the balance of trade touched the maximum figures of 411 and 407 million lire in 1864 and 1865 respectively, dropped to 252 in 1866, and remained around 140 in the next three years, with a minimum of 110 in 1868. The improvement was due only in very small measure to the fall of imports which remained constant at around 900 million, while exports rose from a minimum of 558 million in 1865 to a maximum of 792 in 1869. In fact, as the experience of the last thirty years has shown, devaluation can give only a temporary advantage until prices and wages at home have risen in the same proportion.

If we look at detailed trade figures for 1862-70 and compare the four years preceding the introduction of inconvertibility with the five that followed it, we see that imports fell noticeably only in two commodity groups: 'raw and manufactured silk' from an annual average of 154 million to 102 million lire, and 'grains, flour, pasta etc.' from 134 to 88 million. For the first item, the fall is due in part to the rise in price of foreign silk because of the high rate of exchange, in part to the increased national production of silk cocoons due to improved disease control; and in even greater part to the annexation of Venetia, which removed from the foreign trade figures the considerable influx of Venetian cocoons and raw silk into the Milan silk market. In the same way, for grains, lower imports were due not so much to monetary factors but to a series of good harvests, removing almost totally the necessity of imports from Black Sea markets, which in the preceding years had been considerable.

More closely linked to the changed monetary situation are perhaps some increases in exports, particularly exports of raw silk, which rose from 200 to 250 million lire, cattle from 12 to 13, hemp from 23 to 34; and above all of 'grains, flour and pasta', due mainly to the increased activity of Italian mills and macaroni factories.

The benefits conferred by the introduction of inconvertibility on the conduct of financial policy are less open to doubt than those attributed to it on the balance of trade. Its immediate consequences, lack of confidence in foreign centres and the high rates of exchange, made it extremely difficult to obtain further credit from foreign bankers and forced the Italian State to raise its own revenue to provide for ordinary and, to a great extent, for extraordinary expenditure. It was brought home even to the most reluctant that it was urgent to balance revenue and expenditure in order to extricate the country from a humiliating and dangerous situation. The objective could not be achieved as rapidly as had been hoped; even though effective revenue rose considerably, so that in 1869 it was half as much again as in 1868 (902 million against 609), expenditure continued to rise in 1867 and 1869, especially because of higher foreign exchange rates and the liquidation of war loans. It fell to 1,022 million in 1870, when the deficit was reduced, for the first time in the whole decade, to only 221 million.

More than half the deficit was covered by the issue of paper currency: the State, which in 1865 owed no debts to the *Banca Nazionale*, had to borrow from it in the following five years the sum of 650 million, authorizing the bank to increase the circulation of bank notes by an equal amount.

Normally such a rapid increase of the money supply, brought about not by the needs of trade but to cover the excess in government expenditure, would have burdened the country with an appreciable rise in prices. There was indeed a certain rise, accompanied by the phenomenon, common to periods of rapid inflation, of the complete disappearance of token coinage and the repeated irregular issue of notes of small denomination. But the trend was minimized by the fact that between 1865 and 1870 the trend of world prices had started to fall slightly and, after a rise in the period 1871–3, began again to fall more markedly until 1896. What contributed even more to minimize the effects of increased paper circulation was the very sharp decrease in the circulation of specie because of hoarding and because of the draining abroad of large amounts of gold and silver to pay for bonds repatriated from abroad for sale. It is impossible to estimate even approximately the amounts hoarded; but they must certainly have been considerable, judging by the many concurring reports of depositors rushing to the banks as soon as the rumour spread that inconvertibility was going to be introduced. As for the exodus of coin and precious metal used to buy back from abroad Italian bonds, it is known that in the five years 1866–70 surplus exports of precious metal to France reached the disturbing sum of 452 million, while in the previous five years

H

the much vaunted surplus imports from the same source had only amounted in total to 283 million.

Taking everything into consideration, though the introduction of inconvertibility represented an extremely critical moment in the life of the new Italy and, together with the poor achievements of the railways and the losses of other industrial enterprises financed by foreign capital, gave rise to a serious drop in investments, nevertheless it may also be described as a salutary lesson. It set a new trend in the whole of Italian monetary and financial policy. The two years 1868–70 can be seen as a period of recovery—a recovery which enabled the country to overcome the dangers of the 1871–3 boom and the crisis which broke out at the end of 1873 and fortunately affected only banking and speculation, without damaging the basis of the economy.

# VIII

## STAGNATION OF AGRICULTURAL PRODUCTION

It may seem strange that in this, as in other studies of the economy of the new Kingdom, so much has been said about finance, currency and credit, leaving in second place production, distribution of wealth and social conditions. But the fact is that the state of finance, savings and monetary circulation is not only better known, but had a decisive and unfortunately negative influence on all economic activity. It caused that stagnation so much lamented by the most expert and impassioned observers, which probably turned into decline, not only in comparison with the progress achieved by other nations, but in absolute terms.

This feeling of stagnation, sometimes of decline, strikes any one investigating the conditions of agriculture, in which the majority of the population directly or indirectly found a living. Making all necessary reservations about the agricultural statistics for the period preceding 1907, when for the first time a special statistical service was instituted by the Ministry of Agriculture, one is still struck by the almost constant level of cereal production figures. Before 1870 this was about 35 million hl. for wheat, three million for rye, 7·5 million for barley and oats; that is a total of 54·5 against 222·5 million hl. reached in France. Italian production was higher only for maize, where it reached 16 million hl. against 10 million in France. For its consumption of wheat, which was very modest, owing to substitution of maize meal and chestnut flour, Italy already then was forced to import from five to six million hl. per year.

These figures suggest that wheat production over the whole of Italy only reached an average of seven hl. (less than six quintals) per hectare, compared with an average of 15 quintals per hectare achieved today. They certainly do not give a favourable impression of this most widespread and necessary crop in Italian agriculture, but demonstrate a complete lack of progress. Some branches of agricultural production, however, show more encouraging signs of revival.

The first place must go to silk-worm breeding and to the linked industry of silk throwing, still typically agricultural. These two activities, which between 1855 and 1860 had been reduced by more than half because of the spreading of pebrine were revived after 1860 by large-scale importation of Japanese seeds, immune to the disease. Finally after 1864, thanks to important discoveries by French and Italian entomologists, silk-worm breeding could emancipate itself from Japan and in a few years regain all the lost ground, reaching again peaks of production not touched since 1845. The entire agricultural production benefited from this, since in the silk-worm producing regions, thanks to the very high prices of cocoons and thrown silk, capital was accumulated which would otherwise have been completely lacking.

At the same time, though in smaller measure, rice, flax and hemp production were also helped by price increases, while the American Civil War gave a strong, though ephemeral, impulse to cotton growing in some areas of the South and in Sicily.

Another reassuring sign of agricultural development was the inception of two great projects which were to bring about a considerable increase in production in the following decades: the Cavour Canal, starting where the Dora Baltea flows into the Po and ending in the Ticino, was to enable the irrigation of 500,000 hectares of hills and plains in Piedmont and Western Lombardy; and the reclamation of land by drainage, limited in the first few years to a small area in the Ferrara province, but later to extend to most of the lower Po valley and to the Venetian coast.

But all these improvements, or promises of improvement, were in the period 1865–70 limited to small areas in a few regions, unable to modify the general pattern of stagnation. This was caused partly by limitation of the market, not overcome until many years after unification, but even more by scarcity of capital. This scarcity was aggravated, as we have seen, by the government's financial policy of continually issuing bonds at very attractive terms, and by increasing taxation which did not bring the State much advantage, but weighed intolerably on landlords and tenants and made impossible the investment needed to improve agricultural production.

The sale of ecclesiastical property and of what remained of crown and feudal property was started in 1867; though not completed until much later, it was accelerated in the following years under the spur of financial necessity. This however only contributed to make the situation worse. It had been thought, and in normal times this would have been true, that the availability of expropriated lands on the free market would quickly improve the agrarian economy: the land would be bought by private individuals who would have every interest in increasing its value and reaping the highest possible profits by more economical and rational methods of husbandry. But the peasantry was traditionally hungry for land, especially in the South and in the islands. Since most of the expropriated ecclesiastical and crown lands were in these regions, and given the extreme scarcity of cash, the result was that all available capital, perhaps even more than was actually available, was absorbed by purchases of land. Most owners therefore found themselves completely bereft of the capital needed on their properties, old and new, for improvements or even for maintaining a reasonable standard of cultivation in order to avoid dangerous soil exhaustion.

We still lack an accurate study to establish into whose hands fell the lands expropriated in 1864 from ecclesiastical bodies, religious orders and charitable institutions, and the crown and feudal lands whose distribution had started in 1806, but had proceeded very slowly, so that at the time of unification the greater part had still not been definitely allocated.

For the years we are now considering (1867 to 1870), we have the total figures quoted by Sachs on the basis of official documents, undoubtedly reliable but limited to ecclesiastical property.

| Year | Number of plots | Reserve price (in million lire) | Price at which sold (in million lire) |
|---|---|---|---|
| 1867 | 7,078 | 41·7 | 53·7 |
| 1868 | 25,888 | 122·2 | 162·5 |
| 1869 | 9,717 | 40·8 | 51·4 |
| 1870 | 8,149 | 39·9 | 40·5 |
| Total for the 4 years | 50,832 | 244·6 | 311·7 |

Twenty per cent of the difference between the reserve price and the sale price went to the contracting company; the State therefore must have collected 294 million in the four years.

Of the 50,832 lots disposed of over the four years, more than two-thirds were in the southern provinces and in the islands, and most of the buyers were to be found, not among the rich feudal nobility nor among the poorer peasantry, but among large and middle landowners into whose hands were soon to fall also the few thousand lots sold to small farmers. The final result was thus the creation, along-side the old nobility, of a powerful landed bourgeoisie. This class however did not bring to the management of their new acquisitions more modern or rational standards nor that spirit of initiative which would seem to have been, at least at that time, a necessary attribute of the so-called bourgeoisie. After the expenses sustained to buy the property, this rural bourgeoisie did not want to, and generally could not, invest even modest sums in improving it, but confined itself to securing an income by pressing heavily on those dependent on the land (small tenants, sharecroppers, farm labourers).

At the same time the South, or at least its poorer regions, Molise and Basilicata, at first lost more than it gained from the extension, still incomplete, of the railway network. During the construction period many owners were induced to sell large tracts of their woods. The work of deforestation was favoured by the railways themselves and helped by a simultaneous and considerable rise in wheat prices which induced landowners to put large areas under the plough. These gave large profits for a few years, but were soon to lose their thin layer of humus and become sterile, while deforestation threatened to ruin even the lower-lying plains.

In spite of these undeniable ill-effects, it seems to us quite wrong to attribute the beginning of the southern problem to unification. The economic inferiority of many (not all) southern regions and of the islands compared with some (not all) northern and central regions has its roots in the period of Spanish rule—or probably even earlier in the Aragonese and Angevin periods—and in deep-rooted causes which it would be out of place to re-examine here. There is no doubt however that existing inferiority was aggravated in the immediate period after unification, partly owing to the causes already mentioned, but perhaps even more for subjective reasons.

These subjective causes are effectively suggested by Iacini in his excellent general report, prefacing the results of the agricultural inquest. He says that farm labourers' conditions were probably worse before unification than at the time he wrote (1884), but they were not felt as much and did not give rise to protests. The unification of the country, the railways, internal and external migration, had put the peasants (especially southern peasants) in contact with regions where living standards, although not too prosperous, were so superior to theirs that they felt their hopeless inferiority to be intolerable.

# IX

## POOR PROGRESS OF NORTHERN INDUSTRY; DECLINE IN THE SOUTH; SIGNS OF PARTIAL REVIVAL AFTER 1866

The same causes which determined the stagnation of agricultural development hindered, perhaps even more seriously, the progress of industrial production—which was also damaged, in some of its branches, by concurrent factors. Even Lombardy, which exhibited greater solidity and economic balance than the rest of Italy, and was, as we have seen, in the lead with savings, was still in 1860 very far from that industrial development which was so much discussed, and had been anticipated by twenty years, while in fact it did not appear until the 1880s.

There had been a period of about fifteen years, in the 1830s and 1840s, when it seemed that Lombardy was nearing the triumph of industrialization. But even then the phenomenon had been limited to a few large cotton spinning mills and a few engineering works started in Milan to supply rolling stock for the railways. Those beginnings, interrupted before 1847 by a serious general slump, were not followed up because of the war, and—after the war—because of the crisis in the silk industry, which hit the whole Lombard economy, and because of delay in railway construction. Therefore at the end of 1859 and even at the time of unification, Lombardy was not in a position to reap from the union with the other four-fifths of Italy those immediate advantages which had been fondly imagined; on the contrary, it was going through a difficult economic crisis and was seriously damaged by separation from Venetia.

Industrial activity was certainly not lacking in Lombardy at that time; on the contrary it was widespread and diversified; but for the greater part it was still tied to agriculture. With few exceptions, the separation between industry and agriculture which is a fundamental characteristic of great modern industry had not yet taken place. The link between the two was still very close in the silk industry, where silk-worm breeding and silk throwing were done in the houses of the peasants themselves or in tiny workshops, situated in the countryside, where for 90 days a year from 20 to 50 workers gathered, mainly women who for the rest of the year worked in the fields. Only twisting, spinning and waste-processing were done by middle-sized, if not by large, industry.

The situation was not much different in the other textile industries: even in the youngest, the cotton industry, as had happened in Britain, only spinning was industrialized at first, while weaving was still overwhelmingly done on hand looms, some gathered in large workshops, but most still operated in the peasants' homes, under contract to some big merchant.

But this is not all: the same link with agriculture is found even in some industries where it may appear absurd, as in mining and iron-smelting, where the mines and the foundries were worked only in the winter months, to leave workers free to attend their fields in the busy farming months.

The picture is different in Piedmont and Liguria where Cavour's financial and economic policies (condemned as ruinous and foolhardy by many of his opponents) had succeeded, in less than nine years, in changing the economic structure and outlook of the two regions. Even more than Genoa, already well advanced in this field, did the change affect Piedmont, where next to the old, impoverished and narrow-minded landed aristocracy there arose a new commercial and industrial bourgeoisie which proved capable of new and bold initiatives. To this period belong the 800 km. of the Piedmontese-Ligurian railway network, the founding of the *Ansaldo* works, the first shipyards for the building of iron battleships and of the first steamships, the *Societa Rubattino* for steam navigation, several engineering works, and mills for cotton and silk spinning. But even in the ex-Kingdom of Sardinia, perhaps because of the great effort sustained in the preceding ten years and largely based on credit, economic advantages logically expected from unification were very slow in materializing.

In addition to general financial causes, what contributed to slow down the pace of economic development in Piedmont as in Lombardy was the still unresolved crisis of the silk industry, and an even more serious cotton crisis. The imports of raw cotton for the whole Kingdom fell from 135,000 quintals in 1860 to 109,000 in 1861, 27,000 in 1862, 2,300 in 1864, and disappeared altogether in 1865, when there was a surplus of exports of 16,500 quintals. This reversal in the foreign trade in raw cotton was due to an increase in national production, especially in Sicily, following large investments by Lancashire mill-owners who naturally appropriated part of the crop for their mills. In consequence, Piedmontese and Lombard mills had a hard struggle to secure much smaller quantities of raw material than in the preceding decade.

Finally, a grave blow was struck at the silk weaving industry, centred on Milan and Turin for luxury goods and on Como for more ordinary products, by the loss of the Viennese market and by increased competition from Lyons. The Lyons industry not only deprived Italian weavers of the very modest exports they had been able to supply to Central Europe up to 1860, but easily succeeded in infiltrating the Italian market itself. Thus in Milan the 2,000 looms still operating in 1861 were reduced to 600 in 1864; and the same proportional fall happened in Turin and Como.

If from the three regions which already in those years were considered the leaders of Italian economic development, we pass to the regions of Central and Southern Italy where the agrarian character of the economy was even more marked, the situation appears less and less promising as we proceed southwards. While in Tuscany and in the Marches some famous industries, founded by successful personal initiative, were kept alive, such as the *Ginori* pottery at Doccia, the *Milani* paper-mill at Fabriano and the *Cini* paper-mill at S. Marcello Pistoiese, in the rest of the country there was hardly any breakaway from the pattern of artisan crafts and cottage industry.

In the South there survived, although leading a wretched existence, beset by perpetual difficulties, the engineering works of Pietrarsa and the shipyards of Castellammare; the iron and steel industry in Calabria was destined to die out; while the cotton mills of the upper Liri valley and of Salerno province, as well as the macaroni factories of Torre Annunziata and nearby towns, were able to hold out and prepare for a period of greater development.

Only after 1866 did there appear some slight signs of economic development, at least in the economically more advanced regions. The revival was caused by the disappearance of the frontier between Lombardy and Venetia; by the completion of the railway network, at least of the main lines (Milan, linked with Turin, the French and Swiss frontiers, Genoa, Leghorn, Florence, Rome, Naples, Bologna, Ancona, Brindisi, fully resumed its role as the centre of Italian commerce); by the recovery already mentioned of silk-worm breeding and silk throwing, which in a period of very high prices gave Lombardy, Venetia, Piedmont, and to a lesser extent Emilia, Tuscany and the Marches a steady flow of income which had been almost totally lacking in the preceding decade; by the end of the American Civil War which allowed the resumption of exports of American raw cotton. But the most effective help was given, in particular to some exporting industries, by inconvertibility not so much directly, but because it brought about a heavy rise in foreign exchange rates—a rise which, at least until internal prices and values reached parity again with international prices, gave those industries a premium on exports and protection against imports of manufactured goods.

# X

## CONDITION OF THE WORKING CLASSES.
### FIRST SIGNS OF SOCIAL MOVEMENTS

The backward and generally wretched conditions of agriculture, and the even worse ones of industry, were inevitably reflected in the condition of the workers in both sectors. Unfortunately even today we labour under extreme difficulties in trying to establish accurately real and nominal wages, unemployment figures, constancy of employment, daily and weekly hours worked, etc., in spite of the progress made in this field and the institution of statistical services. These difficulties were even greater on the morrow of unification and were aggravated by the almost universal lack of a dividing line between industrial and agricultural work, so that it is impossible to determine to what extent either activity contributed to the workers' subsistence. However, in spite of the incompleteness and uncertainty of statistical data, there is no doubt that industrial wages, and still more farm labourers' wages, were grievously low. While an adult skilled worker (male) could easily reach and even sometimes exceed a daily wage of two lire on working days (about 300 days in the year), women and children, who made up the majority of the work force in the textile industries, were paid real starvation wages varying from 25 to 50 *centesimi*.

A personal memory prompts me to believe these incredible figures: fifty years later, in 1915, when the cost of living had risen by more than 40 per cent since 1870, women workers in a large hemp mill in Venetia were paid one lira for a ten-hour working day, and by then they could not even supplement this, however modestly, by agricultural labour.

The links still existing in the period 1861–70 between industry and agriculture were an obstacle to the development of common bonds and interests amongst workers in the same industry, which is a prime condition of collective resistance. Mutual-aid societies were in this period the main, or rather the only, expression of a trade union spirit among workers. They were still to a great extent organized by bourgeois or even aristocratic philanthropists and found the bulk of their membership among urban artisans. A few of them were beginning to evolve a programme of industrial action, mainly the printers, who in Piedmont already in 1848 put among the aims of their association the opposition to wage cuts and negotiated with the employers a wage rate which was revised in 1850 and 1851. The same happened in Genoa in 1852. Apart from these exceptions, it was extremely rare for these mutual-aid societies to unite workers from a single industry, and they were completely lacking in the countryside.

As far as workers' agitation in defence of their class interests is concerned, it is true that they started to use the strike weapon to obtain increases in wages or limitations of the working day, but the number of strikes was still very small (132 in the 1860s in the whole of Italy) and their duration very brief: most lasted no longer than 24 hours. They were all purely local in character and the number of strikers was limited. They were not organized by craft unions but by workers' societies among which only a few, all of them from among the typesetters, established strike funds.

If these small and infrequent industrial strikes bore at least a trace of the beginning of trade unionism, this was completely lacking in the much more serious, sometimes tragic, unrest which shook the southern countryside from 1861 to 1865 and the lower Po valley in the winter of 1868–9.

The brigandage which did so much to deepen the painful chasm between North and South was in its first year a political and religious movement marked by the attempt at revenge by the Bourbons who had their headquarters in the Palazzo Farnese in Rome and had enlisted the help of the high ecclesiastical hierarchy. But this aspect disappeared completely in the four following years when the struggle became a pathological manifestation of extreme discontent among all classes of rural society. Though a sure symptom of the acute distress in which the rural population was left, it could not be honestly interpreted as a beginning, however remote, of a social movement consciously aiming at reform and redemption. Nor did the flour riots have any more social significance: they were an outburst of discontent, encouraged by political opposition of the right and of the left, but without any well defined social or economic aim.

More gravely in the South but, with a few exceptions, in the North as well, economic life in the first decade of the Kingdom still moved at an extremely slow pace and was unable to free itself from the straits which had confined it for over two centuries. Only around 1870 are there the first signs of greater dynamism: periods of rapid growth alternate with periods of serious crisis until after 1898 when development was almost uninterrupted for fifteen years—a development which one would find more comforting if it had not taken place north of Rome only and if it had not deepened the already wide gulf between the two halves of Italy.

# Outline of the History of
# German Cartels from 1873 to 1914

ERICH MASCHKE

Translated by Walter M. Stern and Carla M. Wartenberg

EDITORS' FOREWORD

[Though the phenomenon of cartels has international significance, their influence on economic structure has been more decisive in Germany after the crisis of 1873 than in any other country. However, there they had a tradition stretching back over a number of centuries. Hence Professor Maschke has devoted a special study to medieval cartels, 'Deutsche Kartelle des 15. Jahrhunderts' (German Cartels of the Fifteenth Century), in *Festschrift zum 65. Geburtstag von Friedrich Lütge* (Festschrift for Friedrich Lütge's 65th Birthday), 1966, pp. 74–87. Subsequent centuries again and again experienced the rise of cartels, either of producers or merchants. The author was able to ascertain the existence of 33 German cartels in the nineteenth century prior to the 1857 crisis. This continuity in the behaviour of German entrepreneurs, who at different periods and under differing economic conditions invariably tended to react by eliminating competition through combination, led to his paper on 'Deutsche Kartelle im späten Mittelalter und im 19. Jahrhundert vor 1870' (German Cartels in the Late Middle Ages and in the Nineteenth Century before 1870), given at a meeting on economic and social problems of the development of trade in the fifteenth, sixteenth and nineteenth centuries, held in March 1966 by the *Gesellschaft für Sozial- und Wirtschaftsgeschichte*; it will be published in its proceedings. The two above-mentioned studies deal with the history of German cartels prior to 1873, thus supplementing the essay printed here; its German original had a chapter on beginnings and foundations of German cartel history which has been omitted from the English version.]

# I

GERMAN CARTELS IN SLUMP AND STAGNATION, 1873-94

The crisis of 1857, the first world-wide crisis in the history of modern industry,[1]

---

[1] H. Rosenberg, 'Die Weltwirtschaftskrisis von 1857 bis 1859' (The World Economic Crisis, 1857–9), *V[ierteljahrschrift für] S[ozial- und] W[irtschafts-] G[eschichte]*, Suppl. No. 30,

caused setbacks in German industrial development; the crisis of 1873 which followed the so-called 'promoters' years'[2] and the subsequent depression years exerted a far more profound effect on German entrepreneurial behaviour. Economic liberalism had already been fettered by traditions surviving from the pre-liberal era; now, pressure of crisis and depression led to far-reaching departures from liberal economic principles, especially among industrial entrepreneurs. This found its most decisive expression in the protective tariffs of 1879, centring on iron,[3] but was also reflected in the increase of cartels formed in the 1870s, destined henceforth to play a progressively more important part. The same parties which waged the fight for protective tariffs backed the formation of cartels. It was not merely the iron duties which enabled cartellization of the iron industry. This consistent policy became public knowledge for the first time during the Iron Enquiry of 1878 when the rail cartel, existing in a rudimentary form since 1856, was discussed in the context of protective measures for the iron industry.[4]

In the depression following the crisis year of 1873, prices and sales fell off, particularly in raw materials and capital goods industries.[5] Competition became cutthroat, prevailing upon entrepreneurs to put an end to it by combination. Exaggerating dramatically, B. Schoenlank[6] wrote in 1890:

> The bells in Vienna sounding the death knell of the economic boom on 9 May 1873 rang in the birth hour of cartels.

He continued his description of the situation:

> The gamble of production and the limitless price fall of recent decades testified conclusively to the bankruptcy of a policy of unrestricted competition. The fight against overproduction and falling prices emerged as the most urgent and important task; regulatory intervention became the imperative demand born of knowledge matured by bitter experience.

Elimination of ruinous competition which, apart from structural difficulties, existed of course only at times of crisis and downswing thus was the oldest and first economic motive of continuous new cartellization. In his book *The Cartels*, (1883), the first student of cartel theory, the Austrian lawyer Friedrich Kleinwächter, defined them[7] as

1934, esp. pp. 166ff.; A. Spiethoff, *Die wirtschaftlichen Wechsellagen. Aufschwung, Krise Stockung* (Economic Fluctuations: Upswing, Crisis, Stagnation), i, 1955, pp. 118–19; J. Schumpeter, *Business Cycles*, German ed., i, 1955, pp. 342ff.; J. Kuczynski, *Die Geschichte der Lage der Arbeiter unter dem Kapitalismus 11: Studien zur Geschichte der zyklischen Überproduktionskrisen in Deutschland 1825–1866* (History of the Workers' Conditions under Capitalism, xi: History of Crises of Cyclical Overproduction in Germany, 1825–66), 1961, pp. 110ff.

[2] Spiethoff, *op. cit.*, p. 123; Schumpeter, *op. cit.*, pp. 347ff.; Kuczynski, *ibid.*

[3] J. N. Lambi, 'Free Trade and Protection in Germany, 1868–1879', *VSWG*, Suppl. No. 44, 1963; for tariffs cf. F. Kestner, 'Die deutschen Eisenzölle, 1879–1900' (The German Iron Tariffs, 1879–1900), *Staats- u. sozialwiss. Forschungen*, xxi, 3, 1902.

[4] Lambi, *op. cit.*, p. 78, with further references.

[5] Besides Lambi, cf. H. Rosenberg, 'Political and Social Consequences of the Great Depression of 1873–96', *Economic History Review*, 1/2, 1943.

[6] B. Schoenlank, 'Die Kartelle. Beiträge zu einer Morphologie der Unternehmerverbände' (The Cartels. Contributions to a Morphology of Industrial Associations), *Brauns Archiv für soziale Gesetzgebung und Statistik*, iii, 1890, p. 493.

[7] F. Kleinwächter, *Die Kartelle* (The Cartels), Innsbruck, 1883, pp. 126–7; cf. further A. Wolfers, 'Das Kartellproblem im Licht der deutschen Kartelliteratur' (The Problem of

agreements made between producers in a particular line of production, with the object of eliminating to some extent unrestricted competition among themselves, and of regulating output more or less so as to adjust it at any rate approximately to demand; cartels aim specifically at avoiding overproduction.

In a review of Kleinwächter's book A. E. E. Schäffle[8] on the other hand emphasized that the immediate object was 'a monopolistic price level favourable to cartel members', without excluding the long-term aim of 'creating economic equilibrium as between demand and output'.

The earliest theoretical definitions of cartels were based therefore on overproduction and unrestricted competition during a depression.[9] Kleinwächter's epithet for them, 'children of bad times',[10] came to be used again and again even when the business cycle situation did not, or no longer, apply. As late as 1905 Emil Kirdorf described the Rhine-Westphalian Coal Syndicate and the Steelworks Association as 'children of bad times'.[11]

The very first attempts at cartellization showed that it succeeded only in the case of certain commodities. Especially where sale was to be controlled by price agreements, products had to be homogeneous or at any rate standardized. Of all criteria bearing on cartellization, homogeneity of output was considered the most important; the more heterogeneous a commodity, the more difficult or even hopeless was combination.[12] Suitable commodities occurred most obviously within the range of raw materials: coal, iron and potash; it was in these industries that cartellization was achieved first and most completely.

Thus two determinants decisively shaped cartellization in Germany: on the one hand where all producers of a raw material joined a cartel, a perfect collective monopoly ensued, though in practice it almost invariably remained imperfect. Even an only approximate monopoly position however enabled coal and iron cartels to reduce to direct or indirect dependence on them in many respects not only the next, but all subsequent stages of production, and as raw material prices constituted data for the next stage of production,[13] to exert substantial influence on price formation which in a world of cartels had repercussions all along the line

Cartels in the Light of German Cartel Literature), *Sch[riften des] V[ereins für] S[ozialpolitik]*, clxxx, 2, 1931, p. 15. About 10 years later in an article on 'Industrial Associations (Economic)' in *H[andwörterbuch] d[er] S[taatswissenschaften]*, vi, 1st ed., 1894, p. 349, Kleinwächter omitted the idea of unlimited competition and adopted the following definition: 'Cartels are combinations of entrepreneurs in the same branch of industry (or in mutually dependent branches) pursuing the aim of improving the economic position of each member through collective measures by all'. He still does not adopt the monopoly concept.

[8] A. E. F. Schäffle, 'Die Kartelle' (The Cartels), first in *Z[eit]s[chrift] f. d. ges[amte] Staatswissenschaft*, 1883, later in *Gesammelte Aufsätze* (Collected Essays), i, 1885, pp. 150ff., esp. p. 153.

[9] Thus above all L. Brentano, cf. Wolfers, *op. cit.*, p. 15.

[10] Kleinwächter, *op. cit.*, p. 143.     [11] *SchVS*, cxvi, 1906, p. 275.

[12] R. Liefmann, *Die Unternehmerverbände (Konventionen, Kartelle). Ihr Wesen und ihre Bedeutung* (Industrial Associations (Agreements, Cartels): Nature and Meaning), Abhandlungen der badischen Hochschulen, i, 1897 [hereinafter quoted as Liefmann (i)], p. 61; R. Liefmann, *Kartelle, Konzerne und Trusts* (Cartels, Combines and Trusts), 8th ed., 1930 [hereinafter quoted as Liefmann (ii)], p. 36; typical the pronouncements of semi-manufactured articles' consumers in the hardware industry, *K[ontradiktorische] V[erhandlungen]* (Controversial Negotiations within the Government Enquiry into Cartels, 1903–6), i, pp. 194–6.

[13] Liefmann (i), p. 55; for coke and iron prices, *KV*, i, pp. 636ff., 640, 676.

of production.[14] Each producer passed on the prices paid by him to consumers of his output.[15] This created a network of dependence starting from cartellization at the raw material stage.

Dependence at subsequent stages of production on the other hand caused producers there to combine in their turn, in self-defence against pressures proceeding ultimately from the raw material industries, and sometimes at the explicit behest of cartels at antecedent stages.[16] A bird's-eye view shows cartellization progressing from primary to consumer goods production, often involving in its course wholesalers who had rendered themselves dependent on cartellized producers. In some branches of the economy, even retailers were stimulated to combination.

The different types of entrepreneurial combination before 1914 had all been known in the early history of cartels, but in a continuous development certain forms—each form progressively elaborated and increasingly adapted to particular output and market conditions and to the quality of the commodities produced— came to be associated with different periods and different industries. Since entrepreneurs took their cue from prices and since a price fall was the most obvious indicator of depression, producers combined to raise prices collectively by eliminating competition. The price cartel,[17] fixing either minimum or mandatory selling-prices, formed therefore the most immediate, simplest and earliest type in the continuous history of German cartels. Such were a salt cartel in 1868, the first potash cartel[18] (covering potassium chloride production only) of 1876, an 1882 agreement concluded among cement makers,[19] the high-quality puddled iron agreement in Rhineland-Westphalia and Nassau of the same year,[20] the price agreements for coking coal of 1879 and 1881 and for coke of 1882.[21] Similar in form was the 1881 Association of German Brassworks which also laid down delivery

---

[14] E.g. for the price formation of strip iron cf. W. Pieper, *Theodor Wuppermann und die Vereinigung Rheinisch-Westfälischer Bandeisenwalzwerke* (Theodor Wuppermann and the Association of Rhine-Westphalian Strip Iron Rolling Mills), Schriften zur Rheinisch-Westfälischen Wirtschaftsgeschichte, ix, 1963, p. 49 and table after p. 172.

[15] Cf. *KV*, ii, pp. 467–8.

[16] Cf. pp. 237, 238, 250 below.

[17] Liefmann (i), pp. 87ff.; Liefmann (ii), pp. 39–40i H. v. Beckerath, *Der moderne Industrialismus* (Modern Industrialism), Grundrisse zum Studium der Nationalökonomie, xi, 1, 1930, pp. 247–8; *HdS*, x, 1959, *sub* 'Unternehmenszusammenschlüsse' (Combinations of Firms), pp. 552ff.

[18] H. Siegel, *Die Entwicklung des deutschen Kalisyndikats unter besonderer Berücksichtigung der staatlichen Einflussnahme* (The Development of the German Potash Syndicate with special Reference to State Influence), 1941, p. 6.

[19] *Portland-Cement Fabrik Dyckerhoff & Söhne. Der Chronik zweiter Teil, 1896–1924* (Portland Cement Works Dyckerhoff & Söhne. Second Part of the Chronicle, 1896–1924), p. 103. Cf. below, p. 236, with n. 80.

[20] A. Klotzbach, *Der Roheisenverband. Ein geschichtlicher Rückblick auf die Zusammenschluss-bewegungen in der deutschen Hochofenindustrie* (The Pig-Iron Association: a Historical Review of Tendencies towards Combination in the German Blast Furnace Industry), 1926, pp. 23–4. To a very limited extent it also regulated conditions.

[21] *Die Entwickelung des Niederrheinisch-Westfälischen Steinkohlen-Bergbaues in der zweiten Hälfte des 19. Jahrhunderts XI: Wirtschaftliche Entwickelung* (The Development of Coal-Mining in Lower Rhine-Westphalia in the Second Half of the 19th Century, xi: Economic Development), pt. 2, 1904, pp. 316ff.; K. Wiedenfeld, 'Das Rheinisch-Westfälische Kohlensyndikat' (The Rhine-Westphalian Coal Syndicate), *Moderne Wirtschaftsgestaltungen*, i, 1918, p. 18; for the slightly earlier output agreements, cf. pp. 231–2 below.

conditions,[22] as did several other price cartels. Such price cartels significantly soon progressed to superior forms of combination, regulating more than mere prices,[23] though price cartels remained the preferred form of combination at the early stage of organization[24] where they sufficed, e.g. chemicals, or where industries proved unsuitable in structure and type of output for more elaborate forms of cartellization, e.g. parts of textiles.

The first, albeit short-lived, agreement in the chemical industry was a potash agreement of 1876.[25] The first cartel in coal tar dyes was the alizarin agreement of 1881.[26] The earliest regional price cartels for explosives date from about the same time.[27] In the 1880s and early 1890s cartellization made great progress in the chemical industry:[28] by 1897 no less than 82 cartels existed.[29] Price agreements were the predominant type. Since only homogeneous commodities could be cartellized, one at a time, with the object of achieving a uniform market price, a very large number of cartels representing various chemicals—bromide, ferro-cyanide, etc.—were formed. Undertakings producing a number of chemicals belonged to a different cartel for each of these products.

In textiles it was the turn first of semi-finished products, yarns, etc., and of fabrics whose sale could be most easily and uniformly controlled through prices.[30] Cartellization began in spinning mills in the 1880s; jute mills achieved output restriction as early as 1888.[31] A successful step was the conclusion of the all-German Zanella agreement of 1894,[32] subsequently the Association of German Lining Fabrics Weavers. Symptomatic of cartel enthusiasm on the part of manufacturers

[22] W. Jutzi, *Fünfzig Jahre Verbandsbestrebungen in der deutschen Messingindustrie* (Fifty Years of Associative Endeavours in the German Brass Industry), 1925, pp. 35ff.

[23] Cf. pp. 231-3, 238-9 below.

[24] Cement, a recent industry, started pricing agreements in 1882 and 1889: F. Berkenbusch, *Die deutsche Portland-Cement-Industrie und ihre Kartellbestrebungen* (The German Portland Cement Industry and its Endeavours to Cartellize), Heidelberg thesis, 1903, p. 34; F. Ritter, *Entwicklungen und Bestrebungen in der deutschen Portlandzementindustrie* (Developments and Endeavours in the German Portland Cement Industry), 1913, pp. 150–1; cf. n. 19 above. Short-lived price cartels for different types of paper first came about from 1889 onwards: F. Salzmann, *Die Papierindustrie, ihre wirtschaftliche Entwicklung und heutige Lage* (The Paper Industry: Economic Development and Present Situation), 1911, pp. 54, 128; H. Terhorst, *Kartelle und Konzerne in der papiererzeugenden Industrie* (Cartels and Trusts in the Papermaking Industry), Cologne thesis, 1936, pp. 41–2.

[25] L. F. Haber, *The Chemical Industry during the 19th Century*, Oxford, 1959, p. 228.

[26] *Ibid.*, p. 229.

[27] H. Wagenführ, *Kartelle in Deutschland* (Cartels in Germany), 1931, p. 230; F. A. Spiecker, 'Kartellverbindungen im Pulvergeschäft und verwandten Produktionszweigen' (Cartel Links in Powder and Kindred Production Lines), *SchVS*, lx, pp. 237ff.; G. Martin, *Geschichtliche Entwicklung der Kartellbildungen in der deutschen Sprengstoffindustrie* (Historical Development of Cartel Formation in the German Manufacture of Explosives), Heidelberg thesis, 1903, pp. 11ff.

[28] Cf. the historically rather incomplete outline in Wagenführ, *op. cit.*, pp. 213ff.; H. Kretzschmar, *Die Kartellbewegung in der chemischen Industrie* (The Cartel Movement in the Chemical Industry), Heidelberg thesis, 1921, pp. 50ff.; Haber, *op. cit.*, pp. 227ff., with further references.

[29] Liefmann (1), p. 143.

[30] Cf. V. Stern, *Die Kartelle in der Textil- und Bekleidungsindustrie* (Cartels in the Cloth and Clothing Industries), 1909; Wagenführ, *op. cit.*, pp. 262ff., esp. pp. 264, 274, 276.

[31] Liefmann (1), p. 81.

[32] *Denkschrift über das Kartellwesen, bearbeitet im Reichsamt des Inneren* (Memorandum on Cartellization compiled in the Reich Ministry of the Interior), 4 vols., 1906–8, i, pp. 56, 136–7; a combination of five large firms had been in existence since 1878 (*ibid.*, p. 137).

was the umbrella fabrics makers' cartel of 1888.[33] In textiles too, cartellization of one stage of production caused a desire for combination at the succeeding stage.[34] Early in the 1890s when linen thread spinners had formed a cartel, linen weavers tried to follow suit—an attempt which typically misfired.[35] For many years to come, scope for cartellization in textile industries remained limited.

Once the first price cartels existed, it very quickly became apparent in the raw materials industries that this form of cartel was incapable of bringing about the hoped-for improvement in the market situation: markets could not be controlled by means of sales and prices without simultaneously regulating production. As early as 1877 the Mining Association resolved that

the general meeting regards a suitable reduction of output in local mines as an indispensable preliminary to putting a rapid end to the evils of overproduction.[36]

Output agreements of this type prevailed from the late 1870s onwards, especially in the coal industry.[37] A quota cartel constituted a more advanced type than a pure price cartel, rationing output by means of allocating quotas to its members and restricting the volume of total output. The above-mentioned original price cartels soon turned into this new type.[38] Homogeneity of output required separate cartels for different types of coal, a little later for coke and manufactured fuels. In order to achieve any combination at all, wholly based on voluntary participation, such cartels had to take account of the individual requirements of their member firms, hence were often of limited duration.[39]

Even the quota cartel proving inadequate, the way was clear to the highest degree of cartellization, the syndicate which assigns to a common marketing agency the entire output of all firms in the same branch of industry and at the same stage of production.[40] This form had been known in the eighteenth-century iron industry. The Mining Association now endeavoured to impose it on the coal industry; its annual report for 1887 suggested the establishment of a syndicate calling in aid outside capital, in the form of a trading company to take charge on agreed terms of the entire coal output and be solely and on its own account responsible for sales.[41] Several groups of individual coal firms blazed the trail by

[33] Wagenführ, op. cit., p. 276.     [34] Liefmann (I), p. 56.
[35] SchVS, lxi, p. 204.
[36] Die Entwickelung . . . (n. 21 above), p. 91; E. Jüngst, Festschrift zur Feier des Fünfzig-jährigen Bestehens des Vereins für die bergbaulichen Interessen . . . 1858–1908 (Festschrift to Celebrate Half a Century of the Association Safeguarding the Interests of Mining . . . 1858–1908), 1908, p. 88. The first attempts in coal mining began in 1878 and 1879, preceded from 1876 by selling agreements: V. Muthesius, Ruhrkohle 1893–1943. Aus der Geschichte des Rheinisch-Westfälischen Kohlen-Syndikats (Ruhr Coal, 1893–1943: Leaves from the History of the Rhine-Westphalian Coal Syndicate), 1943, pp. 36–7. For quota cartels, cf. Liefmann (II), pp. 40ff.; v. Beckerath, op. cit., p. 249; HdS, x (n. 17 above), pp. 556ff.
[37] Liefmann (I), pp. 91ff.; Die Entwickelung . . . , pp. 90ff.; Wiedenfeld, op. cit., p. 18.
[38] Muthesius, op. cit., pp. 35ff. Conversely combinations lacking the preconditions for a more elaborate form of cartel relapsed into price cartels: Liefmann (I), p. 189.
[39] Die Entwickelung . . . , table xiv; Wiedenfeld, op. cit., pp. 18–19; Muthesius, op. cit., pp. 34ff.
[40] Liefmann (I), pp. 97ff.; Liefmann (II), pp. 41–2; v. Beckerath, op. cit., pp. 249–50; HdS, x, p. 555.
[41] Die Entwickelung . . . , pp. 132ff. for the negotiations which resulted from Hammacher's suggestion. Cf. also R. Passow, Materialien für das wirtschaftswissenschaftliche Studium I: Kartelle des Bergbaues (Materials for the Study of Economics, i: Mining Cartels), 1911, pp. 23ff.

establishing marketing bureaux:[42] in 1890 the Westphalian Coal Syndicate,[43] in 1891 the Manufactured Fuels Sales Association[44] were set up, modelled on the existing Pig-Iron Syndicate. Wearisome negotiations resulted on 16 February 1893 in the Rhine-Westphalian Coal Syndicate,[45] representing 86·6 per cent of total coal production of the Dortmund mining district. This achieved the long-desired dominating position of a large association able to regulate output and sales in a regionally limited market; for only within a so-called 'non-competitive area' was it possible to obtain anything approaching monopoly position.[46] At the same time the syndicate, the supreme type of cartel, had been created in the most essential sector of German raw material production, the Ruhr coal industry.

By its activities and longevity the Rhine-Westphalian Coal Syndicate greatly influenced further cartellization, serving as a model not only for coal industries outside the Ruhr, but for other branches of production capable of syndicalization. When the Brassworks Cartel, set up in 1881 as a price cartel[47] and renewed several times in that form, was dissolved in 1903, one of its former members argued with great conviction:[48]

Price cartels may once upon a time have proved their worth; today they are a wholly retrograde form of combination, out-of-date and no longer effective. Operative associations require support from sales syndicates.

Not only as a model for other syndicates, but also by its market behaviour[49] did the Rhine-Westphalian Coal Syndicate exercise an extraordinary influence on the development of the German economy. Cartellization in iron and steel moved towards the same goal of a syndicate, though other pre-conditions applied. As in coal mining, general cartellization began towards the end of the 1870s—earlier in the Nassau district. The scattered distribution of ore deposits led to regional syndicates,[50] a phenomenon appearing earlier in iron than in coal-mining. Out of various pre-existing combines arose in 1896 the Pig-Iron Syndicate with its seat at Düsseldorf, the most important of these groupings. Iron, as distinct from coal, enjoyed tariff protection after 1879, a significant turning point in German economic policy towards protection after a short free-trade interlude. Henceforth syndicalization of iron-making and iron-using industries proceeded in the shelter of tariff walls and in the comparative isolation of the domestic market.[51]

---

[42] Such as the collieries connected with the Diskonto-Gesellschaft, led by Gelsenkirchen: Wiedenfeld, *op. cit.*, p. 21.
[43] *Die Entwickelung* . . . , p. 240; Wiedenfeld, *op. cit.*, p. 21.
[44] *Die Entwickelung* . . . , p. 250; Wiedenfeld, *op. cit.*, p. 21.
[45] *Die Entwickelung* . . . , p. 264; Wiedenfeld, *op. cit.*, p. 21; Muthesius, *op. cit.*, p. 61.
[46] On competition in 'competitive' areas, cf. Wiedenfeld, *op. cit.*, pp. 78ff.
[47] Cf. pp. 229–30 above.
[48] Jutzi, *op. cit.* (n. 22 above), p. 88.          [49] Cf. pp. 253–4 below.
[50] For what follows, cf. Klotzbach, *op. cit.* (n. 20 above), pp. 22ff.
[51] Liefmann (1), pp. 66–7; Kestner, *op. cit.* (n. 3 above), discusses the formation and behaviour of iron cartels in conjunction with tariffs. R. Sonnemann, 'Die Auswirkungen der Schutzzollpolitik des Deutschen Reiches aus dem Jahre 1879 auf die Monopolbildung in der Eisen- und Stahlindustrie (1879–1892)' (The Repercussions of the German Policy of Tariff Protection of 1879 on Monopoly Formation in the Iron and Steel Industry, 1879–92), *Wiss.Zs.d. Martin-Luther-Universität Halle-Wittenberg*, viii (1958–9), *Gesellsch.- u. sprachwissensch. Reihe*, pp. 615–20, author's summary of a dissertation, yields little information on actual happenings. Cf. p. 227 above.

Between 1879 and 1882 about 18 cartels were formed in the iron industry, covering everything from pig-iron to semi-manufactures, sheets and pipes.[52] These years saw a short-lived upswing,[53] and it is arguable that bitter experience of the preceding crisis years combined with tariffs and particularly present economic improvement in stimulating a wave of cartel formation.[54] In the second half of the 1880s cartellization made considerable progress in the iron-using industries;[55] though cartels were frequently short-lived, the tendency to combine was ubiquitous, reaching far into the finishing branches: chains, locks, ploughshares, ladles and other hardware. Beside the dominant price cartels other types occurred, such as cartels regulating conditions of supply among mechanical engineering works.

Wherever homogeneity of output permitted cartellization, it started at the same time as in coal and iron. Sharp competition in the potash industry,[56] originating in the rise of private alongside State-owned enterprises, led to the formation of the first cartels allocating output quotas—carnalite in 1879, cainite in 1880. In 1888 the Potash Syndicate was established, an elaborate and unsatisfactory association achieved by seven separate agreements involving mines producing, and factories processing, raw materials; this was not replaced by a complete and uniform syndicate until 1899. The history of the Potash Syndicate sheds an interesting light on problems faced by cartels where raw material supplies make possible an increase in output. Price maintenance by the Syndicate encouraged the opening of new potash mines which had to be admitted to the Syndicate and granted quota participation if the combine was to maintain its monopoly position. These accessions perpetuated overproduction and endangered profitability of enterprises which no longer could work to capacity. In 1910 a compulsory government-run syndicate took over control of potash supplies. The Prussian State, by far the largest owner of potash mines, had the same attitude to competition as any private entrepreneur and, especially in the early decades, took the lead in creating cartels and syndicates, all the more as the rise of private undertakings had unleashed ruinous competition. Principles of regulation were only slowly introduced into the cartel policy of the State in respect of potash, always modified by its own financial interests. They gained strength from the world monopoly of potash which Germany possessed up to the end of the First World War.

1893, the year of the foundation of the Rhine-Westphalian Coal Syndicate, was the most fateful in the history of German cartels because the syndicate as a superior form of cartel had taken root in the most important raw material industries and in the heartland of productive industry, the Ruhr. The foundations of the modern cartel movement were laid in the long economic stagnation, from 1874 to 1894;[57] the short spells of upswing—1880-2 and 1888-90—merely confirmed businessmen

[52] Liefmann (1), pp. 66ff.; cf. p. 237 below with n. 86.
[53] Spiethoff, op. cit. (n. 1 above), pp. 125–6; Kuczynski, op. cit. (n. 1 above), pp. 53ff.
[54] Cf. Liefmann (1), p. 54, for the year 1882; generally p. 235 below.
[55] For what follows, F. Grossmann, 'Über industrielle Kartelle' (On Industrial Cartels), *Schmollers J[ahr]b[uch]*, xv, 1891, pp. 236ff.
[56] For what follows, Siegel, op. cit. (n. 18 above) with further references, also p. 229 above; R. Liefmann, 'Kaliindustrie' (Potash Industry), *HdS*, v, 1923, pp. 563ff.; Wagenführ, op. cit., with further references.
[57] Cf. Spiethoff, op. cit., pp. 123ff.; Schumpeter, op. cit. (n. 1 above), pp. 347ff., giving a slightly different timing of business cycles (cf. p. 352); Rosenberg, op. cit. (n. 5 above).

in the consciousness of their dependence on cyclical fluctuations.[58] The shock of the crisis, the drop in prices, the falling-off in sales during the downswing and stagnation which stimulated competition to the point of ruin taught entrepreneurs to meet these evils by voluntary combination. Entrepreneurial reaction to cyclical fluctuations was one of the strongest motives for cartellization. But other factors played their part. Personal and organizational links between entrepreneurs engaged in the same branches of production were strengthened by trade associations arising out of the social insurance legislation of 1884 which were demonstrably a force in cartellization.[59]

# II

## CARTELLIZATION UP TO THE FIRST WORLD WAR

Cartellization continued to make great progress from the middle of the 1890s to the First World War. An important contribution was the clarification of the legal position of cartels provided by the judgment of the Supreme Court of 4 February 1897.[60] It declared cartel obligations to be binding in law and recognized the right to combine in order to raise unduly low prices. Henceforth cartels did not contravene the principles of freedom of trade. Such legalization opened the gates to continued cartellization.

Existing syndicates in part consolidated their organization. Syndicalization of raw materials was completed, and cartellization penetrated ever more deeply into the finishing stages of production and even into consumer goods industries. Particularly between 1903 and 1906, a wave of new cartels filled gaps in branches and stages of production already extensively cartellized and reached out into subsequent production stages, even down to wholesaling, in addition to making new conquests of whole industries down to retail distribution.

As cyclical swings were no longer as violent as in previous decades, the cyclical pattern ceased to play as decisive a part in determining entrepreneurial behaviour as in the period after 1873. Nevertheless the sudden cyclical change of 1900 and the depression of 1901–2[61] left a deep impression on entrepreneurs and consider-

---

[58] Cf. further pp. 235, 252 below.

[59] Schoenlank, *op. cit.* (n. 6 above), p. 497 and n. 1.

[60] Supreme Court Civil Cases, xxxviii, 1897, pp. 155ff., reprinted in *Denkschrift* . . . (n. 32 above), pp. 58ff.; O. Lehnich, *Kartelle und Staat unter Berücksichtigung der Gesetzgebung des In- und Auslandes* (Cartels and State with Reference to Domestic and Foreign Legislation), 1928, pp. 91–2; R. Isay, *Geschichte der Kartellgesetzgebung* (History of Cartel Legislation), 1955, p. 32; further F. Böhm, 'Das Reichsgericht und die Kartelle' (The Supreme Court and the Cartels), *Ordo*, i, 1948, pp. 197ff.; B. Röper, 'Der wirtschaftliche Hintergrund der Kartell-Legalisierung durch das Reichsgericht, 1897' (The Economic Background to the Legalization of Cartels by the Supreme Court, 1897), *ibid.*, iii, 1950, pp. 239ff.; Th. F. Marburg, 'Government and Business in Germany: Public Policy towards Cartels', *Business History Review*, xxxviii, 1964, pp. 81–2.

[61] Cf. Spiethoff, *op. cit.*, pp. 132–3; Schumpeter, *op. cit.*, p. 438; regarding cartels in crisis, R. Liefmann, 'Krisen und Kartelle' (Crises and Cartels), *Schmollers Jb.*, xxvi, 1902, pp. 661ff.; L. V. Wiese, 'Die rheinisch-westfälische Eisenindustrie in der gegenwärtigen Krisis' (The Rhine-Westphalian Iron Industry in the Present Crisis), *ibid.*, pp. 299ff.; cf. Kuczynski, *op. cit.*, pp. 103ff.

ably increased their readiness to form associations in the years of upswing which followed. Thus 1903 and the subsequent period gave an extraordinary fillip to the cartel movement. In the iron industry, 12 new cartels came into being in 1903, six in 1904, 11 in 1905[62]—the largest annual figures ever for new cartels. It is arguable how far they were due to experience derived from the earlier depression. Before 1901 the maximum number of cartels set up in any single year had never exceeded two. Six were formed in the depression years of 1901 and 1902.[63]

Originally, and especially in the two decades after 1873, the readiness of entrepreneurs to combine had been predominantly a reaction to crisis and stagnation. But men react in a variety of ways. Upswing as well as downswing could prompt combination; conversely, both could bring about a collapse of cartels and a preference for competition.[64]

Where cartels had been formed during cyclical depressions as 'children of bad times', entrepreneurs not infrequently reverted to free competition during the upswing. At the height of the period of recovery in 1888 and 1889,[65] the number of cartels dissolved was six times as large as in the two years preceding and following; whereas in 1887 and in 1890 two cartels were dissolved out of 42 and 92 respectively, this happened to 13 out of 68 in 1888, 11 out of 67 in 1890.[66] At the same time 20 new cartels came into being in 1888, even 50 in 1889, corresponding figures for 1887 and 1890 having been 30 and 23 respectively.[67] As in the boom years of 1888–90,[68] so in the prosperous[69] year 1882,[70] an astonishing number of cartels had been established: cyclical upswing could tempt to combination. In the midst of the boom of 1905 members of the dissolved Sheet Steel Association counted on the possibility of renewal due to favourable market conditions and better prices. It was clear that resuscitation of the Association depended on continuation of a favourable cyclical trend.[71] Whereas combination allowed individual entrepreneurs to take collective advantage of a favourable economic climate by means of common price formation, no entrepreneur working on his own could raise prices in a favourable market in the certainty that his competitors would follow suit.[72]

On the other hand, pressure of crisis and depression could also lead to dissolution of existing cartels, since at least the stronger members of any cartel could hope to overcome adverse economic conditions by competition. In 1901–2 and 1907–8

[62] E. Altmann, *Über die Entwicklung und Bedeutung der Kartelle in der deutschen Eisenin, dustrie* (On the Development and Significance of Cartels in the German Iron Industry), Darmstadt thesis, 1909, p. 27, based on *Denkschrift* . . . (n. 32 above).
[63] *Ibid.*
[64] H. Wagenführ, *Konjunktur und Kartelle* (Cyclical Movements and Cartels), 1932, p. 6, in his table showing cyclical movements and number of industrial cartels in Germany gives a survey for the period from 1865 to 1930 which is inadequately differentiated; cartellization at the beginning of cyclical upswings is particularly stressed. Good tables in V. Holzschuher, *Soziale und ökonomische Hintergründe der Kartellbewegung* (Social and Economic Background to Cartellization), Erlangen-Nürnberg thesis, 1963, pp. 65–6, 96.
[65] Spiethoff, *op. cit.*, pp. 127–8; Schumpeter, *op. cit.*, p. 377.
[66] Grossmann, *op. cit.* (n. 55 above), p. 274; his overall figures for cartels in 1888 and 1889 differ from Schoenlank's, *op. cit.* (n. 6 above), pp. 515–6.
[67] Grossmann, *loc. cit.*     [68] Cf. also Liefmann (I), p. 143.
[69] Spiethoff, *op. cit.*, p. 125; Schumpeter, *op. cit.*, p. 377; Kuczynski, *op. cit.*, pp. 54ff.
[70] Liefmann (I), p. 54.
[71] *K[artell-]R[undschau]*, iii, 1905, p. 271.
[72] Liefmann (I), pp. 53–4; Liefmann (II), p. 29.

cartels disintegrated for this reason,[73] although by far the larger number weathered the storm.[74] At times of depression, strong outsiders could often exert sufficient pressure to bring about dissolution. The Pig-Iron Syndicate succumbed in 1908, incapable of enduring at this difficult economic juncture the existence of outsiders, especially of Kraft's Iron Works, of Stettin.[75] But overall, the number and importance of cartels increased continually during the two decades before the First World War.

The large syndicates perfected their organization. The Rhine-Westphalian Coal Syndicate in 1903 incorporated the Coke Syndicate and at last achieved the long-desired accession of the mixed works, which were promised that their own coal consumption would not be counted against their syndicate quotas.[76] The Pig-Iron Syndicate made an agreement in the same year with outside producers, thus tightening its organization.[77] In 1904 the German Steelworks Association was formed, a combination of long pre-existing associations.[78] 27 large German steel works joined in the formation of this association which represented 83·5 per cent of Germany's total steel production. After initial resistance, several sizeable outsiders acceded, including Phoenix A.G.,[79] bringing membership up to, and exceeding, 31.

Syndicates were formed in industries which had up to now contented themselves predominantly with price or quota cartels. The most important regional syndicates in the cement industry were established between 1903 and 1905.[80] After some years of negotiations starting in 1904, a Brassworks Syndicate was set up in 1907.[81] The Printing Paper Syndicate dates back to 1900.[82]

In the coal industry too, cartellization reached a climax. Syndicalization in the Waldenburg colliery district (Lower Silesia)[83] or in lignite production in Central Germany[84] was first achieved around this time. By 1908 the entire German coal industry, with the exception of a relatively small number of outsiders, was organized in large regional syndicates.

---

[73] Cf. *Deutsche Wirtschaftszeitung*, v, 1909, pp. 121ff., vi, 1910, pp. 218ff.; cf. p. 253 below and nn. 221–2.

[74] The textile industry even managed to maintain its conditions: *Deutsche Wirtschafts-zeitung*, v, p. 122.

[75] Klotzbach, *op. cit.* (n. 20 above), pp. 155ff.

[76] Wiedenfeld, *op. cit.*, pp. 146–7; Muthesius, *op. cit.* (n. 36 above), p. 91; for the attitude of mixed works, cf. pp. 246–7 below.          [77] Klotzbach, *op. cit.*, pp. 115ff.

[78] P. Ufermann, *Der deutsche Stahltrust* (The German Steel Trust), 1927, pp. 32ff.; cf. A. Zöllner, 'Eisenindustrie und Stahlwerksverband. Eine wirtschaftliche Studie zur Kartell-frage' (Iron Industry and Steelworks Association. An Economic Study of the Cartel Prob-lem), *Wirtschafts- u. Verwaltungsstudien mit bes. Berücksichtigung Bayerns*, xxix, 1907.

[79] Cf. p. 249 below.

[80] Ritter, *op. cit.* (n. 24 above), pp. 160, 164–6, 172; for earlier sales associations, cf. Berkenbusch, *op. cit.* (n. 24 above), pp. 36ff.; cf. the survey in Wagenführ, *op. cit.*, p. 166.

[81] Jutzi, *op. cit.* (n. 22 above), p. 82.

[82] Salzmann, *op. cit.* (n. 24 above), p. 128; Wagenführ, *op. cit.*, p. 34; Terhorst, *op. cit.* (n. 24 above), p. 42.

[83] Wagenführ, *op. cit.*, p. 34; *Denkschrift . . .* , i, 1906, pp. 76–7, 1903.

[84] M. Heinz, *Kartellbildungen im mitteldeutschen Braunkohlengebiet* (Cartel Formations in the Central German Lignite Region), Heidelberg thesis, 1919, pp. 82ff.; R. Dohm, 'Der gegen-wärtige Stand der deutschen Braunkohlenindustrie und ihrer Syndikate' (The Present Condition of the German Lignite Industry and its Syndicates), *Deutsche Wirtschaftszeitung*, vi, 1910, pp. 753ff.

Increasing cartellization of the iron industry was of special importance for Germany's economy. Associative activities at stages of production subsequent to iron ore extraction were already in full operation in the 1880s,[85] but made decisive and lasting progress in the years after 1900. Among these combinations the Semi-Manufactured Articles Association, set up in 1895[86] and consolidated at the time of its renewal in 1901, had particular significance due to the superiority of joint-product over single-product firms and to the rigid and ruthless price policy made possible by such a structure. With the progressive cartellization of the iron industry, raw material monopolies were joined by a form of association which combined monopsony with monopoly.

Initially entrepreneurs engaged in subsequent stages of production combined chiefly as consumers[87] to hold their own vis-à-vis pressure exerted by the coal and iron syndicates, but also and in particular by the Semi-Manufactured Articles Association.[88] But pure monopsonies generally proved too weak. Hence they soon blossomed out into complete cartels, though remaining clearly far from independent.[89] Around the turn of the century a tendency emerged more strongly among raw materials syndicates to promote in their turn, to demand more imperiously, at times even to enforce cartellization at subsequent stages of production.[90] As raw material syndicates could not tolerate the coexistence of regulation in production with sharp competition in distribution which set at nought the syndicates' price policy, they also brought about combination among wholesalers. Wholesale coal merchants,[91] able in a situation of perfect competition at the appropriate moment in the business cycle to determine coal prices at the pithead, on the foundation of the Rhine-Westphalian Coal Syndicate fell into dependence on it and combined, initially as a measure of self-defence. Subsequently, for the above-mentioned reason, the Syndicate itself set the greatest store by the formation of an association in coal wholesaling[92] which had begun as early as the 1890s, reaching a climax in 1903–5.[93] In iron too, association among wholesalers occurred to some extent at the initiative of producers' cartels.[94]

[85] Cf. p. 233 above with n. 52; Grossmann, *op. cit.* (n. 55 above), pp. 242ff.

[86] H. G. Heymann, 'Die gemischten Werke im deutschen Grosseisengewerbe' (Mixed Works in the German Iron Industry), *Münchner Volkswirtschaftl. Studien*, lxv, 1904, pp. 153–4.

[87] Liefmann (1), pp. 55ff., 73ff., 151; Report on Cartellization in the Domestic Iron Industry, *KV*, iii, 1904, pp. 40 (Pig-Iron Purchasing Association, 1902), 55 (Association to Safeguard the Interests of Consumers of Semi-Manufactured Articles), 550 (Rod Purchasing Association, 1896–1900).

[88] Report ... (n. 87 above), *passim*; Pieper, *op. cit.* (n. 14 above), pp. 107ff.

[89] Report ..., especially pp. 42ff., 56ff., on the fruitless negotiations with the Rhine-Westphalian Pig-Iron Syndicate and the Semi-Manufactured Articles Association; also the discussions on these syndicates during the Controversial Negotiations (n. 12 above) in *KV*, iii.          [90] Cf. p. 250 below.

[91] For what follows, cf. H. Bonikowsky, *Der Einfluss der industriellen Kartelle auf den Handel in Deutschland* (The Influence of Industrial Cartels on Trade in Germany), 1907, pp. 246ff.; cf. K. Wiedenfeld, 'Der Handel und die Industriekartelle' (Trade and Industrial Cartels), *Schmollers Jb.*, xxxiii, 1909, pp. 353ff.; K. Wiedenfeld, 'Das Rheinisch-Westfälische Kohlensyndikat' (The Rhine-Westphalian Coal Syndicate), *Moderne Wirtschaftsgestaltungen*, i, 1912, pp. 30ff.; Wagenführ, *op. cit.*, pp. 41ff.

[92] Cf. *KV*, i, (Coal Syndicate), pp. 134, 137.

[93] Cf. tables in Wagenführ, *op. cit.*, pp. 44ff.

[94] Bonikowsky, *op. cit.*, pp. 262ff.; Zöllner, *op. cit.* (n. 78 above), pp. 88, 153ff.; W. Leisse, 'Wandlungen in der Organisation der Eisenindustrie und des Eisenhandels seit dem

Progressive cartellization of coal meant that in the iron industry, dependent on coal, the combination movement spread from one stage of production to the other, finding its limits only where insufficient homogeneity of output prevented cartellization. This had already proved virtually impossible for the so-called B-products: the light, strongly differentiated products of rolling mills, especially rods.[95] Initially included by the Steelworks Association among output under quota allocation, they were freed in 1912.[96] Consumers of semi-manufactured iron responded to pressure towards cartellization, exerted by syndicates at preceding stages of production, by the contention that it could not in practice be done.[97] Even more limited was the scope for cartellization in the hardware industry, although a number of cartels arose here during the first years of the twentieth century.[98] Cartellization encountered the greatest difficulties in the mechanical engineering industry. When in 1904 the machine tool industry tried to form a cartel[99] to counter combination at the anterior stage of semi-manufactured iron, the great variety of products made to customers' own specifications rendered the attempt extremely difficult. Nevertheless, the bounds of cartellization were pushed farther and farther outward in the iron-using industry.

What was true of mechanical engineering or hardware, applied equally to other industries whose products lacked homogeneity, especially to textiles, including the clothing industry[100] in which the effect of fashion was superadded and where the pronounced individualism of owners of the numerous middling and small firms further impeded cartellization.[101] Attempts made fairly early to cartellize finished articles had failed. After the turn of the century this resulted in a new form of cartel—the conditions cartel,[102] a combination for the purpose of a common policy on conditions of payment, credit, discount and delivery. Like others, this form of cartel had long been known; in the woollen industry the tendency to regulate conditions through combination had appeared as early as 1875.[103] The cloth manufacturers of Brünn in Moravia formed a pure cartel in 1892.[104] Not infrequently price cartels evolved into regulating conditions. But the triumphal progress of

Gründungsjahr des Stahlwerksverbandes' (Changes in the Organization of the Iron Industry and the Iron Trade from the Foundation of the Steelworks Association), *Staats- u. sozialwiss. Forschungen*, clviii, 1912, pp. 140ff. Traders in gas piping combined 1904–5: *KR*, ii, 1904, p. 614; iii, 1905, p. 276. The Gas Piping Syndicate had developed in 1893.

[95] W. Adler, *Die Organisationsbestrebungen in Stabeisenfabrikation und Stabeisenhandel* (The Endeavours to Organize the Manufacture of, and the Trade in, Iron Rods), 1920.

[96] Altmann, *op. cit.* (n. 62 above), p. 48; Adler, *op. cit.*, p. 56.

[97] *KV*, ii, pp. 456–7, 465–6.

[98] Cf. table 1 in Altmann, *op. cit.*; for the 1880s cf. p. 233 above; Leisse, *op. cit.*, pp. 83ff.

[99] *KR*, ii, 1904, pp. 341–2, 429.

[100] For what follows, cf. Stern, *op. cit.* (n. 30 above); H. v. Beckerath, *Die Kartelle in der deutschen Seidenweberei-Industrie* (Cartels in the German Silk Weaving Industry), 1911; R. H. Knopf, *Die Wirkungen der Kartelle der Textil- und Bekleidungsindustrie auf die Abnehmer* (Effects of Cartels in Cloth and Clothing Industries on Buyers), Heidelberg thesis, 1915.

[101] Stern, *op. cit.*, esp. pp. 17–18, 21, 48.

[102] On these cf. Liefmann (II), pp. 44–5, who does not consider them cartels proper; otherwise Wagenführ, *op. cit.*, xi and *passim*; v. Beckerath, *op. cit.*, pp. 246–7; *HdS*, x, pp. 558–9.

[103] F. Bachmann, *Zur Geschichte der Organisation der industriellen Interessen der deutschen Tuch- und Wollwarenindustrie* (Contribution to the History of the Organization of Industrial Interests in the German Cloth and Woollen Industry), Heidelberg thesis, 1915, p. 44.

[104] *SchVS*, lxi, pp. 437ff.

conditions cartels in the textile industry took place only after the turn of the century. Whereas quota cartels could encompass only semi-manufactured textiles and price cartels remained of limited use, the conditions cartel allowed combination of producers, however differentiated their output. Such combination initially received its impetus from the wholesale and retail trades, already organized, and from department stores.[105]

In textile and clothing industries cartellization made ever further headway from the beginning of the century to the First World War. In 1905 the Berlin Chamber of Commerce reported[106]:

> The latest development is the penetration of the cartel movement into the textile industry, hitherto rather averse from it on account of the multiplicity and variety of its undertakings and products.

There was talk in 1905 of 'associative fever' gripping the textile industry; the number of cartels of various types was estimated at 75.[107] *Der Confectionär*, the trade journal, coined the term 'agreement mania'[108] for this cartel enthusiasm. At this time the calculation cartel[109] began to take root[110]—a cartel which established for its members a uniform standard of calculation.

Enthusiasm for agreements similarly seized the leather industry:[111] overall, numerous cartels arose for the most varied commodities in common use. The footwear industry however established hardly any cartels before the First World War,[112] apart from rubber footwear.[113]

A few years after the turn of the century, German industry had been extensively cartellized from raw materials to consumer goods.[114] The Cartel Enquiry of 1905 officially enumerated 385 German cartels, including however 132 regional brickworks cartels. In total[115] it discovered those listed on p. 240. Brickworks apart, this added up to 253 cartels, 92 of them in heavy industry. The real number of cartels was considerably larger.[116]

---

[105] E. Kaufmann, *Zur Kartellierung des Einzelhandels im Textilgewerbe* (On Cartellization in the Retail Trade in Textiles), Heidelberg thesis, 1923, pp. 3ff., 18ff.

[106] Report of Berlin Chamber of Commerce for 1905, quoted from Annual Report of the Association of German Department Stores for 1904–5, p. 17.

[107] *KR*, iii, 1905, pp. 627–8; cf. also pp. 385ff. and *passim*.

[108] Annual Report of the Association of German Department Stores, 1912.

[109] Cf. Liefmann (II), p. 46; v. Beckerath, *op. cit.*, pp. 275ff.; Wagenführ, *op. cit.*, p. 263; *HdS*, x, p. 559.

[110] E.g. Kaufmann, *op. cit.*, p. 5.

[111] *KR*, i and ii, 1904, p. 279 and *passim*; iii, 1905, pp. 33–4, 113 and *passim*. Regarding the Association of German Horse Leather Manufacturers, cf. *Denkschrift* . . . , Appendix F 3 and *KR*, iii, pp. 807, 874.

[112] Here too cartellization of semi-manufacturers occurred relatively early, e.g. combination of Siegen sole leather manufacturers: Grossmann, *op. cit.* (n. 55 above), pp. 271–2.

[113] Annual Report . . . (n. 108 above), 1905–6, p. 17.

[114] Cf. table on volume of cartellization in Germany according to industrial groups as percentage of gross value of production for 1907 in H. König, 'Kartelle und Konzentration' (Cartels and Concentration), in K. Arndt (ed.), *Die Konzentration in der Wirtschaft*, i, p. 311. Figures for processing industries are certain to have been even higher.

[115] *Denkschrift* . . . , i, p. 24; Wagenführ, *op. cit.*, xiii.

[116] König, *op. cit.*, table on number of German cartels in selected industries for 1890, 1891, 1897, 1905, 1910, etc., p. 307. Apart from the works quoted there which offer statistics, cf. also figures for 1888 and 1889 in Schoenlank, *op. cit.* (n. 6 above), p. 515.

19 cartels in coal
62    ,,    ,,  iron
11    ,,    ,,  non-ferrous metals
46    ,,    ,,  chemicals
31    ,,    ,,  textiles
6     ,,    ,,  leather and rubber goods
5     ,,    ,,  timber
6     ,,    ,,  paper
10    ,,    ,,  glass
132   ,,    ,,  bricks
27    ,,    ,,  extraction of stones and ores
4     ,,    ,,  pottery
17    ,,    ,,  food, drink and tobacco
2     ,,    ,,  electrical industry
7     ,,    ,,  others
___
385

# III

### THE TRANSFORMATION OF GERMAN CARTELS UP TO 1914

Cartellization fundamentally modified the structure of the German domestic economy and the attitude of its entrepreneurs. The individual was replaced by the association to which the entrepreneur had voluntarily surrendered freedom of decision. Market competition, though not eliminated, was sufficiently reduced to give cartels control of the market situation. An economy based on freedom of trade had been replaced by what deserves the description of a 'controlled economy'. These fetters had been forged by entrepreneurs themselves, without collaboration from the State, except for potash. This had changed the supplier-customer relationship, most completely in the instance of syndicates which entirely abolished personal contact with customers.

Simultaneously with cartellization, concentration[117] made great progress in the form of amalgamation, especially in vertical integration. It was in this field that the leading industrialists of the time took the initiative most effectively.[118] Concentration is as old as industrialization itself. Alongside the original conception, considering as one all productive processes in any branch of the economy, the dominant early motive for vertical concentration was command, and independence

---

[117] There is no monograph on the history of concentration in German industry; cf. the relevant chapters in A. Sartorius von Waltershausen, *Deutsche Wirtschaftsgeschichte 1815–1914* (German Economic History, 1815–1914), 1923; for the general question also König, *op. cit.* A good survey for the Ruhr is G. Gebhardt, *Ruhrbergbau. Geschichte, Aufbau und Verflechtung seiner Gesellschaften und Organisationen* (Ruhr Mining. History, Growth and Interpenetration of its Companies and Organizations), 1957.

[118] Cf. in general K. Wiedenfeld, *Das Persönliche im Modernen Unternehmertum* (The Personal Element in Modern Entrepreneurship), 2nd ed., 1920, esp. pp. 64–5, 99ff., and references in n. 139 below.

from suppliers, of raw materials. This motive continued to play an important part especially in endeavours of foundry owners to obtain control of coal mines.[119] In addition, cost reduction assumed ever greater importance. Both motives became linked where syndicate prices drove consumers of such syndicalized products to integration of antecedent stages of production, coal or pig-iron, in order to secure these materials at lower costs.[120]

Technical progress as such also made for large-scale production. Demand for capital never ceased to grow and could be satisfied the more easily as the joint-stock form of company had become well-nigh universally accepted. The great joint-stock banks, founded roughly between 1850 and 1870, themselves agents of widespread concentration,[121] came to dominate the business of industrial promotion and exercised strong influence on industry. An almost inextricable network of personal and financial links spread between banks and industry. The general object of expanding concentration was improvement and solidification of market position. Yet up to the First World War no single large-scale undertaking achieved a monopoly; at best the market situation was oligopolistic.

Trustification and cartellization supplemented each other, directed in the same period towards the same object: the creation of large-scale industrial combinations. Entrepreneurial preference between the two varied over time. Though combination to create large-scale industrial organizations was the constant aim and endeavour of leading men, trustification and cartellization were regarded sometimes as alternatives, sometimes as complementary to, and conditional upon, one another. Especially the failure of the earliest cartels formed in the late 1870s, a failure due in no small measure to the scattered units in Ruhr coal-mining, led to a debate among entrepreneurs in the early 1880s, treating cartels and trusts as mutually exclusive alternatives; leading Ruhr mining industrialists demanded integration as the sovereign remedy.

William Thomas Mulvany (1806–85), the Irishman who, in the course of building up the Ruhr industry, made Germany his second home, drew up a memorandum in 1882 on *Amalgamation of Collieries in an Eastern Sector of the Dortmund Mining District*, in which he put the case for 'amalgamation', i.e. combination of numerous small undertakings within a limited area into one large one, in spite of great practical difficulties.[122]

At about the same time Emil Russell in a report of the board of directors of the *Gelsenkirchener Bergwerks A.G.*, drawn up as a preliminary to horizontal integration,[123] based his case on the failure of coal output agreements and contrasted them with

[119] Wiedenfeld, 'Das Rheinisch-Westfälische . . .', pp. 44ff., esp. 47–8; Heymann, *op. cit.* (n. 86 above); Pilz, *Die Hüttenzechenfrage im Ruhrgebiet und Richtlinien für eine Erneuerung des Rheinisch-Westfälischen Kohlensyndikats* (The Question of Collieries Owned by Iron Works in the Ruhr and Guide Lines for a Renewal of the Rhine-Westphalian Coal Syndicate), Münster-Essen thesis, 1910; Leisse, *op. cit.* (n. 94 above), pp. 131ff.; cf. pp. 249ff. below.

[120] E.g. Heymann, *op. cit.*, p. 110 and *passim*.

[121] J. Riesser, *Die deutschen Grossbanken und ihre Konzentration* (The Large German Banks and their Concentration), 4th ed., 1912.

[122] K. Bloemers, 'William Thomas Mulvany (1806–1885)', *Veröff.d. Archivs für Rheinisch-Westfälische Wirtschaftsgeschichte*, viii, 1922, pp. 121–2.

[123] The text of the report of 28 March 1882 in F. A. Freundt, *Kapital und Arbeit* (Capital and Labour), n.d. [1927], pp. 36ff., the sections quoted in the text on p. 38; cf. W. Bacmeister,

the formation of fairly large coal-mining enterprises: 10 to 15 large administrative units besides a number of small collieries.

In the belief that such large organizations would come to free and informal agreements about market needs or output restriction, Russell preferred oligopoly to cartel monopoly, but rejected even 'partial unification', holding that the ensuing monopoly would not be desirable in the interests of the consumers.[124] The Gelsenkirchen Company in fact embarked on planned horizontal expansion, in accordance with the 1882 decisions. Only subsequently did it clearly formulate the connection between this turn towards trustification and its leadership in the movement for syndicalization.[125] In 1902 a declaration of the Gelsenkirchen Company recalled the time when ownership of Rhine-Westphalian collieries had been scattered, continuing:

> It was the purpose and basic principle of the expansion of this Company, begun in 1882, to do away with this evil and achieve, beside the technical advantages of consolidation, a position of power enabling the Company to take a leading part in combining Rhine-Westphalian coal-mining for purposes of marketing.[126]

Eduard Kleine in a memorandum of 1885 went considerably further than Russell: he rejected syndicates as inadequate and proposed as the most effective solution 'a consolidation of all collieries of our district into a single undertaking'.[127] He feared however resistance of State and public opinion to such a dominating market position.[128] After the turn of the century the creation of great trusts, in the United States and in various European countries as well as in Germany, made a growing impact and again brought to the fore the alternatives of cartellization and trustification. This is how Emil Kirdorf considered the decision between trust and syndicate during the Controversial Negotiations on the Rhine-Westphalian Coal Syndicate in 1903,[129] while leaving open the question whether syndicates were a preliminary stage of trustification. At any rate, he approved of syndicates as an economic device for the times. During the same negotiations,[130] and again at the conference

*Emil Kirdorf. Der Mann, sein Werk* (Emil Kirdorf, the Man and His Work), 2nd ed., n.d. [1936], pp. 82ff.; O. Stillich, 'Gelsenkirchener Bergwerks-Aktiengesellschaft' in O. Stillich, *Nationalökonomische Forschungen auf dem Gebiet der grossindustriellen Unternehmung 2: Steinkohlenbergbau* (Economic Research in the Field of Large-Scale Industrial Enterprise ii: Coal-Mining), 1906, pp. 150ff.

[124] Freundt, *op. cit.*, p. 38; cf. Bacmeister, *op. cit.*, p. 84; cf. also p. 250 below.

[125] Bacmeister, *op. cit.*, pp. 49–50, 57–8 (Kirdorf's pronouncement in 1904); Freundt, *op. cit.*, p. 74.

[126] Cf. Heymann, *op. cit.*, p. 303.

[127] Muthesius, *op. cit.* (n. 36 above), p. 32; for a plan of concentration contemplating the formation of three groups (Dortmund, Bochum, Aplerbeck) and submitted in 1886 within the framework of the Mining Association, cf. *Technische Mitteilungen des Vereins für die bergbaulichen Interessen im Oberamtsbezirk Dortmund* (Technical Information by the Association for Mining Interests in the Dortmund District), sifted and published by Bergassessor (retired) Nonne, 3 pamphlets, Berlin, 1886; cf. *Die Entwicklung . . .* (n. 21 above), pp. 111ff. Friedrich Grillo also developed schemes of concentration, cf. W. Däbritz, 'Friedrich Grillo (1825–88)', *Rheinisch-Westfälische Wirtschaftsbiographien*, ii, 1937, p. 84.

[128] Cf. p. 251 below.

[129] *KV*, pp. 252, 264ff.

[130] *Ibid.*, pp. 54–5.

of the Society for Social Policy in 1905,[131] Gustav Schmoller sided decisively with cartels and against trusts, followed by other economists speaking at the conference.

On the other hand Thyssen, one of the leaders in the recent foundation of the Steelworks Association, declared in this same year of 1905 that 'the time of syndicates is already past: we must now proceed to the trust'.[132] The formation in 1904 of the Steelworks Association had again added fuel to the controversy whether development inevitably tended towards the trust or whether the syndicate remained an effective form of comprehensive combination in heavy industry. The conglomeration achieved by the Steelworks Association scarcely differed to the eyes of many beholders from the great American trusts, whereas others laid stress on the basic differences between the two structures.[133]

In a memorandum written in 1903–4 under the impact of a visit to America, Carl Duisberg, founder of I.G. Farben, came down decisively on the side of trustification. He wrote:[134]

The object of any amalgamation of capital and production units between a number of industrial undertakings to form one large corporation under common management must always be the largest possible reduction in the costs of production, administration and sale, with a view to achieving the highest possible profits by eliminating ruinous competition . . .

Other objects were good wages and a high level of social welfare for staff and workers, a favourable return to capital, division of labour and improvement in the firm's world market position. These goals also played a more or less prominent part in cartels, but it is significant that Duisberg claimed for trustification what was in fact the prime object of cartellization: elimination of ruinous competition. He endorsed the competition to which the dye industry in the past had owed its 'admirable versatility',[135] but now proposed to eliminate outside competition, while preserving internal competition by suitable organization.[136] This too fitted the model of cartels, especially quota cartels which did away with external competition while fully maintaining competition within the cartel, particularly for

---

[131] G. Weippert, 'Die wirtschaftstheoretische und wirtschaftspolitische Bedeutung der Kartelldebatte auf der Tagung des Vereins für Sozialpolitik im Jahre 1905' (Importance for Economic Theory and Policy of the Debate on Cartels at the 1905 Meeting of the Society for Social Policy), *Jb. für Sozialwissenschaft*, xi, 1960, pp. 135–6, 156ff. Already in 1894 Brentano had emphasized in Vienna that the question was not whether cartels or no cartels, but whether cartels or industrial concentration: *SchVS*, lxi, p. 180.

[132] *KV*, iv, 1905, p. 269; for Thyssen's attitude to the trust, cf. P. Arnst, 'August Thyssen und sein Werk' (August Thyssen and his Work), supplements to *Zs. f. Handelswissenschaftliche Forschung*, vii, 1925, pp. 60–1. For the problem whether syndicate or trust at this period, illuminating Hj. Schacht, 'Der Stahlwerksverband und die jüngste Kartellentwicklung in Deutschland' (The Steelworks Association and the most recent Development of Cartels in Germany), *Berliner jungliberale Hammacher-Festschrift*, 1904, pp. 273ff. The question was similarly posed as an alternative in many other places.

[133] Cf. the discussions on the Steelworks Association in the Controversial Negotiations of June 1905, *KV*, iv, pp. 235, 269 and *passim*.

[134] Carl Duisberg, *Abhandlungen, Vorträge und Reden aus den Jahren 1882–1921* (Essays, Addresses and Speeches from the Period 1882–1921), 1923, p. 344; cf. Carl Duisberg, *Meine Lebenserinnerungen* (My Reminiscences), 1933, pp. 88–9; H.-J. Flechtner, *Carl Duisberg. Vom Chemiker zum Wirtschaftsführer* (Carl Duisberg: Chemist to Business Tycoon), 1959, p. 190.

[135] Duisberg, *Abhandlungen . . .* , p. 354.

[136] *Ibid.*

quotas. Equally typical of cartels was the goal of maximizing profits.[137] Concentration therefore intended to preserve the most important functions of cartels while embodying them in a single large-scale undertaking. This rendered unnecessary the proliferation of cartels, a characteristic especially of the chemical industry. Duisberg regarded the concentration as an 'agreement for all the products of the chemical industry', far superior to, and rendering superfluous, individual agreements.[138]

In spite of such grandiose conceptions, cartellization and concentration continued to develop side by side, in part complementary, in part developing in close interdependence and interpenetration which had both positive and negative effects. The complementing predominated at the human and personal level. The form of joint-stock organization had given rise to a new type of entrepreneur: managers of great joint-stock companies, men without large personal resources, but bearing great responsibility, running risks, hence feeling responsibilities different from that of the owner or manager of a family business.[139] Hammacher, who took part in the formation of archetypal coal syndicates, Eduard Kleine, a clergyman's son whose intellectual influence was out of all proportion to his financial backing, Anton Unckell (1844–1904),[140] a doctor's son, commercial manager of Tremonia, manager of the Dortmund Coal Association and for more than ten years until his death of the Rhine-Westphalian Coal Syndicate, Emil Krabler (1839–1909), who became a mining engineer in 1867 and joined the Cologne Mining Association in the following year, one of the most active promoters of coal syndicates,[141] all belonged to the new entrepreneurial type. The most outstanding was without doubt Emil Kirdorf (1847–1938),[142] general manager of the *Gelsenkirchen Bergwerks A.G.*, who played a decisive part in syndicalizing Ruhr mining and wholeheartedly believed in cartellizing the economy. 'A salaried employee, such as I am, is in duty bound to fulfil his tasks and defend the interests

[137] For the question of price formation, *ibid.*, p. 359.
[138] *Ibid.*, p. 361.
[139] Cf. W. Zorn, 'Typen und Entwicklungskräfte deutschen Unternehmertums im 19. Jh.' (Types and Motive Power of German Entrepreneurship in the 19th Century), *VSWG*, xliv, 1957, pp. 57ff. and the references given there, esp. works by K. Wiedenfeld and E. Salin; further E. Salin, 'Manager' in *HdS*, vii, 1961, pp. 107–13; F. Redlich, 'Unternehmungs- und Unternehmergeschichte' (History of Enterprises and Entrepreneurs), *ibid.*, pp. 532–49, and the important address by E. Salin on 'Soziologische Aspekte der Konzentration' (Sociological Aspects of Concentration), *Die Konzentration in der Wirtschaft, Verhandlungen des Vereins für Sozialpolitik . . . 1960 SchVS*, n.s. xxii, 1961, pp. 16ff.; cf. also F. Redlich, *Der Unternehmer. Wirtschafts- und Sozialgeschichtliche Studien* (The Entrepreneur: Studies in Economic and Social History), 1964, a beautiful summary of Redlich's essays which contains the works quoted above.
[140] Muthesius, *op. cit.* (n. 36 above), pp. 57ff.
[141] W. Serlo, 'Bergmannsfamilien in Rheinland und Westfalen' (Mining Families in the Rhineland and Westphalia), *Rheinisch-Westfälische Wirtschaftsbiographien*, iii, 1936, pp. 189–90; W. Serlo, *Männer des Bergbaus* (Men in Mining), 1937, p. 89; W. Serlo, *Die preussischen Bergassessoren* (The Prussian Mining Engineers), 1933, pp. 37, 89; C. Matschoss (ed.), *Männer der Technik. Ein biographisches Handbuch* (Technical Personalities: a Biographical Handbook), 1925, p. 144; F. Siebrecht, *Der Köln-Neuessener Bergwerksverein. Ein Rückblick über 75 Jahre* (The Cologne-New Essen Collieries Association: 75 Years' Retrospect), n.d., p. 31, regarding his work for syndicates, pp. 40ff.
[142] For his biography, cf. Bacmeister, *op. cit.*; F. A. Freundt, *Emil Kirdorf. Ein Lebensbild* (Emil Kirdorf: a Biography), n.d. [1921].

of the company',[143] was his call to fellow members at the Mannheim meeting of the Society for Social Policy in 1905, outlining the situation of the dependent entrepreneur with relatively small resources, but great responsibility for other people's capital.[144]

Heads of great family concerns so especially characteristic of nineteenth-century German heavy industry,[145] such as the Krupps, Thyssens and many others, represented the opposite type. They had in general little love for cartellization, preferring maximum independence and a strong market position based on trustification. At least their typical representatives were far from endorsing cartels in principle as an essential part of German economic structure. Their decisions for or against cartellization were taken pragmatically, in the light of individual situations, always keeping their position as strong as possible. Thyssen, Haniel, Stinnes and Krupp were members of cartels for some of their firms, outsiders for others.[146] The same applied to members of the Silesian aristocracy engaged in mining.[147] Franz Haniel who in 1838 had had a share in a coal sales organization with output quotas,[148] built up the first integrated colliery and foundry.[149] Friedrich Krupp kept out of the Rhine-Westphalian Pig-Iron Association set up in 1886.[150] Thyssen was very slow to join the Rhine-Westphalian Hoop Iron Association, having previously been a non-competing outsider,[151] and his *Deutscher Kaiser* remained outside the Pig-Iron Syndicate until 1901.[152] The Kraft Iron Works at Stettin, an outsider extremely troublesome to the Pig-Iron Association,[153] belonged to the Silesian Prince Guido von Henckel-Donnersmark[154] whose Falva Foundry was a member of the Upper Silesian Pig-Iron Syndicate.[155] The late and, compared to Western Germany, weak development of syndicates in Silesian mining was equally characteristic.[156]

Because of their large number and highly developed individualism, middling and small independent entrepreneurs in certain industries, notably textiles, were only with difficulty persuaded to form cartels.[157] As the dividing lines between

---

[143] *SchVS*, cxvi, p. 277; it refers to the interests of the Gelsenkirchen Company. Cf. *ibid.*, p. 272, 'workers in the same enterprise'.

[144] *Ibid.*, p. 273.

[145] Wiedenfeld, *Das persönliche* . . . (n. 118 above), p. 57.

[146] Heymann, *op. cit.* (n. 86 above), p. 271; F. Kestner, *Der Organisationszwang. Eine Untersuchung über die Kämpfe zwischen Kartellen und Aussenseitern* (Compulsory Combination: an Enquiry into the Struggles between Cartels and Outsiders), 1912, p. 21.

[147] A. Perlick, *Oberschlesische Berg- und Hüttenleute* (Upper Silesian Mining and Iron Masters), 1953, pp. 31ff.; Wiedenfeld, *op. cit.*, p. 95.

[148] Muthesius, *op. cit.*, p. 34.

[149] Cf. H. Spethmann, *Franz Haniel. Sein Leben und seine Werke* (Franz Haniel: his Life and Works), 1956, esp. p. 293.

[150] Klotzbach, *op. cit.* (n. 20 above), p. 29. Hoesch took a similar attitude: *ibid.*, p. 119.

[151] Pieper, *op. cit.* (n. 14 above), pp. 52ff.

[152] Heymann, *op. cit.*, p. 271; Kestner, *op. cit.*, p. 21; cf. also Arnst, *op. cit.* (n. 132 above), pp. 61ff.

[153] Klotzbach, *op. cit.*, pp. 85ff. and *passim*; cf. p. 249 below.

[154] On him cf. Perlick, *op. cit.*, pp. 42ff.

[155] Heymann, *op. cit.*, p. 271; Kestner, *op. cit.*, p. 21.

[156] K. Euling, *Die Kartelle im oberschlesischen Steinkohlenbergbau* (Cartels in Upper Silesian Mining), 1939.

[157] Cf. references given in n. 100 above.

manager and family firm owner were imprecise, their activities to a great extent
overlapped: Thyssen, no friend of cartellization, yet was with Adolf Kirdorf co-
founder of the German Steelworks Association in 1904,[158] whereas Emil Kirdorf,
while head of the Rhine-Westphalian Coal Syndicate, at the same time converted
the Gelsenkirchen Company into a mighty combine.[159] Friedrich Grillo (1825–88),
who crowned a life's work by the vertical concentration of coal and iron, collabor-
ated as member of the Mining Association in preparing the ground for the Coal
Syndicate.[160] On the other hand Theodor Wuppermann (1835–1907), head of a
medium-sized family business, in 1896 founded the Rhine-Westphalian Hoop
Iron Association and brought outstanding ability to bear on its management to
the day of his death.[161]

Yet on the whole the difference between the types is unmistakable. Cartellization was above all the work of men in the position and of the calibre of Emil
Kirdorf. Great enterprises, where their influence was strong, headed the movement towards cartellization. The Rhine-Westphalian Coal Syndicate was formed
in 1893, due above all to the efforts of Emil Kirdorf of the Gelsenkirchen Mining
Company and Robert Müser[162] of the Harpen Mining Company, the two largest
coal producers in the Ruhr,[163] whose importance rested on horizontal concentration.[164]

Vertical integration of coal and iron, on the other hand, created great difficulties
in the coal syndicate movement. These arose from mixed works[165] because only
products belonging to a single stage of production were suitable for cartellization.
Mixed works consumed in their own furnaces the coal mined in their own collieries.
As initially it was impossible to obtain agreement within the syndicate on the
counting of internally-consumed coal against quota production, these mixed works
refused to join the Rhine-Westphalian Coal Syndicate at its foundation in 1893[166]
and only became members in 1903[167] on being granted the concession that works-
consumed coal would not be counted against their quotas. By their accession the
influence of large undertakings in the syndicate was further strengthened.

Beyond this, the special position of colliery smelting combines stimulated pure
coal-mining firms to turn to iron-making. The most impressive example was the
Gelsenkirchen Mining Company whose head, Emil Kirdorf, was the founder and
remained the manager of the Rhine-Westphalian Coal Syndicate. Only one year

---

[158] Arnst, op. cit., p. 64.
[159] Cf. references given in nn. 123, 142 above, also p. 254 below.
[160] Die Entwickelung . . . (n. 21 above), p. 133; T. Kellen, 'Friedrich Grillo. Lebensbild
eines Grossindustriellen aus der Gründerzeit' (Friedrich Grillo: the Life of an Industrial
Magnate in the Promotion Period), Die Rheinisch-Westfälische Industrie, i, 1913, pp. 78ff.;
Däbritz, op. cit. (n. 127 above), p. 84.
[161] Pieper, op. cit. (n. 14 above).
[162] For him cf. Serlo, 'Bergmannsfamilien . . .' (n. 141 above), pp. 168–9.
[163] Die Entwickelung . . . , pp. 254ff., esp. 256ff.; Wiedenfeld, op. cit., p. 22; Muthesius, op.
cit., pp. 50, 62; A. Heinrichsbauer, Harpener Bergbau-Aktien-Gesellschaft 1856–1936, 1936,
pp. 99–109.
[164] Cf. Gebhardt, op. cit. (n. 117 above), pp. 194ff., 306ff.
[165] Heymann, op. cit., esp. pp. 242–72: mixed works and cartels; Leisse, op. cit. (n. 94
above), pp. 85–139.
[166] Wiedenfeld, op. cit., pp. 44–5; Muthesius, op. cit., p. 61.
[167] Die Entwickelung . . . , p. 269; Wiedenfeld, op. cit., pp. 46–7; Muthesius, op. cit., p. 92.

after the accession of mixed works to the Syndicate he transformed Gelsenkirchen into a vertical concern.[168] He stressed in 1904 the importance of the accession of colliery smelting combines to the Syndicate, a 'recognition of the road taken by the West German economy', and argued that, because of the privileges accorded them, they would acquire further syndicate mines. The only line of defence open to pure coal mines would be the incorporation of iron works. This combination of cartel and trust planning, so characteristic of him, was for Kirdorf a preparation for the renewal of the Syndicate agreement due to expire in 1915. Even before this development, smelting works had begun to secure their own mines.[169]

Cartels combining undertakings of very different sizes on the one hand protected, but on the other also threatened small firms. Every cartel had to guarantee a certain profit even to its weakest members who enjoyed protection within the cartel, without which they would have succumbed to unrestricted competition. Their production costs, higher than those of large-scale works, had to be taken into account in price fixing. It was particularly these small undertakings which in the Rhine-Westphalian Coal Syndicate were the most decisive opponents of the policy of moderate pricing pursued by Emil Kirdorf.[170]

Cartels with production quotas on the other hand promoted horizontal concentration in that large members bought up and closed down smaller ones to obtain control of their output quotas,[171] a process endorsed and characterized by Brentano as 'euthanasia'.[172] This form of concentration increased rapidly after about 1900,[173] arousing considerable public notice. In any case the importance of larger members stimulated concentration. Of 66 collieries allotted quotas of less than 1 per cent by the Rhine-Westphalian Coal Syndicate in 1893, 46, more than two-thirds, had vanished from the membership list by 1914.[174]

In the Pig-Iron Syndicate, too, the number and importance of mixed works combining blast furnaces and steel works was continually on the increase, giving rise to the same difficulties as in the Coal Syndicate. In the 12 years between 1897 and 1908, the internal consumption of mixed works rose from 50·87 per cent of their production to 67·12 per cent.[175] Syndicates in basic industries were thus increasingly undermined by vertical concentration, a trend exacerbating the discussion on the relative merits of cartel and trust. Pure works, relying on the market for the whole of their output, were left in an ever weaker position.[176]

[168] For what follows, cf. Bacmeister, *op. cit.* (n. 123 above), pp. 58–9; Wiedenfeld, *op. cit.*, pp. 48–9; Stillich, *op. cit.* (n. 123 above), pp. 190ff.          [169] Cf. p. 246 above.

[170] Cf. Emil Kirdorf's typical pronouncements during the Controversial Negotiations (*KV*, i, pp. 58, 93, 181) and at the Mannheim meeting of the Society for Social Policy (*SchVS*, cxvi, p. 280), also Wiedenfeld, *op. cit.*, pp. 41–2. Partly this is not a question of size, but of the difference between pure and mixed works; the latter could manage to offer on the market that part of their output which they did not use up within their works at prices lower than those of the pure works. Cf. p. 254 below.

[171] Liefmann (1), p. 711; Kestner, *op. cit.*, pp. 36ff.          [172] *KV*, i, p. 748.

[173] *Die Entwickelung* . . . , pp. 272–3; Wiedenfeld, *op. cit.*, pp. 144–5. The renewal of the syndicate agreement in 1903 made a considerable contribution.

[174] List of founder members with figures of shares taken in Gebhardt, *op. cit.*, pp. 511ff.; shares taken in 1914 in *KR*, xii (1914), p. 19; cf. Wiedenfeld, *op. cit.*, pp. 38–9, for coke and manufactured fuels, pp. 35ff. on the number of member collieries which had lost their independence before 1912.          [175] Klotzbach, *op. cit.* (n. 20 above), p. 158.

[176] H. Mannstaedt, *Die Konzentration in der Eisenindustrie und die Lage der reinen Walzwerke* (Concentration in the Iron Industry and the Situation of pure Rolling Mills), 1906.

Syndicalization of pig and semi-manufactured iron also helped to promote vertical integration. In addition to reasons already mentioned,[177] the desire of entrepreneurs for competition played a considerable part. Though more or less eliminated from the market by combination, it re-emerged within quota cartels as a struggle within the cartel for quotas.[178] Seeking further outlets, it found them in the development of finishing industries. To evade syndicate ties for at least part of their output, trusts embarked more and more on production of semi- and completely finished goods,[179] where cartellization was difficult, if not impossible. Thus large undertakings resisted syndicalization of bar iron and did their best to keep the so-called B-products out of syndicates, partly by taking up their manufacture themselves.[180]

Another escape into competitive markets occurred via exports, an outlet generally left to each individual firm. Here, especially for pig-iron and semi-manufactured goods, a policy of differential prices was adopted. Whereas the syndicate, protected by tariff, kept domestic prices at a high level, entrepreneurs competed on the world market at low, and even dumping, prices.[181] From an economic point of view this was a doubtful policy, cutting down the export potential of pure works at the stages of production affected.[182] Altogether the difficulties facing pure works, especially pure rolling mills, show most clearly the effects on German heavy industry of combined horizontal cartellization and predominantly vertical trustification.

Neither cartels nor syndicates ever achieved complete monopoly in practice, but their market behaviour around the turn of the century was that of monopolists. In the early stages of the cartel movement entrepreneurs had sought to eliminate ruinous competition and, in a general atmosphere of liberalism, had made the formation of cartels dependent on voluntary accession of all entrepreneurs. The aim of the cartel was monopoly, but the power bestowed by monopoly was not used.[183] The earliest definitions of cartels,[184] such as those of Kleinwächter and Brentano, had referred to limitation of competition by adjustment of output to demand, not to monopoly. By the turn of the century, monopoly was always described in definitions as the essential object of association.[185] Most unambiguous in this respect was the definition by R. Liefmann who in his first book on entre-

---

[177] Cf. pp. 233ff. above.

[178] Liefmann (I), pp. 110–11; Wiedenfeld, *op. cit.*, pp. 44ff.; Klotzbach, *op. cit.*, *passim*; Kestner, *op. cit.*, pp. 30ff.

[179] Cf. *KV*, ii, p. 392; Heymann, *op. cit.*, *passim*; Leisse, *op. cit.*, pp. 59ff.

[180] Cf. the complaints of the pure works, particularly of pure rolling mills, and the discussions in the Controversial Negotiations, *KV*, ii, pp. 431ff., 465–6 and *passim* in *KV*, ii (Association of Semi-Manufactured Articles) and iv (Steelworks Associations). Very illuminating the pronouncement by one of the first steelworks managers in Western Germany reported in the Negotiations about the Association of Semi-Manufactured Articles (*KV*, iii, p. 431) on cartellization of rod iron: 'I am not in favour of a rod iron association; for at least one product I need a safety outlet'. Cf. also Adler, *op. cit.* (n. 95 above).

[181] Liefmann (I), pp. 163ff.; W. Morgenroth, *Die Exportpolitik der Kartelle* (The Export Policy of Cartels), 1907.

[182] Very illuminating on this *KV*, ii, pp. 389–90, 469–70; Mannstaedt, *op. cit.*, *passim*; Morgenroth, *op. cit.*, pp. 45ff.; Leisse, *op. cit.*, pp. 99ff.

[183] Cf. pp. 252–7 below.          [184] Cf. p. 228 above.

[185] Cf. Wolfers, *op. cit.* (n. 7 above), pp. 15–16. Similarly Bücher in Vienna in 1894, also Schäffle in 1898.

preneurial associations[186] in 1897 treated monopoly position as the *conditio sine qua non* for the attainment of cartel objectives. His final definition[187] characterized cartels as

free agreements or associations of entrepreneurs in the same line of business who, while retaining their independence, combine to exercise a monopolistic influence on the market.

From the late 1880s[188] entrepreneurs united in syndicates indeed used the monopoly power arising from monopoly position against outsiders[189] who were to be forced into accession or ruined by cut-throat prices, denial of raw materials and credit, trading boycotts, etc. Borrowed from the field of individual competition, undercutting[190] as the most obvious means of eliminating non-cartellized competitors had all the more prospect of success in that it was collectively enforced. In the early years of the twentieth century, the Cast Pipes Syndicate employed such cut-throat prices against the Mannesmann Tube Works,[191] the Sheet Steel Association against the Thale Works.[192] For years the German Pig-Iron Association thus fought the Kraft Iron Works,[193] belonging to Prince Guido von Henckel-Donnersmark, a Silesian coal magnate sufficiently independent[194] to remain a powerful outsider.

Other weapons were the denial of raw materials and credits, as employed against the Phoenix Company which in 1904 refused to join the Steelworks Association.[195] Phoenix was threatened with denial of supplies of semi-manufactured goods and with withdrawal of the export subsidy allowed by the Coal Syndicate. Decisive pressure was exerted via the great banks which by share purchases succeeded in obtaining a majority in the annual general meeting and in forcing Phoenix into the Steelworks Association. The example illustrates how syndicates by their price and supplies policies supported each other in the fight against outsiders.[196] Pressure on wholesalers could also be used to cut off coal and other primary material supplies from outsiders. In the textile and clothing industries, statutes and decisions of

---

[186] Liefmann (I).

[187] Liefmann (II), p. 9.

[188] Cf. examples in Schoenlank, *op. cit.* (n. 6 above), p. 502, drawn from the years 1887 and 1888.

[189] For what follows, cf. Kestner, *op. cit.* (n. 146 above), whose 2nd ed. by O. Lehnich in 1927, rewritten and modified with regard to subsequent legislation, offers less guidance on cartel history before 1914. G. Lucae, *Aussenseiter von Kartellen. Ein Beitrag zu dem Problem der Wirtschaftsfreiheit* (Cartel Outsiders: a Contribution to the Problem of Business Freedom), 1929, p. 13, for the definition of the outsider.

[190] The older essays on cartels provide numerous examples. In general cf. Liefmann (II), pp. 56–7; Kestner, *op. cit.*, pp. 117ff.

[191] *Kleine Chronik der Mannesmannröhren-Werke* (A Short Chronicle of the Mannesmann Tube Works), 1940, pp. 66ff.; *KR*, iii, 1905, pp. 318, 496 and *passim*. It was the background of these severe struggles that Mannesmann owing to their seamless tubes were superior to the firms united in the syndicate which used obsolete methods of production.

[192] Cf. *KR*, ii, 1904, pp. 535, 748, 801.

[193] Klotzbach, *op. cit.*, pp. 85ff., 131–2; on the Works, cf. Zöllner, *op. cit.*, pp. 121–2; Leisse, *op. cit.*, p. 26.

[194] Cf. p. 245 above.

[195] Kestner, *op. cit.*, pp. 124–5; *Geschichtliche Entwicklung und gegenwärtiger Stand der Phoenix A. G. für Bergbau und Hüttenbetrieb in Hoerde* (Historical Development and Present Condition of *Phoenix A.G. für Bergbau und Hüttenbetrieb* at Hoerde), 1912, p. 52.

[196] Heymann, *op. cit.*, p. 67; Kestner, *op. cit.*, pp. 90–1.

I

associations were enforced all along the line from producers via wholesalers down to retailers by threats, and if necessary application, of boycotts.[197] Other industries acted similarly.

Comparable pressure was exerted to force entrepreneurs at subsequent production stages into cartellization and a uniform dependence. Consumers of semi-manufactured goods were under constant pressure from the Semi-Manufactured Articles Association which demanded their syndicalization.[198] The almost eccentric lengths to which this policy of cartels at earlier stages of production could be carried vis-à-vis their customers in small trades can be seen in the German Spring Steel Association which in 1903 tried to force manufacturers of corset stays and clasps to cartellize.[199]

Export subsidies, beneficial in intention and effect,[200] were similarly used as means of pressure on entrepreneurs at subsequent production stages to join cartels, by being paid only to members of cartels, not to independent entrepreneurs.[201]

The real power of the syndicate lay in its price policy; it could aim at maximum prices without regard either to consumers or to the economic consequences.[202] Even where combined, consumers were the weaker party.[203] In course of time the application of power in the shape of collective cartel power unmistakably increased, giving rise to a sense of power previously absent. When Emil Russell in 1882 had demanded the concentration of Ruhr mining, he had explicitly rejected even 'partial unification' with its ensuing monopoly on account of the consumer interest.[204] Eduard Kleine, who in 1885 went even farther in his demand for concentration, was in no doubt about the immense power wielded by a gigantic horizontal trust, but knew that

there must be grave doubts about concentrating in a single hand such power unchecked by competition.[205]

However, by and after the turn of the century application of, and struggle for, power had become deliberate policy. In the complaints voiced by consumers during the Controversial Negotiations against the Pig-Iron Syndicate, but especially the Coke Syndicate and the Semi-Manufactured Articles Association, terms like 'power', 'terrorism' and others were frequently employed.[206] The formation in 1904 of the Steelworks Association further increased concern at the concentration of economic power, a concern voiced again and again in the Con-

[197] The annual reports of the Association of German Department Stores (n. 106 above) abound with reports of such boycotts.

[198] *KV*, ii, p. 411 and *passim*, but cf. A. Kirdorf, *ibid.*, p. 529. Cf. p. 238 above.

[199] *KR*, i, 1903, pp. 562, 604, 744.

[200] Cf. pp. 255-6 below.

[201] Liefmann (II), pp. 151ff. When the associations for rolled wire, wire nails and sheet steel had dissolved in 1905, the Steelworks Association brought heavy pressure to bear for restoration of the associations by withholding export subsidies from those producers which were not now cartellized; Leisse, *op. cit.* (n. 94 above), pp. 75, 187.

[202] We cannot here deal more fully with the pricing policy of cartels.

[203] Cf. *KV*, ii, pp. 453, 514 and *passim*; Kestner, *op. cit.*, p. 248; cf. pp. 228ff. above.

[204] Cf. p. 242 above.

[205] Muthesius, *op. cit.* (n. 36 above), p. 32; cf. p. 242 above.

[206] *KV*, i: power, p. 654; position of power, p. 611; sense of power, p. 693; compulsion, p. 684; pressure, pp. 460, 472, 653, 658; misuse of force, p. 461; omnipotence, p. 459; terrorism, pp. 521ff.; similar expressions *passim*, also in *KV*, iii and iv.

troversial Negotiations of June 1905 about the Steelworks Association. Though the position of power could not be denied, a spokesman for that Association declared in the course of the Negotiations:

> We know the limits beyond which we must not step and shall take great care not to pit the economic power inherent in the Steelworks Association against the political authority and power of the State.[207]

This recognized the limits of industrial power vis-à-vis the State—but not within the economy.

The problem of the exercise of power by cartels and especially by great syndicates was not yet on the agenda at the conference of the Society for Social Policy held in Vienna in 1894,[208] but occupied the centre of the stage during the Controversial Negotiations[209] and particularly at the Society's Mannheim conference of 1905.[210] There Emil Kirdorf rejected an interpretation equating such power with political power;[211] during the Controversial Negotiations he had admitted to syndicates wielding power, deriving from this an obligation to exercise moderation.[212]

His elder brother Adolf,[213] on the other hand, explicitly endorsed both the power and power struggle concepts. During the 1903 Government Enquiry into cartels, in the course of which he demanded that consumers too ought to be cartellized, he defined the relation between supplier and consumer cartels[214]: 'Power will determine the outcome; he who has the greater power will derive the greater benefit.' Later he again stressed the part of power in the struggle between syndicalized producers, contrasting it with the consumers' sovereignty in the 1870s, which had also been a form of power.[215] His brother Emil supported him in this reference to consumers' sovereignty of that period.[216] Adolf Kirdorf's open admission of the power motive left a profound impression, shown in the following year in the *Memorandum on the Situation of Rolling Mills buying Semi-Manufactured Articles* in the last quarter of 1904.[217] The consumers of semi-manufactured articles realized that 'the Semi-Manufactured Articles Association had every intention of making full use of its power'. Thinking in power terms occurred elsewhere in the economy, though often with different ends in view. The 'chief and fundamental object' of the Gelsenkirchen Company's horizontal concentration was stated in 1902 to be 'the attainment of a position of conspicuous power so as to be able to take the lead

---

[207] *KV*, iv, p. 240.
[208] Cf. G. Schmoller's concluding remarks, *SchVS*, lxi, pp. 236–7.
[209] *KV*, i, pp. 53, 611 and *passim*.
[210] Cf. e.g. the report by G. Schmoller, *SchVS*, cxvi, 1905, p. 241 and *passim*.
[211] *Ibid.*, pp. 276–7.
[212] *KV*, i, p. 663; for a policy of moderation cf. pp. 252ff. below.
[213] On him, cf. W. Serlo, *Westdeutsche Berg- und Hüttenleute und ihre Familien* (West German Mine and Iron Masters and their Families), pp. 148–9.
[214] On 2 December 1903: *KV*, ii, p. 427.
[215] *Ibid.*, p. 474.
[216] *Ibid.*, p. 475. Claus, manager of Thale Iron Works, also emphasized (*ibid.*, p. 455) the irremovable conflict between producers and consumers: 'The stronger takes advantage of his power'.
[217] *KV*, iv, p. 485. Cf. *ibid.* the statement that one of the ruling personalities had said of pure rolling mills: 'Whoever cannot keep up, falls by the wayside; our road passes over dead bodies'; for the contrasting attitude of Voelcker, manager of the Steelworks Association, cf. *ibid.*, pp. 238ff. Cf. also *KV*, iv, p. 453 on Kirdorf's pronouncement.

in uniting Rhine-Westphalian mining in the market area'.[218] In a first letter, taking soundings for his project of amalgamating his own firm with the Augsburg Machine Factory, a project leading ultimately to the formation of *MAN*, Anton Rieppel, head of the Nuremberg Machine Construction Company, wrote in 1898: 'The two firms in combination . . . would represent industrial power in Southern Germany.'[219] Thus there was at the time not merely practical exercise of power in German industry, but a sense of power representative chiefly, though not exclusively, of collective power.

At the turn of the century another attitude on the part of cartels was beginning to appear. In their first attempts at combination entrepreneurs had reacted to crisis and downswing, but the psychological reaction which determined their attitude to cartellization derived not so much from crisis, recession and recovery as such as from the persistence of cyclical changes. Early in the cartel movement elimination of ruinous competition had played a dominant part. Although elimination of competition featured as a continuing theme in cartel articles of association,[220] cartels now served as a weapon against unhealthy, unsound and harmful competition and cut-throat pricing. Moderate, adequate, appropriate, realistic, remunerative prices—these were variations on the theme of the purpose of combinations. The Upper Silesian Coal Agreement of 1898 emphasized price maintenance in times of recession. Many cartels proclaimed price regulation to be the sole object of their existence. The chief economic task was adjustment of output to demand, as attempted by quota cartels. In a draft of 1885 for an Association of German Rolling Mills to be achieved only a little later, this object was formulated with particular precision: 'to bring output . . . into balance with the capacity of the domestic market'. It was obvious that such adjustment of production to market conditions would serve to keep prices up as far as possible in times of crisis and downswing.

But in time the tendency to maintain price stability, even at periods of cyclical upswing, increased. Already in 1882 the Westphalian Coke Syndicate had aimed at 'indispensable profitability of coke works . . . without reducing coke consumption by artificially and unhealthily raising prices'. After its renewal in 1901 the Semi-Manufactured Articles Association defined its object as 'the attainment of appropriate, moderately remunerative prices and the moderation of sudden upswings in prices when the market is favourable, as this has proved to be detrimental'. Articles of various cartel associations gave as their object constant or stable prices, i.e. they opposed price fluctuations. By combining, entrepreneurs sought to moderate as far as possible the swings of the economic pendulum and to obtain stable prices, where necessary, by output manipulation. There was a tendency among newly-formed cartels, especially at times of upswing, to fix their prices at

[218] Cf. p. 242 with n. 126.
[219] F. Büchner, *Hundert Jahre Geschichte der Maschinenfabrik Augsburg-Nürnberg* (Centennial History of the Augsburg-Nuremberg Machine Factory), n.d. [1940], p. 115; G. Strössner, 'Die Fusion der *Aktiengesellschaft Maschinenfabrik Augsburg* und der *Maschinenbau-Actien-Gesellschaft Nürnberg* im Jahre 1898' (Amalgamation of the Machine Factory Augsburg Ltd. and the Machine Building Company Nuremberg Ltd. in 1898), *Tradition*, v, 1960, p. 105.
[220] What follows is taken from *Denkschrift* . . . (n. 32 above), i and supplementary volume; for the draft agreement of 1885 for the Association of Rolling Mills, cf. Heymann, *op. cit.*, p. 325.

a very high level. Experience generally soon taught them that there were limits even to monopoly prices. The first German Rolling Mills Association, set up in the years of upswing 1887–8, foundered on its unduly high prices as soon as the turning point of the cycle came.[221] For the same reason the West German Sheet Steel Association of 1888 dissolved two years after its formation.[222]

Market opportunities for newly-formed cartels, owing to their more or less pronounced monopolistic position, were too alluring not to tempt members to push prices to their maximum possible limits. Basically all entrepreneurs were tarred with the same brush. Pure rolling mills, which during the Controversial Negotiations had complained bitterly about the pricing policy of the Semi-Manufactured Articles Association, had not behaved differently 15 years earlier as members of the German Rolling Mills Association. Schmieding, manager of a rolling mill, during the Negotiations said about that Association:

This type of behaviour appears to be characteristic of all of us iron masters; I need only remind you of the Sheet Steel Syndicate to which I belonged in the late 1880s which misused its power of fixing prices.[223]

He went on to regret that by contrast with the Rhine-Westphalian Coal Syndicate,

we in the iron industry have not yet learnt to accept that mutual consideration of each other's interests is a necessary condition of life,

and referred to the example of the Rhine-Westphalian Coal Syndicate, thus giving expression to a change in entrepreneurial attitude; their horizon was beginning to extend beyond the interests of their own associations.

In the cartels and especially in the larger syndicates the tendency to stabilize prices became progressively more dominant: prices were only moderately raised at times of upswing, only moderately reduced at times of downswing. Theory and practice did not, of course, always coincide. The price policy of the Semi-Manufactured Articles Association, which in the articles of association of 1901[224] had explicitly committed itself to the object of moderating price rises at times of upswing, nevertheless came under justified heavy attack from users of semi-manufactures on account of its high prices. Buyers however always find prices excessive.

After the downturn of the cycle in 1900, the large syndicates in heavy industry maintained during the years of downswing of 1901 and 1902 prices at the level previously reached, but now too high.[225] This drew more public attention to the part played by cartels in the economy; a *Reichstag* debate[226] ensued, followed by an official enquiry into cartels.[227] There is no doubt that the syndicates of the early

[221] O. Caro, 'Der Deutsche Walzwerksverband' (The Association of German Rolling Mills), *SchVS*, lx, 1894, pp. 41ff.

[222] Heymann, *op. cit.*, p. 80.

[223] *KV*, iii, p. 519.    [224] Cf. p. 252 above.

[225] Especially for pig-iron: Klotzbach, *op. cit.* (n. 20 above), pp. 102, 106; Altmann, *op. cit.* (n. 62 above), pp. 59ff. The behaviour of cartels in the 1900–1 crisis furnished material for comment: cf. n. 61 above; in general, the comprehensive enquiry by the Society for Social Policy: 'Die Störungen im deutschen Wirtschaftsleben während der Jahre 1900ff.' (The Disturbances of German Economic Life during the Years 1900 and After), *SchVS*, cv–cxii, 1903.

[226] Lehnich, *op. cit.* (n. 60 above), pp. 94ff.; Isay, *op. cit.* (n. 60 above), pp. 33–4.

[227] *Denkschrift* . . .

years of the twentieth century were a failure. Their leading men, headed by the Kirdorf brothers, admitted the mistakes they had made.[228] Cartels as a form of large-scale combine in German industry, they argued, were comparatively young. They lacked a scientific method of economic forecasting; price fixing among large combines was too slow and inflexible.

In the general criticism of cartels, no syndicate fared as well in the discussions of those years as the Rhine-Westphalian Coal Syndicate,[229] regarded as a model. According to one rolling mill owner,

we could all learn something from the most powerful German syndicate so far, the Coal Syndicate . . . as far as consideration of everybody's interest is concerned.[230]

Standing at the source of all production processes, its organization a model for other syndicates, the Coal Syndicate was of immense significance for the German economy. It sought to stabilize prices not only during periods of downswing, but also at times when upswings tempted it to raise them to the maximum extent. Already in the early days of the Ruhr cartels, at a meeting of the Bituminous Coal Association for the Dortmund District held in 1889, Anton Unckell formulated the principle by pointing to the object of the association, 'not to maximize prices for all coal, but to take as a guiding line moderation of prices'; in the long run sound business could only be built up by 'a policy of reasonable moderation, taking into consideration the interests of other industries'.[231]

From Unckell, whose part in the creation of syndicates he rated very highly,[232] Emil Kirdorf adopted the policy of moderation. It was due to Kirdorf that the Syndicate did not practise a monopoly price policy and that other syndicates copied its example to a greater or lesser extent. Time and again Kirdorf emphasized moderation—'moderation vis-à-vis consumers', 'moderation of prices with due regard for the general economic situation' were among his most characteristic phrases.[233] In the report to the general meeting of the Gelsenkirchen Company held in 1904, announcing the Company's policy of vertical concentration, Kirdorf deduced the duty of moderation from its strong position:

Our resources not only put us in one of the most influential positions, notably in the Coal Syndicate . . . but enabled and indeed compelled us to acknowledge and carry out a policy of moderation, no less in the interest of our particular trade than of the economy as a whole.[234]

Kirdorf referred to the responsibility imposed upon him by his position[235] and stressed the importance of the economy as a whole. In the cyclical changes around the turn of the century, when prices oscillated greatly, he achieved that the Rhine-Westphalian Coal Syndicate raised coal prices only moderately—in the face of the general upward tendency—but also lowered them only a little during downswings.[236]

[228] KV, ii, p. 399, iii, pp. 158ff., 327 and passim; Kirdorf at Mannheim in 1905: SchVS, cxvi, p. 275.

[229] KV, i, pp. 62–3, 124–5, 162, 193.          [230] KV, iii, p. 519.

[231] Die Entwickelung . . . (n. 21 above), p. 202.

[232] Bacmeister, op. cit. (n. 123 above), pp. 89–90; Muthesius, op. cit., p. 57.

[233] KV, i, pp. 63, 102 and passim.

[234] Bacmeister, op. cit., p. 59.

[235] SchVS, cxvi, pp. 291; cf. p. 244-5 above.

[236] Wiedenfeld, op. cit., pp. 114–5.

Eventually the Steelworks Association came to pursue a similar pricing policy,[237] in spite of disappointment and criticism from among its members at its failure to raise prices sufficiently in the upswing.[238]

Thus did the leading men through consideration for the general economy and a sense of responsibility transform the sectional selfishness of business associations. The new principles were generally accepted, though practice, especially in periods of recovery, lagged behind. This is how Voelcker, manager of the Steelworks Association, formulated the aims of his cartel during the Controversial Negotiations of 1905:

> We regard it as one of our tasks to pursue a stable price policy in cooperation with the other great combines—the Coal, Potash and other Syndicates. We have no intention of continually adjusting our prices to cyclical fluctuations: we do not intend to raise our prices suddenly and unduly at favourable times nor to yield to falling demand in bad times by reducing prices. We aim to hold a middle course.[239]

Economic stability through stabilization of output, sales and prices had been raised to the status of an economic principle.

Symptomatic of this attitude were the export subsidies[240] paid by syndicates at earlier production stages to firms at subsequent stages in order to raise the latter's exports. They represented 'the refund of the excess domestic price paid by the exporting processer, i.e. of the difference between cartel and world market price, that is, of the so-called cartel surcharge'.[241] The High-Quality Puddled Iron Convention of Rhine-Westphalian Blast Furnaces formed in 1882, a body about which otherwise little is known,[242] in the year of its foundation came to an agreement with rolling mills on a discount for pig-iron processed for export.[243] Similar agreements followed in subsequent years.[244] Later, export rebates were substituted. The Pig-Iron Association in principle recognized the justice of the demand, put forward by wire and other rolling mills in 1897, for export rebates to compensate for the low export prices of pig-iron, yet failed to meet it.[245] Export rebates however became increasingly popular, and in 1902 the Rhine-Westphalian Coal Syndicate, the Semi-Manufactured Articles Association and the Steel Girder Association set up a clearing house for exports.[246] The close co-operation of these associations through their policy of export rebates is illustrated by the example of the Wire Nail Association. The sums which this Association passed on to its exporting members were composed of rebates from the Coal Syndicate, the Pig-Iron Syndicate and the Steelworks Association, as well as of export subsidies paid by

[237] Consumers of semi-manufactured goods felt bound however in the first place to maintain the complaints which they had raised in 1903 during the Controversial Negotiations against the Semi-Manufactured Articles Association, vis-à-vis the recently (June 1905) formed Steelworks Association: *KV*, iv, p. 413 and *passim*.

[238] W. Treue, *Die Geschichte der Ilseder Hütte* (The History of Ilsede Foundry), 1960, p. 365.

[239] *KV*, iv, p. 242.

[240] Altmann, *op. cit.*, p. 63; Liefmann (II), pp. 151ff.; Morgenroth, *op. cit.* (n. 181 above), pp. 51ff.

[241] Zöllner, *op. cit.* (n. 78 above), p. 144.

[242] Klotzbach, *op. cit.*, pp. 23ff.

[243] Liefmann (I), p. 192; the pig-iron agreement of Siegerland furnaces established in the same year, though surviving only a few months, similarly granted an export subsidy to its customers: Heymann, *op. cit.*, pp. 71–2.

[244] Liefmann (I), p. 192.      [245] Klotzbach, *op. cit.*, pp. 98–9.

[246] Morgenroth, *op. cit.*, p. 53; Leisse, *op. cit.* (n. 94 above), p. 186.

the Rolled Wire Association and the Wire Nail Association itself.[247] As cartellization of consumers of pig and semi-manufactured iron was made a condition of payment of such rebates or subsidies,[248] they were a method of enforcing cartellization on these consumers and of keeping them in a state of perceptible dependence.[249] But in considering these consumers' export interests, they served primarily as a means of establishing a balance between producer and consumer, domestic and foreign markets.

Despite a great many conflicting tensions of interests and associations, German heavy industry progressively adopted measures which in a different economic system would have been incumbent upon the State. The increase in new economic thinking is shown in the initial articles of association of the syndicate formed in 1907 as Association of German Brassworks[250] which said:[251]

Anxious to adjust output in their particular branch of industry to demand and by creating a stable relationship between the price of brass and those of the raw materials to afford members of this Association a moderate return without taking advantage of the consumer or injuring his ability to compete in world markets, the members of this Association agree to the following articles . . .

Such words, explicitly within the programme of a syndicate taking account of world economic conditions, would have been unthinkable in a cartel agreement even a few years earlier.

In the textile and clothing industries there was also a tendency to strike a balance between associations at the producing and those at the distributing stages. After bitter battles the Association of German Tie Fabrics Manufacturers and the Association of German Tie Manufacturers, a combine of purchasers from the former, concluded a reciprocity agreement in 1906.[252] A similar agreement was made between the Association of Ladies' and Girls' Overcoats Manufacturers, immediately after its establishment in the crisis year of 1907, and the Association of Silk Manufacturers, followed in the next year by one with the Association of Manufacturers of Blouses, Costumes and Kindred Products, also founded in 1907.[253] In 1909 an attempt was made to unite manufacturers, wholesalers and retailers of sewing cotton, 'to bring about order in the wholesale and retail trade', but it misfired.[254]

Recognition of the need, and readiness, for negotiation were already almost universal by the time of the Controversial Negotiations. Once the habit of association had spread throughout the economy, negotiations between associations became more and more the rule; and if they did not always lead to results, this was only a parallel to the early and ineffective stages of more general cartellization when cartels often dissolved as rapidly as they arose.

[247] *Ibid.*, p. 189.

[248] *KV*, i, pp. 162ff., 177, esp. typical p. 199. Cf. the pronouncements of rolling mill owner Rudolf Springmann, iv, pp. 300–1.

[249] Cf. p. 250 above.

[250] Cf. p. 236 above.

[251] Jutzi, *op. cit.* (n. 22 above), p. 89; similarly previously other non-ferrous metal syndicates (*Denkschrift*, i, pp. 111, 113) and the Upper Silesian Pig-iron Syndicate (*ibid.*, suppl. vol. B 17).

[252] Kaufmann, *op. cit.* (n. 105 above), p. 5.

[253] *Ibid.*, p. 8.

[254] Annual Report of the Association of German Department Stores for the Year 1909.

The economic vision of the Kirdorf brothers was a German economy consistently cartellized down to, and including, the exporters.[255] Only complete cartellization could create a balance, even though in Adolf Kirdorf's opinion it entailed power struggles. For the structure of German industry in its most crucial sector, the heavy industry, and from there radiating outwards throughout the whole economy, it was indeed decisive that there were not isolated cartels in a monopoly position, but a system of bilateral monopolies in which organized suppliers faced organized consumers, the supplier cartel also being a consumer cartel, except at the initial stage of production. Bounds were thus set to the monopoly situation and monopoly powers restricted. Achievement of a balance between cartels at successive or otherwise interdependent stages of production and distribution became necessary and possible. Negotiations were increasingly used to bring about this adjustment. Liefmann's definition[256] of the cartel, a definition specifically based on German cartels, ceased to be valid in the last years before the outbreak of the First World War, as did every other definition of the isolated cartel as such. For, as the result of extensive cartellization of the German economy and increasing adjustment between cartels at various production stages, cartels by means of methods which remained controversial had begun more and more effectively to assume marketing functions whose object was above all the stability of the economy. Such functions became similarly evident in particular sectors: delimitation of regional markets; standardization of freight charges; adjustment and coordination of production programmes—endeavours not discussed in this article. As the government—a policy of tariff protection excepted—did not interfere, this development was the result of private enterprise. This extraordinary organizational achievement, unique in the world economy up to the First World War, had sprung from the private initiative of entrepreneurs.

In return, entrepreneurs had sacrificed the right of making personal decisions. In voluntary association abandoning individual opportunities of gain, they had sought first to eliminate ruinous competition, then later come widely, though not universally, to expect enjoyment of monopoly prices from cartellization. What they aimed at by and large, was not maximization of individual profits at high risk, but more moderate profits within the security of an association.

What had been lost was individual freedom. Gustav Schmoller, during the Controversial Negotiations within the framework of the official enquiry of 1903, put it this way:[257]

A large portion of the freedom of trade and the free economy on which 30 years ago we prided ourselves has been buried through cartels, not legally, but in fact.

Entrepreneurs could renounce their freedom only because the economy as such was free. Even more all-embracing was the other pre-condition: that general and,

---

[255] Emil Kirdorf during the Controversial Negotiations, *KV*, ii, p. 449: 'a syndicate which does not also dominate the export trade is not a syndicate'.—The continuation of this economic policy led the way into international cartels. In this context we have not gone into them. Liefmann (1), pp. 142–3, gives a catalogue of international cartels existing before 1897 in which Germany took part.          [256] Cf. p. 249 above.

[257] *KV*, i, p. 259; a weakened version already at the Vienna meeting of the Society for Social Policy, 1894, *SchVS*, lxi, p. 235, further at the same Society's Mannheim meeting, 1905, *SchVS*, cxvi, 1906, pp. 251–2.

12

in particular, political freedom was not endangered; had these been lost, a whole economy ruled by cartels would have been in peril of unfreedom. Twice in the history of the German cartel movement did this happen, but after our period: in the First World War when cartels provided the framework, and the means, of steering the war economy,[258] and, after a new great growth of cartellization during the 1920s, reaching an estimated maximum of 3,000,[259] under the National Socialist régime which used cartels to guide and plan the economy.[260] Before the First World War the German economy had been fundamentally different. But even then the nature and function of cartels had not remained static. Their metamorphosis forms a leading chapter in German economic history before 1914.

[258] R. Liefmann, *Die Kartelle vor und nach dem Kriege* (Cartels before and after the War), 1918.

[259] Liefmann (II), p. 38.

[260] Cf. V. Voigt, 'German Experience with Cartels and their Control during the Pre-War and Post-War Periods', in J. P. Miller (ed.), *Competition, Cartels and their Regulations: Studies in Industrial Economics*, iv, Amsterdam, 1962, pp. 169ff., with further references.

# Structural Change
# and Economic Growth:
# Sweden in the Nineteenth Century

LENNART JÖRBERG

Sweden, like other European countries, underwent drastic economic changes during the nineteenth century. Economic expansion in Sweden during this period had many features common to European experience; others differed from the general pattern.

The example usually taken for European economic expansion is that of England, but England was in many ways unique. Her initial situation differed vastly from that of Continental countries; for although, as the first country industrialized, she influenced economic growth in other countries, the factors which started her on the path to industrialization were not the same as those which initiated development on the Continent. Hence neither in Sweden nor on the Continent of Europe did the pattern follow that of England.

# I

SYNOPSIS

The rate of economic growth in Sweden accelerated during three decades, the 1850s, the 1870s and the 1890s. The first period to a large extent focussed on agriculture: international demand for Swedish grain greatly contributed to the changes. The 1870s saw the industrial breakthrough, strongly enhanced by the prevailing international boom, whereas the expansion of the 1890s reflected increasing domestic demand. Swedish industry began its phase of self-sustained growth, though international development remained very important in explaining the spurts and lags in the Swedish economy.

At the beginning of the nineteenth century, Sweden was agrarian like all European countries, perhaps more so than most. Agriculture provided employment for more than 80 per cent of her population, whose growth was relatively slow; agricultural production scarcely sufficed to maintain it. Sweden depended on grain imports up to about 1830, though to a diminishing degree. Then a change occurred: such was the productive capacity achieved by Swedish agriculture that it not only fed a population increasing by more than 30 per cent between

1830 and 1860, but produced an export surplus; over the same period agricultural exports multiplied tenfold. For a short while, agriculture contended with iron for second place in the league of export revenue earners, timber remaining in the lead. We do not know whether the living standard of the population fell, i.e. whether such exports were achieved at the expense of the home market. Though it is generally asserted that the so-called lower classes in agriculture were proletarianized, no proof has been adduced. Indeed, certain factors, such as the increase of the birth rate and the reduction of the mortality rate manifest after 1845, indicate on the contrary that that period saw a positive improvement in the national economy.

Signs of industrial growth simultaneous with expanding agricultural yields can be detected after 1830. Iron-ore mining, production of pig and bar iron all expanded at about three per cent *per annum* between 1830 and 1860; there was a very pronounced upward trend in the textile industry: production of cotton yarn multiplied more than twentyfold, while the output of cotton and linen fabrics rose in value by about 20 per cent *per annum*. Industrial statistics indicate that the number of workers employed in factories increased by about $3\frac{1}{2}$ per cent *per annum*, whereas value of output rose by about ten per cent *per annum*, implying a substantial improvement in productivity.[1] This could be taken to mean that an industrial breakthrough had been achieved, but it would be unwise to draw that conclusion. Very large percentage increases in this instance indicate no more than a very low base and modest absolute changes yielding impressive proportional figures. The iron industry, long and well established, received a veritable jolt, intensified by enormously increased competition from England and such continental countries as were beginning to industrialize. The Swedish timber industry began to develop at the same time. Its exports multiplied fivefold between 1830 and 1860, and traditional water-driven sawmills were gradually replaced by steam-driven mills with larger capacity. This enabled the industry to move from inland waterfalls to the coast.

TABLE 1
SOME DATA ILLUSTRATING SWEDISH ECONOMIC
GROWTH, 1870–1914[2]

| | Annual Growth (%) | Absolute figures (in millions) | |
| | | 1870 | 1914 |
|---|---|---|---|
| Population | 0·7 | 4·2 | 5·7 |
| Town population | 2·3 | 0·5 | 1·5 |
| National income | 2·8 | 800 | 3,300 |
| Industrial output | 4·4 | 320 | 2,200 |
| Gross investment | 5·0 | 50 | 450 |
| Investment in machinery | 4·0 | 10 | 90 |
| Exports | 3·1 | 140 | 790 |
| Imports | 3·2 | 150 | 800 |

(National income through Imports braced together as Kronor)

[1] *Report on the Economic and Financial Development of Sweden during the Years 1834–1860* (Finance Committee's Report), Stockholm, 1863: appendix tables.
[2] L. Jörberg, *Growth and Fluctuations of Swedish Industry, 1869–1912, Studies in the Process of Industrialization*, Lund, 1961, p. 27. Percentage growth calculated exponentially by the method of least squares.

The economic expansion of the 1870s on the other hand deserves the description of an industrial revolution, if by revolution we mean a rapid change in economic structure. The conditions for this rapid change had of course been created during previous decades. In this essay, we will not dwell on these conditions, but concentrate on short-term changes taking place during the brief period of take-off. Extremely rapid expansion took place in most industries in the 1870s. Investment reached new heights, concentrated in a few industries and transport which were strategic from the economic point of view.

From the 1870s to the First World War, Swedish national income rose at a rate of about three per cent *per annum*, i.e. it more than doubled during this period. Industrial growth was even faster. At the outbreak of the First World War, industry contributed a considerably larger share to national income than agriculture. More than 30 per cent of the population depended on industry, whereas agriculture employed about 50 per cent.

Analysis of this development must deal with some long-term changes before investigating in detail the situation in the 1870s and the evolution up to 1914. It will be necessary to introduce factors whose significance for economic growth can be neither isolated nor quantified.

# II

## POPULATION DEVELOPMENT

In 1800, Sweden had a population of 2·3 million. This increased by 23 per cent up to 1830 and by 34 per cent during the thirty-year period which followed, 1830–60; population then totalled 3·9 million. The increase was strongly differentiated geographically: in eight counties population increased by less than 30 per cent, in seven by more than 40 per cent. It was greatest in the south and west of Sweden and in Norrland; the eastern and central counties had the lowest growth rates. During the next forty-year period up to the turn of the century, the increase was approximately as great as during the thirty-year period 1830–60, i.e. 33 per cent. Sweden now boasted a population of over five million, more than twice that at the beginning of the nineteenth century. Moreover, in the latter half of the century more than a million people had emigrated—a movement which began on a small scale in the 1850s and reached its maximum during the 1880s. In addition, population proved very mobile even before the period of emigration. In some counties net migration, especially in seasons of bad harvests, amounted to several thousand *per annum* during the years 1830 to 1860. While it is difficult to assess the contribution which mobility of population made to equalizing employment opportunities and recruiting workers for new industries, it must obviously have helped to raise levels of output and productivity and to prevent diminishing returns which would have had a deadening economic effect. A labour force shifting from industries with low to those with higher productivity achieved considerable transfer gains accruing to the gross national product.

In assessing the influence of population changes on economic development, we must take account of modifications in age structure. A large increase in non-productive population during the pre-industrial phase must have helped to delay

TABLE 2
PERCENTAGE CHANGE IN THE SIZE OF DIFFERENT
AGE GROUPS, 1800–1910[3]

|        | 1800–10 | 1810–20 | 1820–30 | 1830–40 | 1840–50 | 1850–60 |
|--------|---------|---------|---------|---------|---------|---------|
| 0–14   | − 0·4   | +10·4   | +22·6   | + 2·9   | + 8·7   | +12·7   |
| 15–39  | +5·2    | + 8·3   | + 6·6   | +14·1   | +14·9   | + 7·6   |
| 40–64  | +2·6    | + 2·3   | + 5·6   | +11·3   | + 6·9   | +17·4   |
| 15–64  | +4·3    | + 6·1   | + 6·2   | +13·0   | +12·0   | + 9·1   |
| 65 +   | − 7·7   | +13·8   | + 9·3   | − 2·0   | +12·0   | +19·8   |
| Total  | +2·1    | + 7·8   | +11·7   | + 8·6   | +10·9   | +10·8   |

|        | 1860–70 | 1870–80 | 1880–90 | 1890–1900 | 1900–10 |
|--------|---------|---------|---------|-----------|---------|
| 0–14   | + 9·7   | + 4·8   | + 7·0   | + 4·5     | +5·0    |
| 15–39  | + 0·8   | +11·2   | − 0·4   | + 9·0     | +9·8    |
| 40–64  | +17·4   | +11·4   | + 2·1   | + 5·5     | +6·9    |
| 15–64  | + 6·6   | +10·8   | + 0·5   | + 7·7     | +8·7    |
| 65 +   | +12·6   | +18·7   | +36·7   | +16·9     | +8·4    |
| Total  | + 8·0   | + 9·5   | + 4·8   | + 7·3     | +7·5    |

a rise in national product. (Despite our having, compared to other countries, unusually complete material for population study, the development of population in
Sweden has not yet been thoroughly investigated.) A substantial increase in population of working age, however, does not necessarily lead to greater production:
in a pre-industrial phase, it may equally well result in more or less hidden unemployment or in a reduction in wages which in turn reduces consumption or
savings and thereby investment. This repercussion could occur even in an industrialized society, though the depression would be of shorter duration. In
Sweden, the number of people of working age—defined as the 15–64 age group—
increased more than the total population during the 1830s, 1840s, 1870s, 1890s and
in the first decade of the twentieth century; during the 1850s, the growth rate
almost equalled that of total population. Thus at times of accelerating economic
growth, increase in working population exceeded or almost equalled increase in
total population, whereas during decades of less marked economic expansion, the
1810s, 1820s, 1860s and 1880s, the number of potential workers increased noticeably more slowly than that of total population.

If we consider changes not only in the size of age groups, but also in the proportion of potential workers to total population, the picture looks different, though of
course the main features emerge unchanged. The proportion of potential workers
decreased from 1850 to the 1870s, but increased from 1890. It was during the

TABLE 3
AGE GROUP 15–64 AS PERCENTAGE OF TOTAL
POPULATION, 1800–1910

| 1800 | 1810 | 1820 | 1830 | 1840 | 1850 | 1860 | 1870 | 1880 | 1890 | 1900 | 1910 |
|------|------|------|------|------|------|------|------|------|------|------|------|
| 62·0 | 63·3 | 62·2 | 59·2 | 61·6 | 62·2 | 61·2 | 60·5 | 61·5 | 59·0 | 59·2 | 59·9 |

[3] *Swedish Historical Statistics*, Pt. 1, Stockholm, 1955, Table A 16.

1880s that the most wide-ranging increase in Swedish manufacturing industry occurred, i.e. number of workers rose more rapidly than accumulation of real capital.

Changes in population structure could obviously influence the rhythm of economic growth, though in the present state of demographic knowledge we cannot be dogmatic about the causal nexus. In asserting that this increase in population was sufficiently large to constitute an expansive force in the growth process, but not large enough to obstruct it, we touch upon the most crucial aspect of the population problem in economic growth. As in other European countries, growth of population in Sweden did not in general outrun increase in output, thus making possible even before 1870 a rise in real incomes, in spite of the modest nature of expansion up to that time. Of the rise in Swedish national income, we can attribute about 30 per cent to increased population, the other 70 per cent to the greater productivity achieved in the years 1872–89; up to 1912 enhanced productivity exerted even more influence and accounted for over 80 per cent of the rise in national income.[4]

# III

## THE TRANSFORMATION OF AGRICULTURE

During the preliminary phase before 1870, Swedish society underwent radical structural change. The relatively large increase in population may well have led to overpopulation and thus to a degree of proletarianization of the lower classes in rural areas during the period up to 1840, i.e. rise in national income lagged behind increase in population. In other words, average productivity per head may have fallen, though there are no grounds for assuming that marginal productivity equalled zero. During the period 1750–1840, the number of farmers grew by about 16 per cent, whereas the increase in lower-class population amounted to about 240 per cent.[5]

At the same time, however, extensive land reclamation took place and led to expansion of agricultural output. The usual explanation for this land reclamation is the speeding up of enclosure activities after about 1830 when a law regulating enclosure was enacted. This unquestionably contributed to land reclamation, but alone does not explain why farmers were so ready to enclose their villages; to account for this, population growth must also be brought into the picture. It was not the enclosure movement which caused population increase; rather did a settled agrarian community respond by land redistribution to the impact of a greater demand from an increased population for food. Where population growth remained relatively slight, enclosure came later than in areas of rapidly increasing population. It may have been the same in Western Europe: redistribution of land took place in countries whose populations grew rapidly. e.g. England and Germany, but not in a country where population stagnated, like France. Enclosure necessitated considerable investment: new buildings, new roads, new fences demanded much capital outlay over relatively short periods; though farmers did much of the work themselves, using timber drawn from their own forests, this new

[4] L. Jörberg, op. cit., p. 20.
[5] E. Hojer, Svensk befolkningsutveckling (Swedish Population Growth), Stockholm, 1959.

investment must have stimulated the economy and generated a multiplier effect. In addition agriculture became more capital-intensive around 1850, with new implements, such as reaping or threshing machines, coming into use; more capital-intensive production must have led to an increase in the growth of investment and income.

This calls for a discussion of the availability of, and access to, capital. Had it proved impossible to mobilize resources for enclosure and land reclamation at this time, Swedish agriculture would either not have been transformed at all or at least would have assumed a different shape. Surprisingly, rural areas appear to have had fairly easy access to capital. The growth of rural savings banks was to some extent a reaction to the refusal of urban savings banks to allow the rural population deposit facilities, on the grounds that investment outlets for more capital than could be saved by the small number of urban inhabitants did not exist. That this was a misconception is clear from the rapid growth of savings banks in rural areas. Their number increased between 1834 and 1860 from 31 to 146, their capital from 2·3 million to 29·0 million *kronor*.[6]

Another source of funds came with the development of mortgage societies. The first of these in a farming community was founded in 1836; by the middle of the century most counties in South and Central Sweden had their own. At the end of 1858 these societies had borrowed from abroad 52 million *kronor* out of a total bonded debt of 72 million *kronor*.[7] It goes without saying that such large imports of capital in the pre-industrial phase played a large part in facilitating agriculturat transformation.

In considering sources of capital, we must not forget exports of grain which began on a small scale around 1830, growing in importance to a zenith in the 1870s. Their main component was oats of which England bought the largest share, using it to 'fuel' its contemporary omnibuses. Thus, in addition to feeding the population, Swedish agriculture earned a large income from abroad.

Assuming that farming had worked at full capacity, the change in foreign demand made possible greater grain sales. The addition to farming revenues through the multiplier effect increased income formation in other sectors of economic life, helping to speed up home demand for industrial goods and creating scope for the establishment of a consumer goods industry. Furthermore opportunities to borrow abroad improved because imports of agricultural products ceased to be of importance in the 1830s; had they continued, foreigners might have been unwilling to lend.

Early agricultural development may have been impeded by the relatively even distribution of different types of grain throughout the country, which prevented specialization and expansion of the national trade in cereals. (Uneven distribution of natural resources would have increased trade, raised profits and enhanced the share of trade in economic growth.) Instead, imbalance in production was brought about by exports, but not without creating fresh problems for future development.

Agricultural transformation constituted one of the more important matters in economic growth. Its impact on population was more obvious than on industrialization which was making only slow progress at the time: it contributed to the growth of capital and improved opportunities for rationalizing agriculture. Up to

[6] Finance Committee's Report, Table xxii.          [7] *Ibid.*, p. 83.

1875, prices rose during the greater part of the period, with inflationary peaks during the Crimean War and at the beginning of the 1870s, no doubt rendering investment more profitable. Credit institutions looking upon agriculture as their best customer co-operated in putting export profits at the disposal of enterprising farmers.

All these factors in combination explain why Swedish agriculture was transformed before industry; that these two changes did not occur simultaneously makes the phenomenon of growth easier to understand. By the time industrial expansion took place, the problem of feeding the increasing non-agrarian population had been largely solved. Not that agriculture had dealt with all its problems, but structural tensions had been reduced. Around 1880 Sweden once again imported grain, and industrial development up to 1914, combined with emigration, appears to share the responsibility for reducing the agricultural labour force more rapidly than productivity improved. Perhaps the agricultural crisis of the 1880s and 1890s was not solely a reflection of changed world markets.[8]

By transforming agriculture earlier than industry Sweden, a country poorly endowed with capital, succeeded in concentrating investment at different periods in different sectors of her economy. Though low elasticity of agricultural supplies as a rule stands in the way of rapid expansion, Swedish agriculture responded to increased international demand with surprising speed. Especially during the 1850s and 1870s this elasticity of supplies may have been due to land reclamation and redistribution through enclosure reforms, with its attendant gains in productivity, at the beginning of the 1890s to the elimination of wasteful methods, such as excess feeding of cattle. In any case, ability to increase agricultural supplies was an important factor in Swedish economic development which thus did not depend solely on the country's industrial capacity, but equally on its ability to transform the agricultural sector.

One of the consequences of agricultural development was railway construction which began during the 1850s, inspired to some extent by the demand of agriculture for improved transport from inland areas to ports. The export industry added its own demand, and during the 1870s Sweden experienced a railway boom of unsurpassed proportions.

# IV

## INTERNATIONAL ADAPTATION

Up to the 1870s industrial development in Sweden was more adaptation to events outside its frontiers than independent economic expansion. Typical was the iron industry, struggling against foreign competition and adapting itself with some difficulty so as not to drop out of international markets. To an even greater extent did the expansion of the sawmill industry prior to the 1870s reflect the larger demand from England and those continental countries which were undergoing industrial development. Exports of sawn timber, amounting to 200,000 cubic metres at the beginning of the 1830s, reached 1 million around 1860. The development of sawmill exports can be illustrated by a logistic curve, with the turning point in the

[8] G. Fridlizius, *Swedish Corn Export in the Free Trade Era*, Lund, 1857. Cf. also Jorn Svensson, *Jordbruk och depression 1870–1900*, Lund, 1965.

1880s, the subsequent rate of increase flattening out to the First World War.[9] Growth in the sawmill industry in Sweden before 1870 surpassed that in almost any other sector of the economy. Its forward and backward linkages made its multiplier-accelerator of crucial importance for industrial development: backward into the capital goods industry which equipped sawmills with machinery and in its turn increased the demand on the engineering industry for other products, forward into the consumer goods industry which responded by a boom.

Export industry thus came to be a driving force in economic growth. Foreign demand for Swedish products furnished opportunities to exporters and producers to expand activities and reduce costs of production. In a community such as Sweden, with a low national income and poorly developed communications, it was easier for industries supplying foreign than home consumers to expand, because export expansion could precede the development of a social infrastructure. Industrial expansion in the home sector was delayed, not only by low real income, but also by poor communications between regions. An integrated home market would require in the initial phase of industrialization investment in communications in order to improve the mechanism of distribution. Because demand for industrial products came from foreign markets, industry could begin to expand before these investments had been made. Industrial breakthrough in the 1870s coincided with the rapid development of internal communications.

Being first in industrial development, export industry had no immediate need to compete for labour and capital with industries working for the home market. Later, competition between the two sectors stimulated mainly industries supplying the home market by providing them with an incentive to increase productivity by innovation.

Expansion in the export sector thus encouraged growth in other sectors, partly owing to the multiplier-accelerator effect of bigger demand for export products on other branches of industry, partly owing to external economies.

Walter Hoffmann at the beginning of the 1930s investigated the proportion of capital goods and consumer goods industries during the process of industrialization.[10] He concluded that consumer goods preponderated at the earlier stage, but that their share was later reduced and exceeded by capital goods industries; Hoffmann assumed that this phenomenon had general validity. For Sweden this 'law' is not entirely correct. Around 1870, even before industrialization had seriously begun, the weight of the two sectors in industry was approximately equal, whereas in Hoffmann's scheme such a constellation ought not to have been reached until considerably later. But it is easy to show why Sweden fails to fit the general pattern.

Swedish industrialization was a reflection of, and an adaptation to, conditions outside Sweden. Branches working for exports predominated in the capital goods industry, with sawmills and ironworks responsible for the larger part of the output. Their growth stimulated in its turn an expansion in the consumer goods industries. This poses the question: why did not the Swedish economy become a 'dual economy', with an advanced industrial sector working for export and an under-developed sector supplying the home market?

[9] E. Söderlund, *Svensk trävaruexport under 100 år* (Swedish Timber Exports during 100 Years), Stockholm, 1951.

[10] W. Hoffmann, *Stadien und Typen der Industrialisierung*, Jena, 1931 (English edition: *The Growth of Industrial Economies*, Manchester, 1958).

# V

## STRUCTURE AND FINANCE OF ENTERPRISES

One reason for avoiding this degeneration has already been discussed: not only industry, but also agriculture derived an income from exports; this spread favoured balanced economic expansion. Another factor of considerable importance was the emergence of an entrepreneurial class in Sweden.

Industrial expansion entails by definition a high proportion of investment. Investment can be investigated from different angles: who invests? how is investment used? what decisions motivate investment?

Investment can further be classified as either private or public. In Sweden the State assumed responsibility for heavy fundamental investment in communications and education, both spheres of investment essential for economic growth. In enquiring into industrial growth, however, interest must focus on the activities of the private entrepreneur. With understandable exaggeration, Professor Arthur Cole has called the entrepreneur 'the central figure in modern economic history, and in my view the central figure in national economy'. To understand Swedish industrial expansion, we must study its entrepreneurial history.

Swedish industrial entrepreneurs were recruited from a relatively small group. Commercial houses, i.e. wholesalers, constituted the most progressive founders of businesses in Sweden.[11] Most sawmills as well as enterprises in other industries were established at the initiative of merchants; this small group trained a larger number of entrepreneurs for the industrial breakthrough. Being both importers and exporters, wholesalers had an international outlook, recognizing the needs of foreign markets and responding rapidly by founding, or helping to found, new export enterprises.

Iron and timber industries, with plants of already considerable size, were the earliest to be in need of large amounts of capital. Few new enterprises were promoted in the iron industry. It was rather a question of firms of long standing being modernized by commercial houses which invested capital resources as owners or reorganizers. In the timber industry on the other hand, merchants promoted new firms; in the engineering industry, too, trading companies started on the ground floor. Within this latter branch, the initiative often came from technical experts, with commercial houses providing finance. Financing often took the form of short-term credits, for instance guarantees by means of promissory notes; but continual renewal turned short-term into long-term credit, though of course it squeezed the liquidity of the debtors.

For a long time it was believed that much of the working capital came from foreign countries. Professor Torsten Gårdlund's investigations of Swedish industrial finance have shown this not to be the case;[12] foreign capital undoubtedly played a large part, but probably because it furnished the marginal loans which were of greater importance to firms than their actual amount indicated.

[11] T. Gårdlund, *Industrialismens samhälle* (The Society of Industrialism), Stockholm, 1942.
[12] T. Gårdlund, *Svensk industrifinansiering under genombrottsskedet 1830–1913* (Swedish Industrial Finance during the Breakthrough Period 1830–1913), Stockholm, 1947.

A factor not discussed by Gårdlund is the importance of foreign short-term credits which played a large part in the sawmill industry and in grain exports.[13] Foreign trading houses paid in advance for future deliveries, thus facilitating the finance of business; such short-term loans could be of considerable size. Without them, Swedish industry could not have financed its operations as successfully as it did.

Commercial houses were able to engage so strongly in the promotion and finance of industrial enterprises because they not only had large capital resources, but made large profits in trade. Up to the turn of the century, trading remained the core of their business; thereafter, the centre of gravity shifted to financial operations. These large profits resulted not so much from the loans made to industry as from their monopoly of sales of industrial products from which they were able to extract substantial commissions.

Merchants and commercial houses thus clearly played a decisive part in the spread of entrepreneurial operations in Sweden; their attitude towards, and opinions concerning, entrepreneurial activities were more modern, their planning more far-sighted, than that of most leading entrepreneurs in other countries. Sweden's long-standing association with the European market, established chiefly through earlier iron exports, became of crucial importance because it enabled Swedish enterprises to recognize opportunities for expansion and to use their foreign connections in order to relieve the country's shortage of capital by allowing foreign buyers to assume responsibility for part of the finance of production in the form of advance payments and short-term loans.

In discussing finance of production, we must mention incorporation. It reduces the risks to individual financial backers and simplifies capital accumulation by (a) facilitating capital concentration through increasing the willingness of capitalists to invest; (b) enabling owners of small funds to associate themselves with productive investment; (c) limited company status often being a condition for substantial bank loans and for the issue of debentures.

From the introduction of the limited companies Act of 1848 to the 1860s, the State adopted a restrictive attitude to limited company status; many applications were refused. The attitude changed after the 1860s; during the 1870s and 1880s, practically all applications were granted.[14] However, the role of the State throughout remained regulatory; it neither encouraged nor supported company formation. The number of new limited companies—whether newly formed enterprises or conversions of firms already in existence—rose sharply during the first half of the

TABLE 4

NUMBER OF NEWLY FORMED LIMITED COMPANIES
IN INDUSTRY BETWEEN 1866 AND 1910[15]

| 1866–70 | 155 | 1881–85 | 259 | 1896–1900 | 976 |
| 1871–75 | 505 | 1886–90 | 394 | 1901–05 | 1073 |
| 1876–80 | 234 | 1891–95 | 545 | 1906–10 | 1486 |

[13] E. Söderlund, *op. cit.*, and *Skandinaviska banken 1864–1914*, Stockholm, 1964; also G. Fridlizius, *op. cit.*

[14] C. A. Nilsson, 'Business Incorporations in Sweden 1849–1896', *Economy and History*, II, Lund, 1960.　　　[15] L. Jörberg, *op. cit.*, p. 198.

1870s; dynamically accelerating development during the 1890s resulted in figures which for the first time exceeded those of the 1870s.

The increase during the twentieth century is due above all to even small enterprises now adopting limited company form. Earlier it had chiefly been large enterprises which had taken advantage of opportunities of safeguarding their owners against the dangers of unlimited responsibility and which required large accumulations of capital for their operations. It is not clear whether the twentieth-century figures reflect rising economic activity or merely a change in attitude towards the adoption of limited company status.

TABLE 5
PERCENTAGE INCREASE IN NUMBERS OF
INDUSTRIAL WORKERS EMPLOYED BY LIMITED
COMPANIES AND OTHER FORMS OF ENTERPRISE,
1872–1912[16]

| | Limited Companies | Other forms | | Limited Companies | Other forms |
|---|---|---|---|---|---|
| 1872–80 | +37·1 | + 8·0 | 1897–1903 | +29·8 | − 4·2 |
| 1880–89 | +82·6 | +49·8 | 1903–12 | +24·1 | +6·0 |

The growth of Swedish industry naturally entailed not only an increase in output and in the number of industrial workers, but also changes in the structure of production and ownership. The limited company was both a driving force and during certain periods a consequence of industrial development. It created greater opportunities for risk bearing; to an increasing extent industrial output came from enterprises which had adopted limited company form. In 1872, 45 per cent of all workers were employed by limited companies; in 1912, the figure had risen to almost 80 per cent.

This relatively novel form of ownership facilitated the promotion of large-scale firms. Alexander Gerschenkron has pointed out that, the more backward a country at the outset of industrialization, the more likely its first enterprises are to be on a large scale. To some extent, this reasoning applies to Sweden. The largest firms in Sweden had a greater share of output in their respective industries at the beginning of the 1870s than later. This does not mean that these businesses were large by international standards, only that in a country where enterprises remained few

TABLE 6
PERCENTAGE CHANGES IN THE NUMBER OF
INDUSTRIAL WORKERS EMPLOYED IN FACTORIES
WITH LESS THAN 100, WITH 100–500, AND WITH
MORE THAN 500 WORKERS, 1872–1912[17]

| | Total | − 100 | 100–500 | 500 + |
|---|---|---|---|---|
| 1872–80 | +13·6 | +25·4 | − 1·6 | +25·9 |
| 1880–89 | +66·0 | +51·9 | +67·8 | +97·0 |
| 1897–1903 | +19·1 | +25·5 | +13·0 | +22·8 |
| 1903–12 | +16·3 | +12·8 | +17·8 | +22·1 |

[16] *Ibid.*, p. 201.
[17] *Ibid.*, p. 150. Figures prior to 1897 do not include the sawmill and iron and steel industries, owing to lack of statistical information regarding these industries.

and the range of products restricted, it was easy to capture a large share of any one market. In 1872 more than two-thirds of all workers in Swedish industry were employed in firms which had more than 100 workers. As industrialization progressed, this proportion fell.

What was the volume of initial investment required in order to commence production economically? A business faced with strong or differentiated demand might require only small capital in order to reach a profitable level of production; even relatively small firms could survive in competition where economies of scale did not count for much. There are on the other hand industries, for instance railways, where investment has to be on a large scale: initial costs are heavy, and not until the railway has commenced operating can income be expected. This capital-intensive type of investment was largely provided by the State, thus leaving the capital market free to concentrate on enterprises with a shorter gestation period and requiring lower initial outlay.

This economic structure was conducive to development. Specialization demanded relatively large firms, and the nature of many new industrial products called for heavy investment, such as could be provided only by substantial enterprises. Beginning without serious competition, these could exact high prices for their output and foster development by ploughing substantial profits into new ventures. A characteristic of large enterprise at this time was the small share of profit accruing to owners, compared to gross profit.

Not all aspects of this development were favourable to growth. With communications remaining poor, firms requiring a national rather than a regional market to grow to full size could never reap all the advantages of large-scale operation. By international standards their optimum scale of production remained small.

Nor was productivity any higher in the larger than in the small firms; in many instances, the opposite was true, particularly in the early stages of industrialization. This was apparently due to the difficulty of scientific management as well as to shortages of skilled workers and technical experts—all of more consequence to large than to small firms.

A high degree of concentration is not synonymous with the leading enterprise dominating the market. The degree of market domination depends on the number and size of sellers, product differentiation, cartel formation, integration, and finally on the existence of foreign competition. To measure the degree of concentration requires a study of the market as a whole, not merely of the share of particular firms in national output.

High concentration in Swedish export industries for instance did not enable

TABLE 7

AVERAGE NUMBER OF INDUSTRIAL WORKERS
EMPLOYED IN FACTORIES OWNED BY LIMITED
COMPANIES AND OTHER FORMS OF ENTERPRISE,
1872-1912[18]

|  | Limited Companies | Other forms |  | Limited Companies | Other forms |  | Limited Companies | Other forms |
|---|---|---|---|---|---|---|---|---|
| 1872 | 163 | 32 | 1889 | 117 | 31 | 1903 | 82 | 29 |
| 1880 | 108 | 26 | 1897 | 101 | 33 | 1912 | 75 | 26 |

[18] *Ibid.*, p. 202. Cf. comment to n. 17.

these exporters to dominate the market. Concentration in any line of production has little meaning where substitutes can easily be provided. Moreover, market domination is set at nought where demand increases rapidly or technical change takes place quickly or where there is market or product differentiation.

In this context it is interesting to consider the attempts in Sweden to control by cartel formation what industrialists considered a threat of over-production. Cartellization may not only appear desirable to entrepreneurs when over-production has become a fact, but already when equilibrium between supply and demand is threatened.

Cartels were conspicuous in industries working for the domestic market; agreements between exporters occurred more rarely. The type formed was predominantly that of the price cartel. Proposals for stricter cartellization were made very early; the sugar industry for instance discussed trustification already in the 1870s,

TABLE 8

SHARE IN THE OUTPUT (BY PERCENTAGE OF VALUE) OF THE THREE LARGEST ENTERPRISES IN CERTAIN INDUSTRIES, 1872–1912[19]

| Industry | 1872 | 1880 | 1897 | 1912 |
|---|---|---|---|---|
| Margarine | — | — | 89 | 71 |
| Flour milling | — | — | 23 | 31 |
| Sugar refining | 54 | 59 | 43 | 98 |
| Cotton | 29 | 21 | 26 | 27 |
| Woollen | 29 | 26 | 29 | 25 |
| Leather | 30 | 24 | 23 | 31 |
| Footwear | — | 95 | 36 | 17 |
| Sawmilling | — | — | 11 | 7 |
| Paper and pulp | 50 | 20 | 15 | 13 |
| Cement | — | 100 | 84 | 72 |
| Matchmaking | 59 | 56 | 57 | 82 |
| Engineering (except electrical) | 40 | 24 | 11 | 10 |
| Electrical engineering | — | 100 | 92 | 92 |
| Iron and steel | — | — | 23 | 24 |

but did not act until 1907. Some of the more specialized engineering branches tried to include Norwegian firms in their cartels—a plan not realized in practice, but very advanced in conception. In the economic recession of the 1880s, the sawmill industry experimented with an international cartel by trying to draw Finnish and Russian firms into an agreement for the limitation of output.

The greater industrial concentration, the easier it proved to form cartels. However, many industries working for the home market had only a small degree of concentration, such as the footwear and ready-made clothing industries; engineering also belonged to this group and was more concerned with product differentiation than with cartellization.

The end of the 1880s saw a policy of tariff protection introduced in Sweden. Several authors consider it to have been an important element in the growth of Swedish industry. Industries working for the domestic market may well have derived some advantage from tariffs which conferred an element of monopoly at home, while on the other hand preventing industrial concentration. There is however no proof of this tariff having played a decisive part in industrial develop-

[19] *Ibid.*, p. 170.

ment: as industrialization proceeded rapidly and demand expanded quickly, it was only during some downswings that depression rendered tariff protection useful.

Integration and amalgamation of firms occurred in the wake of technical developments; they were hardly of decisive importance for industrial growth. When good communications were established (in which we include railways as well as postal and telegraph services), managements could supervise firms with several factories in different locations; these did not make a general appearance on the Swedish industrial scene until the 1890s. Similarly, cartels proved ineffective until members found it easy to communicate with, and supervise, one another; hence quite a number of cartels were established in the 1870s and 1880s, but dissolved after a short existence.

THE BOOM OF THE 1870s

The 1870s mark the beginning of Sweden's industrial breakthrough. 'Breakthrough' in this sense does not signify the beginning of industrialization; this can be traced back to the 1830s. 'Breakthrough' characterizes an acceleration in the movement so marked as to change the trend; an upswing in production, moreover, accompanied by a change in institutional structure, so that the Swedish economy faced a new situation from the boom of the 1870s onwards. Extensive investment occurred in almost all Swedish industries in the 1870s, including railways and residential building.

Agricultural exports increased rapidly at the end of the 1870s. The output of the capital goods industries more than doubled in the boom period up to 1875; industrial investment increased by more than 80 per cent, national income, measured at constant prices, by more than 30 per cent, all during the period 1871–5: an increase almost double that for any quinquennium up to 1914.

TABLE 9
ANNUAL PERCENTAGE CHANGES IN THE VALUE OF EXPORTS, IMPORTS AND INDUSTRIAL OUTPUT, 1869–79[20]

|         | Exports | Imports | Industrial output |
|---------|---------|---------|-------------------|
| 1869–71 | +20     | +10     | + 5               |
| 1871–74 | +14     | +27     | +17               |
| 1874–75 | − 9     | −13     | − 5               |
| 1875–77 | + 2     | + 7     | 0                 |
| 1877–79 | − 8     | −14     | −10               |

Economic expansion was fostered by strong foreign demand for Swedish exports; expansion was stronger in industries working for exports than in those supplying the domestic market. Inflation at the beginning of the 1870s brought substantial profits to entrepreneurs, largely used to make further investments. Moreover, low rates of interest dominated the money market: a situation typical of the Swedish capital market during the last decades of the nineteenth century and due to expansion being 'imported', in the sense of large profits from export industries being transferred to the capital market.

Extension of railways was unquestionably important for industrial development. Transport costs fell considerably; the development of communications changed the

[20] Ibid., p. 224.

cost structure of business at the same time as it facilitated marketing of output. Lower transport costs resulted in cheaper raw materials which in turn reduced prices of finished goods; this in many instances contributed to a fall in the costs of railway construction—cheaper fuel for iron works, for example, making for cheaper steel, with a resulting drop in the costs of rails and other railway materials.

Swedish railways did not always cross areas already densely populated. The main line from Scania to Stockholm passed through relatively under-developed thinly populated country. Much social capital was therefore sunk in the extension of new communities developing around railway stations, often far from old centres of settlement. Such investment contributed to the acceleration of economic development in the 1870s, leading to a vigorous creation of additional income in other sectors of industrial life. Railways contributed to a substantial relocation of population, shifting it from areas of relatively low to those of higher productivity. Transfer gains from this shift may have been as great as those due to direct investment in railway construction.

Railways were financed chiefly through foreign loans arranged by the State. This kept intact the supply of domestic capital for other investments. State grants towards railway construction during the period 1855–60 amounted to almost 34 million *kronor*,[21] but it was during the 1870s that railway construction experienced its real boom, extending the permanent way by an average of 14 per cent annually, i.e. trebling it during the decade and reaching a total in excess of 5000 kilometres. The subsequent rate of extension up to 1914 came to about 3 per cent *per annum*.

At the same time as the communications network was decisively improved in the 1870s, structural changes occurred in industrial investment. Production became more capital-intensive; because investment was especially heavy in capital goods industries, repercussions were felt in other sectors. The iron and steel industry made large investments at the beginning of the 1870s to take advantage of the Bessemer process and other technical improvements. Cost reduction due to such technical changes had effects more far-reaching than price reductions in consumer goods industries. True, they demanded fairly heavy non-recurrent infusions of capital, often on a scale larger than justified by immediate demand; but they resulted in cheaper production and increased capital available for investment in other industries which were users, among others, of iron and steel products.

Imports of coal and coke can serve to some degree as an index of increasing industrial mechanization; they rose by 150 per cent between 1869 and 1878, but only by 66 per cent between 1880 and 1890. These imports reflect the order of magnitude of investment and the technical changes underlying expansion, though some of them were absorbed by the rapid railway extension of the 1870s.

Export industries, with the exception of iron and steel, succeeded in raising output practically in step with demand, but production in heavy industry stagnated during the years 1871–3 while prices continued to rise, both internationally and in Sweden. This was due to the longer gestation period and the heavier capital required in heavy industry than for instance in sawmilling which by and large managed to keep abreast of increasing international demand. Growth in the export sector changed factor distribution and raised productivity, entrepreneurs to a large extent re-investing increased incomes productively.

[21] Finance Committee's Report, p. 118.

The depression at the end of the 1870s was the first to have an unmistakable effect on the Swedish economy; it remained also the most severe up to 1914. Owing to Sweden's close links with the international market, it would be reasonable to expect both timing and amplitude of its business cycles to correspond to international ones; this proved generally true for the chronology, but not for the severity. Swedish economic development proceeded with unusual evenness, manifesting only slight fluctuations. Exports naturally fluctuated more than production and were subject to shorter waves than industry working for domestic markets—shorter than seven to eleven years.

TABLE 10
ANNUAL PERCENTAGE GROWTH IN THE VALUE OF
OUTPUT OF SELECTED INDUSTRIES, 1867/69–1912[22]

|  | *1867/9–1892/5* | *1896–1912* |
|---|---|---|
| 1. Paper, pulp and paper-using | 6·1 | 11·0 |
| 2. Gravel, stone, clay and allied | 6·0 | 5·3 |
| 3. Food and tobacco | 5·1 | 4·0 |
| 4. Chemicals | 4·5 | 7·3 |
| 5. Metal and engineering | 3·7 | 7·0 |
| 6. Timber | 3·7 | 2·0 |
| 7. Iron and steel | 3·2 | 2·2 |
| 8. Textiles | 2·6 | 5·6 |
| 9. Leather, non-textile fibres, rubber | 1·7 | 10·0 |
| 10. Capital goods | 5·2 | 6·2 |
| 11. Consumer goods | 3·3 | 6·1 |

How far growth, once triggered off, was sustained by the vigorous increase in demand for agricultural produce when industrial progress faltered at the end of the 1870s, it is difficult to judge, but in fact the expansion of the 1870s continued up to 1914, though with slight variations in the growth rate of industry as a whole; the stories of individual industries were more involved.

Though Swedish expansion follows a pattern customary in Western Europe, it started later and proceeded more quickly than for instance that of France or Germany. This fits the general theory of underdeveloped countries: the later the start of growth, the more rapid industrialization will be; they borrow and apply ideas and techniques from their more advanced neighbours.[23] Sweden was undoubtedly backward, compared to Western Europe; this provided her with certain initial advantages, such as capital imports from England and France which paid for costly investment in economic infrastructure. Scarce domestic capital could concentrate on industry. The wage level of Swedish workers being lower than that in Germany and considerably lower than that in England, Swedish business, though not the Swedish worker, benefited in competition. As regards technical knowhow, Sweden imported a fair number of experts, chiefly from England, for employment in textiles, engineering and railway construction; when a Swedish rubber industry was established in the 1890s, Russian experts were brought in. But the technical gap between different European countries in the nineteenth century was much smaller than it is between underdeveloped and advanced

[22] L. Jörberg, *op. cit.*, pp. 61, 63.
[23] A. Gerschenkron, *Economic Backwardness in Historical Perspective*, Cambridge (Mass.), 1963; W. Fellner, *Trends and Cycles in Economic Activity*, New York, 1956.

ountries today. Though Sweden reaped advantages from importing technical nowledge, they could not have been decisive for industrialization.

Nor can we conclude from the speed of Sweden's industrial development in the 870s that she was necessarily far more backward than other Western European ountries. National income calculations for the period are notoriously unreliable nd provide little evidence for the general standard of living. If Kuznets's calulations can be believed, the difference in this respect between Sweden and Western Europe was slight, in spite of a national income *per capita* lower in Sweden han in most Western European countries.[24]

Sweden's rapid development in the 1870s should thus not be attributed mainly ɔ her backwardness, but to other reasons. The simplest explanation is her ability ɔ satisfy foreign demand for Swedish exports from a limited sector of her economy. 'here were a number of reasons for this ability: the changes preparing the way ɔr economic development, for example in the field of agriculture, rooted in the receding decades; the high status, by international comparison, accorded to ?aching and education; the development of communications, even though railway onstruction did not have its first large-scale upswing until the 1870s; the long truggle of the iron industry to concentrate output in larger and more rational nits; modernization of business legislation and abolition of the old restrictive ?gal framework fettering industry. Only so far as England, the leading industrial ation, rendered considerable assistance to all other European countries in their conomic expansion, did Sweden derive direct advantage from her late start in ndustrialization.

URTHER DEVELOPMENT, 1880–1914

ABLE 11
·ERCENTAGE DISTRIBUTION OF SWEDISH EXPORTS
;Y COMMODITY GROUPS, 1881–1913[25]

| | *1881–5* | *1891–5* | *1901–5* | *1911–13* |
|---|---|---|---|---|
| Timber | 40·4 | 37·1 | 38·5 | 26·1 |
| Iron and steel | 16·2 | 9·5 | 10·2 | 9·3 |
| Grain | 11·7 | 4·7 | 0·4 | 0·3 |
| Butter | 6·3 | 12·0 | 8·9 | 6·0 |
| Paper and pulp | 4·6 | 8·3 | 12·9 | 17·6 |
| Iron ore | — | 0·4 | 5·0 | 8·0 |
| Engineering products | 2·6 | 3·1 | 6·7 | 10·5 |
| Others | 18·7 | 22·8 | 17·6 | 21·6 |

Between the middle of the 1880s and the start of the First World War, the volume f Swedish exports increased by 150 per cent. The composition of exports changed: he proportion of old staple goods fell, grain exports ceased and were replaced by neat and dairy produce, chiefly butter. Home processing of timber resulted in the ubstitution of paper and pulp for some timber exports. A new raw material, iron ·re, made its appearance on the market and, together with the products of the ngineering industry, constituted the most rapidly expanding sector. While iron

---

[24] S. Kuznets, 'Quantitative Aspects of the Economic Growth of Nations, I–II', *Economic* )evelopment and Cultural Change, vol. v, 1956–7.
[25] G. Fridlizius, 'Sweden's Exports 1850–1960', *Economy and History*, vi, Lund, 1963.

ore stood for the old type of Swedish exports, raw materials, the output of the
engineering industry represented a novel type, proving that Swedish economic
development had reached the point of being largely independent and self-sustained

One element of considerable assistance to the Swedish economy was the move
ment of the terms of trade in her favour throughout almost the entire period after
1860. During the 1870s the terms of trade were extremely advantageous to Sweden
the prices of her exports rose much farther than those of her imports up to about
1875; between that date and the depression of 1879 the terms deteriorated
Thereafter followed new improvement, very considerable for a short period from
the end of the 1880s, to an extent of about 20 per cent. On this occasion, it was not
Swedish export prices which rose, but import prices which dropped considerably
whereas Sweden succeeded in holding the prices of her exports steady.

Arthur Lewis has pointed out that terms of trade moved against raw material
producing countries after 1883,[26] explaining it by increased output, immigration
re-allocation of land, capital investment in these countries as well as reduction in
transport costs. While he is probably right in this argument, it must be remembered
that export prices were quoted f.o.b., import prices c.i.f.: a substantial fall in
transport costs, such as happened at the end of the nineteenth century, did not
necessarily lead to a fall in the prices received by primary producers. Lowered
transport costs could lead to an improvement in terms of trade both for industrialized and primary producing countries. The fall of raw material prices in industrialized countries is therefore only a part, hardly even the most important, of an
explanation why primary producing countries ceased to expand.

Raw materials accounted for about one-half of Swedish exports, more from the
1890s onwards when iron ore began to be shipped in larger quantities. Both raw
materials and manufactures exported by Sweden benefited from improvement in
her terms of trade. Her raw material exports enjoyed a strong demand in the
European market, being in many instances essential to industrialization; this
accounts for terms of trade moving in her favour.

Improved prices for Swedish exports provided purchasing power for a greater
volume of imports; Sweden managed not only to pay the bill for rapidly increasing
imports, but also to service and repay the substantial loans floated for railway and
other constructional purposes.

Rising prices contributed to economic growth, both by facilitating capital
accumulation and by easing social mobility; falling prices had the opposite effect
In Sweden prices were rising throughout the greater part of the nineteenth cen
tury; when they fell, as happened after the depressions of the 1870s, 1880s and up
to the middle of the 1890s, decline was less sharp than in many other European
countries. This development may well have facilitated Swedish economic expan
sion during the period up to 1914. Though industrial profits in Sweden in the
1880s were not as high as earlier or later, the volume of industrial output showed
hardly any recession during that decade. Whereas investment in the 1870s, even
more in the 1880s, had been extensive, spreading employment of capital into wider
and wider fields, it subsequently turned intensive, providing more capital per
worker; the index of capital intensity is the degree of mechanization. This showed
little variation during the period, justifying the argument that the greater economic

[26] W. A. Lewis, *Economic Survey, 1919–1939*, London, 1963.

ifficulties of the 1880s provided the driving force towards increased mechani-
ation. While the increase in the number of workers lagged substantially behind that
the amount of horse-power used in all sectors of industry, the increase in horse-
ower per worker was slower during the 1880s than during the previous decade.
Iechanization was an important growth factor, coupled with the ability to keep
p the prices of Swedish exports and the improved productivity which enhanced
e competitive power of Swedish industry. Thus both mechanization and price
evelopment bear responsibility for rapid economic expansion.

ABLE 12
ERCENTAGE CHANGES IN POPULATION
MPLOYED IN THE ECONOMY, 1870–1910[27]

|  | 1870–80 | 1880–90 | 1890–1900 | 1900–10 |
|---|---|---|---|---|
| Total | +10 | +5 | +7 | +8 |
| Agriculture | +3 | -4 | -5 | -5 |
| Industry | +30 | +31 | +37 | +24 |

Occurring while all countries in Western Europe added substantially to their
idustrial potential, economic expansion in Sweden in part merely reflected inter-
ational development. For a country strongly dependent on its foreign trade,
bolition or reduction of tariffs and other trade barriers was important (Swedish
mber exports first grew to really large proportions when tariff reductions, later
ee trade, were introduced in England and France in the middle of the nineteenth
entury). During the 1880s a policy of protective tariffs was initiated in most

ABLE 13
NNUAL PERCENTAGE CHANGES IN THE VALUE OF
XPORTS, IMPORTS AND INDUSTRIAL OUTPUT,
393–1900[28]

|  | Exports | Imports | Industrial output |
|---|---|---|---|
| 1893–5 | +2·5 | +3·4 | +4·0 |
| 1895–7 | +7·4 | +8·5 | +13·0 |
| 1897–8 | -4·8 | +11·8 | +9·9 |
| 1898–1900 | +6·4 | +8·5 | +8·7 |

uropean countries, including Sweden, due among other reasons to the sufferings
f European agriculture in competition with the United States and other overseas
ountries. Such increased tariff protection ought to have acted as an obstruction to
ontinued expansion in the 1880s and 1890s, but it is no easier to measure the
ifluence of foreign tariff protection on the development of Swedish exports than
ie importance of Swedish tariff protection in fostering Swedish industry. A re-
istribution of exports undoubtedly took place, but need not have been a conse-
uence of increased duties; it might equally well have resulted from increasingly
educed transport costs making Swedish commodities competitive also in extra-
uropean markets.
During Swedish industry's third acceleration period, that is in the 1890s, the
ome market assumed greater importance than in the earlier ones. It expanded at

[27] *Swedish Historical Statistics*, Part I.    [28] L. Jörberg, *op. cit.*, p. 186.

the same rate as did export industries, being responsible for about half the value of total output before the First World War—the same proportion as it had had around 1870. Swedish industry became sufficiently competitive to resist the incur-sions of foreign countries on the Swedish market; evidence is provided by the ability of industry before 1914 to carry competition into foreign markets in respec of goods typically made for domestic consumption, such as textiles and footwear Moreover, Sweden kept an increasing proportion of the output of her capital good industries within her frontiers.

Erik Dahmén in his book *Svensk industriell företagarverksamhet* (Entrepreneuria Activity in Swedish Industry) claims that limitation of domestic outlets were a hindrance to Swedish industrial development before the First World War; too restricted a market may have prevented the spread of industrial innovation; the products of some innovations could be sold at a reasonable price only in market wider than the Swedish. In his view, this was the situation in several branches o the engineering industry during the initial phase of industrialization.

However, during the 1890s the engineering industry entered to some extent a new phase. Expansion was in some cases based on Swedish inventions: separators turbines, internal combustion engines, gas accumulators and ball bearings. The structure of the engineering industry was unbalanced: the sector based on Swedish inventions and subject to international competition expanded powerfully, the sector working for a regional market and only slightly specialized grew slowly. The latter often consisted of small firms of low profitability, owing partly to lack o specialization, partly to strong domestic competition. Whereas exports of engineer-ing products increased by more than 50 per cent in each five-year period after 1889, imports increased by scarcely half that proportion. The Swedish engineering industry was obviously expanding at a rate fast enough simultaneously to satisfy an increasing part of the growing home demand and to augment exports.

Textiles, particularly woollens, provide a further example of the capacity of Swedish industry to supply the home market. Output value increased from about 20 million *kronor* around 1890 to 70 million around 1910. While at the end of the 1880s 65 per cent of Swedish consumption had come from home production, the figure had gone up to 80 per cent on the eve of the First World War.

Innovations spread most vigorously during typical boom years, which also saw the foundation of many new businesses. The pattern of investment activity varies over business cycles. During the 1880s, regarded as a 'poor' decade because o falling prices, in spite of output increasing by about five per cent *per annum*, invest-ment was clearly extensive, capital/worker ratio rising only slowly: increase in output was due to the growing number of workers. A development similar to that of the 1880s occurred after the accelerated expansion of the 1890s; there followed a slowdown of investment within the larger firms; rather were extensive invest-ments undertaken, broadening the base of industrial development by establishing new businesses.

Variations in exports were obviously of the utmost importance in explaining fluctuations in Swedish industry. Variations in industry's export income reacted on formation of domestic income via the multiplier repercussions of changes in exports. The crisis at the end of the 1870s was naturally affected by international depression. However, it also owed something to the discovery that the investment boom (broken by economic decline) had led to a large volume of misinvestment, because the economy as a whole required more time to change from an agrarian to a partly industrial society. Hasty establishment of new industries created serious problems of imbalance. 'Development blocs' were not ready; this created 'tensions' which industry found difficult to solve. Demand proved insufficient to enable many industries to operate profitably.

The effect of fluctuations in retarding industrial expansion was comparatively light. Except for the depression in the 1870s, downswings were mild. The explanation of such stability is complex; we can indicate only some of the forces which moderated and levelled out the impact of fluctuations on industry.

Between the middle of the nineteenth century and the First World War, expansion of industry changed Sweden's economic structure by increasing its share in the national product, changing the composition of its output and improving productive techniques. By maintaining a demand for Swedish products, such as iron, timber and paper, the international market led to increased Swedish exports and facilitated Swedish industrialization by its secondary effect of stimulating expansion in other parts of industry. New products, new methods and new markets appeared; such new industries often represented growth sectors which helped to carry expansion over periods of stagnation in export industries.

Examples of such new industries are beet sugar at the end of the 1880s, ready-to-wear clothing, rubber, furniture, paper pulp and superphosphates in the 1890s; also new products of the engineering industry, such as dairy machinery and internal combustion engines; the iron industry developed new ingot steel processes which in turn stimulated rapid expansion of iron-ore mining, and so on.

As the market expanded, industrial production increased, resulting in lower cost and some import substitution by domestic output. To this substitution the policy of tariff protection of 1888 and 1892 may have contributed by clearing a space for home production, for instance in the footwear and jute industries, though the effect of the tariff is difficult to evaluate.

Not until the initial difficulties of a restricted home market and poor communications had been overcome, could industry enter upon its phase of self-sustained growth: by the 1890s it generated incomes so large as to relegate to minor importance fluctuations in other sectors of economic life as well as in exports; they were overshadowed by the demand of Swedish industry for Swedish industrial products. Though that demand continued to some extent to depend on the development of the export industries, their importance for the generation of income within the country via the multiplier effect was diminished by the stability of industries catering for the home market. Industrialization expanded production at the expense of imports: industries supplying the home market grew faster, especially during the 1890s, than demand. Consumer goods industries being less sensitive to business cycles than those supplying exports, this increase in economic independence helped to level out fluctuations and facilitated industrial expansion.

Another partial explanation of stability is furnished by investments in railway construction and housing at periods of economic decline. Similarly agricultural exports, up to the turn of the century amounting to about one-fifth of total exports, were largely of a counter-cyclical nature. Of Swedish population, almost three-quarters around 1870 and almost one-half around 1910 lived by agriculture. This sector of the economy has a stabilizing effect on industrial output because its demand is largely unaffected by fluctuations in industry. In addition the introduction

TABLE 14

PERCENTAGE CHANGES IN THE VALUE OF EXPORTS,
IMPORTS, INDUSTRIAL OUTPUT AND THE NUMBER
OF WORKERS IN INDUSTRY, 1871–1909[29]

|  | 1871–4 | 1876–8 | 1881–3 | 1885–6 | 1887–9 |
|---|---|---|---|---|---|
| Total exports | +43 | −19 | +14 | − 8 | +20 |
| Total imports | +82 | −18 | +16 | −12 | +29 |
| Exports of industrial goods | +51 | −18 | +12 | −10 | +27 |
| Imports of industrial goods | +87 | −22 | +16 | −11 | +29 |
| Industrial output | +37 | −16 | +14 | − 1 | +13 |
| Number of industrial workers | +15 | −10 | + 7 | + 2 | +23 |

|  | 1890–3 | 1898–1900 | 1900–1 | 1904–7 | 1907–9 |
|---|---|---|---|---|---|
| Total exports | +10 | +13 | −10 | +26 | −10 |
| Total imports | −12 | +18 | −13 | +17 | − 9 |
| Exports of industrial goods | + 8 | +18 | −11 | +24 | − 8 |
| Imports of industrial goods | −17 | +14 | −12 | +24 | −14 |
| Industrial output | +10 | +18 | − 2 | +27 | − 7 |
| Number of industrial workers | − 1 | + 8 | − 1 | + 8 | − 5 |

of protective tariffs in the 1880s may well have prevented reduction of agricultural incomes.

Industrial growth, however, concentrated on a few well-defined boom periods, identifiable by accelerated expansion in output and real wages of industrial workers. In the forty-year period up to 1910, the largest expansion of output occurred during the boom periods of 1871–4, 1898–1900 and 1904–7; rises in real wages concentrated on three limited periods: 1869–75, 1881–7 and 1892–6.[30] The latter thus did not entirely coincide with the pattern of output expansion, because real wages did not always rise in step with money wages; this may also help to explain the relative mildness of depressions during the 1880s and 1890s.

These periods of expansion coincided with international economic developments. But the contribution of exogenous factors in facilitating Sweden's expansion does not explain the ability of the Swedish economy to change or to exploit the opportunities created by change. We have stressed the part played by agriculture as well as the importance of entrepreneurs, further the responsibility for basic investments assumed by the State—investments made largely by means of capital borrowed abroad which helped the formation and relieved the scarcity of domestic capital. To this we added technical development leading to the establishment of a number of industries based upon Swedish inventions.

Population development was an element facilitating change from an agrarian to an industrial society. Emigration, instead of being merely negative in impact, may have simplified the transformation. Our conclusion must be that Swedish society had abundant capacity for change and showed distinct ability in inaugurating a development distinguished by stability.

[29] Ibid., p. 338.
[30] G. Bagge, E. Lundberg and I. Svennilson, Wages in Sweden, 1886–1930, I–II, Stockholm, 1935.

## Date Due

| MAY 23 1988 | | | |
|---|---|---|---|
| | | | |
| | | | |
| | | | |
| | | | |
| | | | |
| | | | |
| | | | |
| | | | |
| | | | |
| | | | |
| | | | |
| | | | |
| | | | |
| | | | |
| | | | |
| | | | |